Monsters of the Market

Zombies, Vampires and Global Capitalism

Contemporary Materialism

Historical Materialism Book Series

More than ten years after the collapse of the Berlin Wall and the disappearance of Marxism as a (supposed) state ideology, a need for a serious and long-term Marxist book publishing program has arisen. Subjected to the whims of fashion, most contemporary publishers have abandoned any of the systematic production of Marxist theoretical work that they may have indulged in during the 1970s and early 1980s. The Historical Materialism book series addresses this great gap with original monographs, translated texts and reprints of "classics."

Editorial board: Paul Blackledge, Leeds; Sebastian Budgen, London; Jim Kincaid, Leeds; Stathis Kouvelakis, Paris; Marcel van der Linden, Amsterdam; China Miéville, London; Paul Reynolds, Lancashire.

Haymarket Books is proud to be working with Brill Academic Publishers (http://www.brill.nl) and the journal *Historical Materialism* to republish the Historical Materialism book series in paperback editions. Current series titles include:

Alasdair MacIntyre's Engagement with Marxism: Selected Writings 1953–1974, edited by Paul Blackledge and Neil Davidson

Althusser: The Detour of Theory, Gregory Elliott

Between Equal Rights: A Marxist Theory of International Law, China Miéville

The Capitalist Cycle, Pavel V. Maksakovsky, translated with introduction and commentary by Richard B. Day

The Clash of Globalisations: Neo-Liberalism, the Third Way, and Anti-Globalisation, Ray Kiely

Critical Companion to Contemporary Marxism, edited by Jacques Bidet and Stathis Kouvelakis

Criticism of Heaven: On Marxism and Theology, Roland Boer

Criticism of Religion: On Marxism and Theology II, Roland Boer

Exploring Marx's Capital: Philosophical, Economic, and Political Dimensions, Jacques Bidet, translated by David Fernbach

Following Marx: Method, Critique, and Crisis, Michael Lebowitz

The German Revolution: 1917–1923, Pierre Broué

Globalisation: A Systematic Marxian Account, Tony Smith

The Gramscian Moment: Philosophy, Hegemony and Marxism, Peter D. Thomas

Impersonal Power: History and Theory of the Bourgeois State, Heide Gerstenberger, translated by David Fernbach

Lenin Rediscovered: What Is to Be Done? in Context, Lars T. Lih

Making History: Agency, Structure, and Change in Social Theory, Alex Callinicos

Marxism and Ecological Economics: Toward a Red and Green Political Economy, Paul Burkett

A Marxist Philosophy of Language, Jean-Jacques Lecercle, translated by Gregory Elliott

Politics and Philosophy: Niccolò Machiavelli and Louis Althusser's Aleatory Materialism, Mikko Lahtinen, translated by Gareth Griffiths and Kristina Köhli

The Theory of Revolution in the Young Marx, Michael Löwy

Utopia Ltd.: Ideologies of Social Dreaming in England 1870–1900, Matthew Beaumont

Western Marxism and the Soviet Union: A Survey of Critical Theories and Debates Since 1917, Marcel van der Linden

Witnesses to Permanent Revolution: The Documentary Record, edited by Richard B. Day and Daniel Gaido

Monsters of the Market

Zombies, Vampires and Global Capitalism

David McNally

Haymarket Books
Chicago, IL

First published in 2011 by Brill Academic Publishers, The Netherlands
© 2011 Koninklijke Brill NV, Leiden, The Netherlands

Published in paperback in 2012 by
Haymarket Books
P.O. Box 180165
Chicago, IL 60618
773-583-7884
info@haymarketbooks.org
www.haymarketbooks.org

ISBN: 978-1-60846-233-9

Trade distribution:
In the US, Consortium Book Sales, www.cbsd.com
In Canada, Publishers Group Canada, www.pgcbooks.ca
In the UK, Turnaround Publisher Services, www.turnaround-psl.com
In Australia, Palgrave Macmillan, www.palgravemacmillan.com.au
In all other countries, Publishers Group Worldwide, www.pgw.com

Cover design by Ragina Johnson.

This book was published with the generous support of
Lannan Foundation and the Wallace Global Fund.

Printed in the United States with union labor.

10 9 8 7 6 5 4 3 2 1

Library of Congress Cataloging-in-Publication data is available.

 (28)

 SUSTAINABLE Certified Sourcing
FORESTRY ─────────────
INITIATIVE www.sfiprogram.org
SFI-01234

For Liam

Contents

Acknowledgements

This book has been a long time coming. I hope it is better for the wait. I first started work on it in 2003, only to have my labours interrupted by a three-year stint (2005–8) as chair of the Department of Political Science at York University. When I resumed this study, global capitalism had entered into its most profound crisis since the 1930s, adding a special resonance to the themes I explore here.

While there are many sources for the reflections developed here, my ideas on several of these topics developed in a sort of dialogue with the work of a number of outstanding scholars, comrades and friends: Himani Bannerji, Susan Buck-Morss, Robin D.G. Kelley, Peter Linebaugh, and Ellen Meiksins Wood, in particular. In some cases, their influence on this book will be obvious, in others less so. But all of them have figured importantly in shaping the very questions I have posed and some of the ways I have tried to answer them.

Parts of this work have been presented at seminars sponsored by the Center for Theory and Criticism at the University of Western Ontario, the Historical Materialist Research Network at the University of Manitoba, and at conferences in London, Toronto and Amherst organised by the journals *Historical Materialism* and *Rethinking Marxism*. I thank all the organisers and participants at these events for their comments and criticisms. Thanks also to Pablo Idahosa, who generously read an early version of what is now Chapter Three and offered invaluable suggestions and criticism, not all of which I have heeded, as he probably expected. I would also like to extend my appreciation to Ben Fine who greatly encouraged me in this project and provided thoughtful comments on the whole manuscript, and to Ben Maddison and Alan Sears for the abiding interest they took in this work. Huge thanks as well to Véronique Bertrand-Bourget whose incredible conscientiousness and good humour when it came to checking footnotes and references helped preserve my sanity as I prepared the final manuscript for publication.

As befits a work about monsters, this book had a bizarre birth, having been twice rejected, much like Frankenstein's Creature, by publishers who had initially embraced it. Notwithstanding universally favourable reviews, this 'hideous progeny', to use Mary Shelley's term for her great novel, was thus twice orphaned. Its monstrous transdisciplinarity – crossing social history, cultural studies, political economy, and literary theory – scandalised some publishers, while uncertainty about its marketability discouraged others. I was fortunate throughout these experiences to receive ongoing encouragement from Sebastian Budgen and Peter Thomas, who urged me to bring this work to the distinguished *Historical Materialism Book Series* with Brill and Haymarket. That I have now done, with great thanks to both of them.

The people with whom I most intimately share my life have been unwavering in their love and support over the years in which *Monsters of the Market* took shape. I had the great joy, yet again, of sharing all phases of my work on this project with my partner, Sue Ferguson, who offered advice and steadfast support every step of the way, while reading and commenting on various drafts. I hope I have adequately conveyed my gratitude to her. Our sons Adam, Sam and Liam have been most intrigued by the idea that their dad is writing about monsters, none more so than Liam, who at a very early age has developed his own fascination with rebel-monsters from Malcolm X to the outlaw-pirates of the eighteenth-century Flying Gang. It is only fitting that I dedicate this work to him.

List of Figures

Introduction

We live in an age of monsters and of the body-panics they excite. The global economic crisis that broke over the world in 2008–9 certainly gave an exclamation-mark to this claim, with *Time* magazine declaring the zombie 'the official monster of the recession', while *Pride and Prejudice and Zombies* rocketed up bestseller-lists, and seemingly endless numbers of vampire- and zombie-films and novels flooded the market.[1] As banks collapsed and global corporations wobbled, and millions were thrown out of work, pundits talked of 'zombie banks', 'zombie economics', 'zombie capitalism', even a new 'zombie politics' in which the rich devoured the poor.[2] But while zombies took centre-stage, vampires too made their mark, so to speak, particularly in one American journalist's widely-cited declaration that Goldman Sachs, America's most powerful investment bank, resembled 'a great vampire squid wrapped around the face of humanity, relentlessly jamming its blood funnel into anything that smells like money'.[3] Having colonised much of mass-culture, monsters also infiltrated the discourse of world-leaders. 'We know very well who we are up against, real monsters',

---

1. Grossman 2009; Austen and Grahame-Smith 2009. See also Bilson 2009, and Edgcliffe-Johnson 2008. Also on the proliferation of vampires in mass-culture see Schneller 2009.
2. See Fine 2009, pp. 885–904; Harman 2009; Giroux 2009.
3. Taibbi 2009.

proclaimed the president of Ecuador in late 2008 in a stinging attack on the international banks and bondholders who hold his country's debt.[4] Only a few days earlier, Germany's president told interviewers that 'global financial markets are a monster that must be tamed'.[5] Compelling as such proclamations are they also risk trivialising what is genuinely monstrous about the existential structures of modern life. For modernity's monstrosities do not begin and end with shocking crises of financial markets, however wrenching and dramatic these may be. Instead, the very insidiousness of the capitalist grotesque has to do with its invisibility with, in other words, the ways in which monstrosity becomes normalised and naturalised via its colonisation of the essential fabric of everyday-life, beginning with the very texture of corporeal experience in the modern world. What is most striking about capitalist monstrosity, in other words, is its elusive everydayness, its apparently seamless integration into the banal and mundane rhythms of quotidian existence. This is why the most salient representations of the capitalist grotesque tend to occur in environments in which bourgeois relations are still experienced as strange and horrifying. In such circumstances, images of vampires and zombies frequently dramatise the profound senses of corporeal vulnerability that pervade modern society, most manifestly when commodification invades new spheres of social life. As the following chapters demonstrate, the persistent body-panics that run across the history of global capitalism comprise a corporeal phenomenology of the bourgeois life-world. Throwing light on the troubled relations between human bodies and the operations of the capitalist economy, such panics underline the profound experiential basis for a capitalist *monsterology*,[6] a study of the monstrous forms of everyday-life in a capitalist world-system. In what follows, I seek to track several genres of monster-stories to explore what they tell us about key symbolic registers in which the experience of capitalist commodification is felt, experienced and resisted.

Yet, it is a paradox of our age that monsters are both everywhere and nowhere. Let us begin with the everywhere.

---

4. Reuters 2008a.
5. Reuters 2008b.
6. I prefer the term *monsterology* to the more common 'teratology', given the latter's connection to the normativising study of birth-defects.

No great investigative rigours are required to discover zombies and vampires marauding across movie- and television-screens, or haunting the pages of pulp-fiction. Tales of bodysnatching of abduction, ritual-murder and organ-theft traverse folklore, science-fiction, film, video and print-media.[7] As with all such cultural phenomena, these stories and legends speak to real social practices *and* to the symbolic registers in which popular anxieties are recorded. After all, organ-selling is in fact a growing industry, based on commercial clinics that harvest parts, like kidneys, from poor people in the global South on behalf of wealthy buyers in the North.[8] Here, then, we have monstrosities of the market enacted in actual exchanges of body-parts for money. But, the revulsion elicited by such transactions often occludes the much wider range of monstrous experiences beginning with the everyday-sale of our life-energies for a wage that define life in capitalist society. And this brings us to the nowhere-ness of monsters today. For, effectively, nowhere in the discourse of monstrosity today do we find the naming of *capitalism* as a monstrous system, one that systematically threatens the integrity of human personhood. Instead, monsters like vampires and zombies move throughout the circuits of cultural exchange largely detached from the system that gives them their life-threatening energies.

One purpose of this book is to bring the monsters of the market out of this netherworld by exploring the zones of experience that nurture and sustain them, that provide them the blood and flesh off which they feed. Central to this exploration is the claim that tales of body-snatching, vampirism, organ-theft, and zombie-economics all comprise multiple imaginings of the risks to bodily integrity that inhere in a society in which individual survival requires selling our life-energies to people on the market.[9] Body-panics are thus,

---

7. For a highly influential novelistic riff on this theme see John le Carré, *The Constant Gardener* (2001) subsequently released in 2005 as a major film of the same name, directed by Fernando Meirelles.

8. The literature in this area is growing rapidly. For important accounts, see Scheper-Hughes and Wacquant 2002; Andrews and Nelkin 2001; Sharp 2000, pp. 287–328; and Scheper-Hughes 1996, pp. 3–11. Singapore has recently legalised payment for organ-'donations'; see Gutierrez 2009.

9. Amongst the more illuminating treatments of these issues see Comaroff 1997, pp. 7–25. Nancy Scheper-Hughes (see note 8 above) leans to a more purely literal treatment of these fears – a move which is laudatory given the postmodern amnesia about real corporeal damage done to the poor, but which tends to ignore the importance of these rumours as ways of imagining a wide range of other 'disembodying'

I submit, cultural phenomena endemic to capitalism, part of the phenomenology of bourgeois life. But, because liberal ideology typically denies these quotidian horrors, apprehensions of the monstrosities of the market tend to find discursive refuge in folklore, literature, video and film. Once we turn to these media, however, we also realise that monsters of the market operate on each side of body-panic, as both perpetrators and victims. In the former camp, we have those monstrous beings – vampires, evil doctors, pharmaceutical companies, body-snatchers – that capture and dissect bodies, and bring their bits to market. In the camp of the victims, we find those disfigured creatures, frequently depicted as zombies, who have been turned into *mere bodies*, unthinking and exploitable collections of flesh, blood, muscle and tissue.

At its heart, this book is about these monsters of the market and the *occult economies* they inhabit. In the chapters that follow, I argue that a whole genre of monster-tales, both past and present, manifest recurrent anxieties about corporeal dismemberment in societies where the commodification of human labour – its purchase and sale on markets – is becoming widespread. In making this argument, my study ranges from popular opposition to anatomists in early-modern England, an opposition captured in the poetics of Mary Shelley's *Frankenstein*, to vampire- and zombie-tales in contemporary Sub-Saharan Africa. In so doing, our investigation tracks themes of dissection, mindless labour, and the vampire-powers of capital across writers from Shakespeare to Dickens, from Mary Shelley to Ben Okri. And it re-reads Karl Marx's *Capital* as, amongst other things, a mystery-narrative that seeks out the hidden spaces in which bodies are injured and maimed by capital. Across all these readings, it shows how and why fears for the integrity of human bodies are so ubiquitous to modern society.

Today, Sub-Saharan Africa is the site of some of the most resonant legends of market-monstrosity. Ravaged by the forces of globalisation, the African subcontinent is rife today with tales of enrichment via cannibalism, vampirism and extraordinary intercourse between the living and the dead – of paths to private accumulation that pass through the mysterious world of the occult. In various parts of the African subcontinent, we encounter tales of magical coins

processes. Comaroff is more sensitive to these registers, though she does not share my emphasis on the commodification of labour as a crucial experiential underpinning of these panics.

that turn people into labouring zombies, of credit-cards that provide instant commodities without registering debt, of enchanted currencies that leave cash-registers and return to their owners after every commodity-exchange.[10] In Nigeria, newspapers carry reports of passengers on motorcycle-taxis who, once helmets are placed on their heads, mysteriously transform into zombies that spew money from their mouths – into human ATMs.[11] From Cameroon, Tanzania, South Africa and elsewhere come stories of witches who, rather than devouring their victims (as in older witchcraft-genres), turn them into zombie-labourers on invisible plantations in an obscure nocturnal economy. And, in all these countries, there is an epidemic of stories of dismemberment and murder for the purpose of harvesting body-parts which can be used in magic-potions that guarantee enrichment, or can be sold as commodities for the same purpose.[12]

Mainstream social science has a long tradition of characterising such tales as premodern superstitions that refuse to accommodate the disenchantment of society that is integral to modern life.[13] Yet such dismissals enact a mystification, denying as they do the systematic assaults on bodily and psychic integrity that define the economic infrastructure of modernity, the capitalist market-system. And that is why we need disruptive fables of modernity like those circulating throughout Sub-Saharan Africa today. For such tales disturb the naturalisation of capitalism – both of its social relations and the senses of property, propriety and personhood that accompany it – by insisting that something strange, indeed life-threatening, is at work in our world. So normalised has capitalism become in the social sciences, so naturalised its historically unique forms of life, that critical theory requires an armoury of de-familiarising techniques, a set of critical-dialectical procedures, that throw into relief its fantastic and mysterious processes. Discussing Freudian theory's attempts to unearth concealed mechanisms of psychic repression, Theodor

---

10. Geschière 1997, pp. 148, 152–5, 165; Fisiy and Geschière 1991, pp. 261, 264–6; Geschière 1999, pp. 221–2; Comaroff and Comaroff 1999b, p. 291.

11. Drohan 2000. The comparison of these zombies with ATMs is made in this article by Professor Misty Bastian.

12. On Nigeria see Drohan 2000; for South Africa see Comaroff and Comaroff 1999b, p. 290.

13. The classic formulation of the disenchantment-thesis belonged to Max Weber, but it has now even infiltrated the ostensibly 'critical' theory of Jürgen Habermas. See Habermas 1984, Chapter II.

Adorno once intoned that 'in psychoanalysis only the exaggerations are true'.[14] The structures of denial that dominate conscious life in modernity are so habitual, the intellectual and cultural web that normalises the repression of unconscious desires so intricate, that only images with explosive power can break the web of mystification. This is why psychoanalysis (at least in its most genuinely radical version) is compelled to *dramatise*, to use a metaphorical language and imagery that shocks the modern mind.[15] And what is true of the psychic conflicts in the life of individuals applies with markedly greater force where the traumas attendant on the commodification of everyday-life are concerned. 'The feeling of atomization and bondage which is the phenomenology of the market-based system'[16] has become so normalised, the buying and selling of all imaginable goods and human capacities, including body-parts, so routinised, that a genuinely critical theory must operate by way of estrangement-effects, via procedures that make the everyday appear as it truly is: bizarre, shocking, monstrous.[17]

But this means, as I argue across the chapters of this study, that critical theory must be capable of developing a *dialectical optics*, ways of seeing the unseen. For the essential features of capitalism, as Marx regularly reminded us, are not immediately visible. To be sure, many of their effects can be touched and measured. But the circuits through which capital moves are abstracted ones; we are left to observe things and persons – boxes of commodities, factories full of machines, workers straining inside the sweatshop, lines of people seeking work or bread – while the elusive power that grows and multiplies through their deployment remains unseen, un-comprehended. This is why critical theory sets out to see the unseen, to chart the cartography of the invis-

---

14. Adorno 1974, p. 49, translation modified.

15. Of course, psychoanalysis has itself undergone a sort of bourgeois domestication at the hands of 'neo-Freudian revisionists'. For a critique of this current see Marcuse 1955.

16. Taussig 1980, p. 27. Taussig's book, the first sustained interrogation of the intertwining of commodity-fetishism with precapitalist magical beliefs, is a pioneering work. While its theoretical framework suffers from uncritical use of the concept of 'natural economy', it remains of enormous importance for everyone interested in the issues I am exploring here.

17. This is one of the great strengths of the epic theatre of Bertolt Brecht as a form of radical aesthetic practise. On this see 'The Modern Theatre is the Epic Theatre' and 'Indirect Impact of the Epic Theatre' in Brecht 1964, and Benjamin 1973. I discuss Brecht and his decisive influence on Benjamin in McNally 2001, pp. 190–1.

ible. 'Invisible things are not necessarily not-there', observes Toni Morrison.[18] And it is the demonic power of such invisible things, the unseen operations of capital, that at least some fantastic legends seek to map.

'The fantastic might be a mode peculiarly resonant with the forms of modernity', observes China Miéville.[19] After all, straightforward narrative strategies regularly fail to register the reality of the unseen forces of capital; they assume that what is invisible is necessarily 'not there'. But this is to miss the essential: the hidden circuits of capital through which human capacities become things, while things assume human powers; in which markets 'rise' and 'fall', and in so doing dictate who shall prosper and who starve; in which human organs are offered up to the gods of the market in exchange for food or fuel. 'The reign of the market shapes conditions of life and death in a zombie economy', argues Henry A. Giroux.[20] And this means that invisible powers – market-forces – are at the same time *fantastically real*. Market-forces constitute horrifying aspects of a strange and bewildering world that represents itself as normal, natural, unchangeable. For this reason, fantastic genres, be they literary or folkloric, can occasionally carry a disruptively critical charge, offering a kind of grotesque realism that 'mimics the 'absurdity' of capitalist modernity' the better to expose it.[21]

As the global unleashing of unrestrained market-forces intensifies anxieties about the integrity of the body and generates horrifying images of bewitched accumulation, of occult forces exploiting zombie-labour, critical theory thus needs an alliance with the fantastic.[22] In seizing upon fabulous images of occult capitalism, critical theory ought to read them the way psychoanalysis interprets dreams – as a necessarily coded form of subversive knowledge whose decoding promises radical insights and transformative energies. Mining a popular imaginary populated by vampires, zombies and malevolent corporations that abduct and dissect people, critical theory needs to construct shock-effects that allow us to see the monstrous dislocations at the heart of

---

18. Morrison 1989. Avery F. Gordon (1997) takes up the question of invisibility in a powerfully compelling way. The notion of dialectical optics that I employ owes much to the work of Walter Benjamin and its interpretation by Buck-Morss 1989.

19. Miéville 2002, p. 42.

20. Giroux 2009.

21. Miéville 2002, p. 42.

22. This has been a theme of surrealist Marxism, of course. For a recent and exciting intervention in this area see Kelley 2002, Chapter 7.

commodified existence. And, because modern bourgeois consciousness was decisively shaped by its colonialist horror over African peoples and their customs, it is fitting that our investigation should culminates in Chapter Three with an interrogation of the poetic knowledge animating fables of monstrosity that emanate today from Sub-Saharan Africa.

'Poetic knowledge', urged Aimé Césaire, the legendary poet-writer-political theorist from Martinique, 'is born in the great silence of scientific knowledge'. And, since liberal-bourgeois rationalism pivots on a disdain for bodies, corporeal experience, and material practices, it is these that poetic wisdom seeks to capture.[23] 'What presides over the poem', Césaire continued, is 'experience as a whole'.[24] Yet, 'the great silence of [social] scientific knowledge' concerns the very experiential texture of life in a marketised society. Incapable of a dialectical optics that sees the unseen, it focuses on the observable: measures of output, employment, trade and gross national product. Meanwhile, the invisible processes of exploitation, and unmeasurable experiences of psychic and corporeal disintegration are occluded by its investigative lens. Popular folklore, however, occasionally becomes the preserve of poetic knowledge about what capitalism does to people at the deepest levels of corporeal and psychic existence. Rather than being treated as 'an eccentricity', folklore, as Gramsci insisted, deserves to be studied as 'a conception of the world and of life'.[25] In the chapters that follow, I seek to observe this injunction by attending to a variety of symbolic registers through which people come to know global capitalism, as it shapes bodily experience, sensibilities and freedom dreams.

Of course, Africa is not the only space of such folkloric knowledge. As I demonstrate in Chapter One, similar imaginings of monstrosity characterised the rise of capitalism in early-modern England, and found literary expression in works by Shakespeare, Dickens and Shelley, amongst others. And such imaginings are no mere relics of the past in the global North, as the explosion of vampire- and zombie-tales in film, video and pulp-fiction attest. Indeed, the

---

23. For an assessment of bourgeois rationalism in these terms see the Introduction to McNally 2001.

24. Césaire 1996. For a brilliant overview of Césaire's life and work, see Kelley's 'Introduction' to Césaire 2000, as well as Kelley 2002, Chapter 7.

25. Gramsci 1985, pp. 191, 189.

idea that something monstrous is at work in the operations of global capitalism is never far from the surface today, especially amongst social groups for whom intense commodification has not been utterly normalised.

Consider two cases of folkloric reactions by indigenous peoples in the Andean region of South America to debt-driven economic crises. In 1982–3, panic swept parts of Bolivia, where it was said that gringos, in cahoots with the country's president, had been sent by the World Bank on a mission to extract fat from peasants in order to repay foreign debts. Later in the decade, rumours circulated in Ayacucho neighbourhoods in Peru that children were being abducted by machine-gun wielding gringos equipped with instruments for tearing out eyeballs to be sold abroad in order to pay off foreign debts.[26] Here, we encounter another potent folkloric representation of the threats posed to bodily integrity by the financial circuits of global capitalism. After all, across the course of the 1980s – as neoliberal policies of privatisation, wage-cutting and 'structural adjustment' were being implemented – a staggering 50 million Latin Americans fell below the poverty-line. Homelessness, hunger and malnutrition stalked the continent, at the same time that billions were sent to financial institutions in the global North to pay off foreign debts.[27] Rather than premodern superstitions, therefore, fantastic depictions of global capitalism as a vampire-system that extracts and sells body-parts capture something very real about the economic universe we inhabit.

In so doing, contemporary fables of monsters of the market remind us of the etymology of the word monster itself, which derives from the Latin *monere* (to warn). Amongst other things, monsters are warnings – not only of what may happen but also of what is already *happening*. Yet, as we have seen, cultures often repress and deny the most profound warnings of monstrous happenings. 'Monsters of disaster', note two social theorists, 'are harbingers of things we do not want to face, of catastrophes'.[28] At the same time, as psychoanalysis tells us, at the same time as we repress these things we also crave to know them, indeed *need* to know them, if we are to change ourselves and our world.

---

26. Wachtel 1994, pp. 86–7, 82–3.
27. McNally 2006, p. 128.
28. Gordon and Gordon 2009, p. 10.

It is in this spirit that I read tales of monstrosity across different times and spaces of global capitalism, in an effort to unlock the critical energy lurking within fantastic narratives that interrogate the mysteries surrounding the creation and accumulation of wealth in modern society. And I urge that these fables be deployed as a means of mapping the cryptic transactions of global capital with human bodies that define our age. But this critical strategy is not without its difficulties, precisely because of the ubiquity of monsters today, their proliferation throughout mass-culture – and cultural theory.

Indeed, in cultural studies, a giddy embrace of monstrosity is underway, as monsters are positioned as heroic outsiders, markers of nonconformity and perversity, representing all those marginalised by dominant discourses and social values. Arguing that monstrous otherness is projected onto those who do not conform to cultural codes and norms – those, for example, whose language, sexuality or skin-colour are 'different' – postmodern theory tends to celebrate monsters, seeing them as the excluded who bind together dominant (normative) identities.[29] 'I am on the side of the monsters as signifiers of the radical destabilization of the binary processes of identity and difference that devalue otherness', writes one theorist.[30] There is certainly something to be learned from such readings of monstrosity. By using tropes of monstrosity to probe constructions of normality – be it with respect to ability, gender, sexual, racial or ethno-national identity – such studies often do critical work. However, in merely valorising the monstrous, postmodernist readings collapse into a kind of one-dimensional thought. Rather than seeing the arena of monstrosity as a site of contestation, instead of recognising that monster-images are multi-accentual, the postmodern celebration of the monstrous flattens out a field in which different social accents and values contest one another.[31]

---

29. As Richard Kearney notes, for postmodern social theory 'monsters are to be celebrated rather than demonized'. See Kearney 2002, p. 120. A crucial text in the development of the celebratory attitude toward the monstrous was Michel Foucault, 'The Order of Discourse' (1981, pp. 48–7), a lecture originally delivered in 1970. One notable work in this vein includes Gibson 1996, Chapter 7.

30. Shildrick 2002, p. 129. Shildrick's emphasis on the body is quite interesting and yields some real insights, but her deconstructive celebration of monstrosity wears thin in its one-sidedness. Antonio Negri, too, tends merely to valorise the monster. See Negri 2008, pp. 193–218. While Negri rightly links monstrosity to labour-power, he too loses sight of the monstrous appropriation of labour's powers by capital.

31. My notion of multi-accentuality draws upon the work of V.N. Voloshinov and Mikhail Bakhtin. See Voloshinov 1986; and Bakhtin 1981. I discuss these works in detail in McNally 2001, Chapter 4.

Postmodern accounts of monstrosity are thus disabled in two key respects. First, their obsession with identifying binary relations – in this case, self versus other and its plural form, us versus them – tends to lapse into what Hegel called *monochromatic formalism*, a tedious procedure in which the same conceptual schema is slapped over all phenomena.[32] The social and historical specificity of distinct forms of experience effectively vanishes in the reduction of all social relations to general categories of *us* and *them*. It is true that if I affirm my identity (or that of my 'country') as white, I embrace an us/them binary that excludes all who are non-white. However, the same is *formally* true if I passionately embrace an identity as an anti-racist, thereby defining racists as the 'others' against whom I and my companions (say, my anti-racist co-thinkers and activists) position ourselves. But in concrete social-historical circumstances, needless to say, the two forms of identification operate rather differently. One reinforces racial identities and practices while the other, at least in principle, challenges them. And this brings us to the second flaw with the postmodern approach: the way its universal injunction to be on the side of monsters tends to trivialise real ethico-political choices, sometimes dangerously so. It is one thing, after all, to be on the side of monstrous others like people of colour or sexual 'deviants' in the face of political persecution and repression. But it is quite another thing where multinational corporations, racist gangs or an imperial war-machine are the monsters in question. Yet, much postmodern theory, as one highly sympathetic commentator notes, offers us no guidelines for assessing 'the difference between benign and malignant others'. As a result, it evades 'our legitimate duty to try to distinguish...between saints and psychopaths'. And this inability to draw socially informed distinctions incapacitates much postmodern theory, leading it 'less to praxis than paralysis' in the face of the actual decisions that must be made on the terrain of real ethico-political life.[33]

Put simply, not all monsters are equal, and this is especially so where the monsters that stalk this book are concerned. It is all very well (and sometimes insightful) to delineate the horrors of the 'split self' – the human subject that projects unpalatable aspects of its self onto despised others. But it is

---

32. Hegel 1977, p. 9.
33. Kearney 2003, pp. 67, 70, 107–8. Kearney, whose orientation is heavily indebted to deconstruction, makes these criticisms with respect to the ethics of Jacques Derrida and Emmanuel Levinas.

something else again to analyse the horrors of a *split society*.[34] Yet it is precisely here that crucial aspects of modern horror originate, in the painful and traumatic processes through which non-capitalist social bonds are dissolved, individuals subjected to market-forces, and impersonal economic relationships created between the dominated and the dominant. In such circumstances, images of monstrosity track the intertwined experiences of corporeal fragmentation and social apartheid that characterise modern capitalism.

Something is decidedly lacking, therefore, in an approach that cannot differentiate distinct forms of monstrosity, and which cannot grasp the ways in which subaltern groups in capitalist society attach images of monstrosity to oppressive powers, not just subversive ones. Lacking a critical theory of capitalism, much of cultural studies is hampered when it comes to explaining the intertwining of monsters with markets, and the genuinely traumatic (monstrous) experiences of subjugation and exploitation that occur when people find themselves subordinated to the market-economy.

The vampire and Frankenstein's Creature constitute the two key-monsters that make their literary emergence with industrial capitalism – and which continue to haunt the modern imaginary. Products of early nineteenth-century capitalist industrialisation in Britain, these monsters, and the anxieties they register, have significant parallels – and, as we shall see, some critical differences – with those prowling Sub-Saharan Africa and Latin America today. *Frankenstein*, I argue in Chapter One, is in important measure a story about the monstrous practices of grave-robbing, body-theft, and dissection – in short, about corporeal dismemberment. And the resonance of this story owed much to actual phenomena, which became points of contestation at the gallows in eighteenth-century London, as the urban crowd fought to save the bodies of the hanged from anatomists seeking to procure corpses for dissection. For the British working class, anatomists, surgeons and resurrectionists were all part of a general conspiracy to degrade and oppress the poor in both life and death through kidnapping, murder, grave-robbing and dissection. But these popular anxieties about body-snatching involved more, I submit, than the fear of one's corpse being plundered. With the original accumulation

---

34. However, as I argue in Chapter 1 in my analysis of Mary Shelley's *Frankenstein*, it is also possible to dialectically link problems of psychic and social division.

of capital in Britain – principally achieved through dispossessing millions of the poor of their land – huge numbers of people could henceforth survive only by selling their bodily capacities on the labour-market. This unprecedented and deeply traumatising experience was profoundly resented and contested. And rescuing the corpses of the poor from those who would claim them as private property in order to chop them up offered a rare victory in the battle to save working-class bodies from commodification. It is in this light, I contend, that we need to read Mary Shelley's *Frankenstein*. Arguably 'the classic fictional account of the bodysnatching era',[35] Shelley's novel drew upon images of monstrosity that were the stock-in-trade of the popular culture of the English working class.

Part of the genius of Karl Marx is to have intuited something of this plebeian culture and to have mobilised it for critical purpose in his monumental analysis of the capitalist system. Numerous commentators have noted Marx's propensity to enlist images of monsters to depict how capitalism operates. Describing the way in which it expands by appropriating the unpaid labour of workers, Marx writes that 'Capital is dead labour which, vampire-like, lives only by sucking living labour'. Elsewhere, he describes capital's 'werewolf-like hunger for surplus labour' and its 'vampire thirst for the living blood of labour'.[36] Typically, formulations of this sort are seen as mere rhetorical flourishes; rarely has their strategic-theoretical purpose been divined, nor its connection to the theme of corporeal dismemberment. As Marx searched for a means of depicting the actual horrors of capitalism – from child-labour, to the extermination of North America's indigenous peoples, from the factory-system to the slave-trade – he reworked the discourse of monstrosity that emerged with the rise of capitalism. Pillaging popular and literary imagination, from vampire-tales to Goethe's *Faust*, he cast capitalism as both a modern horror-story and a mystery tale, each inexplicable outside the language of monstrosity.

More than this, one of the absolutely crucial concepts of Marx's *Capital*, that of *abstract labour*, to be discussed at length in Chapter Two, pivots on notions of separation and dismemberment. To capital, argues Marx, all workers and the labours they perform are effectively interchangeable. The distinctive

---

35. Marshall 1995, p.14.
36. Marx 1976, pp. 342, 353, 367.

character of workers and their labours matter nothing when commodities enter into competition on the market. Specific goods, from bread to blue jeans, computers to cars – count merely as means to accumulate wealth. Similarly, specific acts of production – tailoring, assembling computers, building cars – are in principle all the same process, the production of surplus-value. As a result, radically different concrete work processes are reduced to a single standard: commodity-producing, profit-generating labour. So, when Marx claims that capitalism is organised on the basis of *abstract* labour, he also has the literal sense of the word in mind. To abstract [Latin: *abstrahere*, 'to draw away'] is literally to separate, detach, cut off.[37] And capitalism abstracts (detaches, cuts off) labour and its products from the concrete and specific individuals who perform unique productive acts, treating all work as effectively identical and interchangeable. The capitalist system of production and exchange thereby homogenises all forms of waged work, reducing them to pure quanta of qualitatively undifferentiated human labour in the abstract. This, as I explain below, is an abstraction that actually happens – a process of *real abstraction* – in a world of universal market-exchange governed by money.

All of this has important implications where workers are concerned. It means that rather than their own life-force, their fundamental human creative energy, workers' labouring power becomes a commodity, a separable and detachable thing that can be sold, handed over to someone else. As a commodity, labour is not seen as integral to human personhood but, instead, as something that can be isolated and given to a buyer for a stipulated period of time. In buying labouring power, then, capital takes possession of labour, effectively draining it of its substance as a series of unique and unrepeatable acts tied to specific human personalities. Commodified abstract labour is thus effectively *disembodied*, detached from the persons who perform it. This detachability of commodified labour allows capitalists to break up and dissect work-processes into their component parts, confining individuals to the repetition of a limited number of human movements. As identical and interchangeable units of homogeneous labour-power, workers' skills and bodies are dissected, fragmented, cut up into separable pieces subjected to the direction of an alien-force, represented by a legion of supervisors, and embedded

---

37. See the *Oxford English Dictionary Online* 1989, and the quite useful discussion by Rader 1979, pp. 150–9.

in rhythms and processes of work that are increasingly dictated by automatic programmes and systems of machinery.[38] In analysing these processes, Marx resorts repeatedly to the language of monstrosity. Capitalist manufacture 'mutilates the worker', he writes, 'turning him into a fragment of himself'. Describing capital's appearance in the form of the modern automated workplace where machines dominate workers, he refers to it as 'a mechanical monster whose body fills whole factories', and he denounces its 'demonic power' over living labour.[39]

Contrary to a widespread misunderstanding, one of Marx's great insights was to discern that capitalism could not be understood merely in terms of new techniques for producing goods. To think in such terms is to *fetishise*, to interpret transformations in human social relations as if they simply involved new interrelations amongst things (machines and commodities). Commodified labour involves a profound and thorough-going restructuring of human experience: people's sense of their very bodies, of their capacities and creative energies, of the interrelation of self and things, and of self and others – all of these are utterly transformed by commodification. 'The capitalist epoch is therefore characterized', writes Marx, 'by the fact that labour-power, in the eyes of the worker himself, takes on the form of a commodity which is his property'.[40] But workers do not submit to this new reality without resistance. Because it ruptures established customs, social relations and senses of personhood, the rise of capitalist labour-markets invariably meets with potent opposition. More than this, it inspires amazingly creative efforts by subaltern groups to map just what is happening to the very corporeal and social fabric of their lives.

African witchcraft-tales are, as we shall see, amongst the most vivid contemporary expression of such efforts. And this makes them especially compelling in an age in which capitalism has become as invisible as the air we breathe. In their insistence that something not-quite-real is at work within global capitalism, some occult process of exploitation that conceals itself, these tales carry a *defetishising* charge. Across these stories, real bodies are implicated and at risk: they perform unseen zombie-labour; they are possessed by evil spirits that

---

38. Marx 1976, p. 302.
39. Marx 1976, pp. 482, 503.
40. Marx 1976, p. 274n4.

turn them into money machines; they are dissected for marketable parts. A hermeneutics of suspicion animates these folktales, a mistrust of the self-satisfied narratives of bourgeois culture. And this should come as little surprise at a time when the per capita incomes in Sub-Saharan Africa have contracted by fully twenty-five per cent in the space of a decade, while the continent is bled of hundreds of millions of dollars *per day* to repay debts to world-banks. For all their involvement with witches and spirits, contemporary vampire-tales in urban Africa are driven by a materialist impulse to search out the sites where real bodies are at risk. And, in seeking out those bodies, African discourses of witchcraft detail the ways in which they are enmeshed in dangerous logics of exploitation and accumulation – nowhere more life-threatening than in Sub-Saharan Africa itself.

To be sure, as I argue further below, all such tales are multivalent. They are about more than the threats to bodily integrity posed by labour-markets in the era of capitalist globalisation. Gender-anxiety, colonial histories, memories of slavery, the depredations of an HIV-AIDS pandemic – all this and more animates some of these tales. Yet, while these fables of modernity are not reducible to existential anxieties associated with mysterious transactions between money and labouring bodies, neither can they be adequately grasped outside these modes of experience. Indeed, as I try to show, they provide crucial symbolic registers in which these experiences are received, handled and resisted.

Moreover, as I show throughout the chapters that follow, such tales have appeared at a number of compelling moments in the global rise of capitalism, and have been reworked in powerful works of literary imagination by the likes of William Shakespeare, Charles Dickens, Mary Shelley and, most recently, Ben Okri. By reminding us that commodified social relations unleash monstrous forces of death and dismemberment, such literary creations harbour a poetic wisdom we can ill afford to squander. As capitalism globalises war, hunger and environmental destruction, we would be well advised to heed their warning that monstrous forces prowl our planet. It is the central argument of this book that we need this wisdom, dialectically worked up, not merely to understand the world in which we live, but also to nurture critical resources for remaking it.

Chapter One

Dissecting the Labouring Body: *Frankenstein,* Political Anatomy and the Rise of Capitalism

> But suppose that many of our common Thieves were not to be buried at all, and some of them made Skeletons.... What if it was a Disgrace to the surviving Relations of those, who had Lectures read upon their Bodies, and were made use of for Anatomical Preparations?[1]

The author of these lines, Dr. Bernard Mandeville, was amongst those 'respectable' citizens who attended public hangings at the gallows at Tyburn, roughly three miles from London's notorious Newgate prison. Like many of his sort, Mandeville was appalled by the raucous opposition to authority he observed there. His letters of 1725 (first published in the *British Journal* and later issued together as a pamphlet, *An Enquiry into the Causes of the Frequent Executions at Tyburn*) lament the tumult surrounding public executions. Rather than solemn rituals that impress the lower classes with the gravity of the law, public hangings had become occasions for turbulent displays of solidarity with the condemned by thousands of the London poor. Deploring the 'scene of confusion' that reigned in the streets, Mandeville complains that the jailors are regularly assaulted

---

1. Mandeville 1964, p. 27.

by 'the most resolute and sturdy of the Mob'. He bemoans 'the loud laughter' and 'oaths and vile expressions' of a riotous crowd that overflows with
drunks and gin-sellers, cats and dogs. Ticking off the terrible effects of this
boisterous, chaotic whirl of bodies and animals, he enumerates the 'blows that
are struck, the heads that are broke, the pieces of swinging sticks, and blood,
that fly about'. Having completed his horrible picture, Mandeville turns to
the commotion that ensues once the hanging is complete: 'The Tragedy being
ended, the next Entertainment is a Squabble between the Surgeons and the
Mob, about the dead Bodies of the Malefactors.... They have suffer'd the Law
(cries the Rabble), and shall have no other Barbarities put upon them.'[2]

The barbarity in question is, of course, dissection – the very reason for the
presence of the 'surgeons' – which, as the eighteenth century progressed, was
practised on growing numbers of corpses of the poor. Addressing this issue,
Mandeville's rhetoric changes register. No longer the outraged observer of the
tumultuous rabble, he strides forward as a dispassionate scientist, extolling
dissection as necessary to the progress of knowledge. To his dismay, however, the royal road to science is blocked by the unruly mob, which battles the
surgeons for the corpses of the condemned:

> ...the superstitious Reverence of the Vulgar for a Corpse, even of a Male-
> factor, and the strong Aversion they have against dissecting them, are preju-
> dicial to the Publick; For as Health and sound Limbs are the most desirable
> of all Temporal Blessings, so we ought to encourage the Improvement of
> Physick and Surgery. The Knowledge of Anatomy is inseparable from the
> Studies of either....[3]

This argument leads the good doctor to a proposal that anticipated the whole
direction of ruling-class opinion on these matters for the next hundred years:
routine dissection of the bodies of all who have been condemned. While
pitching his proposal as a scientific duty, Mandeville does not conceal the
social agenda it enacts. Dissection, it turns out, ought also to be a source of
disgrace and dishonour:

> But suppose that many of our common Thieves were not to be buried at
> all, and some of them made Skeletons.... What if it was a Disgrace to the

2. Mandeville 1964, pp. 24, 26.
3. Mandeville 1964, p. 26.

surviving Relations of those, who had Lectures read upon their Bodies, and were made use of for Anatomical Preparations? The Dishonour would seldom reach beyond the Scum of the People.... The University of *Leyden* in *Holland* have a Power given them by the Legislature to demand, for this Purpose, the Bodies of ordinary Rogues...[4]

The mask is now off. Stepping forward we recognise the bourgeois ideologue lurking in the guise of the disinterested scientist. Dissection, first extolled for the advancement of knowledge, now emerges as a means of disciplining and punishing proletarian bodies. The interconnection of power and knowledge (in this case, anatomy) could scarcely be more blatant – but, *contra* Michel Foucault, this bourgeois discipline was not to be achieved by massaging minds to conform with authority, but by directly (and punitively) imprinting bodies.[5] Mandeville's striking expression, *'lectures read upon their bodies'*, is especially worthy of note. After all, bodies are not just being subjected to the optical gaze of power – they are being marked, cut, dismembered. The multiple meanings of Mandeville's intriguing term 'lectures' are instructive in this regard. While the word refers to the action of reading and to public discourse, it also carries the sense of admonition and correction, as in being lectured by someone.[6] And Mandeville's reference to the 'disgrace' of having 'lectures read upon their bodies' clearly intends the moralising and disciplinary effects of this ostensibly scientific practice. As in Kafka's *Penal Colony*, where prisoners are forced to have messages written on their bodies, the moral instructions comprise corporeal warnings, monstrous injunctions written on the flesh.[7] In the case in question, these entail threats as to the physical fate – dissection – that awaits plebs who dare defy the law.

Before the working-class body can be read, however, it must first be written, it must be marked as a certain kind of 'text'. Mandeville, for one, had no doubt as to what this entailed: the grueling disciplines of wage-labour. From childhood, he argued, the poor must be put to 'Dirty Slavish Work' for as many hours as possible – 'most Days in the Week, and the greatest part of the

---

4. Mandeville 1964, p. 27.
5. Foucault's seminal, but in important respects misleading, account of bodies and power received its first systematic sketch in Foucault 1979, especially Part III.
6. See the entries in the *Oxford English Dictionary Online* 1989, under 'lecture'.
7. Kafka 1961.

Day' – and for the lowest possible wages.[8] Across the eighteenth century, this programme proceeded unrelentingly, as proletarian bodies were inscribed ever more thoroughly by the disciplines of wage-labour, and forced to submit to the intrusions of capitalist control. Popular hostility to dissection of the poor can be adequately understood only in this context – as one expression of a powerful hatred of the corporeal régimes of wage-labour (including its associated system of crime and punishment). Whatever else this hostility entailed, it signalled hatred of the persistent 'lectures read upon' working-class bodies'. And at the gallows, the London crowd fought to insure that in death 'no other Barbarities' should be inflicted upon the bodies of the poor.

'Save my body from the surgeons'

Awaiting death by hanging in 1737, Henry Bosworway, a sawyer, implored a workmate 'to save my body from the surgeons'. Sentenced to death two years later for theft, Richard Tobin, a drawer, entreated his former master to take 'into Consideration my poor body' by insuring that it should be 'saved from the Surgeons'. Family-members and friends often needed no such prompting, regularly assuring loved ones awaiting the gallows that 'we shall take Care of your Body'. As Peter Linebaugh has brilliantly shown, saving the bodies of the condemned from dissection was a central aspect of a working-class culture of solidarity against the law and the authorities.[9] To this end, the labouring poor created two unique 'forms of working-class cooperation in the face of death': the Friendly Societies to which workers contributed pennies to fund a proper burial, and the riot against the surgeons.[10]

The riot at the gallows was one of the most distinctive features of social life in eighteenth-century London, without parallel in any other European city. Its uniqueness signalled three things: widespread contempt for the law; an insurgent culture of resistance; and a deeply felt anxiety about the integrity of the labouring body.

---

8. Mandeville 1970, pp. 307, 281–2, 294. For more on Mandeville see McNally 1993, p. 47.
9. See Linebaugh 1975. The three quotations cited all come from Linebaugh's pioneering article, pp. 82, 83, 84.
10. Linebaugh 1975, p. 83.

The contempt of the London poor for law and authority was rooted in a centuries-long battle to defend common rights against incursions by the ruling class. Much ostensible 'crime' was perceived by the lower classes as simple defence of longstanding rights, as survival-strategies sanctioned by centuries of custom. Stealing, poaching and smuggling from the parks and forests of the rich – many of them once sites for the exercise of common rights, such as hunting, fishing and gathering of wood, berries and herbs – were routinely celebrated. The Ordinary of Newgate remarked in 1735, for instance, that 'It has for some years been a Practice amongst a parcel of the idle dissolute Fellows in defiance of the Laws, to associate themselves together in Parties in order to rob Gentlemen's *Parks, Chases* &c., of Deer.'[11] Contemptuous of the new forms of bourgeois property in whose name they were persecuted and prosecuted, the labouring poor glorified defiant thieves, like Dick Turpin and Jack Sheppard, who regularly eluded arrest and escaped from jail. Turpin, a famous highwayman, dealt extensively in stolen horses, cattle and sheep – the very species whose breeding was bound up with the displacement of the poor from the land. Moreover, the places where highwaymen often lived, common lands and forests near roads between towns, spoke directly to what had been stolen from the poor, as if their thefts were meant to symbolically reverse the famous expropriation of the peasantry from the land. Underlining these class-contestations, many highwaymen preyed deliberately on the rich and powerful, ignoring those of modest means.[12]

Popular opinion celebrated such criminals. Ballads and rhymes extolled their feats, and children were named and nicknamed in their honour. And, if the poor could do little to aid them in life, they took up their cause in death. Once Turpin had finally been captured, convicted and hanged, the London poor sought a justice of sorts for him in death, rushing the gallows to seize his body before the surgeons could claim it. A few days after his burial, when rumours circulated that his body had been stolen and dissected, a crowd quickly gathered at the burial sight, exhumed Turpin's body and, on finding it there, carried it victoriously through the streets of York.[13] Similarly, the 1724 execution of Jack Sheppard, whose escapes from captivity were the stuff

---

11. As quoted in Linebaugh 2003, p. 202. The classic study of such poachers and thieves and their treatment by the upper classes, is E.P. Thompson 1975.
12. Linebaugh 2003, p. 203, n. 36.
13. Moore 1997, p. 225.

of folklore, was the occasion for the largest outpouring of the London crowd in 75 years. As thousands thronged the gallows, a plebeian guard fought off the surgeons. Battles continued throughout the afternoon and evening until, around midnight, Sheppard's body was buried at St. Martin-in-the-Fields.[14] Although his corpse was badly damaged and torn by the crowd who fought to claim it, this seems not to have perturbed its protectors. Bodily damage inflicted by the crowd was tolerable, as was digging up a corpse and parading it through the streets – so long as it was saved from dissection by the surgeons.

It seems, therefore, that something other than religious or spiritual belief was at issue in these contests. Although many commentators have invoked 'traditional religious beliefs in the sanctity of the corpse' as the explanation for the furore aroused by dissection, the evidence supporting this interpretation is decidedly thin.[15] In fact, many popular attitudes to the bodies of the hanged owed more to pragmatic concerns with life, not afterlife. Hanging, as Linebaugh reminds us, was a notoriously uncertain means of ending a human life. The noose was meant to cause death by asphyxiation; but tied loosely or inexactly, it often induced loss of consciousness, rather than loss of life. The London poor were well aware of cases – such as that of 'Half-Hanged Smith' – where men and women were revived hours after having been pronounced dead at the gallows.[16] In fighting for the bodies of the hanged, therefore, the crowd may in part simply have been trying to save lives, rather than displaying 'superstitious reverence' for the corpse, as Mandeville claimed. Furthermore, the willingness of the crowd to damage Jack Sheppard's body so long as they kept it from the surgeons, suggests that it was *control* over the plebeian body that was at stake, more than its physical integrity. To be sure, longstanding burial-practices were concerned with appropriate means of entering the afterlife; but eighteenth-century anxieties about dissection appear to have been fairly recent. Rather than a defence of longstanding traditions, the riot

---

14. Linebaugh 2003, pp. 38–9; Moore 1997, pp. 224–5; Linebaugh 1975, p. 105.

15. Moore 1997, pp. 224–5. Ruth Richardson's important work attempts to summarise popular attitudes toward death and the corpse, yet much of the evidence rests on an assessment of 'a popular theology' prevalent in the eighteenth and early nineteenth centuries (Richardson 1987, p. 7; see also p. 90), when, as I argue below, such beliefs were almost certainly undergoing important transformations.

16. Linebaugh 1975, pp. 103–4.

against the surgeons would seem to register much newer sensibilities about the commodification of human life. As E.P. Thompson astutely observed:

> ...we cannot present the rioter as an archaic figure, motivated by the 'debris' of older patterns of thought, and then pass the matter off with a reference to death- superstition and *les rois thaumaturges*.... The code which informs these riots, whether at Tyburn in 1731 or at Manchester in 1832, cannot be understood only in terms of beliefs about death and its proper treatment. It involves also class solidarities, and the hostility of the plebs to the psychic cruelty of the law and to the marketing of primary values.[17]

Reference to plebeian hostility toward 'the marketing of primary values' seems particularly apposite. For, just as the human corpse was becoming a new kind of commodity throughout the eighteenth century (a point to which I return later in this chapter), so were the living bodies of the poor. The rise of capitalism involved an unrelenting commodification of the labouring body and its powers. Progressively deprived of non-market means of survival – common lands, common rights and various perquisites – the poor had little option but to turn to the market, as sellers of their own labouring power, in order to secure their subsistence. To be sure, the working poor fought this reduction of their labour to just another marketable good among many; but, over the long haul, capital proved largely victorious. At the gallows, however, the plebeian crowd could gather in their thousands to publicly reclaim prole-tarian bodies from market-forces. In wresting the corpse from the surgeons, the crowd struck a blow – both symbolic and real – against commodification and for the integrity of the proletarian body, male and female, if only in death. In burying it intact, they claimed a moral victory over the dismembering powers of capital.

The culture of dissection: anatomy, colonisation and social order

Dissection of human corpses was not always frowned upon in medieval and early-modern Europe. Indeed, from the eleventh through the eighteenth centuries, members of the upper classes often left instructions in their wills that

---

17. Thompson 1978, p. 157. Ironically, Moore 1997 cites this article in support of the claim that the issues involved concerned traditional religious beliefs.

they should be dismembered and their body-parts be buried at different sites. Choice of dissection usually had a twofold purpose: first, to leave something of their remains near loved ones (parents, spouses, siblings, children) who were buried at disparate locations; and, secondly, to receive more prayers (delivered by members of religious orders at each site) which might aid them in their afterlives. So popular with the upper classes was the practice of dismemberment and burial at multiple sites that it not only persisted, but even increased in frequency, despite a ban imposed in 1299 by Pope Boniface VIII.[18] Moreover, in the early-modern period, one encounters a growing aesthetic fascination with the isolation and separation of body-parts: we find them visually depicted on blazons that adorned armour, and lyrically represented in poetry.[19] Lack of concern for the integrity of the cadaver is further indicated in the routine use of dissection to establish cause of death in the cases of kings, nobles and church-officials.[20]

Following the Reformation, a powerful current of hostility toward care for the corpse swept English culture. To Puritans, ritual mourning, tombs and epitaphs all constituted idolatrous practices, typical of a popish confusion of material things (in this case, cadavers and items designed to commemorate them) with those of the spirit. Embalming or mummifying the corpse encountered special resistance. In light of this disdain for the materiality of the corpse, English funeral-rites generally became sparer, so much so that, in 1649, one commentator described them as 'in a manner profane, in many places the dead being thrown into the ground like dogs, and not a word said.[21] Although there may have been a partial return to earlier practices after the Restoration (1660), there is little evidence that traditional concerns for the sanctity of human remains fuelled popular opposition to dissection in eighteenth-century London. Indeed, what evidence there is suggests that eighteenth-century hostility to anatomy was of recent vintage. For instance, the records of the Company of Barber-Surgeons of London, which had performed public anatomies since 1540, indicate that seizing corpses for purposes of dissection 'was undisputed until the early eighteenth century'.[22]

---

18. See Brown 1981, pp. 222–6, 241, 263, 251.
19. See, for example, Vickers 1997.
20. McManners 1981, p. 41.
21. As quoted by Thomas 1971, p. 605.
22. Creegan 2008, p. 20.

Although dissection was performed routinely throughout the medieval period in Europe, largely on the remains of those from the upper class, it was not until the last decade of the fifteenth century that post-mortems were widely used to acquire anatomical knowledge. Before then, theoretical anatomy in Europe eschewed dirtying its hands with the empirical work of dissection and anatomisation. The occasional task of dissecting human bodies was left to less than reputable groups such as barber-surgeons, executioners, and bath-keepers, who seem to have performed those punitive dissections of criminals for which we have records from the middle ages on. With the Renaissance, however, a decisive shift occurred in the status of anatomy. As new generations of intellectuals sought to remake the natural sciences on the basis of empirical observation and experiment, anatomy came to occupy a privileged position. The year 1543 looms large in this regard: in addition to seeing the publication of Copernicus's *On the Revolutions of the Celestial Spheres*, it also witnessed the appearance of a path-breaking text in anatomy, Andreas Vesalius's *On the Workings of the Human Body*, published in Basel. Advertising his proficiency at dissection by performing public anatomies, Vesalius prided himself on having recast his science by overcoming the medieval prejudice against manual work. Woodcuts adorning Vesalius's text, which was repeatedly translated and reprinted, portrayed the anatomist cutting into human corpses.

The mapping of the body was more than a new trend in the natural sciences – it also became a central cultural event, one which energised the arts as well. Attendance at public anatomies became a mark of enlightenment; and artists, philosophers and civic leaders took up dissection. Not only is Leonardo da Vinci said to have performed up to thirty anatomies, but René Descartes frequented Amsterdam butcher-shops in search of carcasses for dissection, and Rembrandt owned arms and legs that had been anatomised by Vesalius.[23] Interest in anatomy became an index of intelligence, wit and education; indeed, it was not uncommon in eighteenth-century France for a wealthy man to have his own private dissecting room.[24] Denis Diderot, for instance, not only authored the article on anatomy in the *Encyclopédie* of the

---

23. On Da Vinci see Heckscher 1958, p. 45. On Descartes and Rembrandt, consult Sawday 1995, p. 148.
24. Áries 1981, p. 366.

French Enlightenment, but also assisted at dissections.[25] So pervasive was the influence of anatomy that it underwent a semantic inflation, emerging as a paradigm for all sorts of investigations in the arts and human sciences. Infiltrating philosophy, literary criticism, political economy and botany, the term featured in the titles of one significant work after another: *The Anatomy of Wit* (1578), *Anatomy of Absurdity* (1589) *The Anatomy of Melancholy* (1621), *The Political Anatomy of Ireland* (1672), *Comparative Anatomy of the Trunks of Plants* (1675), and so on.

Emerging in Padua in the late fourteenth century, dissection for the scientific study of human anatomy spread rapidly throughout much of Europe in the following century, becoming a feature of virtually all major universities.[26] Yet, alongside scientific anatomy, a curious offshoot developed: the public anatomy. Again Padua took the lead, with the first known public dissection being performed there in 1497. And *performed* is the operative word. A public anatomy, invariably conducted on the body of an executed criminal, was a meticulously theatrical event. Presented at night in an 'anatomy-theatre' to packed houses of 200 to 300 fee-paying spectators, the performance was enacted on a stage (or an anatomy-table that served as such), often to musical accompaniment. The event, which typically lasted four to five days, was generally an annual one – and usually performed in January, during the traditional carnival-season. Yet, especially in Protestant Europe, the festive anatomy was governed by bourgeois order and decorum and obeyed a carefully regulated script. As if to underline the seriousness of the occasion, the Ordinances of the Surgeons of Amsterdam, ordained in 1605 and 1625, specified that the audience refrain from laughing and talking. In such regulations, we glimpse the role of public anatomy in the formation of a bourgeois civic culture.

All forms of class-power are bound up with aesthetics of rule, and the public culture of the European bourgeoisie was no exception. Like feudal domination, bourgeois authority required its unique social spaces, architectural and artistic forms, symbolic displays and civic rituals. The public anatomy played

---

25. Landes 2004, p. 167.
26. Harley 1994, p. 4, and Ferrari 1987, p. 55. It is important to note that temporary anatomy-theatres had existed in Italy and Germany since the twelfth century. But their integration with universities comes later, and the first permanent anatomy-theatres not until the late sixteenth century – 1594 in Padua and 1597 in Leiden. On the early history, see Brockbank 1968, pp. 371–84.

a key role in this regard, theatrically enacting the forms of bourgeois power developing in the rapidly growing, and often socially volatile, urban spaces of early-modern Europe.[27]

'Aesthetics is born as a discourse of the body', Terry Eagleton has reminded us[28] – and this is perhaps nowhere more evident than in the ceremony of public anatomy. Not only were a group of respected scientists and civic leaders gathering to display their talents for the edification of hundreds of respectable, paying spectators, they were also literally inscribing the rule of law – of property rights and 'free trade' – on the body of an executed member of the lower ranks of society. Such events partook in an aesthetics of domination, a pleasurable (and, for those from the lower classes, masochistic) identification with the victors and their laws. One of the elements involved was clearly 'a delight in particularisation' – a joy in partitioning and mapping – that lay at the heart of the Renaissance 'culture of dissection'.[29] But this joy in dissecting and particularising was equally bound up with the celebration of power – especially the new kinds of class- and colonial power that emerged during the age of anatomy.[30] And this aesthetics of authority was regularly and symbolically enacted on the bodies of the poor.

It is particularly noteworthy that the anatomical 'mapping' of the body took off in the sixteenth century, the era that saw a great burst of European colonisation. Moreover, the language of anatomy and that of colonialism meshed with each other, sometimes via an erotics of dissection. The aesthetic pleasures of anatomisation, of claiming, appropriating and partitioning 'virgin'-territory is especially evident in the poetry of John Donne, where the erotically anatomised body is linked with the penetrated and appropriated

---

27. It should be noted that bourgeois cultures can emerge without the establishment of a fully-fledged capitalist mode of production. The northern Italian city-states of the fifteenth and sixteenth centuries, for instance, had well-developed commercial bourgeoisies even though the mode of production was by no means capitalist.

28. Eagleton 1990, p. 13.

29. Sawday 1995, pp. viii, 2–3.

30. As I explain below, the development of early-modern cultures of bourgeois rule in urban settings should not be taken to mean that the capitalist mode of production had taken root in all these contexts. Urban-bourgeois power sometimes existed in a complex, subordinate relationship to feudal domination, as in France. In other cases, such as the Netherlands in the seventeenth and early eighteenth centuries, forms of commodity-production coexisted with powerful interests based on merchant's capital and bourgeois rent-seeking. England provides the first case of a decisive transformation of the entire mode of production along capitalist lines.

female body, itself described as America. In Donne's poems, we also see how the anatomists' delight in particularisation articulated the English experience of enclosing, mapping, dissecting, particularising and privatising common lands.[31] To delight in anatomy was, therefore, to revel in a new social project of colonising and mapping domestic and foreign lands – along with domestic and foreign bodies. Public anatomy, it is worth reminding ourselves, had no scientific value. Its purpose was, instead, a civic display of bourgeois rule enacted on the body of paupers and criminals, a ritual designed to inscribe social control over the bodies of the labouring poor.[32] Its practice in the Netherlands illustrates this clearly.

During the seventeenth century, Leiden University became the leading centre of anatomy, supplanting Padua. Every year, the Guild of Physicians and Surgeons publicly anatomised the body of a criminal executed in the city, a practice intimately entwined with the deep worries of the Dutch bourgeoisie about the growth and disposition of the urban rabble (the *grauw*). As social inequality mounted and the ranks of the urban poor expanded, bourgeois attitudes toward the destitute became increasingly harsh, leading a number of Dutch writers in the second half of the sixteenth century to advocate forced labour for the idle poor. Such proposals had become social policy by century's end: a workhouse for men was launched in Amsterdam in 1589, while one for the female poor opened its doors seven years later. Over the next century, twenty-six Dutch towns followed Amsterdam's lead.[33] In the shadows of its celebrated golden age, the Dutch bourgeoisie erected an unrelentingly cruel régime of punishment for the poor. Compelled to languish for years in the House of Correction, able-bodied beggars were subjected to draconian regimes of forced labour.[34] But confinement in a House of Correction was among the lesser worries of those who fell afoul of the law. Harsh corporal punishment was the ultimate deterrent: 'Young delinquents were branded

31. See the excellent discussion of this theme in Sawday 1995, pp. 24–8. While Sawday does not pursue these important connections with enclosure, he does see how the agrarian-capitalist language of 'improvement' becomes the idiom in Donne of a colonising ethos.

32. Ferrari 1987, pp. 90–4. As William S. Heckscher observed (1958, p. 24), public anatomy served 'moral-didactic rather than scientific-didactic purposes'.

33. Lis and Soly 1979, pp. 118–19.

34. See Schama 1987, pp. 17–20. While Schama tends to underemphasise the harsh and punitive attitudes toward the poor that characterised the Dutch bourgeoisie, a point to which I return, his summary here is quite helpful.

with red-hot irons, pedlars of dirty books were dragged through the streets, or pilloried, murderers were burnt alive; the rack, whip and torture-chamber were in constant use.'[35] Public anatomy was bound up with disciplinary practices designed to alleviate bourgeois anxieties through the ritual exercise of class-power over the proletarian body. A remarkable case study in this regard is provided by Rembrandt's famous painting, *The Anatomy of Dr. Nicolaas Tulp* (Figure 1).

Rembrandt's painting was composed in the early months of 1632, on behalf of the Guild of Surgeon-Anatomists of Amsterdam and in celebration of a public anatomy performed by their chief anatomist, Dr. Nicolaas Tulp, on the corpse of a young man, Adriaen Adriaenszoon (also known as Aris Kindt), convicted of stealing a coat. The timing is significant, as Amsterdam was then in the midst of its transformation into the pre-eminent commercial and banking centre in Europe. Indeed, the city was effectively rebuilt during this period, with traditional signifiers of bourgeois status marking its ascent: its *Illustre School*, soon to be a university, opened in 1632, the year Rembrandt immortalised Tulp's anatomy, while its full-time anatomy-theatre was completed seven years later. January 1632 was also the month in which the theologian and poet Caspar Barlaeus delivered a memorable speech inaugurating the city's *Illustre School*. Entitled 'Mercator Sapiens' (The Cultured Merchant), the speech praised the wedding of wisdom and commerce characteristic of his bustling bourgeois metropolis.[36] Tulp's 1632 anatomy was equally meant as a civic marker of Amsterdam's coming of age.

It was not a city that was coming of age, of course, so much as its ruling class. And the group portrait played a crucial role in this regard, expressing and shaping new corporate, civic and class-identities. Where aristocratic portraiture had concentrated on individuals and their family ties, the group-portrait was a means by which male representatives of the urban middle class could forge a civic identity as builders of a new economic, political and cultural space centred on the bourgeois town. Captured together in the act of meeting, conferring, adjudicating, governing and banqueting, bourgeois élites presented themselves as a new breed of publicly-spirited Christian rulers. The group-portrait sought to link their temporal efforts to eternal life. As much as they might participate in the profane things of the world, these groups sought

---

35. Wilson 1968, p. 58.
36. Heckscher 1958, p. 111.

to portray themselves as spiritual shepherds enforcing the laws that would lead their flock to everlasting life in God – while punishing those who strayed. In their immortalisation by Rembrandt, the Guild of Surgeon-Anatomists staked their claim to membership among the natural rulers of humankind.

To this end, they sought their self-reflection in the scientific and spiritual virtues of their *praelector*, Dr. Nicolaas Tulp, who alone wears a hat in Rembrandt's painting. And Tulp was an ideal cipher for these desires. For a quarter century (1629–53), he served as a magistrate (or city-councillor). He was city-treasurer eight times, and Burgomaster on four occasions. He also performed duties as Orphan Master, Curator of the Latin School, and Curator of the University. In short, he embodied the bourgeois ideal of the civic-minded man of science, an anatomist who handled city-finances, disciplined the children of the poor, and superintended the city's educational institutions. In addition, he performed at least five public anatomies – and these too need to be seen as essential to his role in maintaining social order in Amsterdam. Too often, however, the role of public anatomy in the theatre of class-power has utterly escaped commentators. Simon Schama, for instance, in his influential study, *The Embarrassment of Riches: An Interpretation of Dutch Culture in the Golden Age* refers to Tulp on seven occasions without so much as mentioning his profession as an anatomist. More striking, Schama does not have even a single entry for anatomy in the index of his book, despite the crucial purpose it served in the symbolic enactment of law and class-power during the Dutch golden age.

Consider, for instance, the four acts in the theatre of power associated with public anatomy. Act One was the public execution of the condemned criminal. Act Two consisted of the public anatomy of the criminal who had been hanged the day before, an Act stretching as long as five days.[37] Act Three involved a semi-private banquet of the Guild of Surgeon-Anatomists on the concluding night of the anatomy, while the final Act consisted of a torch-lit parade following the banquet.[38] We observe here carefully orchestrated ceremonies of

---

37. Where a full-time anatomy-theatre did not exist (Amsterdam's opened in 1639), public dissections were typically undertaken in chapels.

38. See Heckscher 1958, p. 33. Heckscher combines the banquet and torch-lit procession into a single act whereas, for reasons discussed below, I prefer to treat these as distinct acts.

class-power. To begin, the criminal is executed in a public demonstration of the rule of law, one which claims its ultimate sanction on the gallows, thereby proclaiming its terrifying power before the rabble. Second, and as a continuation of the punishment, the criminal's naked corpse is dissected before an audience of paying customers. Gathered on the anatomy-stage are a group of bourgeois citizens (members of the anatomists' guild) who, as much as they observe the dissection, are in turn meant to be themselves observed as incarnations of law and social power. This group then superintends the inscription of that power on the corpse of a transgressor, a pauper who has run afoul of the law. Throughout the performance, the chief anatomist delivers a lecture literally read upon the body of the condemned. Third, the representatives of law and order retreat from public observation to reconstitute their unity and corporate identity with a banquet, the traditional ritual of the privileged and the powerful, which sharply demarcates them from the hungry rabble whom they govern. Having retreated from public view, this group them re-emerges at night, the typical time of terrors, carrying torches as if to ward off all evil spirits of transgression against religion and property. Taken together, these acts comprise a *political anatomy of the body-politic*. Having demonstrated its power over life by publicly executing a poor thief, the ruling class engages in a lengthy moral instruction centred on corporeal dissection.

Just as body-parts are being mapped, so are social parts. Each group is appropriately positioned: Dr. Tulp, as representative of the ruling class, faces his peers and, at one remove, a respectable, paying audience absorbs and affirms the moral instruction on offer. Naked, displayed for all to observe, is the pitiful body of the condemned, undergoing slow and systematic dismemberment. But not only is a human body being destroyed; in and through this destruction, a social order is being reconstituted. A threat – theft of property – has been eliminated, a transgressor ripped to pieces. In the process, the body-politic has been symbolically reaffirmed, social order restored. If the criminal has died for his sins, his blood is also a sacrifice intended to redeem all human sinfulness – a reason, perhaps, why woodcuts and paintings of dissected criminals often gesture to the bodily sufferings of Christ. The theatrics of public anatomy thus activated a multi-levelled script through which bourgeois class-rule was symbolically enacted in violence against the body of one who violated the law.

Figure 1   *The Anatomy Lesson of Dr. Nicolaes Tulp* by Rembrandt (1632)

Now let us return to Rembrandt's painting. Although anatomy-painting had a long tradition in Europe from which he could draw,[39] Rembrandt's *Anatomy of Dr. Tulp* has a number of highly distinctive features. We have already observed the decisive position accorded to Tulp who alone wears a hat and, along with the corpse, visually dominates the scene. The anatomist is clearly the driving force of the scene. But, alongside Tulp, the painting is also dominated by the dramatic portrayal of the corpse, whose diagonal position, adapted from paintings of Christ and martyred saints, had long been an indicator of 'the suffering, surrender, and passivity in general of the defenseless, the dying and the dead'.[40] Expressions of passivity and surrender are especially salient where a criminal, one who actively defied the law, is concerned. Of course, the reference to Christ may also indicate Rembrandt's well known 'sympathy for poor people':[41] a sympathy that runs through his remarkably sensitive paintings of beggars and outcasts. But, unlike those paintings, which highlight the personality of a pauper, here the victim is effectively anonymous. Rembrandt's characteristically powerful use of light and shadow is noteworthy in this regard. The light falls across Tulp and his fellow-anatomists, highlighting their faces, their concentrated attention, their intelligence. The face of the corpse, however, is covered by shadow, stripping the dead man of individuality and rendering him an abstract, undifferentiated representative of the rabble.

Let us turn, finally, to perhaps the most unique aspect of Rembrandt's painting: the fact that Tulp has commenced his anatomy with the corpse's left arm. As the artist would well have known, this was anything but standard anatomical procedure. Renaissance anatomies began in the abdominal region with the *venter inferior*, precisely as Rembrandt portrayed it in a later painting, *The Anatomy Lesson of Dr. Joan Deyman* (1656). As numerous commentators have suggested, it is probable that Rembrandt has Tulp first dissect the hand in order to compare the Amsterdam anatomist with Vesalius, whose famous text was often adorned with a woodcut of the author dissecting an arm. Yet, there is a decisive difference between the two images. Unlike Vesalius, Tulp grasps a tool (a forceps) with which he manipulates the *flexorum digitorum* muscles of

39. See Heckscher 1958, especially Chapters 3–6, and Sawday 1995, p. 151.
40. Heckscher 1958, p. 36.
41. Clark 1988, p. 43.

Kindt's left hand. Indeed, Tulp can be seen pulling on these muscles, causing the corpse's fingers to curl in imitation of his own (Figure 2). We have here, I want to suggest, a portrayal of the paradigmatic relationship between capital and wage-labour.[42] The superintending will (in this case Tulp's), employs a tool with which it directs the movements of the labouring body – or, rather, of a body that ought to have devoted itself to labour. As we would expect in seventeenth-century Holland, the paradigm is that of manufacture, where movements of the human hand animate the production-process, not the fully developed capitalist form of industry in which machinery drives a process to which human bodies adapt. But the relationship of domination and control is quintessentially capitalist: the movement of the pauper-body is being directed by a will external to it, a will whose control over the tools of production (in this case, those of anatomical production) is the key to its command over the bodies of the poor.

Rembrandt's portrayal transforms the genre of anatomy-painting, recasting older traditions in the context of social relations where control of labouring bodies is conferred on those with a monopoly of science and technology. What is on display in *The Anatomy of Dr. Tulp* is thus more than just bourgeois authority over the bodies of those who have fallen afoul of the law. Rembrandt's heroic rendering of Tulp's manipulations of the criminalised body solicits admiration for the ultimate victory of capital: its control over the physical movement of labouring bodies. Bourgeois authority is cast as a heroic, even godlike power that ennobles all involved. In a characteristic antinomy of class-society, intelligence is attributed to those with social power, while the labouring classes are reduced to brute bodies awaiting a superintending will.[43] Indeed, in a quintessentially capitalist inversion, the labouring body is rendered lifeless while capital is animated – in the form of Tulp and his forceps, itself a product of dead labour. As if to emphasise the contrast, Tulp is bathed in light while the face of the body he manipulates remains in shadow, a longstanding signifier of death. With this use of light, Rembrandt underlines the utter insignificance of the individuality of the labourer to the object lesson on display: the dynamic, world-transforming powers of bourgeois

---

42. I am indebted here to Sawday's insightful analysis of this painting (1995, p. 153), although the emphasis on the tool as mediating capital's control over labouring bodies is entirely mine.

43. See the Introduction to McNally 2001.

society. In their daily exchanges with capital, workers count simply as bearers of labour-power, the powers of muscle and brain that are appropriated by capital (indeed, it is suggestive in this regard that Rembrandt's later painting in this genre shows Dr. Deyman anatomising the brain of an executed criminal). Bourgeois appropriation is not merely sanctified here in the name of justice and law, it is exalted as an index of civilisation.

Before proceeding, a few comments about social and economic developments in the Netherlands are in order. While the Netherlands of the seventeenth century was a commercially prosperous, urbanised bourgeois republic it had not undergone a fully-fledged capitalist transformation of the sort that was utterly remaking social relations in England. Dutch society was bourgeois by virtue of the fact that political power resided in the hands of a class of merchant-capitalists whose domestic power derived from domination of foreign trade and markets. While the Dutch economy of the period did see considerable industrial growth – in pottery, malting, brewing, sugar-refining, paper-making, glass, printing and armaments – by and large 'machinery was uncommon and was largely limited to hand-operated looms'.[44] More significant, by the early eighteenth century, Dutch industry underwent a marked regression as control of world-trade shifted to rivals, most notably England. The Dutch commercial republic had always depended on a system of economic protection which was 'closer in ethos to medieval or Renaissance trade' than to fully capitalist domination of markets based on minimising costs of production.[45] Yet, such systems of international protectionism rest ultimately on military might, on the control of geographical spaces, commodity-flows, shipping routes, and trade-networks. The fate of such a society pivots not on labour-productivity and the rate of accumulation, but on the fortunes of military might. Once its military power was constrained, Dutch merchants lost their privileged position as intermediaries in world-exchanges. The result was a declining commercial empire that persistently lost ground to its fully capitalist rival, England. Unable to dominate markets through economies of production, rather than through commercial protectionism, the Dutch bourgeoisie became an increasingly *rentier*-class, living off profits on speculative

---

44. Wilson 1968, p. 31.
45. Schama 1987, p. 341. Indeed, Eric Hobsbawm (1965, p. 42) goes so far as to call the Netherlands of this time a 'feudal business' economy. Ellen Meiksins Wood (2003, pp. 61–72) has analysed these features of the early-modern Dutch economy.

activity while turning toward 'the systematic exploitation of public office' and its fruits.[46] Of course, in the context of the world-market of the eighteenth and nineteenth centuries dominated by British capital, the Netherlands did undergo a systematically capitalist transformation. But its economy did not drive the global process, while Britain's agrarian and industrial capitalism did.[47]

Nevertheless, during its golden age, the Dutch republic was the site of a flourishing bourgeois culture. Innovations in architecture, philosophy, natural science, painting and public culture expressed the social values and power of a class of merchant-capitalists who sought to remake the world according to science and Christian virtue. Many of these innovations became part of the cultural stock of European capitalism, just as Descartes's philosophy, itself deeply indebted to Dutch anatomy, provided a conception of the human body as a divisible extended thing, a 'machine' composed of an agglomeration of distinct parts, all subject to an external will, and contributed thereby to a distinctively capitalist sense of the proletarian body as a bearer of powers susceptible to direction by representatives of reason.[48] The Dutch anatomy-paintings are a crucial inheritance in this regard, encapsulating the political aesthetics of a bourgeois culture preoccupied with social control of the labouring poor. As rendered by Rembrandt, these paintings anticipated the thoroughgoing domination of the physical movements of labouring bodies which was to be fully realised in England, as agrarian and industrial transformation ushered in a full-fledged system of capitalist production and a modern industrial proletariat. And, as that class created its culture of resistance, it converted the bourgeois rituals of public hanging and anatomy into points of social contestation. Europe's first industrial capitalism thus became a laboratory of 'sensational revolts against the surgeons and anatomists'.[49]

---

46. Wilson 1968, p. 44.

47. The nature of the Dutch transition to capitalism is the subject of an important debate between Robert Brenner and Ellen Meiksins Wood. See Brenner 2001, and Wood 2002. It is beyond the scope of this study to enter into this debate. What I would add to it is the claim that, under the competitive pressures of a new British-centred world-market, the Dutch economy did undergo a complete capitalist transformation during the eighteenth and nineteenth centuries.

48. Descartes 1968, p. 73. Descartes explicitly refers to anatomy on p. 66.

49. Ferrari 1987, p. 60. While correctly pointing out that Italy did not see such 'sensational revolts', Ferrari errs, in my view, by treating the occasional revolt in France as justifying its treatment on the same terms as England.

Political anatomy, wage-labour and destruction of the English commons

It is often forgotten that capitalism fully emerges only where older, communal forms of economic life have disintegrated, or, more accurately perhaps, where they have been *dissected*. For capitalism to develop, customary ties between people and the land must be severed, and communal obligations among people disrupted. Throughout most of recorded history, the majority of human beings have lived as peasants, organised into family-units whose members work the land collectively (usually along patriarchal lines) and share resources within the community. Access to land in such societies generally required the performance of services for powerful lords and masters. But, on such terms, such access was usually heritable. Peasants thus typically possessed land as their primary means of producing the goods of life, and often enjoyed access to common lands open to nearly all members of the village-community. The subsistence of people in such rural societies was largely secured, therefore, without recourse to the market. Because almost every household held land, and usually had access to communal lands as well, they could directly procure the foodstuffs, fuel and materials necessary for survival (barring drought or violent appropriation of their produce). While people might go to the market to sell surplus-goods and acquire specific items, their survival did not depend upon market transactions.

Capitalism, by contrast, is a society of systematic market-dependence, one in which survival depends upon individuals finding a buyer for a good or service (usually labour) that they offer on the market. What distinguishes capitalism, therefore, is not the existence of markets, but the unique imperatives of *market-compulsion* in which owners and labourers have no means of reproducing themselves other than by selling and buying.[50] And, for the majority of people, such compulsion arises only where they have been *detached* from direct access to the means of life of the sort provided by family-plots and common lands. Once the majority is so subjected to markets, including the market in labour, people become both regular sellers (of their labour-power) and regular buyers (of the subsistence-goods they require). Capitalists, too,

---

50. No one has stressed the centrality of market-dependence to capitalism more clearly than Ellen Meiksins Wood (see Wood 2002 and 2003). I have addressed the crucial question of market-regulation in McNally 1993, Chapter 6.

become market-dependent; they purchase their means of production (labour, raw materials, tools and machines) on the market, just as they sell there the goods whose production they supervise. Although the market-experience is radically different for each group – a potential source of profit for the capitalist and a constant site of exploitation for the worker – it is the central regulator of social-economic life for both.

The rise of such a market-system required the destruction of the older village-economy, whose death knell was sounded with the widespread enclosure of land, particularly common lands, and the extinction of the open-field system. At the most basic level, enclosure involved a spatial reorganisation of land-ownership and use. The traditional feudal economy had been organised around the lord's manor with most land in the hands of peasants who held leases (usually as either freeholders or copyholders, whose terms and obligations were outlined in manor-documents), and were obliged to pay rents and services to their lord. Family-holdings were often geographically dispersed (a given owner possessing scattered strips of land) and much land was organised as *open fields* available to the entire village-community after harvest and in fallow seasons. In addition to open fields, the manorial economy contained common fields, forests and 'wastes' where any inhabitant could graze livestock; hunt; fish; pick fruit, berries and herbs; glean grain; gather wood (for both building materials and fuel) as well as peat, coal and stones; and pick bulrushes that could be woven into mats, baskets, seats for chairs, or used for bedding. These rights of the community (or of most of its members) were regulated by an assembly of cultivators – either the manor-court or a gathering of the village-community.[51]

The reader may have noticed that I have used the word 'held' rather than 'owned' in my description of peasant-possession of land. Under classical feudal law, all land belonged to the king of the realm. Individuals, including lords, had rights to *use* land only if they rendered proper service to their superiors. Rights to property were thus conditional; the idea of absolute private property simply had no place in such a society. Indeed, historians have been unable to find a clear definition of 'property' in English legal writings prior to

---

51. See Thirsk 1976, p. 10. For a description of the way in which communal rights might be regulated, see the outstanding study by Neeson 1993, pp. 2–3. For discussions of some of the limits that might be imposed on participation in common right see Becket 1991, p. 3; and Wood 1997, pp. 48, 50.

the eighteenth century.[52] Nevertheless, long leases, which were typical in the period 1450–1700, gave peasant-households a stability of possession, and their common rights gave them an enduring sense of community-membership. Moreover, because privately-held fields were generally open, and sometimes subject to a variety of communal rights, the peasant-economy was both public and shared.[53]

The early enclosure-movement initiated a long process by which common rights and the open-field economy were displaced by capitalist forms of private property. Not that any of this could have been clear at the outset to those wealthy tenant-freeholders in search of larger farms, or lords looking for higher rents, each of whom began to concentrate and enclose land. Yet, in facilitating the construction of spatially unified properties bounded by hedges and fences, the first enclosures began the dissolution of communal rights. Spatial concentration of land may have made possible the application of new techniques – which were often cost-effective only if applied on a relatively large scale – but it also went hand in hand with its *social* concentration, as poor peasants were bought out (often when land was demanded as debt-payment), defrauded of land (in cases where there were no written records of their tenancies), or forced out by jacked up rents or entry-fees when leases expired. In arranging local enclosures to the benefit of wealthy tenants, lords deepened divisions within the village-community, exacerbating the disparity between rich and poor peasants, and weakening the capacities of communities to resist collectively. As some of the earliest enclosers, rich tenants or yeomen also undermined their poorest neighbours, for whom enclosure was frequently disastrous.[54]

By 1500, almost half of England was enclosed. But, in addition to spatially enclosing, landlords also *engrossed*, amassing ever larger amounts of land under their direct control. Lands that had, for centuries, been subject to communal customs – let out to peasant-households that, in return for rent and service, received legal and military protection, as well as use of land and commons rights – were now treated as market-assets to be rented to the highest bidder, usually wealthy farmers who hired rural wage-labourers. The result

---

52. Manning 1988, p. 5.
53. As pointed out eloquently by Neeson 1993, p. 2.
54. Hilton 1975, pp. 161–73. For a major scholarly appreciation of Hilton's work, see Byres 2006, pp. 17–68.

was 'land-hunger for the dwarf and family farmers...while the capitalist farmers bid against each other for the tenancies of medium and large farms able to return high profits'.[55] As enclosure picked up steam over the next 150 years, more and more poor peasants found their old way of life disappearing in the wake of the new class-structure emerging in the countryside. The upshot was a growing class of semi-proletarianised cottagers who, lacking holdings adequate to support their families and deprived of common rights, increasingly resorted to wage-labour.

Following the period of civil war and revolution (1640–60), landlords remobilised, enclosing fully one-third of all English lands in the century after 1660. The scale of the transformation that occurred over one hundred and fifty years was staggering: whereas peasants had occupied two thirds of all lands at the Restoration (1660), they held a mere ten percent by the end of the next century.[56] But the process was far from over, since growing numbers of lords were setting their sights on the vast commons (perhaps a quarter of all English land) where peasants had rights to hunt, fish, pick fruit and berries, gather wood and graze animals – all entitlements without which millions could not have supported themselves and their families, given the meagreness of their landholdings.[57] The resulting wave of parliamentary enclosure – in which landowners introduced bills in Parliament seeking legislative authority (which they readily received) to enclose common lands around their estates – saw a further six million acres privatised between 1760 and 1830.

Enclosure and engrossment radically transformed both class- and gender-relations. Their combined effect was to push poor peasants onto smaller and less fertile morsels of land, forcing them into occasional, seasonal and sometimes permanent labour for wages. Whereas only 12 per cent of English peasants engaged in wage-labour in 1550, by 1640 the figure was in the range of 40 per cent, and over 50 per cent by 1688.[58] With the privatisation of commons,

---

55. Kerridge 1953, p. 19.
56. Allen 1992, Chapter 5.
57. On the chronology of enclosure of the English commons, see Yelling 1977; Butlin 1979, pp. 65–82; and Wordie 1983, pp. 483–505. Neeson 1993 rightly points to parliamentary enclosure of the common lands as the process that sealed the fate of commoners, irreversibly proletarianising them – a point to which I return.
58. Lachmann 1987, p. 17. My own sense, as I argue in McNally 1993, pp. 17–18, is that many of these labourers (that is, those of the period 1550–1688) continued to combine work for wages with some degree of self-provisioning from their own small plots of land and/or their access to commons.

peasant-households which had managed to survive on small plots and cottagers who subsisted on little more than a garden (thanks to the self-provisioning made possible by customary rights to game, fish, berries and wood from common lands) now lost indispensable means of survival. And these transformations registered powerful gendered effects. Many forms of production on the commons – gleaning; gathering of fruits, berries, nuts, wood and turfs; and milking of cows that grazed on common lands – were performed by women, often with the assistance of their children.[59] The products of these labours both fed the household (in fact, milk disappeared from many poor families' diets after enclosure of commons eliminated their grazing rights) and fetched money on the market. In both these ways, labour on the commons significantly reduced the dependence of the household on wages; a cow, for instance, could be worth almost half the annual wages of a labouring man.[60] Not surprisingly, then, male workers frequently refused wage-labour in order to contribute to household work on the family-plot or the commons. But such refusals became less and less viable as the commons disappeared – and wage-dependence became the order of the day. Simultaneously, the economic contributions of women to the reproduction of the household contracted and new gender-relations emerged.[61]

For many of the English poor, enclosure of the commons thus represented a point of no return after which the only alternatives to wage-labour were theft and begging. Many certainly tried their hands at these. But increasingly draconian laws against theft and vagrancy rendered such strategies more and more unattractive. Squeezed unrelentingly, the English peasantry metamorphosed into a rural proletariat. 'Evidence indicates,' writes one historian of rural England, 'that in most of the important industrial and forested areas of seventeenth-century England the cottagers...had ceased to be peasants and had become members of a rural proletariat',[62] a process that both accelerated and widened after parliamentary enclosure of common lands. The transformation from peasants to proletarians signified nothing less than a socio-economic revolution, one which ushered in the world's first capitalist society. And the driving force was clearly the transformation of property-relations,

---

59. See the important article by Humphries 1990, pp. 17–42.
60. Humphries 1990, pp. 24, 31.
61. In addition to Humphries, see the classic study by Pinchbeck 1985.
62. Sharp 1980, p. 158.

particularly the destruction of the common lands, not demographic growth. Indeed, while the English population grew sevenfold between 1520 and 1850, the proletariat (those reliant on wages) grew perhaps twenty-three-fold.[63]

As we might expect, this transformation was often registered in the conceptual language of anatomy and monstrosity. For the poor, of course, the loss of land and commons, and the pauperisation these produced, was truly monstrous. For the ruling class, it was stubborn, sometimes violent, resistance to enclosure, privatisation and marketisation that comprised a monstrous threat to societal well-being. And, in the pamphlet-wars and social conflicts in which the discourse of monstrosity was contested, anatomy provided a salient discursive frame. Throughout the centuries of enclosure, after all, land was persistently anatomised – mapped, measured, cut up, enclosed, reassembled. If, before 1500, local maps were rare, by the end of the sixteenth century a near craze for mapmaking had emerged, as the ruling class sought to document the topography of private ownership.[64] In opposition to custom and annual perambulations in which field- and village-boundaries were committed to collective memory, maps provided the figurative system that represented the new geography of private power. Not surprisingly, the term *political anatomy* emerged during the 1650s, as the new order of property gave rise to an unprecedented cartography of English lands. It is especially instructive that political anatomy made its appearance in the title of a work devoted to Cromwellian and Restoration efforts to measure, chart and expropriate the lands of Irish Catholics in order to distribute them to English landowners.[65] Mapping had been a central technology for the assertion of English power in Ireland since the sixteenth century,[66] and anatomy became the discursive frame in which the cutting up of Irish society was described and analysed. The same technology of power and representation was applied to English lands.

As we have seen, it was not just the physical landscape of rural England that was radically altered in this way; more significant was the transformation of social geography. Land had long been an extension of people; people and their village- and kinship-networks were grounded in concrete places and

---

63. Levine 1984, pp. 87–128.
64. Johnson 1996, pp. 90–2, 114–16.
65. On the term 'political anatomy', see McNally 1988, pp. 43, 46. The specific text in question is William Petty's *Political Anatomy of Ireland* (1672).
66. Johnson 1996, p. 94.

spaces – and truly inconceivable outside the land of which they were a part (and which was a part of them). The bourgeois sense of self – an enclosed, individuated personality strictly demarcated from others and from the world around it – had no place in such a community, nor did the classical notion of the enclosed body. Instead, the popular body was conceived as open, untidy and fluid. And, to an emergent ruling class intent on enforcing order, establishing limits and distinctions, and defending privatised property, this expansive body of the common people assumed a grotesque character. In the era of ascendant capitalism, the non-enclosed body appeared to them as monstrous, unfinished and transgressive, an intrusive, invasive thing 'not separated from the world by clearly defined boundaries'.[67]

For the ruling class, all that was common was dangerous, unruly, subversive – the common people as much as common lands. Indeed, the word *commons* was used to denote both lands and people, a semantic slippage that highlights the very lack of demarcation between people and land that was at issue. Just as *commons* referred to land that was unenclosed and communal, land that defied the exclusive rights of private property, so it also referred to the 'uncivilised' poor, the unruly commoners. 'We can get no work, nor have we no money,' the rebellious woolen-weaver Edward White reportedly intoned in 1566, 'but we will have a remedy one of these days, or else we will lose all, for the commons will rise…'.[68] For these sentiments, he and three others were hanged. The same usage repeatedly makes its appearance in the drama and literature of the era. In his *Part Two of King Henry the Sixth*, a play I discuss below, Shakespeare presents us with rebel-leader Jack Cade exhorting his followers with the words, 'you that love the commons, follow me'.[69] Such evidence suggests that the lower orders embraced the term and, at least implicitly, affirmed common property as integral to a plebeian (non-enclosed) sense of self.

---

67. Bakhtin 1984, p. 27. I have discussed this text and others by Bakhtin in McNally 2001, Chapter 4.

68. As quoted by Emmison 1970, pp. 63–4.

69. William Shakespeare, *Part Two of King Henry the Sixth* Act IV, Scene II, lines 195–6. All citations of Shakespeare's plays will refer to *The Oxford Shakespeare* (Oxford: Oxford University Press, 2006). Henceforth this play shall be referred to as 2 *Henry VI*, in accordance with standard scholarly practice. Also following scholarly practice, I will continue to refer not to page numbers but to Acts, scenes and lines in these plays.

As capitalism restructured patriarchal relations, this non-enclosed body of the common people was given both a class- and a gender-identity. While the bourgeois male self was constructed as a possessive individualist, owner of a demarcated, enclosed body and possessor of property and the rights that accrued to it, the body of the common people was feminised and animalised, treated as a deficient type, a leaky vessel inadequately separated, differentiated and defined.[70] The idealised bourgeois male body was constructed as an appropriating unit, an accumulator of privatised property, while the demonised/feminised body of the commons was a dangerously porous one, seeping into enclosed spaces, transgressing limits and boundaries. This delineation of the grotesque body of the people was underwritten by the active role of women in many anti-enclosure riots, an indication that rebellious women did not know their place (or perhaps knew it all too well) – both geographically and socially.[71] In fact, during the years of the English Civil War, female rebellion, manifest in challenges to religious hierarchy and gender-roles, was directly linked to anti-enclosure riots. 'The women in this country begin to rise,' bemoaned one frightened commentator in 1642, 'I wish you all to take heed of women, for this very vermin have pulled down an enclosure.'[72]

In its campaign to impose social order, the ruling class persistently feminised this untidy, spatially rambunctious body of the people, identifying women with unruliness, even ungodliness. Aided by prosperous men of the middling sort, England's rulers sought to impose more sharply patriarchal gender-relations. A war against riotous women was launched, with particular vigour during the period 1560–1640, in an effort to rigidify gender-norms, persecute communal practices and suppress rebellion. Assertive women were demonised, publicly ridiculed (as in Shakespeare's *Taming of the Shrew*) and punished by mechanisms such as the cucking-stool, a teeter-totter type apparatus for ducking offenders in rivers or ponds.[73] In contrast with much

---

70. On this point see Stallybrass 1986, pp. 123–42; and Paster 1987, pp. 43–65. Both authors rightly emphasise the absence of a gender-dimension to Bakhtin's pioneering analysis.

71. See Wood 1997, p. 56; Humphries 1990, pp. 22, 38. See also Neeson 1993, pp. 198, 200–1.

72. Margaret Eure, writing to her nephew, May 1642, as quoted by Cressy 2004, p. 54.

73. See Underdown 1985.

of Europe, English trials against accused witches seem to have revolved most frequently around their insistence on communal obligations – to alms from neighbours in particular, but also to rights to glean and to gain access to the commons. As individualised notions of property took hold and many villagers refused older communal responsibilities, claims to traditional rights were depicted not only as illegitimate, but as evil. At the same time, to aver possession of occult powers was often the only weapon remaining to poor women, particularly the elderly and widows, the only means with which they might back up demands for observance of customary entitlements.[74] In persecuting witches, and imposing ever more rigid gender-roles, the wealthy were thereby attacking communal practices, and identifying them with monstrous women.

Like communal lands, then, the common people were portrayed as wild, open, primitive and uncontrolled – and none more than poor women. 'Civilising' the poor thus required the particularising procedures of political anatomy – separating them from their land and communal rights, closing off their leaky, feminised bodies (and the non-private entitlements they sought) in order to reconstitute them as discrete property-owners (of labour-power) forced to rely on their individual market-resources.

---

74. See the excellent discussion in Thomas 1971, pp. 552–69. In her important and provocative book, Silvia Federici (2004) argues that the whole of the European witch-hunt was about the imposition of bourgeois control over proletarian bodies. There are powerful insights to much of this analysis, but Federici's interpretation involves a certain over-generalisation, particularly in her tendency to see the whole of Europe, even Germany, as involved in capitalist development from the fifteenth century. In my view, the case that England underwent the first capitalist transformation has been powerfully substantiated both theoretically and empirically (see Robert Brenner's contributions in Aston and Philpin (eds.) 1985, and Wood 1999). Federici's own interesting analysis sits uneasily with her attempt to correlate the European witch-hunts *as a whole* with the rise of capitalism. As she notes, Europe's witch-hunts began in the middle of the fifteenth century (p. 165), well before the capitalist mode of production was emergent outside of England, and started in southern France and northern Italy – not England (pp. 165, 177–9). Indeed, only in England were witchcraft-trials principally about the struggle over customary obligations in the face of encroaching capitalist property-relations. Moreover, as Thomas (1971, p. 569) notes, sexual offences did not figure prominently in English witchcraft-trials. In short, there is something distinctively protocapitalist about the persecution of English witches, a fact which undercuts Federici's attempt to squeeze continental Europe and England into the same explanatory matrix.

The poor generally experienced all of this as little more than monstrous destruction, as a demonic process by which they and their communities were dissected and devoured. Enclosures, wrote Philip Stubbes in a book provocatively titled *Anatomy of the Abuses in England* (1583), have created a horror in which 'rich men eat up poore men, as beasts doo eat grasse'.[75] In invoking images of the rich as beastly and cannibalistic annihilators of the poor, Stubbes contributed to the secularisation and politicisation of the discourse of monstrosity. No longer imagined as ghosts, spirits or bizarre beings from unknown realms, monsters were here pictured as fully human and close at hand. Their defects were social, not natural in character. What characterises monstrous humans in such a discourse is their role as destroyers of social bonds and obligations. To violate communal obligations, Shakespeare will suggest, is to challenge fate, to invite tragedy. And this was so for both sides in the polemics over enclosure and the new economics, which became a staging ground for just such a secularised discourse of monstrosity. If enclosure became identified in the eyes of the poor with cannibalism (the rich eating the poor), for the rich the anti-enclosure riot came to symbolise monstrous transgressions against property, law, church and state. Across these decades, a new grammar of monstrosity thus emerged as a secular rhetoric of social contestation, a shift encapsulated in Samuel Purchas' contention in the early seventeenth-century that 'Man himselfe is this Monster'.[76] And, in the era of the English Civil War, these new idioms of monstrosity were to become crucial rhetorical figures through which struggles over political power were played out, only to be reworked and reanimated as means of interpreting the conflicts of the French Revolution, nearly a century and a half later. But, throughout the early-modern period, the secular stream of the discourse of monstrosity never lost contact with the debate over enclosure.

With their livelihoods and communal properties under siege, the resistance of the poor flared into violence throughout the Tudor era, as they tore down fences, trampled hedges, invaded forests and fields. 'The enclosure riot,' notes one historian, 'remained the pre-eminent form of social protest during the period from 1530 to 1640.'[77] In the face of the relentless pressures of enclosure,

---

75. Stubbes 1877–9, p. 117.
76. Samuel Purchas, *Purchas his Pilgrim* (London, 1619), p. 324, as cited by Burnett 2002, p. 30.
77. Manning 1988, p. 27. See also Charlesworth 1983; and Sharp 1980, Chapter 6.

ever-growing numbers of the poor gravitated to those remaining sites where subsistence and sociality could be enjoyed. Forests and commons became the refuge of a variety of rebels and outcasts – squatters, highwaymen, itinerant craftspeople and day-labourers. These spaces nourished a rebellious popular culture and rugged practices of communalism. At moments of social upheaval, these practices could assume a more explicitly political expression, as during Kett's Rebellion of 1649, when tens of thousands of rebels set up campsites across lowland-England and demanded that 'henceforth no man shall enclose any more'.[78] Not surprisingly, restoration of the commons was the central motif of all radicalism of the period, enjoying a utopian inflation at the hands of the most revolutionary dissenters, for whom all private property was illegitimate and common property the solution to society's ills.[79] But, just as the poor rallied to defend (and sometimes extend) the commons, the dominant classes depicted them as nests of evil and corruption. An alarmed King James warned in 1610 that the multiplying cottages to be found in forests and commons were 'nurseries and receptacles of thieves, rogues and beggars'.[80] Forty years later, an anonymous pamphleteer elaborated the political threat posed by these gardens of thieves, proclaiming that 'common fields are the seat of disorder, the seed plot of contention, the nursery of beggary'.[81] The commons thus became sites of contesting monstrosities: breeding grounds of insolence, crime and rebellion in the eyes of élites, cherished buffers against the depredations of the market-economy for the poor.

Of course, the victors painted their dissection of the old village-economy in noble terms, lauding its destruction as a great moral improvement. The privatisation of the commons was presented, as it is today in the era of neoliberal capitalism, as a cure for the intractability of the poor, a means to propel them into the age of industry and improvement. One seventeenth-century advocate urged that enclosure 'will give the poor an interest in toiling'; by depriving them of subsistence it would thus accomplish what 'terror' could not.[82] Rapacious property-grabs and the crushing of common rights and village-customs

---

78. See Fletcher and MacCulloch 1997, pp. 144–6.
79. See Hill 1972. For an important selection of writings from the agrarian-communist and Digger Gerard Winstanley, see Hill 1973.
80. As quoted by Hill 1972, p. 51.
81. As reprinted in Thirsk and Cooper 1972, p. 144.
82. Adam Moore, *Bread for the Poor*, p. 39, as quoted by Hill 1972, p. 52.

assumed the robes of a momentous civilising mission. Rather than sources of
new profits, enclosure and wage-labour were extolled as cures for the laziness
and insubordination of the lower classes, as tonics that would render the poor
industrious and respectable. 'The use of common lands by labourers operates
upon the mind as a sort of independence', bemoaned a Mr. Bishton to the
Board of Agriculture in 1794. Elimination of the commons would, however,
break this spirit of independence and insure that 'the labourers will work
every day in the year', that 'their children will be put out to labour early', and
that the 'subordination of the lower ranks' would be 'secured'.[83] The moral
improvement of the poor thus became synonymous with their subordination to the disciplines of wage-labour. Cottages, gardens and common lands
became markers of laxity and insubordination, of resistance to the uplifting rigours of waged work. In a sly semantic move, independence and self-
sufficiency were cast as obstacles to moral progress, and respectability framed
in terms of *dependence* on one's betters. The campaign to destroy communal
property and enthrone capitalist property-rights assumed its moral colouration in these discursive terms.[84] And, while the debate was first framed in
relation to land, it was readily extended to cover other rights to non-capitalist
property. The struggle over wood-chips offers a compelling case in point.

Throughout the seventeenth and eighteenth centuries, workers in England
regularly exercised claims to a variety of industrial goods and by-products. In
shipbuilding, labourers' appropriation of 'chips', scraps and waste produced
in the course of hewing, chopping and sawing ship-timbers, which had been
a customary right since 1634, augmented money-wages by a third to a half
(much being sold for firewood). However, the Navy, the great employer of
shipyard-labour, loathed the practice of 'chips' – a term which referred as
much to the workers' *right* of appropriation as to the wooden bits themselves.[85]
In this, the Navy embodied the emergent logic of capital, and its hostility to
all notions of workers' rights to any of the products (including by-products)
of their labour. At the heart of capitalism, after all, is the complete separation/

---

83. As cited by Hammond and Hammond 1978, p. 9.

84. At the time of the New Poor Law Act (1834), dependence began to be recast in
terms of reliance on poor relief – and thus as an evil. On this point, see McNally 1993,
Chapter 1.

85. See the excellent discussions in Linebaugh 2003, pp. 378–80, and Linebaugh
1982, pp. 319–28.

alienation of workers from the means of production and the products of labour – all of which adhere to capital by virtue of its property-rights. The pure form of capital is established where workers' subsistence is derived from money-wages alone. But industrial by-products buffered workers from the pressures of total proletarianisation by providing economic resources outside the matrix of the wage-relation. In treating some of the products of labour (chips) as non-capitalist property, workers subjected these products to dual claims, setting the stage for intense battles between contending rights to property. Using Parliament and the courts, the Navy was able throughout the 1790s to redefine more and more cases of chip-taking as 'theft', pushing all the time for harsher punishments. In 1795, Samuel Bentham was appointed Inspector-General of the Naval Works. In the utilitarian spirit of his famous brother, he quickly drew up an anatomy of shipbuilding, defining the multiple operations and procedures by which wood was worked into ships, reorganising the labour-process on 'scientific' lines, and introducing machines wherever possible. At the same time, he introduced shift-work on a twenty-four hour schedule and, despite resistance in the form of a mass-strike, established piece-work in 1801, the very year the custom of chips was finally eliminated.[86]

Here again, the establishment of fully capitalist property-relations rested on criminalising workers' customary property-rights. And chips were not the only form of non-capitalist property so contested. Similar battles were fought over weavers' right to 'thrums', the weft-ends left on the loom after the removal of finished cloth, or over the practices through which porters, seamen and coopers 'socked', or pocketed, bits of the tobacco they packed, loaded and unloaded on ships. In one trade after another, masters and employers formed associations for the prosecution of 'embezzlement,' modelled on those mounted by the rural gentry to enforce game-laws and prosecute 'poachers'. Deploying inspectors to search workers' homes for 'stolen' materials, these associations also provided masters with funds for prosecutions. And, as more workers were prosecuted, so were they also subjected to stiffer sentences. By 1777, the penalty for embezzlement was increased from two weeks to three months in a house of correction.

Part and parcel of the destruction of customary rights, then, was a new legal code that, by outlawing all non-market claims to wealth, subordinated

---

86. Linebaugh 2003, pp. 397–9.

workers ever more powerfully to the regimes of wage-labour. As customary property-rights lost protection under the law, previously sanctioned practices were transformed into criminal offences. Workers invariably resisted the redrawing of these boundaries between the legitimate and the illegitimate, glorying in 'theft' and 'pilfering', while symbolically trampling down these new hedges and enclosures. In response, stiffer punishments were introduced, new police-forces constructed, and new prisons built, all in an effort to force compliance. The gambit of laws and punishments enacted to secure this régime and to criminalise practices of resistance is staggering: the Riot Act (1715), designed to clamp down on all public disturbances; the Transportation Act (1719), which instituted deportation of felons for purposes of slave-labour on West-Indian or North-American plantations; the Combination Act (1721), whose purpose was to criminalise workers' associations; the Workhouse Act (1723) by which parishes could set up workhouses to confine the poor and their offspring and put them to forced labour; the notorious Black Act (1723); and the Vagrancy Act (1744). Not only did these new laws outlaw a wide range of social activities – public protest, worker-organisation, begging, hunting and fishing on former common lands – they also introduced draconian punishments for their transgression. The number of offences punishable by death rose ominously and persistently during the consolidation of agrarian and industrial capitalism – from about 50 in 1688, to 160 by the middle of the eighteenth century, and to about 220 early in the next century, virtually all of them having to do with crimes against property.

The Black Act, which criminalised various acts of hunting, stealing and poaching from forests, as well as the felling of trees, created more than fifty new offences subject to capital punishment, making it one of the most punitive pieces of legislation passed by any legislature anywhere.[87] That these laws were designed, in large measure, to compel the poor to accept the rigours of wage-labour was never in doubt to their framers. Game-laws, for instance, often opened with preambles like the following, which bemoaned the 'great mischief [which] do ensue by inferior tradesmen, apprentices and other dissolute persons neglecting their trades and employments who follow hunting, fishing and other game to the ruin of themselves and their neighbours'.[88] In

---

87. See Thompson, 1975.
88. Richard Burn, *Justice of the Peace and Parish Officer*, 1st edn. (London, 1755) v. 2, p. 445.

defiance of this onslaught against customary economies, the poor displayed a stubborn preference for survival-strategies that evaded the disciplines of the market. Determined to close off all such options, legislators used the 1744 Vagrancy Act to endow magistrates with the power to whip or imprison beggars, peddlers, gamblers, strolling actors, gypsies and 'all those who refused to work for the usual and common wages'. As if this were not enough, the Act also conferred on them authority to imprison 'all persons wand'ring abroad and lodging in alehouses, barns and houses or in the open air, not giving a good account of themselves'. Interestingly, it also extended vagrancy to 'endgatherers', i.e. individuals who travelled about collecting odd bits of cloth or wool.[89]

As adjunct to this harsh criminal code, the ruling class built new prisons to house the growing army of transgressors. At the same time, it sought to equip the law with new terrors. To this end, it enlisted the services of anatomy.

Anatomy and the corpse-economy

The English ruling class did not grasp the punitive possibilities of dissection as early as its counterparts elsewhere, but, having done so, it refined punitive anatomy into an ominous weapon of class-discipline. In 1540, Henry VIII conferred on the newly united companies of Barbers and Surgeons the right to four corpses of hanged felons annually. In the next century, Charles II hiked the group's annual entitlement to six corpses. Through these royal enactments, anatomy became part of the repressive armoury of the state, and public dissection of felons part of the theatre of power. It is especially intriguing that the blueprint for London's first permanent anatomy-theatre was drawn up in 1636 by Inigo Jones, who had designed the city's Phoenix playhouse and was perhaps the most celebrated designer of masques and spectacles of the day.[90] Public anatomy was deliberately organised as dramatic performance and mounted in theatres in the round that simultaneously entertained, instructed, and warned – all the while reproducing forms of class-authority. And, as poverty grew with the rise of capitalism, so did the numbers threatened with punitive dissection.

---

89. Radzinowicz 1947–56, pp. 68–71.
90. See Billing 2004, p. 1, and Holzapfel 2008, pp. 3–4.

The whole drift of English social policy throughout the seventeenth and eighteenth centuries was toward treating poverty as an offence against the laws of nature and the market. To be desperately poor was to be insubordinate, to refuse to adapt to the market-economy. In this spirit, poor-law policy increasingly punished the destitute for their indiscipline – and soon enlisted dissection to this end. In 1694, the London town-council for the first time decreed that abandoned bodies of the poor – found dead in the street, or unclaimed after violent deaths – could be provided to the anatomists.[91] Still, as anatomy boomed and medical education increasingly emphasised direct experience of dissection, the supply of corpses failed to keep pace. The result was twofold: first, a steady rise in the price of corpses, which more than tripled in the twenty years after 1720;[92] and, second, considerable growth in the practices by which they were illicitly procured – grave-robbing, murder and the purchase (from relatives and friends) of the bodies of the condemned on hanging days at Newgate. By the 1720s, corpse-stealing had become a full-time profession whose practitioners (known as 'resurrectionists') could make a comfortable living. And, as the market increased, so did evidence of murder, particularly of street-youth, in order to sell their corpses for dissection.[93] The result was a *corpse-economy* in which human bodies, increasingly commodified in life, assumed in death the status of commodities pure and simple. So extreme was the reification involved that a corpse intended for the market was dubbed a 'Thing'. In this spirit, the commodity-corpse was subjected to pricing policies as subtle as those applied to most goods. During the 1790s, for instance, one gang of resurrectionists listed separate prices for the corpses of adults and children – the latter selling for six shillings for the first foot, and nine pence for every inch beyond that – alongside prices for specific organs and body parts, known as 'offcuts'. As Richardson observes,

> Corpses were bought and sold, they were touted, priced, haggled over, negotiated for, discussed in terms of supply and demand, delivered, imported, exported, transported. Human bodies were compressed into boxes, packed in sawdust, packed in hay, trussed up in sacks, roped up like hams, sewn in canvas, packed in cases, casks, barrels, crates and hampers,

---

91. Sawday 1995, p. 58.
92. See the calculations by Linebaugh 1975, p. 77.
93. See, for one set of examples, Wise 2004.

salted, pickled, or injected with preservative.... Human bodies were dismembered and sold in pieces, or measured and sold by the inch.[94]

By granting judges in murder-trials discretion to substitute dissection for gibbeting in chains, the Murder Act of 1752 augmented the supply of corpses and drove down their price, at least for a while, since demand kept rising, what with four hospital-medical schools, seventeen private anatomy-schools and countless private dissection-courses all in the market.[95] But any loss to the resurrectionists (in terms of income) represented a gain to the state – in the form of an alarming new capacity of the law to terrorise. Echoing Mandeville, the text of the Murder Act described dissection as a 'further Terror and peculiar Mark of Infamy', thus underlining its punitive, rather than scientific, inspiration. Equally significant, in an attempt to clamp down on the riots against the surgeons, it also declared rescue or attempted rescue of a corpse to be punishable by transportation to the colonies or American plantations for seven years, return before such time being punishable by death.[96] That the punitive nature of public dissection was never in doubt can be gleaned from observing William Hogarth's famous 1751 illustration, 'The Reward of Cruelty' (Figure 2). Let us start with its accompanying text before analysing the illustration itself:

Behold the Villain's dire disgrace,
  Not death itself can end:
He finds no peaceful burial place;
  His breathless corse, no friend.
Torn from the root, that wicked tongue
  Which daily swore and curs'd!
Those eye-balls from the sockets wrung,
  That glowed with lawless lust.
His heart, expos'd to prying eyes,
  To pity has no claim;
But dreadful! from his bones shall rise
  His monument to shame.

94. Richardson 1987, p. 72.
95. Wise 2004, p. 25 and p. 314 n. 2.
96. Richardson 1987, pp. 36–7.

Several interconnected themes animate these verses. First, there is the notion that death itself is not the end of punishment: after expiring, the villain's body will know neither peace nor friend. One encounters, second, a description of anatomised body-parts – tongue, eyeballs, heart – which is clearly meant to be both frightening and demeaning. Finally, a discourse of disgrace and shame runs throughout, underlining the publicity of the criminal's humiliation: exposed to 'prying eyes' bereft of pity, the corpse is subjected to scorn and contempt. I shall return to some of these themes shortly. But let us now turn to the illustration itself, beginning with the actual social-physical context. The site is the London anatomy-theatre of the Company of Surgeons, whose walls, as Hogarth faithfully demonstrates, were framed by the skeletons of two actual felons, Canonbury Besse and Country Tom, executed in 1635 for robbery and murder. The insignia of royal power hovers above everything, while a throne bearing an authoritative figure presides over the process, directing things by means of a pointer. Insignia, throne and setting all decisively link anatomy to the exercise of state-power, one inscribed by colonial and racialised motifs.[97]

Turning now to the corpse, known as Tom Nero, we detect a number of curiosities. First, the anatomised villain still has the hangman's rope around his neck, a clear suggestion by Hogarth that, far from having ended with death, the punishment continues with the anatomy. Note next that the victim's entrails are being funnelled into a barrel and that whatever parts of his innards spill upon the floor are being gobbled up by a dog – becoming dog-food, in short. Indeed, Hogarth compounds the indignity by serving up the condemned man's heart, typically considered the very seat of life, as the dog's victuals. Not only does this threaten law-breakers with public humiliation, it also animalises the transgressor by incorporating him into the dog. Moving to the corpse's head, we observe it being raised by a dissecting tool inserted into a pulley. Pain, even after death, is clearly intimated by the grimace on the corpse's face. Perhaps more significant, as in Rembrandt's *Anatomy of Dr. Tulp*, the manipulation of corpse by a mechanism suggests the subordination of the bodies of the poor to the instruments of production: the corpse's movements are directed by an apparatus that obeys the wills of the ruling class, whose representatives supervise the anatomy. Staying with the head, note the

---

97. On racialised motifs in Hogarth see Dabyden 1985.

Figure 2   *The Reward of Cruelty* by William Hogarth (1751)

two-sided optics of terror: while the corpse is being subjected to the gaze of the 'prying eyes' of the anatomists, its own eyes are being extracted. In symbolic terms, the poor are being blinded, deprived of means to see the world around them, while sight is assigned exclusively to those who govern social life. Meanwhile, another anatomist appears ready to dissect the corpse's feet, the organs of locomotion, of self-movement through the world.

Two other features of the illustration are noteworthy for our purposes. First, at the back left, a single figure points to one of the skeletons adorning the hall, as if to warn potential transgressors of the fate that awaits them. Moving to the front left of the illustration, we find an even more remarkable feature: a boiling cauldron of skulls and bones from which arises an ominous smoke. Here is our clearest indication that a ritual of social magic is being enacted, a reminder that public anatomy is intended not only to punish and terrorise, but also to exorcise ruling-class anxieties. By means of this exorcism, the social body is cleansed of the disease of crimes against property and bourgeois order. Just as the anatomists painted by Rembrandt conclude their activities with a torchlight-procession, so the Company of Surgeons brews a magic potion meant to ward off evil.

The horrors aroused in the poor by dissection were thus anything but simple products of traditional religious ideas about the body and its afterlife, even if these may have played some role. Hatred of body-snatching and dissection seem largely to have derived from vigorous opposition to public humiliation and degradation of the poor. Indeed, as Thomas Laqueur has shown, a measurable shift in popular attitudes towards death and funerals occurs in the middle of the eighteenth century when, in efforts to further demean the destitute, the pauper-funeral was created.[98]

Prior to the consolidation of capitalism, funerals recorded different social statuses by enacting distinctive rituals. Those of the rich and powerful signalled their subjects elevated public standing – for example, in the number of mourners allowed and the sort of banners carried – while those of the poor, largely eschewing public display, revolved around post-burial feasts. But, as the new social hierarchies of capitalism developed, funerals were commodified and refashioned as occasions for the display of purchasing power – and

---

98. Laqueur 1983, pp. 109–31. The following paragraph largely draws upon Laqueur's seminal article.

thus determined by money, not traditional social standing. Burial-plots, caskets, monuments and processions all became prised commodities indulged by the rich. For the poor, meanwhile, funerals became markers of destitution, of what they lacked in a capitalist society. And, in seeking to penalise poverty, officials stripped away customary entitlements in this area too. While the law traditionally gave anyone dying in a parish a right to burial in its churchyard, new institutions – such as workhouses, which took over responsibility for regulating the unemployed – redrew (and diminished) funeral- and burial-rights. The same officials who sought to humiliate the poor in life, also undertook to degrade them in death. By combining the funerals of several paupers (denying the family control over time and place and treating the deceased as an interchangeable unit of a larger group of the destitute), by depositing corpses in cheap and unmarked parish-coffins (publicly displayed, so that all might see), and by stacking coffins of the poor on top of one another in graves, everything was done to strip the pauper-funeral of any sense of the identity of the deceased. In these ways, the authorities publicly exposed the poor in death to the very anonymity that haunted them in life. The pauper-funeral became thereby yet another badge of abasement, a public declaration of their moral failings.

Two further indignities faced the poor in death. One was body-snatching, whose purpose, as we have seen, was dissection. As the corpse-economy grew, the rich developed a whole armoury of protections: burial at remote cemeteries outside the city core; vaults and private chapels; triple coffins (wood, lead, wood); guards hired to protect their graves. Indeed 1818, the year the first edition of *Frankenstein* appeared, also saw the marketing of a metal coffin, explicitly meant to thwart body-snatchers.[99] The poor, of course, could not afford these luxuries. Their only recourse was collective self-organisation. Not only did they organise to light and protect their graveyards, they also rose up against the resurrectionists, frequently inflicting physical injury on them.[100] The second indignity threatening the poor in death was the delivery of their bodies to the anatomists. And, with the Anatomy Act (1831), this became the potential fate of all poor people who died in workhouses, should

99. Richardson 1987, p. 81. For more on body-snatching see Quigley 1996, pp. 292–8.
100. Richardson 1987, pp. 82–92.

their bodies be unclaimed. Once a punishment for murder, dissection now became a penalty for poverty and obscurity.

Anatomisation was literally the last straw, the final indignity. And the poor mobilised against it wherever possible. Indeed, protest against the corpse-economy became a recurrent theme in popular culture, as evinced by the remarkable success of Edward Ravenscroft's play, *The Anatomist or the Sham Doctor*. First performed at the New Theatre in London's Lincoln's Inn fields in November 1696, the play was almost permanently on the London stage for the next one hundred years.[101] *The Anatomist* explores the dilemma that becoming a corpse – commodified flesh – is the route to money and pleasure in modern society. This dilemma is dramatically highlighted by the presence on the stage of a body, about to be anatomised, that rises up and denounces its apparent fate. Indeed, this character attacks the whole corpse-economy, declaring 'I had rather be a Sot than an Anatomy, I will not have my flesh scrap'd from my Bones. I will not be hung up for a Skeleton in Barber-Surgeons-Hall.' The London crowd celebrated such protests – on the stage and on the streets.

This theme continued to occupy a central place in plebeian culture for the next century and a half. In the 1830s, for instance, the influential radical William Cobbett railed against surgeons, the 'cutters up', as he called them, suggesting they treated the poor as fodder for their scalpels, just as capitalists considered them fodder for industry.[102] And, in the same vein, the best-selling mid-century serial, *The, Mysteries of London* (1844–56), served up an enduring villain known as 'The Resurrection Man'.[103]

So, if anatomy comprised a bourgeois weapon against violation of the laws of property and the market, for the working class it symbolised everything they loathed about the new market-economy. Body-snatching, dissection and the trade in corpses were proof that the monstrosities of the market respected no limits; they demonstrated that the market-economy happily embraced what one trade-unionist called the 'odious and disgusting traffic in human flesh'.[104] The corpse-economy thus became a symbolic register of all that was objectionable about emergent capitalism, of its demonic drive to exploit human life and labour, of its propensity to humiliate and demean in both life

---

101. See the insightful discussion by Sawday 1995, pp. 44–8.
102. William Cobbett, *Cobbett's Political Register*, 28 January 1832.
103. Wise 2004, pp. 307–8.
104. James Doherty, *Poor Man's Advocate*, 1 September 1832.

and death. 'Not content with the people's toil while living,' wrote a radical in *The Poor Man's Advocate*, 'the rich insist upon having their bodies cut up and mangled when dead.'[105]

Monsters of rebellion

While the poor found the market-economy and its agents monstrous, the ruling class, as we have seen, perceived monstrosity in the mob. With enclosure and the rise of capitalist farming forcing people off the land (or onto the margins of forests and wastes), growing legions of masterless women and men crisscrossed the English landscape. A veritable army of 'forest squatters, itinerant craftsmen, and building labourers, unemployed men and women seeking work, strolling players, minstrels and jugglers, quack doctors, gipsies, vagabonds, tramps'[106] prowled the country, answering to neither lord nor master. Severed from the social order of the village-economy, they were also disconnected from the regulatory gaze of their 'betters'. Eschewing the disciplines of regularised wage-labour and the established Church, they fended for themselves in matters of body and soul, establishing dissenting congregations and makeshift-communities. Throughout the country, hordes of homeless people set up camps wherever they could – 'in fields and farm buildings; in city streets and suburban hovels; even on the doorsteps of Parliament and the monarch's court'.[107] England's governors were filled with horror and revulsion at the sight of these battalions of vagrants. Statute after statute was drawn up to regulate, whip, brand and jail them. Discussing the authorities' obsession with vagrancy, R.H. Tawney observed that 'the sixteenth century lived in terror of the tramp'.[108] And the terror persisted into subsequent centuries – witness the twenty-eight statutes passed between 1700 and 1824 in an effort to classify and punish a growing body of practices defined as vagrancy.[109]

The horror of the propertied classes was fuelled in large measure by the persistent waves of anti-enclosure protest and food-rioting that swept

---

105. John Doherty, *Poor Man's Advocate*, 15 September 1832.
106. Hill 1972, pp. 48–9.
107. Beier 1985, p. 85.
108. Tawney 1967 [1912], p. 268.
109. See Rogers 1994, pp. 104–5.

England during the rise of capitalism. The hatred of the poor for the rich may, indeed, have been more intense during this period of English history than at any other.[110] And nothing inflamed the downtrodden more than the spatial aspects of society's transformation: the growing propensity of the rich to keep them out of common lands and open fields, to hem them in, to enclose and imprison them. By the eighteenth century, if not earlier, fences, hedges, jails, locks and keys had become decisive symbols of capitalist order, and dissection a pre-eminent image of bourgeois domination. Yet, these technologies of the grotesque had their counterparts in the anxious horrors of the élites concerning the violent antipathy of the plebs for their rulers. Lurking within the interstices of polite society, the ruling class perceived 'a new-created race of masterless men, of beggars and vagabonds wandering the roads, homesteading on the dwindling common wastes, poaching and fence breaking at will', a monstrous mob ever-ready to transgress boundaries and overturn order, property and civilisation.[111]

Here, again, we encounter the early-modern secularisation of monstrosity, as monsters step forward not as bizarre creatures from other realms, but as disturbing humans who threaten lives, customary obligations and social order. To be sure, this secular grotesque maintained continuities with older monstrous genres. Early-modern images of monstrosity frequently drew on medieval representations of unsettling hybrids, strange combinations of body-parts from different species – human bits conjoined to those of dogs, horses or pigs – or on images of corporeal distortion, such as multiple heads and oversize limbs or body parts. Imagery based on the Book of Revelations also loomed large in both medieval and early-modern accounts of monsters in Europe. Social-geographical foreigners might be pathologised and monsterised in these terms, as Africans and the Irish frequently were. But monstrosity could also be located closer to home, attributed to neighbours and kin whose social behaviour was deemed aberrant, particularly those who, through their dress, behaviour and comportment, blurred class- and gender-differences.[112]

---

110. On this point, see the comments by Sharp 1980, p. 36. For evidence of the rebellious, oppositional culture of the poor, see also the studies by Manning 1988, and Rule 1982.

111. Carroll 1994, p. 38.

112. On medieval monsters, see Bildhauer and Mills 2003; Jones and Sprunger 2002; Platt 1999; and Friedman 1981. Greta Austin (2002) convincingly challenges the

Notwithstanding such continuities, the secularised monsters of the early-modern period were unique in three respects. First, they were clearly human, not non-human, in nature, however deviant and disturbing their behaviour. Secondly, whereas medieval monsters were largely interpreted in theological terms, as created by God in order to warn or punish humankind, secularised monsters were human creations, symptoms of degenerate social action and relations. Third, corporeal distortion and abnormality were no longer essential to their being; social behaviour became the prime index of monstrosity, not bodily form.

The new discourse of monstrosity owed something to the scientific orientation of the European Renaissance, which produced studies of 'monsters' as indicators of the marvellous diversity of nature. It also owed something to a popular tradition of the comic-grotesque, in which creatures composed of improbable and over-sized conjugations of parts and species provoked laughter more than horror.[113] In both of these scientific and popular genres, rather than inducing fear and horror, monsters exercised an aesthetic and scientific fascination. They were widely displayed in public exhibitions, where they could be viewed for a small fee; and, in death, their skeletons or skulls filled the cabinets of curiosities assembled by wealthy patrons of the sciences.[114] But perhaps the most important cause of the new secular discourse of monstrosity was its reshaping as an idiom for expressing the teeming social tensions that emerged in Tudor England with enclosure and the rise of agrarian capitalism. From the 1570s on, in response to these tensions, 'a shift appeared within the rhetoric of monstrosity', as Tudor commentators reworked it to describe horrifying attitudes and practices – from greed and enclosure, on the one side, to riot and treason on the other. Incarnated in frightful behaviour more than grotesque bodies, monstrosity was now less visible, more obscure.[115] Its cryptic signs had to be deciphered and explained, less its socially-destructive tendencies should undermine society itself. Rather than individual bodies, it was the *body-politic* that was now at risk of becoming grotesque – headless or

---

idea that modern concepts of race are appropriate to the understanding of medieval monsters.

113. See Semonin 1996, pp. 76–80.
114. See Guerrini 2005, pp. 153–68, and Ochsner 2005, pp. 252–74.
115. See Brammall 1996, p. 15.

multi-headed in the fearful images of conservatives, rapacious or cannibalistic in the eyes of radicals and reformers.

One intimation of this new rhetoric can be found in a fascinating document of the late 1590s, Luke Hutton's *The Black Dog of Newgate*. A convicted highwayman, Hutton had been condemned to Newgate Prison and there wrote his text. Subtitled, 'or the Discovery of a London Monster,' *The Black Dog of Newgate* is a harrowing tale of a monstrous human who appears to have been responsible for Hutton's capture and arrest. While likened to a black dog, it is clear that Hutton's monster – and he repeatedly uses this word – bears no visible markings. Indeed, an angel advises him,

> Hutton, be bold; for thou shalt see and hear
> Men devils, devils men, one both, all deluding[116]

The devils to be feared are thus humans, Englishmen in fact, who deceive and oppress the poor. 'Bribery his hand, spoil of the poor his trade', says Hutton to describe his horrible creature.[117] Although his monster is said to transform from human to animal and back, Hutton offers no description of physical abnormalities, no physiognomy of the grotesque. The horror lies in social behaviour – entrapment, deceit, bribery, extortion, and oppression – not corporeal form. We hear the secular version of monstrosity echoing here, now worked into a plebeian idiom of revulsion against prisons and confinement.

The multiple strands of the early-modern discourse of monstrosity find no more sensitive registrar than Shakespeare. As did Rabelais, Shakespeare interweaved popular speech-genres and belief-systems with classic literary sources, to produce a new, polyphonic language of immense artistic power.[118] His grammar of monstrosity typically draws on popular idioms, though primarily in a secular vein, to portray fractures in human social relations. In *Richard III*, this involves figuring corrupt political aspirations as corpo-

---

116. Hutton 1930, p. 267.

117. Hutton 1930, p. 269. Of course, the use of the term 'black' carries racial connotations, but here we need to be cautious, as the modern concepts that underpinned 'scientific' racism had not yet congealed. As Michael Wood reminds us in discussing Shakespeare's description in his sonnets of his lover as 'black', this 'was a very complicated word in Elizabethan literature, where it can even be used as a euphemism for Catholic'. See Wood 2005, p. 203.

118. For a useful summary of the popular and classical sources that entered into Shakespeare's artistic language see Wood 2005, Chapter 3.

real distortion, as corruption of individual physiognomy, while, in *Othello*, typical European monsterisations of Africans are ambiguously mobilised to highlight the horrifying dimensions of envy and resentment.[119] In much of the playwright's usage, monstrosity is a moral defect emanating from violations of kinship. In *King Lear*, for instance, Cordelia's ostensible lack of love for her father is described as 'monstrous', while Edgar is named a 'monster' for his apparent betrayal of his father and of the natural obligations that ought to obtain among people in a well-ordered, hierarchical society.[120] Not infrequently, Shakespeare uses the term to signify excessive appetites for personal pleasure and gain, desires that break the bonds of reciprocity. Monstrosity thus takes the form of ruptures in social convention and obligation induced by unbridled individualism. In this vein, Shakespearean characters denounce 'monstrous envy' and 'monstrous lust' (*Pericles*), 'monstrous arrogance' (*The Taming of the Shrew*) and 'monster ingratitude' (*King Lear*).[121] Perhaps no emotion figures more ominously than jealousy, which the poet describes in *Othello* as 'the green-eyed monster'.[122]

Shakespeare also deploys political meanings of monstrosity, extending their reach from the realm of familial obligation into that of the body-politic. Deploying a patriarchal model of political obligation, Shakespeare depicts kings as fathers of their people. For commoners to rebel is, therefore, to behave like Lear's ostensibly ungrateful daughter, to transgress proper relations between father and child, ruler and ruled. In *Coriolanus* we are instructed, for example, that 'Ingratitude is monstrous; and for the multitude to be ingrateful, were to make a monster of the multitude' (2.3.9–11).[123] Yet, Shakespeare is no simple apologist for patriarchal power. The king and nobility have obligations too – to protect their dependents, to rule justly, to listen to the pleas of the poor, to eschew faction and intrigue in the interests of the commonwealth. Great realist that he is, Shakespeare well knows that the aristocracy frequently betrays these obligations. And, when they do so, they have only themselves to blame

---

119. For insightful readings of *Richard III* and *Othello* in this regard see Burnett 2002, Chapters 3 and 4.

120. William Shakespeare, *King Lear*, Act 1, Scene 1, lines 250 and 253, and Act 1, Scene 2, line 99.

121. For these and other examples see Baldick 1987, pp. 11–15.

122. William Shakespeare, *Othello*, III.iii.168.

123. William Shakespeare, *Coriolanus*, II.iii.9–11. *Coriolanus* will be discussed in more detail below.

for the tumult that ensues. While this is not a justification of popular rebellion, it does allow us to sympathise with its participants. Take, for example, what is perhaps Shakespeare's most interesting history play in this regard, *Henry Sixth, Part 2* (often indicated as *2 Henry VI*), probably first performed in 1590, and in which we encounter contending secular versions of monstrosity.

The play traces the short-lived success and ultimate failure of a major uprising of the people – modelled significantly on the English Peasants' Rebellion of 1381 – which transpires in the midst of intrigue, faction and murder among the aristocracy, as well as a rebellion in Ireland. Commentators have disagreed sharply about this play, reading it as both a mockery of the popular rebellion led by Jack Cade and as a declaration of sympathy for the rebels.[124] Arguably, it is both of these, a sympathetic portrayal of the restive commons that nonetheless dismisses the egalitarianism of the rebels, urging the lower orders to leave the business of ruling to those properly qualified – the patriotic aristocracy and upper gentry. Yet Shakespeare exhorts these élites to behave virtuously, as publicly spirited citizens, not rapacious accumulators of property and power. Indeed, a crucial part of the Shakespearean message seems to be that plebeian rebels mimic the factional behaviour of their natural rulers. If revolt is to be quelled, then England's rulers must eschew individualism and factionalism, and unite for the commonwealth.

Depicting the intense dynamics of social conflict, Shakespeare's language carries a high voltage-charge. Ruling-class attitudes toward the common people fairly pulsate with disgust: members of the élite denounce the plebeians as 'the giddy multitude'; 'an angry hive of bees'; 'the rude multitude'; 'rebellious hinds, the filth and scum of Kent'; and 'the rascal people'.[125] But, if Shakespeare gives such sentiments their due, he equally lends voice to the sufferings of the common sort and their pleas for justice. He portrays a rebellion led by clothiers, tanners, butchers and weavers – the very sorts who were found in the van of riots throughout England's cities and towns, as well as in the crowd that would surely have made its way to the theatre. The poet also

---

124. Among those who see Shakespeare as mocking popular rebellion are Tillyard 1991, and Greenblatt 1983, p. 23. Michael Hattaway (1988, p. 15), offers a view of the early Shakespeare as 'a radical'. An intermediate position is taken by Cartelli 1994, pp. 48–67.

125. William Shakespeare, *Henry the Sixth, Part 2*, I.iii.21; III.ii.125; III.ii.135; IV.ii.134; IV.iv.51.

sympathetically highlights the hardships endured by rebel-leader Cade, which would have been familiar to many of the common people. We are informed that Cade was born homeless ('under a hedge'), abused by the authorities ('whipped three market days together', probably for begging), and maimed in defence of property ('burnt I' thee hand for stealing of sheep').[126] More-over, once the rebellion is crushed and Cade escapes, one of his comrades suc-cinctly expresses the dilemma confronting a poor insurgent: 'Alas! He hath no home, no place to fly to',[127] a dilemma to which the poet returns in *King Lear*. But more than this, although occasionally laced with mockery, Shakespeare provides a fair description of the political sentiments of the insurrectionary commons: 'All the realm shall be in common'; 'there shall be no money'; the jails shall be broken open in order 'to let out all the prisoners'; 'ancient free-dom' shall be recovered.[128] Still, because rebellion cannot ultimately be coun-tenanced, the rebel must die if the wound in the body-politic is to be healed. And the form of that death is surely instructive.

Escaping to Kent, Cade scales a brick-wall and enters the garden of Alex-ander Iden, 'a Kentish gentleman.' Having gone five days without a morsel of bread (the staple food of the poor), the intruder hopes to 'eat grass or pick a sallet'. Instead, he is confronted by Iden in the company of his servants. A battle ensues over the rights of property, which has been at the very heart of the struggle between commons and rulers throughout the play. The land-owner's outrage vibrates with the poetics of enclosure. He denounces Cade's attempt 'to break into my garden', and describes him as 'a thief come to rob my grounds/Climbing my walls in spite of me the owner'.[129] Overcome by hunger and fatigue, Cade is no match for the well-fed gentlemen, and dies at his hands. Then, in a series of acts that symbolically restore the order of property, Iden mutilates Cade's remains, decapitates him, buries his headless corpse in 'a dunghill', and presents the rebel's head as a trophy to the king. The fissure in the social order is dramatically healed by mutilating, dissecting and confining the rebel-body.

---

126. William Shakespeare, *Henry the Sixth, Part 2*, IV.ii, 57–8, 65, 70–1.
127. William Shakespeare, *Henry the Sixth, Part 2*, IV.viii.41; IV.
128. William Shakespeare, *Henry the Sixth, Part 2*, IV.ii.77; IV.ii.81–2; IV.iv.16; IV.viii.28–9.
129. William Shakespeare, *Henry the Sixth, Part 2*, IV.x.35–7.

So, while depicting the monstrous suffering – homelessness, whipping and branding – that foments rebellion, Shakespeare nevertheless holds that the greater monstrosity of rebellion must be slain. Fittingly, upon learning it is Cade that he has killed, Iden denounces him as 'that monstrous traitor'.[130] Nevertheless, 2 *Henry VI* is exceptional in its brilliant depiction of the over-arching social conflict in early-modern England: the struggle between common rights and the claims of private property. The play dramatically pits the rebel for whom 'all the realm shall be in common' against a landowner defending his property from the depredations of 'a thief come to rob my grounds'. With his acute sense of the transformations of his age, Shakespeare portrays Cade's rebellion as a contestation between the communal and the enclosed. He also vividly grasps the symbolic registers in which these conflicts are lived. Whereas Cade's crimes involve breaking into gardens and climbing walls, spatial transgressions that make possible theft against duly constituted property, the restoration of order is achieved by mutilating and dissecting the rebel-body. That body – one that, having been whipped and branded, bears the marks of the new order of property – is punished with dissection and enclosure. And, in enclosing he who violated enclosure, the class- and spatial boundaries of private property are reaffirmed, and social order monstrously restored.

Fifteen years later, Shakespeare returned to the issue of homelessness and, within a year or two more, to the problem of popular rebellion. Homelessness, as we have seen, was no mere literary conceit. Waves of enclosures, particularly in the English Midlands, had swept hundreds of thousands of people into poverty, homelessness and 'vagrancy'. Popular discontent was mounting, be it in anti-enclosure riots or petitions to authorities. In 1604, for instance, the people of Northamptonshire, not far from Shakespeare's home-town of Stratford, petitioned the House of Commons to intervene against enclosure and depopulation of the area. It is hard to imagine that Shakespeare could have been unaware of these developments; indeed, literary evidence suggests he was far from unmoved by them. *King Lear*, for instance, his magnificent tragedy of 1605, contains some of the most profound and stirring commentaries on homelessness ever committed to paper. As a powerful storm whips up, the old and tortured Lear meditates on the plight of the dispossessed:

---

130. William Shakespeare, *Henry the Sixth, Part 2*, II.x.65.

Poor naked wretches, wheresoe'er you are
That bide the pelting of this pitiless storm
How shall your houseless heads and unfed sides,
Your looped and windowed raggedness defend
you
From seasons such as these? O, I have ta'en
Too little care of this. Take physic, pomp.
Expose thyself to feel what wretches feel,
That thou may'st shake the superflux to them
And show the heavens more just.[131]

This call for a 'more just' society, in which the rich share their surpluses ('the superflux') with 'poor naked wretches' certainly did not express any sort of insurrectionary sentiment. It nonetheless conveyed deep sympathy with the victims of displacement and poverty. Part of Shakespeare's agenda thus seems to have involved moral reform of the ruling class – an injunction to more fairly share the wealth so that 'each man have enough'.[132] Bonds of reciprocity could be restored, and tumult avoided, if only the rich would resume their traditional obligations to the poor. By restoring the poor to the protection of their masters, hunger, resentment and class-conflict would be alleviated. But, less than two years after the writing of *King Lear*, the hardships of enclosure, dearth and hunger combined to stoke a mass-upheaval throughout the Midlands, one of whose centres was Shakespeare's own county of Warwickshire. The largest plebeian uprising in nearly half a century, the Midland Revolt of May–June 1607 saw thousands of peasants and rural poor, many of them armed, gather in encampments with the intent to tear down enclosures. But the wealthy were not interested in repairing the bonds of reciprocity. Rallying instead in defence of the rights of property, and quickly arming their retainers, they responded with unrelenting violence. Up to fifty poor rebels were killed in the fighting, while others were publicly hanged, drawn and quartered in market-towns throughout the offending region.[133]

Shakespeare appears to have been well informed about these events. He sought out a copy of the manifesto produced by the so-called Warwickshire

---

131. William Shakespeare, *King Lear*, III.iv.33–41.
132. William Shakespeare, *King Lear*, IV.2.81.
133. See Martin 1986, Part III, and Martin 1983.

Diggers to justify their cause, and its echoes can be found in the memorable opening scenes of the play he wrote that year, *Coriolanus*. Alone among Shakespeare's texts, *Coriolanus* opens with a plebeian riot, and the crowd remains a central actor throughout the play. Equally compelling, images of body-parts and tropes of dismemberment dominate the script. And the convergence of these elements – plebeian revolt, body-images, tropes of dismemberment – is electric.[134] It is possible that Shakespeare's personal exposure to the theatre of dissection played some role here – he lived for some time no more than fifty yards from the Barber Surgeon's hall in London, where, as we have seen, public anatomies on convict-corpses were performed four times a year.[135] But it is equally likely that he drew such imagery from his extraordinary ear for the popular vernacular. Whatever the case, *Coriolanus* is exceptional for the way it deploys the body as the central motif for divining the dynamics of popular rebellion.

The play explores the mutual hatred between the Roman crowd, wracked by hunger, and Caius Marcus (later dubbed Coriolanus), at the time the republic's greatest military leader. This dialectic of hostility is corporeally inscribed and enacted. At the most immediate level, it involves the mobilisation of discourses of the body. While Coriolanus's rhetoric of contempt for the poor is predictable – he demeans them as 'curs', 'rabble', 'rats', herd', 'monster', 'barbarians', and as animated by 'fires of the lowest hell' – it is distinguished by persistent comparison of the people to parts, wounds or diseases of the body. Across the text, he describes the plebeians as 'scabs', 'measles', 'tongues', 'the beast with many heads', or as rotting corpses, 'the dead carcasses of unburied dead'. As if rehearsing the political anatomy of Shakespeare's day, Coriolanus threatens to tear the rebels' bodies apart, vowing to 'pluck out the multitudinous tongue', and warning one of the tribunes of the people that he will 'shake thy bones out of thy garments'.[136] In a remarkable image, resonant with the politics of punitive anatomy, he lambastes the crowd as 'you fragments'. Yet, while the military leader threatens the crowd with dissection, Shakespeare warns that the people too can partake in this game. Indeed, the play revolves

---

134. Some utterly fascinating gender-themes, having to do with the ambivalence of 'self-made' males for their maternal origins, also run through the play. For an insightful treatment of these, see Adelman 1980, pp. 129–49.

135. See Wood 2005, p. 269.

136. William Shakespeare, *Coriolanus*, III.i. 155–6, 177–8.

around contending politics of dissection as part of its competing imageries of
the body. And, in the end, it is the great military leader himself who is torn
apart by the crowd.

But, before analysing those later scenes, let us explore Act One, Scene One
of the play, which so fascinated Bertolt Brecht.[137] Alone among Shakespeare's
plays, *Coriolanus* opens with a popular uprising. The cause is hunger: the rebels are 'resolved rather to die than to famish'.[138] More than this, and contrary
to many later interpretations, the rebels are politically articulate. Analysing
the causes of their hunger, one of the insurgents offers a political economy of
class exploitation:

> *First citizen*: We are accounted poor citizens, the
> patricians good. What authority surfeits on would
> relieve us…
> …the leanness that afflicts us, the object of
> our misery, is as an inventory to particularize their
> abundance; our sufferance is a gain to them. Let
> us revenge this with our pikes ere we become
> rakes. For the gods know I speak this in hunger
> for bread, not in thirst for revenge.[139]

This is not an irrational mob, a 'rabble' intent on mere destruction. A 'rebellion of the belly it may be', to use a term that would soon be coined by Francis
Bacon, but its participants comprise an articulate group of commoners, united
against hunger, and capable of strategic action to lower the price of grain.
They have analysed their situation; they have identified those who oppose
their demands; they have developed a rudimentary class-analysis, expressed
in the First Citizen's declaration that 'our sufferance is a gain to them'.

These thinking rebels of the belly are soon confronted by a parable of the
body-politic that is meant to disarm them. Arriving at the scene of the insurgency, patrician Menenius Agrippa endeavours to quell the uprising with a
fable of the body and its members. In hopes of persuading them that the patricians are not to blame for their hunger, Menenius informs the insurgents that

---

137. See 'Study of the First Scenes of Shakespeare's "Coriolanus"' in Brecht 1964,
pp. 252–65.
138. William Shakespeare, *Coriolanus*, I.i.4–5.
139. William Shakespeare, *Coriolanus*, I.i.15–25.

the nobility are like the belly of the body; while ingesting food, they simultaneously distribute its nutrients to all the limbs and organs of the body. Consequently, for the poor ('the body's members') to rebel against the patricians (the belly) is to threaten the very organ that nourishes them. In Plutarch's account, which Shakespeare had been reading prior to writing *Coriolanus*, this fable of the body-politic placates the rebels. Yet, as some commentators have noted, Shakespeare's reworking destabilises the parable, rendering it considerably less effective. After all, this is a rebellion *of* the belly and, as one commentator has observed of Menenius's story, in Shakespeare's version 'its claim is inept, food is clearly and literally not being distributed and the people, not the patricians, have to make do with the bran'.[140] In short, there are contested politics of the body at work here: plebeian claims of the belly challenge a patrician fable of the belly.

'He's a disease that must be cut away', one of the people's tribunes declares of Coriolanus,[141] not so subtly turning their adversary's own dissecting rhetoric against him. But, as we have seen, it is bodies that are at stake in this contest, not just rhetorics. And so the great military leader who sought to cow a tribune by threatening to 'shake thy bones out of thy garments', discovers that what will be scattered are his own bones. 'Tear him to pieces', cries the crowd in the play's final scene,[142] turning the English ruling class's favoured terror-tactic against a member of the nobility. Where a plebeian rebel, Jack Cade, suffered the indignity of dissection in *2 Henry VI*, in *Coriolanus* such is the fate of a sneering member of the ruling class. Shakespeare thus creates here a compelling dialectic of monstrosity. By failing to heed the plight of the poor, the hungry and the homeless, England's rulers, like Coriolanus, risk creating a rebel-monster that will turn the world upside down by using the methods of political anatomy against the rich. As we shall see below, a similar dialectic of monstrosity emerges in Mary Shelley's *Frankenstein*.

But for the moment, let us continue to explore the linguistic ferocity of the ruling class toward the multitude, which, if anything, Shakespeare may have understated. In Philip Sidney's *Arcadia* (1598) the people are 'the many-headed multitude' or 'the mad multitude' which appears both elementally

---

140. Brockbank 1976, p. 39. See also Patterson 1991, Chapter 4.
141. William Shakespeare, *Coriolanus*, III.i.293.
142. William Shakespeare, *Coriolanus*, V.vi.121.

vicious, 'like enraged beasts', 'like a violent flood', and utterly stupid, as if 'an unruly sort of clowns'.[143] As we move toward the tumult of the English Civil War of the 1640s, two themes come to dominate the construction of the monstrous crowd. First, the multitude is portrayed as a 'headless' beast (one that has lost its mind, as represented by the monarch) or, what is meant as the same thing, as 'many headed', a reference to its democratic proclivity for rule by the many. In addition, the mob is said, secondly, to consist of a monstrous 'confusion' of parts, detached bits lacking order and form. Having broken up the body-politic by rebelling, the rabble cannot reconstitute an organic whole; instead, it comprises a monstrous assemblage of disorderly fragments of humanity. For Sir Thomas Browne in 1642, the multitude encompassed 'that numerous piece of monstrosity which...confused together make but one great beast'.[144] This confusion was regularly figured in images of spatial transgression, of overflowing of boundaries. And enclosure was enlisted as the great restorer of boundaries, order, property and authority. 'Anarchical confusions and fearful calamities' await us, urged James Howell in 1642, 'unless with the pious care which is already taken to hinder the great Beast to break into the vineyard there be also a speedy course taken to fence her from other vermin and lesser animals.' Without such fences, 'the many-headed monster' was sure to lay England open to 'waste, spoil and scorn'.[145]

Perhaps no scholar devoted so much attention to the many-headed monster as did Francis Bacon.[146] Much of the motivation here was political, both domestic (to tame the unruly English mob), and colonial (to justify foreign conquests). As Linebaugh and Rediker point out, in his effort at a comprehensive account of monstrosity, Bacon enumerated a series of 'multitudes' whose destruction was recommended: West Indians; dispossessed commoners ('Canaanites'); pirates; land-rovers (such as squatters, itinerant labourers and highwaymen); assassins; Amazons (almost certainly a reference to rebel-women who led food-riots and anti-enclosure-riots); and Anabaptists (who

---

143. Sidney 1922, pp. 311, 34.
144. As quoted by Hill 1966, p. 301.
145. As quoted in Hill 1966, pp. 307–8, 310.
146. See Park and Daston 1981, pp. 20–4; and Dubois 1994, pp. 175–91. While providing much useful contextual material, Park and Daston err in suggesting that educated élites dismissed monster-tales as superstitions after the seventeenth century. Instead, they often reconstructed them as tales of the marvellous, the aesthetically and scientifically curious and fascinating.

were widely presumed to favour common ownership of all property).[147] We find in Bacon the whole project of political anatomy: a plan for empire based, first, on the extermination of the monsters of the colonial world and the expropriation, mapping and particularisation of their lands and resources; and, second, a proposal for war against the rebellious monsters infecting the English body-politic – commoners, squatters, riotous women, agrarian communists.[148] Gender, class, race and colonialism all intersect in this early-modern anatomy of monstrosity. Riotous women, pirates, masterless commoners, communists and West Indians all comprise people of the belly, and Bacon intimates as much when, in his essay on sedition, he declaims that 'The rebellions of the belly are worst'.[149]

If the discourse of monstrosity reached a fever pitch during the English Civil War,[150] it was in the eighteenth century that the rhetoric of dissection came to dominate it. Cromwell, of course, had famously pledged to dismember the radical mass-movement of the 1640s, the Levellers, enjoining that 'you have no way to deal with these men, but to break them to pieces'. But it was during the next century that dissection emerged as the central trope of calls for the elimination of riot and disorder. As anatomy became ever more intimately a part of the practice of criminal justice in England, calls to 'cut off' the offending members of the body-politic gained wide currency. 'The corrupt members of a community must be cut off by the sword of justice', implored Samuel Moody in 1737. Three years earlier, George Osborne had likewise opined that magistrates possessed the right to 'cut off' the vicious members of society. Writing in 1742, Samuel Russell urged that 'the poisonous example' offered by criminals be eliminated 'by cutting them off by the hand of Justice'. And, in the next decade, Joshua Fitzsimmonds could be found exercising the same metaphor: 'The infected limb must be cut off', he declared.[151]

---

147. Linebaugh and Rediker 2000, pp. 37–40, 61–5.
148. On Bacon's role in shaping the project of political anatomy see McNally 1988, pp. 36–8.
149. Bacon 1870, p. 409.
150. See Cressy 2004, pp. 40–65, and Knoppers 2004, pp. 93–125. See also Burns 1999.
151. Samuel Moody, *The Impartial Justice of Divine Administration* (London, 1736), p. 7; George Osborne, *The Civil Magistrates Right of Inflicting Punishment* (London, 1733), pp. 5, 9; Samuel Rossell, *The Prisoner's Director* (London, 1742), pp. 30–1; Joshua Fitzsimmonds, *Free and Candid Disquisitions on the Nature and Execution of the Laws of*

But the episode that most alarmed the ruling class during this century was the Gordon Riots of June 1780, when buildings blazed and the prisons were thrown open by the London crowd. Over 100 houses were levelled or seriously damaged; Parliament and the Bank of England were attacked; up to 500 people killed (mainly by troops firing on the crowd). 'The Gordon Riots have come down to us in images of smoke and fire', notes one historian.[152] Perhaps nowhere is this more true than in Charles Dickens' novelistic account, *Barnaby Rudge* (1841), subtitled *A Tale of the Riots of 'Eighty*, where we fairly hear the roar of the flames and the cracking of the timbers. Describing 'the reflections in every quarter of the sky, of deep, red, soaring flames, as though the last day had come and the whole universe were burning', Dickens informs us that 'it seemed as if the face of Heaven were blotted out'.[153]

Dickens writes that the 'vast throng' that rampaged through the streets was 'composed for the most part of the very scum and refuse of London'. Moreover, 'the mob raged and roared, like a mad monster as it was…'.[154] Drawing on longstanding images of filthy, unkept vagrants, he portrays a gang of rebels 'covered with soot, and dirt, and dust, and lime; their garments torn to rags; their hair hanging wildly about them'. Behaving 'like hideous madmen', the rabble was driven by 'an unappeasable and maniac rage.'[155] 'A mob,' proclaims Dickens, 'is usually a creature of very mysterious existence, particularly in a large city…the ocean is not more fickle and uncertain, more terrible when roused, more unreasonable, or more cruel.'[156] 'A moral plague ran through the city', he declares in invoking rhetorics of disease; 'the contagion spread like a dread fever: an infectious madness…seized on new victims every hour, and society began to tremble at their ravings'.[157]

Dickens's description is intriguing not just for his anxious constructions of the monster-mob, but also for the way he characterises the rioters themselves. After all, if his reference to 'the scum and refuse' of London is meant to

England (London, 1751), pp. 41–2. All these citations can be found in McGowen 1987, pp. 660–4.

152. Rogers 1990, p. 39.
153. Dickens 2003, Chapter 68, p. 569. Given the many editions available, I will provide chapter-references in the body of my text, followed by page-references to the Penguin edition cited above.
154. Dickens 2003, Chapter 49, p. 408.
155. Dickens 2003, Chapter 50, p. 419 and Chapter 68, p. 569.
156. Dickens 2003, Chapter 52, p. 429.
157. Dickens 2003, Chapter 53, p. 438.

designate the unemployed, pickpockets, prostitutes, beggars and thieves, then it is highly misleading about the social composition of the rioters. As George Rudé painstakingly demonstrated, the majority of those arrested during the Gordon Riots were in fact employed labourers.[158] Yet, Dickens may be onto something in his intimation that many of the labouring poor shared much with the unemployed – irregular work, poverty, resort to 'crime' to make ends meet, a defiant popular culture. Indeed, it is instructive that much of the drama of Dickens's novel revolves around apprentices – among them Simon Tappertit, apprentice to a locksmith – precisely the group that astute observers of the time considered to have been in the forefront of the uprising.[159] By the eighteenth century, apprenticeship had become more a form of semi-bonded labour for young workers than initiation into a lifelong trade.[160] Masters and apprentices increasingly confronted one another across a class-divide, rather than as members of a common profession. Appropriately, Dickens depicts a group of unruly apprentices shouting 'Death to all masters, long live all 'prentices', as he sets the stage for the riots.[161] So separated is the world of the apprentices from that of the masters that, when Tappertit attends a meeting of the subversive 'Prentice Knights', it is as if he has entered a foreign land, a space outside the geography of civilisation; he is led through an obscure alley into 'a blind court or yard, profoundly dark, unpaved, and reeking with stagnant odours'. Ominously, the ground seems to 'open at his feet' revealing 'a ragged head', and he is ushered into a meeting.[162] In this resonant description, Dickens spatialises the class-divide that racked London, contrasting its well-lit commercial and wealthy residential districts with dank, smelly back-alleys and unlit courtyards.[163]

The riots themselves had roots in religious bigotry, originating in the agitation of Lord George Gordon against a bill that would have relaxed legal restrictions on Catholics.[164] Yet, as events unfolded and the action of the crowd

158. Rudé 1974, pp. 280–3.
159. Even Horace Walpole admitted as much, while including 'convicts and all kinds of desperadoes' in his description. See Rudé 1974, p. 280.
160. See Linebaugh 2003, p. 62.
161. Dickens 2003, Chapter 8, p. 72.
162. Dickens 2003, Chapter 8, p. 70.
163. For some insightful reflections on these issues see Connor 1996, pp. 211–29.
164. Of course, anti-Catholicism was always also a political sentiment, 'Popery' having long been associated with monarchical absolutism and tyranny.

became increasingly autonomous, the religious dimension receded and the movement's class-character came to the fore. As Rudé noted, there was no general attack on the Catholic community, 'the victims of the riots' being distinguished by the fact they were 'on the whole, persons of substance'.[165] Moreover, as the uprising shook off its primarily religious colouration, new strata of the oppressed were drawn in, most notably segments of London's African population, many of whose members played leading roles in the popular movement.[166]

The event which most clearly defined the transition in the character of the riots – from being a purely anti-Catholic movement toward one based on 'a groping desire to settle accounts with the rich, if only for a day'[167] – occurred on 6 June, when the crowd turned its sights on Newgate Prison, arguably the most hated symbol of ruling-class power in London. Smashing through gates and doors, destroying locks, the insurgents liberated hundreds of prisoners while setting the hated dungeon ablaze. Yet, the destruction of Newgate merely fuelled the crowd's hunger for revenge against loathed institutions. Again, Dickens captures something of the sentiment when an angry youth exclaims that the crowd must attack 'Not that jail alone…but every jail in London'.[168] And so, in fact, it did, sacking additional prisons and jails, along with other institutions of confinement: 20 crimping houses (where impressed, or forcibly conscripted, sailors were held prior to setting out on ship), and private debtors' prisons ('spunging houses').[169]

Among other things, these attacks involved an effort to smash open the closed structures of bourgeois space. If agrarian capitalism in England centrally involved the enclosure of land, the whole of capitalism, rural and urban, entailed the spatial enclosure of property and the confinement of those who would violate it. Indeed, as we have seen, the enclosure of the rebel-body of Jack Cade serves for Shakespeare to represent both the protection of property and the confinement of the transgressor. It is no accident, then, that the valiant master of Dickens's story is a locksmith whose apprentice joins the riots and

---

165. Rudé 1974, p. 287.
166. Linebaugh 2003, pp. 348–56. Linebaugh's pioneering work in drawing attention to this neglected dimension of the Gordon Riots represents a major scholarly achievement.
167. Rudé 1974, p. 289.
168. Chapter. 60, p. 504
169. Linebaugh 2003, p. 335.

pays with parts of his body – losing his legs when the soldiers repress the crowd. If social order is to be restored – once again at the expense of proletarian bodies – then the régime of locks and keys must be preserved. As Linebaugh perceptively notes,

> The control of space is the essence of private property, and its architecture became more complex: yards, fences, railings and gates formed an outer perimeter; stair-wells, doors, rooms and closets an inner one; bureaux, chests, cabinets, cases desks and drawers protected the articles of private property themselves. Each space was controlled by locks, and access to each required a key.[170]

More than this, locks and keys were also (as they remain) key instruments for punishing those who transgressed the laws of property. To seize the keys of Newgate, as Francis Mockford did that historical June night in 1780, was to symbolically challenge the entire machinery of confinement that protected property and power. By brandishing them before the crowd, Mockford scorned the control of space upon which bourgeois property rests.[171] Once more, albeit disapprovingly, Dickens astutely captures the sentiment of the insurgent crowd, their desire to de-enclose. The rebels, he writes, were 'breaking open inviolable drawers, putting things into their pockets which didn't belong to them…wantonly wasting, breaking, pulling down and tearing up: nothing quiet, nothing private…'.[172]

As with Shakespeare, whatever Dickens's sympathies for the poor, he could not condone rebellion. Moreover, not only should his novel's rebels be punished; they must be publicly humiliated. And Dickens knew well the terms of punishment and ridicule: dismemberment. It is the fate of the locksmith's apprentice, Simon Tappertit, his legs having been crushed in the panic when soldiers opened fire on rioters, to undergo amputation. 'Shorn of his graceful limbs,' he henceforth ambles about London 'on two wooden legs', a theme Dickens repeats in *Our Mutual Friend* (1864–5), where he again creates a character without a leg, this time using anatomy to depict the working-class monster as a multiracial hybrid of Indian, African, British and animal parts.[173] In

---

170. Linebaugh 2003, p. 336.
171. On Mockford's actions at Newgate and after see Linebaugh 2003, pp. 345–6.
172. Dickens 2003, Chapter 54, p. 450.
173. Dickens 1989, Chapter 7.

Barnaby Jones Dickens proceeds to ratchet up the index of humiliation, exploiting the phallic imagery available in dissection of legs to suggest castration and loss of 'manhood'. We are informed in the final chapter that Tappertit's wife would mortify her husband by removing his legs in public places, thus exposing him to the ridicule of passers-by.[174] In this image of woeful degradation, Dickens tames the riotous rabble. The rebel-body is dissected and abased, thus transforming the mob that had terrified the bourgeoisie into an object of pity, an ugly but harmless, deformed monstrosity. But, if the riotous monster of 1780 was tamed, it was only temporarily so. It would be only a matter of years before the terrifying rebel-body would once again haunt the bourgeois imagination.

Jacobins, Irishmen and Luddites: rebel-monsters in the age of *Frankenstein*

Perhaps no event so re-energised the discourse of monstrosity as did the French Revolution of 1789–99. Élite-opinion in Britain was at first largely unperturbed by the French events, often seeing them as a replay of Britain's 'Glorious Revolution' of 1688, in which monarchs had been changed without a popular upheaval. But, by 1792, ruling-class opinion had shifted, coming over to the virulently anti-revolutionary sentiment of Edmund Burke. Two events in particular had driven the ruling circles into unremitting hostility to the French Revolution and its British supporters. First was the 'second revolution' in France, the popular upheaval of 1792 that overthrew the monarchy and gave the impetus to radical forces allied to the Paris poor. Next was the appearance of Part Two of Thomas Paine's *Rights of Man*. If Part One (1791) of Paine's work, with its attack on all forms of hereditary power, had been troubling, Part Two was positively incendiary in its proclamation that people naturally possessed economic as well as political rights. Declaring that the poor had a right to public support (in the forms of family-allowances, maternity-benefits and old-age pensions) and a decent standard of living, Paine opened a radical breach in the liberal doctrine of rights. The poor, he submitted, may demand economic support not as an appeal to charity, but

---

174. Dickens 2003, Chapter 82, p. 684.

as the 'exercise of a *right*'.[175] Given his commitments to market-relations and private property, Paine probably did not appreciate all the radical implications of this claim. But a new generation of working-class radicals did. At the hands of theorists associated with the London Corresponding Society (LCS), Paine's message was extended and radicalised, pushed to the very borders of socialism.

And a pervasive message it was. Historians estimate that 200,000 copies of Part Two of the *Rights of Man* were sold within a year.[176] Weavers, shoemakers, miners and others snatched up copies in Norwich, Manchester, Nottingham, Selby, Edinburgh, Oldham and dozens of other localities. Meanwhile, recruitment to the militant LCS soared. Sensing that they faced a burgeoning revolutionary movement, the authorities cracked down, charging radical activists with sedition, imprisoning some, transporting others. *The Rights of Man* was prosecuted in 1793, its author convicted in absentia of sedition. In May 1794 the government intensified its assault, suspending *habeus corpus* and arresting a series of writers and agitators. Momentarily knocked off balance, the radicals quickly regrouped when dearth and hunger ignited a new wave of protest the following year. More ominously for their rulers, radical speakers and writers began to deepen their critique of bourgeois private property. Under the influence of the likes of LCS leader John Thelwall, himself arrested in 1794, of the increasingly revolutionary Thomas Spence, publisher of the weekly *Pig's Meat*, and of former LCS secretary Thomas Evans, protosocialist ideas found a growing audience. And such ideas were soon part of a revolutionary blend as, in the face of tightening repression, many activists began to discuss the merits of a British uprising allied with rebels in Ireland.[177]

It was in this context that the inflamed rhetoric of Burke's *Reflections on the Revolution in France* gained currency among Britain's rulers. While Burke's theoretical analysis was never fully embraced,[178] his language of monstrosity was widely employed. In the first instance, Burke simply mobilised standard tropes about the monstrous mob. Writing to his son in October 1789,

---

175. Paine 1984, p. 243.
176. Royle and Walvin 1982, p. 54; Williams 1968, p. 67; Thompson 1963, pp. 107–8.
177. See Wells 1986; Chase 1988; McCalman 1988; Ashraf 1983; Dickinson 1982; Gallop 1982; Hampsher-Monk 1991, pp. 1–20. On the connection between Irish radicalism and the French Revolution, see Elliott 1982.
178. See McNally 2000, pp. 427–48.

he described the 'portentous State of France' as one 'where the Elements which compose Human Society seem all to be dissolved, and a World of Monsters to be produc'd in the place of it'.[179] His *Reflections* continued in this vein, denouncing the 'monster of a constitution' the revolutionaries had adopted, abusing the municipal army of Paris as 'a monster', and echoing a French politician who had described the French assembly as 'a species of political monster'.[180] But, on top of these usages, Burke decisively innovated, appropriating popular anxieties about grave-robbing and dissection into his counter-revolutionary discourse of monstrosity.

Invoking the imagery of dissection, Burke extols that 'wise prejudice', trampled by the Jacobin revolutionaries of France, which teaches people 'to look with horror on those children of their country who are prompt rashly to hack that aged parent into pieces'. He then mixes the image with references to magic, alchemy and 'resurrection', arguing that the murderous, anatomising children of France hope to put the dismembered patriarchal body 'into the kettle of magicians' who seek, with the aid of 'wild incantations', to regenerate the body politic. Exploiting images of evil spirits that shed old forms to reappear in different guises, he accuses the Jacobins of manufacturing 'new organs' which allow malevolent ghosts to 'transmigrate'.[181] Returning to the attack six years later in his widely read *Letter to a Noble Lord* (1796), Burke jostles together charges of cannibalism, sorcery, grave-robbing and alchemy. France is governed by 'legislative butchers' under the influence of a 'cannibal philosophy', he exclaims. Never having raised his voice against the actual dissection of the poor, he seethes hatred for 'the Sans culotte Carcase Butchers' who ostensibly chop up the nobility 'into all sorts of pieces for roasting, boiling, and stewing'. In addition to dissecting people, these deranged revolutionists also rob graves. Not even 'the sanctuary of the tomb is sacred', to those low enough to deny the departed 'the sad immunities of the grave'.[182] To top things off, these plebeian resurrectionists have brought forth evil spirits with their meddling in the graveyards: 'Out of the tomb of the murdered monarchy in France has arisen a vast, tremendous, unformed spectre', he cries.

179. Cobban and Smith 1967, p. 30.
180. Burke 1986, pp. 313, 350, 333.
181. Burke 1986, pp. 194, 248.
182. Burke 1991, pp. 175, 180, 147.

Burke's attack on the French Revolution is significant for mobilising plebeian anxieties about grave-robbing and dissection on behalf of a rhetorically charged defence of the old order.[183] In an important sense, the motifs of tombs and spirits he deploys situate his counter-revolutionary discourse in the Gothic tradition.[184] In addition to portraying a world haunted by ghosts and phantoms, a central device of Gothic literature was the reversal of pursuer into pursued, a disorienting, horrifying inversion of the everyday-world. And Burke, perhaps unconsciously, traces precisely such a reversal, albeit without the irony that pervaded the Gothic. He portrays a scene of horror in which the dissectors are themselves threatened with dissection. The result is an anxious, aristocratic Gothic shorn of irony, one that depicts a world under the sway of murder and mayhem. With the revolution in France, evil spirits have been unleashed, spectres whose orgy of cannibalistic subversion threatens to devour both the living and the dead. Burke appears obsessed, a man who cannot sleep in the knowledge that our world is haunted by sinister forces – cannibals, revolutionary anatomists, sacrilegious grave-robbers – bent on total devastation. His *Reflections* is, in this respect, a Gothic novel, a work whose author endures 'the unbearable Awakeness' of those who 'see and hear the Ghosts' which others do not.[185] But, if Burke had mobilised popular idioms for anti-popular purposes, he was soon to discover that others could play this game of rhetorical reversal.

His greatest intellectual adversary, Thomas Paine, did precisely this to great effect. In a single passage in *Rights of Man*, for instance, Paine serves up three aristocratic monsters in four sentences. He begins with claims for aristocratic cannibalism. Pointing out that the feudal law of primogeniture required that all noble property descend to the first-born male, he pronounces that this amounts to disowning all other offspring. 'Aristocracy never had more than *one* child', he avers. 'The rest are begotten to be devoured. They are thrown

---

183. Of course, as the Jacobin Terror took off in 1793, the revolutionaries were increasingly associated with the guillotine and body-chopping. See, for example, Landes 2004. But Burke, as we have seen was exploiting these popular tropes as early as 1789–90.

184. The idea that Burke's political texts need also to be read in literary and aesthetic terms is an important innovation of some recent scholarship. See, for example, De Bruyn (1996), which does not, however, address the Gothic motifs in Burke's attack on the French Revolution.

185. Witt 1979, p. 42. For some reflections on the nature of the Gothic, see Punter 1980, Chapter 1.

to the cannibal for prey.' In a deliberate provocation of Burke, he portrays the French revolutionaries as *slayers* of cannibal-monsters. 'To restore, therefore, parents to their children, and children to their parents – relations to each other and man to society – the French constitution has destroyed the law of primogenitureship. Here, then, lies the monster; and Mr. Burke, if he pleases, may write its epitaph.' Having identified noble property as the real monster, Paine then extends the criticism to aristocracy in general: 'whether we view it before hand or behind, or sideways, or anyway else, domestically or publicly, it is still a monster'.[186]

Paine's contemporary, Mary Wollstonecraft, also Mary Shelley's mother, similarly deployed the language of monstrosity in her attack on the *ancien régime* in France. Known today principally for her *Vindication of the Rights of Woman* (1791), Wollstonecraft was also author of two works on the French Revolution, *Vindication of the Rights of Man* (1790) and a subsequent, more ambivalent set of reflections, *An Historical and Moral View of the French Revolution* (1794). In the latter work, she exploits the rhetoric of monstrosity to anti-Burkean purposes. Describing the old order in France as a degenerate body-politic, rife with monstrous excess and vice, she condemns its 'nocturnal orgies', 'flatigious immorality', 'sickly appetites' and 'atrocious debaucheries', while accusing it of 'despotism' and 'butcheries'. All of these she asserts are nothing more than 'the excrescences of a gigantic tyranny', the result of 'the demon of despotism'.[187] Distancing herself from the violence of the revolutionary mob, Wollstonecraft assigns responsibility for their excesses to the old older. By dulling the mind and corrupting manners, French despotism had produced two degenerate types, the 'devouring beast' and the 'spiritless reptile'.[188] The excesses of the French Terror are thus refluxes of an *ancien régime* that engaged in dissection and murder, 'cutting off the heads, or torturing the bodies' of its opponents. Dabbling in 'sanguinary tortures, insidious poisonings, and dark assassinations', the rulers of France inevitably metamorphosed into 'a race of monsters in human shape'.[189] In the same vein, in his influential *Enquiry Concerning Political Justice*, William Godwin opined that all

---

186. Paine 1984, pp. 82–3.
187. Wollstonecraft 1993, pp. 313, 314, 325, 317, 323.
188. Wollstonecraft 1993, p. 383.
189. Wollstonecraft 1993, pp. 379, 384.

systems of hereditary property and power comprised 'a ferocious monster', one expert at 'devouring' all authentic human attributes and virtues.[190]

Burke thus encountered in Paine and Wollstonecraft two literary radicals as adept as he at deploying the language of monstrosity. But, whereas *The Rights of Man* appeared before Jacobin dominance, and thus avoided the problem of the revolutionary Terror, Wollstonecraft's 1794 work responded by extending the analysis of monstrosity to the oppressed classes, arguing that despotism produced grotesque effects among the downtrodden. Since people are a product of circumstances, the lower orders of France, deprived of civil and political rights, were inevitably corrupted. By dividing society into separate orders, one tyrannising the other, the old régime sundered 'ties of affection', 'sullied' human dignity and blunted the moral sentiments.[191] The result was two monstrosities: domineering tyrants, on one side, a class of slaves who felt no moral obligations to their rulers on the other. If the rule of the former is always barbaric, 'the retaliation of slaves is always terrible'.[192] Yet, while the system of despotism is ultimately responsible for the frightening retaliation of slaves – a theme embraced by her daughter, Mary Shelley – this does not reduce the horror of the latter's violence. And this dilemma, this dialectic of monstrosity, would reappear across the greatest of English Jacobin novels, *Frankenstein* among them.

It was Mary Shelley's father, William Godwin, author of *Political Justice* (1793), who composed the most successful English 'Jacobin novel' during the revolutionary era.[193] The term 'Jacobin' is, however, something of a misnomer, a term largely applied to these British reformers by their opponents. Godwin, Wollstonecraft and their associates certainly supported the French Revolution. They defended Thomas Paine and proudly declared themselves advocates of the rights of man. But, unlike many plebeian radicals, they were not revolutionary by temperament or association, favouring literary work over political organising. Contrary to Jacobinism, they rejected violence and embraced a progressive gradualism. As Godwin put it in *Political Justice*, progress 'should take place in a mild and gradual, though incessant, advance, not by violent

---

190. Godwin 1985, p. 476.
191. Godwin 1985, pp. 340, 386.
192. Godwin 1985, p. 386.
193. Among the best treatments of this group is Kelly 1976, and Johnson 2004.

leaps'.[194] While these writers and dissenting ministers from the educated middle class tended toward republicanism, they feared the excesses of the crowd. Intellectual enlightenment was their work, not political agitation and mobilisation, and to this end they produced, particularly during the 1790s, a string of novels that sought to advance the cause of intelligent social reform.

The most noteworthy of these so-called Jacobin novels was Godwin's *Things as They Are, or the Adventures of Caleb Williams* (1794). This highly influential work spawned a tradition of early nineteenth-century 'Godwinian' novels.[195] A stylistic innovator, Godwin designed a confessional novel that utilised a number of Gothic conventions – particularly the doublings and reversals between pursuer and pursued that disturb the reader's sympathies with either of the lead characters. In so doing, he put into question the social circumstances that generated these characters, their motivations and their behaviours. The result was a sort of *radical Gothic* that mobilised characters of psychological complexity caught in a perplexing whirl of intrigue and suspense.

Central to *Caleb Williams* are problems of property, law and class, embodied particularly in relations between masters and servants. Indeed, one especially powerful scene brings all three of these together by portraying a lord's persecution of a tenant under the Black Act, a section of which is quoted in order to expose its extraordinarily repressive character.[196] At the centre of the story is the persecution of Caleb Williams, falsely accused of theft by his lord/master/employer, Ferdinando Falkland, because he has divined the murderous secret the latter conceals. Having pursued the truth about his master, Williams himself is soon pursued – by his employer, the courts, and a variety of bounty-hunters. The dynamics of the novel revolve around the reversals and doublings that characterise the relationship between Falkland and Williams. Godwin shows us how each is a captive of his social role – and of the other. As much as they alternately pursue and flee, they are bound together in a fateful venture. At the same time, the class-divide destroys each. Indeed,

---

194. Godwin 1985, p. 269.
195. See Kelly (1976, p. 18) for an assessment of the success of the novel. On the influence of the book see the editors' introduction to the excellent critical edition: Handwerk and Markley 2000, pp. 9, 37–41. Throughout this chapter, I will refer to this novel by its now customary title, *Caleb Williams*. Further references to the novel will be given with the volume-number, followed by the chapter-number, concluding with page-numbers from this edition.
196. Godwin 2000, v. 1, Chapter 9, pp. 139–40.

we can read Godwin as tracing a whole series of effects of political anatomy, of the partitioning of society. For the socially weaker party, Caleb Williams, the results are especially devastating. Young, intelligent and resourceful though he may be, he is no match for the power of money supported by the law. Consequently, he must hide from virtually all of human kind in order to avoid arrest, imprisonment and a probable death-sentence. In reciting his enforced detachment from society, Williams employs the language of dissection, describing himself as 'a solitary being, cut off from the expectation of sympathy', as a person 'cut off from the whole human species', and as 'cut off from the friendship of mankind'.[197] Once on the run, Williams adopts a series of disguises adapted from marginalised outsiders. Choosing to blend in with outcasts from respectable society, he appears at different times as a beggar, a Jew and an Irishman – in short, he assumes the forms of various 'monsters' that threatened bourgeois sensibility.

The transformation of the oppressed outcast into a grotesque being is arguably the most important Godwinian theme taken up and radicalised in *Frankenstein*. The *monsterisation* of the Irish, one of the peoples whose identity Caleb Williams adopts, was particularly significant in the era of *Frankenstein*. England's first colony, Ireland had been subjected to the rigours of political anatomy, its lands expropriated, mapped and partitioned. As part of the legitimation-strategy entwined with this project, the Irish were racialised, depicted as a violent, disorderly and uncivilised breed. In fact, in his provocatively titled *Political Anatomy of Ireland* (1672), William Petty had described Ireland as 'a Political Animal' susceptible to anatomisation of the sort carried out on 'common Animals'.[198] The Irish were rebel-monsters in every sense. At home they plotted insurrection, never more dangerously than in 1798 when the United Irishmen made common cause with revolutionary France in its war with Britain.[199] The fact that many English Paineites had extensive personal and political connections with Ireland and its rebel-movement only increased their notoriety. And the Godwins and the Shelleys were among the most notorious in this regard. Daughter of Mary Wollstonecraft and William Godwin, Mary Shelley shared this notoriety. Not only was Mary Wollstone-

---

197. Godwin 2000, v. 3, Chapter 7, p. 343, Chapter 14, p. 408 and p. 414.
198. Petty 1963, p. 129.
199. See Elliot 1982.

craft's mother Irish, but Godwin had dined with Irish republicans, including Colonel Despard and Robert Emmett, both of whom went to the gallows in 1803. And these associations had directly domestic consequences in England. The Irish, after all, were more than an 'external' enemy; inside England, as migrant-labourers, they constituted a tumultuous core of the unruly mob. For their efforts, they figured prominently among the London hanged.[200] In a context of established anti-Irish ideology, one indicator of Mary Shelley's radical alignments, and those of her partner and husband, the poet Percy Shelley, is their sustained commitment to the cause of Irish freedom.[201] In addition to consorting with Jacobins, this daughter of Godwin and Wollstonecraft was also suspect for her alignments with the monstrous Irish.

One further beast featured decisively in forming the political context for *Frankenstein*: Luddism. A movement without a central leadership or overarching organisational structure, Luddism terrified the British ruling class across the years 1811–17.[202] Erupting, quickly subsiding, then surging forward again, the Luddite movement constituted a heroic insurgency against the consolidation of industrial capitalism, particularly in the woollen industry. Throughout this industry and many others, work-reorganisation was displacing much human labour and rendering what remained a mere appendage of a mechanised production-system. While generally identified with machine-breaking – which did indeed figure centrally – Luddism was a multi-faceted response to the manifold ways in which labour was being devalued, mechanised, cheapened and more thoroughly subordinated to capital. In addition to attacks on machines, Luddites also organised food-riots and armed uprisings. The movement peaked in April 1812, as riots swept towns and cities across Lancashire, Yorkshire, Cheshire, and Derbyshire, including centres like Manchester, Coventry, Birmingham and Sheffield. 'These few days,' observes one historian, 'had seen the simultaneous insurrections of populations of working

---

200. Linebaugh 2003, pp. 93–4

201. See O'Brien 2004. While efforts have been made since Victorian times to de-radicalise Mary Shelley, the evidence overwhelmingly suggests that she subscribed throughout her life to the left-leaning Enlightenment-liberalism of her parents, Mary Wollstonecraft and William Godwin, whose influences also figured centrally in the political-philosophical formation of her husband, P.B. Shelley. For an excellent treatment of these issues see Bennett 1998.

202. For a detailed chronology of the movement see the Appendix to Thomis 1970, pp. 177–86.

class on a scale England had never before experienced.... Larger and larger groups of weavers, croppers, cotton printers, colliers and other workmen, meeting no longer in hidden places, but on open moorland and near towns, some in gangs of several hundred, were being reported from every one of the northern manufacturing towns.'[203] According to one recent estimate, Luddites destroyed over 100,000 pounds worth of property between 1811 and 1813: 1,200 stocking frames in the Nottingham area, at least 200 shearing frames and gig-mills, the entirety of two factories in Lancashire and Cheshire, two large houses (which were burned to the ground), and untold amounts of cloth.[204] The sight of smouldering factories testified to the eruption of a full-fledged class-war – as did the response of the ruling class.

With capitalist property besieged, England's rulers turned to class-terror. Fully 35,000 armed men were sent into the rebel areas. Shooting, maiming, arresting and imprisoning, these troops re-established bourgeois order. By the end of 1813, well before the movement's final battles, probably three dozen workers had been killed, 24 sent to the gallows, and 51 sentenced to Australia. Of the 21 men and one woman condemned to hang by Special Commissions in Chester and Lancaster in June 1812, three received the death-penalty for having stolen bread, cheese and potatoes – a reminder that property took precedence over life. Coordinated repression on this scale required unprecedented efforts to install military force throughout the country. To this end, the year 1812 saw barracks built for 138,000 soldiers in London and for over 160,000 in Liverpool, Bristol, and Brighton combined. If English liberalism had once prided itself on the absence of a standing army, threats to capitalist authority induced a new conceit, converting men of property to the virtues of an overweening military presence.[205]

The Luddite revolts and the repression they induced are pivotal to the context in which *Frankenstein* took shape. The book originated in a ghost-story contest between Percy Shelley, the poet Lord George Byron, his physician John Polidori, author of the first published vampire-tale in English, and Mary Shelley, as they spent the summer of 1816 together outside Geneva. There can

---

203. Reid 1986, p. 124.
204. Sale 1995, pp. 191–2.
205. On numbers of troops mobilised in 1812 see Reid 1986, p. 152. On numbers sentenced see Reid 1986, pp. 168–70, and Sale 1995, p. 190. On barrack-building see Foot 1984, p. 36.

be little doubt that repression of the Luddites arose in the group's conversations that summer. Byron himself had eloquently denounced state-violence against the rebels in his maiden-speech in the House of Lords in February 1812, attacking Tory proposals to apply the death-penalty to machine-breaking. Challenging the Lords to forsake repression, he declared

> ...all the cities you have taken, all the armies that have retreated before your leaders are but paltry subjects of self congratulation *if your land divides against itself*, and your dragoons and executioners must be let loose against your fellow citizens. You call these men a mob. It is the mob that labour in your fields, serve in your houses – that man your navy and recruit your army, that have enabled you to defy all the world, and can also defy you when neglect and calamity have driven them to despair.[206]

Percy Shelley too had rallied against anti-Luddite repression, participating with his (then) wife Harriet in fund-raising efforts for the families of 14 Luddite men executed in 1813. For Byron and Shelley, as for all radicals of the period, the Luddites, whatever their errors, were victims of a reactionary, anti-democratic ruling class that sanctified the rights of property above all others. While the Godwinian radicals, unlike their plebeian counterparts, recoiled from Luddite violence, they nonetheless blamed the tyranny of Britain's rulers for the desperate revolts of the many-headed multitude.[207] Perhaps equally significant, they identified the drive for accumulation at the expense of human well-being as an inherent feature of Britain's anti-democracy, thus opening the way for a critique of property-relations. So warped were the values of England's rulers, Byron had proclaimed in his famous speech, that they were prepared to see men 'sacrificed to improvements in mechanism'.

For radical liberals of the Wollstonecraft-Godwin variety, Luddite revolt and government-repression were merely different symptoms of the sickness inherent in Britain's system of monarchy, aristocracy and rule of the propertied. Class- and civil war, violence and repression were predictable outgrowths of an authoritarian *ancien régime*. Jacobin terror, Irish insurrectionism, Luddite uprisings may all have been terrifying, but, as Wollstonecraft had warned,

---

206. Lord Byron, 'Framework Bill Speech' (1812) in Byron 1991, my emphasis.
207. For an insightful treatment of P.B. Shelley's lack of identification with Luddite rebellion, despite his sympathy for them as victims, see Foot 1984, pp. 163–4.

they were the inevitable horrors produced by a grotesque system of oppression. These themes cannot have been far from Mary Shelley's mind while she worked on *Frankenstein*. After all, her novel can be said to revolve around the plight of a land that 'divides against itself', one in which people are 'sacrificed to improvements in mechanism'. Moreover, by figuring the creation of the proletariat in the idioms of grave-robbing and dissection, *Frankenstein* constituted a horror-story in which class-oppression was registered in the language of political anatomy. The monstrosities of the market were thus subtly deciphered through the horrific 'lectures' read upon working-class bodies and minds by nascent capitalism. Such considerations would only have been reinforced by the hanging of yet more Luddite rebels in April 1817, as she was making final revisions to her manuscript.

The rights of monsters: horror and the split society

It has been perceptively observed that 'the literature of terror is born precisely *out of terror of a split society*, and out of the desire to heal it'.[208] The monster and the vampire, who we have come to know as Frankenstein and Dracula, had their literary births on the same night in 1816. In reply to the ghost-story challenge laid down by Lord Byron at the Villa Chapuis near Geneva, John Polidori's 'The Vampyre' and Mary Shelley's *Frankenstein* were simultaneously conceived.[209] If Shelley's creation is immensely superior to Polidori's, it is in no small part because of the imaginative power with which she thematises the problem of the split society. To be sure, Shelley's novel explores complex and enduring problems of identity, gender, self and other. But, as I shall demonstrate, it does so while framing these issues in consciously social and political terms. Notwithstanding its omission from most critical commentary, the problem of class-injustice permeates Shelley's novel. Yet, as befits an aesthetic work of this order, class-relations are subtly inflected in *Frankenstein*, refracted through the specific experiences of complex individuals.

---

208. Moretti 1983, p. 83.
209. Ibid. See Polidori 1997, pp. 1–24. Polidori's text was first published in 1819 and erroneously attributed to Byron. Shelley's *Frankenstein* first appeared in 1818. Only in 1823 did an edition (published by her father, William Godwin) appear with her name attached. A revised edition was published in 1831. In a wonderful example of doubling and reversal, the Creature of Shelley's novel is often erroneously identified as 'Frankenstein', the name of its human creator.

The problem of the split society acquires much of its aesthetic force in Shelley's novel due to the way she internalises it in the psychic lives of her two principal characters, Victor Frankenstein and his Creature. A split society, she warns, fractures the individual psyche, creating terrible internal tensions, even schizoid psychoses, in the human agents who compose it. Disowning a whole section of humankind, hating, despising and persecuting them, the oppressor invariably disavows an integral part of himself (and it is largely *him*selves with which she is concerned, as we shall see), and diminishes his own humanity. Pathological hatred participates in the very monstrosity projected onto abject others. In Shelley's dialectic of monstrosity, violence and oppression rebound on the oppressors – distorting their own personalities and marring their judgment, while also creating, as Wollstonecraft had warned, an enraged underclass intent on retribution. Through this dialectic, Shelley probes the dynamics of the split society at the level of interpersonal relations. In constructing a *microcosmics* of class- and gender-division, she lends a personal immediacy to social questions, much as Godwin had done in *Caleb Williams*. As the editor of a recent edition of her works points out, believing 'that the sociopolitical inequities of her day were mirrored within the individual and the family', Shelley's strategy involves 'coalescing the public and private'.[210] However, this subtle coalescence of the private and public has eluded many commentators who have privatised her literary politics, reducing *Frankenstein* (and other of her novels) to purely domestic tales.[211]

One critic insists, for instance, that, while Mary Shelley retains the monster-metaphor, she 'purges it of virtually all reference to collective movements', relocating rebellion 'within the family' and thus shifting 'from politics to psyche'.[212] Yet this is to miss the politics *of* the psyche (and the family) at work in *Frankenstein*, as social conflicts are registered and enacted in the psychic lives of the main protagonists. Indeed, as I suggest below, it is precisely this intricate interweaving of the political and the interpersonal that enables Shelley to map gender and class as mutually constituting modes of social exclusion and oppression. In delineating power-structures, she uses the novel to map macro-relations onto the micro-dynamics among individuals. As if to

---

210. Bennett 1998, p. 3.
211. This was bound up with strategies of 'Victorianising' Mary Shelley, as Bennett (1998, pp. 103, 120–1) points out.
212. Sterrenburg 1979, pp. 157, 159.

remind her readers that they are not witnessing a merely private drama, at a crucial moment in the novel, the Creature cautions Frankenstein that, if his creator continues to reject and isolate him, the consequence will be an evil 'so great, that not only you and your family, *but thousands of others*, shall be swallowed up in the whirlwinds of its rage'.[213] Animating these claustrophobic personal relations is a great social drama, one whose effects, Shelley warns, are sure to be wide-ranging. Indeed, the novel's social implications are further highlighted when, as we shall see, a mass-revolt of sailors averts a final calamity as the story draws to a close.

Structurally, too, *Frankenstein* is organised on collective lines, revolving around the accounts of three different narrators – ship-captain Robert Walton who takes Victor Frankenstein aboard his craft, Victor Frankenstein himself, and the Creature. Organised as a polyphonic novel, *Frankenstein* destabilises the authorial position, to use a recent jargon, taking the reader through multiple narratives, none of which is granted moral authority. As befits a dialogical novel, the ending is highly ambiguous. The reader is given enormous interpretive range, as generations of radically contending readings suggest. Consequently, multiple analytical frames – feminist, psychoanalytical, post-colonial, Marxist – can illuminate *Frankenstein*.[214] To add yet another layer, the novel also problematises its own generation and birth, suggestively spanning a nine-month period, the time frame of a typical human pregnancy, and mapping this frame onto crucial happenings in the author's own life. Events in the novel begin in December 1796, the month in which Mary Shelley was conceived, and the book ends on 11 September 1797, the day after the death of her mother, Mary Wollstonecraft, who perished eleven days after giving birth to *Frankenstein*'s future author. Equally suggestive, these dates corre-

---

213. Shelley 1999, Volume 2, Chapter 2, p. 127. Further citations from this scholarly edition, based on the original 1818 text, will be given according to volume, chapter- and page-number. Like most scholars, I will take the 1818 edition as the 'classic' versions. Doing so also foregrounds the original context, locating the text decisively in relation to the Luddite uprisings.

214. This is not to suggest that all readings are equally reasonable or plausible. Multivalent as *Frankenstein* is, it is clearly a work in the Wollstonecraft-Godwin tradition, as any reading responsive to social and literary history and personal biography indicates. On this overall positioning of the novel, see Clemit 2003, pp. 26–44. My own reading highlights the themes of class and gender as they are refracted through the thematics of grave-robbing and anatomy.

spond closely to those of Mary Shelley's own third pregnancy.[215] So, while recounting the birth of a monster, the text also ruminates on its own birth as a novel – 'my hideous prodigy', as the author was to describe her book in the Preface to the 1831 edition. As if to foreground the self-reflexive character of the work, of the way it narrates the story of its own writing,[216] Walton's letters are written to his sister, Margaret Walton Saville, who just happens to bear the same initials (MWS) used by Mary Wollstonecraft Shelley, as the author of *Frankenstein* typically called herself.[217] Quite appropriately, many critics have productively read the text in highly psychoanalytical terms, exploring perceived connections between authoring and the death of the mother.[218] Much romantic writing manifested precisely such a heightened self-consciousness about authorship and the act of artistic production. But, by situating the problem of self-authoring within the terrifying dynamics of the split society, *Frankenstein* takes this impulse to a higher level, exploring the dilemmas of literary production in an atomised society.

This latter problem – production of the self in a society rife with atomic individualism – crucially frames multiple dimensions of the text. Contrary to conservative readings, it is atomism, not science and the pursuit of knowledge, which comprises the axis of danger in the novel. What the book criticises is not so much the pursuit of science as the dangers of intellectual, artistic and scientific production in a society fraught with possessive individualism. In such a social order, scientific investigation all too easily serves personal aggrandisement, not societal well-being. As the Creature remarks upon being first warmed then subsequently burnt by fire: 'How strange, I thought, that the same cause should produce such opposite effects!'[219] It is this insight – the opposite effects to which human invention can give rise in different settings – that informs the text. Fire is, in fact, a decisive example here, given the full title of the novel, *Frankenstein; or, the Modern Prometheus*. In the version of the Prometheus-myth most familiar to her – that prepared by her father (under the pseudonym Edward Baldwin) in a children's book of 1806 – Mary Shelley

215. See Mellor 1988, p. 54.
216. This aspect is highlighted by Johnson 1982, p. 7.
217. Mellor 2003, p. 12.
218. For an interesting psychoanalytical reading, see, for example, Mulvey-Roberts 2000, pp. 197–210.
219. Shelley 1999, Volume 2, Chapter 3, p. 130.

would have encountered Prometheus stealing fire from the chariot of the sun in order to animate a human being he had formed out of clay.[220] But, whereas Prometheus's enterprise was successful, catastrophe ensues when Victor Frankenstein, the modern Prometheus, attempts something of the same order. The problem is not science, any more than it is fire; the difficulty attaches to the form of social organisation.

Just as the novel is not anti-science, neither, contrary to another conservative reading, is it anti-Godwin. Not only did Mary Shelley dedicate the book to her father (who was so delighted with it that he published a second edition in 1823), but, despite the anonymity of its author, many early-nineteenth-century readers quickly grasped its Godwinian character. The Tory *Quarterly Review* sneered that the book was 'piously dedicated to Mr. Godwin and…written in the spirit of his school', while the *Edinburgh Review* described it as 'formed in the Godwinian pattern'.[221] The doubling of the central characters, the reversals of pursuer and pursued, the emphasis on circumstance in character-formation, the distortion of all parties in an anti-democratic society, and an abiding concern for justice all mark *Frankenstein* as a Godwinian text, albeit an exceptionally innovative one that, in its powerful use of Gothic elements and its remarkable self-reflection, achieves something highly original and distinctive. While Mary Shelley's novel may well have offered a commentary on aspects of her own upbringing – the death of her mother, frictions with her stepmother, disappointment over her father's opposition to her elopement with Percy Shelley – it was anything but a repudiation of Godwinism. Indeed, it is arguable that, for all its critical reflection on the father-daughter relation, the book also represented a deliberate affirmation of her father's worldview.

At the same time, *Frankenstein* is also deeply indebted to the author's mother, whose works she was reading and re-reading before and during the composition of the novel.[222] Mary Shelley's book develops an insight to which her mother had converted Godwin: the critical role of the social sentiments

---

220. Baldwin [William Godwin] 1806, pp. 93–5.

221. These reviews are described and cited in part by St. Clair 1989, p. 437. While Godwin's influence on *Frankenstein* is enormous, the considerable influence of Wollstonecraft and her novel *Matilda* is often neglected. For a more balanced and nuanced view see Clemit 2003. Bennett (1998, pp. 71, 79, 83–4, 90–1, 114) convincingly documents Mary Shelley's sustained commitment to the radical liberalism of her parents.

222. Indeed, Shelley re-read her mother's *Vindication of the Rights of Woman* in 1816, the year she composed *Frankenstein*. See Jones 1947.

and affections in the formation of both enlightened individuals and a just society. Prior to his relationship with Wollstonecraft, Godwin professed an austere intellectualism in which reason's task is to subdue and dominate the passions. In this spirit, he had treated familial relations as detracting from the individual's duties to society. But, under the impact of his love for Wollstonecraft, Godwin came to appreciate her insistence that sentiment united with reason produced the strongest of social bonds. He would never relinquish this insight. Indeed, in a revised edition of *Political Justice*, he publicly acknowledged the deficiencies of his earlier views, arguing that, rather than subtracting from civic duty, happy domestic relations reinforced it.[223] With this in mind, we can readily perceive Mary Shelley's *Frankenstein* as foregrounding Wollstonecraft's contribution to Godwinian liberalism. The great weakness of Victor Frankenstein is not that he thirsts for scientific knowledge but that he pursues it in unhealthy, even dangerous, isolation from social affections and interactions.[224] It is not science the novel condemns, but individualistic enterprise detached from social obligations and responsibilities.

It is telling that Victor Frankenstein's troubles originate with the death of his mother, after which he is sent to school in southern Germany.[225] 'I was now alone', he writes. Separated from family and friends, living in a 'solitary apartment', the natural sciences became, he tells us, 'nearly my sole occupation'.[226] As Frankenstein embarks on his experiments in creating a living being, he becomes even more isolated – in spatial as well as social terms. 'In a solitary chamber, or rather cell, at the top of the house, and separated from all the other apartments by a gallery and a staircase, I kept my workshop of filthy creation', he intones.[227] In withdrawing into his own world of (self-) creation, Frankenstein retreats from nature and social intercourse: 'my eyes were insensible to the charms of nature. And the same feelings which made

---

223. See the discussion of this point in St. Clair 1989, pp. 211–12.

224. I dissent here from the interpretation of Mary Poovey who sees Mary Shelley as identifying self-denial, in opposition to self-assertion, as the key to healthy identity-formation. In my reading, rather than counterposing these two principles, Shelley aspires to connect and balance them. See Poovey 1987, p. 88, reprinted from Poovey 1984.

225. Also involved here is Frankenstein's flight from his promise, delivered to his mother at her deathbed, to marry his cousin, Elizabeth. Among other things, Frankenstein flees from this pledge, the sexual intimacy it entails, and the incest it implies.

226. Shelley 1999, v. 1, Ch. 2, p. 74 and Ch. 3, p. 77.

227. Shelley 1999, v. 1, Ch. 3, p. 88.

me neglect the scenes around me caused me also to forget those friends who were so many miles absent'. Separation from others – an inherent feature of the enclosing, separating and privatising tendencies of capitalist society – carries with it a dangerous social pathology. 'If the study to which you apply yourself has a tendency to weaken the affections,' he observes while retrospectively recounting his fate, it is 'not befitting the human mind'. Divided from the social passions, detached from domestic relations, the mind grows deranged. And therein reside sources of great destruction. 'If no man allowed any pursuit whatsoever to interfere with the tranquility of his domestic affections', he observes retrospectively, humanity could avert great disasters, on the scale of the colonial destruction of Mexico and Peru.[228]

Here, a crucially gendered dimension enters Shelley's analysis as she advocates breaking down the division between the (ostensibly male) sphere of intellectual and artistic creation and the (ostensibly female) domain of domestic relations. Patriarchal bourgeois society severs and partitions the two. Detaching and enclosing these spheres, the prevailing system of class and gender treats all production as private activity (and all products as private property) to be jealously guarded from others. The value of the male individual is determined not by his contribution to communal well-being, but by his personally accumulated wealth and honour. The result is a manic drive for utter separation (enclosure) of self from others, for a form of absolute autonomy in which the individual aspires to be author of his own private world of glory. The pathology involved here is that of the *self-birthing male*, an individual so fanatically committed to individuation and private accumulation as to deny dependence on all others, particularly the female others responsible for his birth, nurturing and social well-being.[229] Just as capital presents itself as capable of generating wealth on its own, thereby denying the productive powers of labour, the self-birthing male seeks to appropriate to itself the procreative powers of female bodies. And, in making his creature without the involvement of another soul, Victor Frankenstein stakes just such a claim, all the while obsessively separating himself from others,

---

228. Shelley 1999, v. 1, Ch. 3, pp. 83–4.
229. For more on the concept of the self-birthing male see McNally 2001, Chapter 1.

particularly women, systematically avoiding his fiancé and procrastinating about marriage (and sex).[230]

The manic drive to separate, enclose and isolate that Shelley portrays in *Frankenstein* rehearses the delight in particularisation that fuelled the Renaissance-rage for anatomy. Moreover, anatomy and dissection figure more decisively in the novel than has often been appreciated. Victor Frankenstein informs us early on that he is both an anatomist and a grave-robber. 'I became acquainted with the science of anatomy,' he explains, and spent 'days and nights in vaults and charnel houses.'[231] Combining body-parts stolen from corpses with others from dissected animals, he cobbles together his monstrous creation:

> Who shall conceive the horrors of my secret toil, as I dabbled among the unhallowed damps of the grave, or tortured the living animal to animate the lifeless clay?...I collected bones from charnel houses; and disturbed, with profane fingers, the tremendous secrets of the human frame.... The dissecting room and the slaughter-house furnished many of my materials.[232]

In aligning him with the surgeons, anatomists and grave-robbers reviled by the labouring poor, Shelley stamps a decidedly anti-working-class identity on Frankenstein. And, in the anatomist's assembly of the monster, she imaginatively reconstructs the process by which the working class was created: first dissected (separated from the land and their communities), then reassembled as a frightening collective entity, that grotesque conglomeration known as the proletarian mob. 'Like the proletariat,' notes Moretti, 'the monster is denied a name and an individuality.... Like the proletariat, he is a *collective* and an *artificial* creature.'[233] Consistent with this plebeian identity, all three figures

---

230. These themes have produced a plethora of feminist analyses of *Frankenstein*. For a helpful introduction to much of this literature see Hoeveler 2003, pp. 45–62. A particularly insightful analysis of Victor Frankenstein's fear and loathing of the maternal body is provided by Mulvey-Roberts 2000. Barbara Johnson (1982, pp. 7–9) has suggested that Mary Shelley's life experiences, particularly the death of her own mother as a result of postpartum-complications after Mary was born, may have given her a unique sensitivity to the issue of self-authoring as a sort of murder/replacement of the mother.

231. Shelley 1999, v. 1, Ch. 3, p. 79.

232. Shelley 1999, v. 1, Ch. 3, p. 82.

233. Moretti 1983, p. 85.

who address the monster refer to him as 'wretch', a common expression of class-snobbery.

That anatomy, dissection and grave-robbing should feature so centrally in Mary Shelley's account of the monster is not especially surprising. Anyone with even a tenuous connection to popular politics would have been aware of the widespread hostility of the poor toward anatomy. But there were more specific connections where Shelley was concerned. Barely a hundred yards from the house in which she grew up, her family could hear the shouts of the crowd at the executions that took place every few weeks at the New Drop of the Old Bailey. Exposed to public executions and the tumult they provoked, it is also likely that Mary Shelley was keenly aware of the practice of grave-robbing. She was, after all, a regular visitor at St. Pancras Churchyard in London, site of her mother's grave – and a haunt of resurrectionists. As someone who frequented cemeteries at a time when over a thousand corpses a year were being stolen from burial grounds in England and Scotland, she could hardly have been unaware of the public outrage over grave-robbing. Further, not only did she spend hundreds of hours reading at her mother's grave, but of the books she most frequently devoured there, her father's *Essay on Sepulchres* occupied a favoured place. Written years after the death of Mary Wollstonecraft, that essay offers a non-religious defence of reverence for burial-sites. Proceeding from principles of sense-experience, Godwin justifies the special attachment we feel for the places where loved ones are buried. In my desire for enduring connection with the deceased, he proclaims,

> it is impossible that I should not follow by sense the last remains of my friend; and finding him nowhere above the surface of the earth, should not feel an attachment to the spot where his body has been deposited. His heart must be 'made of impenetrable stuff' who does not attribute a certain sacredness to the grave of the one he loved…[234]

And such sentiments must surely have been shared by Mary Shelley. Having never known her mother, Shelley regularly sought maternal connection at her grave. St. Pancras Churchyard became a revered site, an emotional centre point of her life. She and Percy Shelley would read there to each other for hours from her mother's writings, and it was here that they first declared

---

234. William Godwin, *Essay on Sepulchres* (London, 1809), pp. 16–18.

their mutual love. Given this enduring emotional attachment to a grave-site, Mary Shelley would almost certainly have shared the horror at grave-robbing and dissection that permeated the London working class, and have powerfully sympathised with the victims of the anatomists and resurrection-ists. Interestingly, her last novel, *Falkner*, opens with a child defending her mother's grave from a mysterious stranger. Strikingly, the protagonist of that novel describes with disdain the anatomists' reduction of the human body to a mere collection of parts: 'To the surgeon's eye, a human body sometimes presents itself merely as a mass of bones, muscles and arteries...'[235] This, of course, is precisely how the human body appears both to capital and to anato-mists. And it was her acute representation of this bourgeois worldview – of reified body-parts and beings detached from the organic wholes in which they inhere – that gave *Frankenstein* much of its resonance. Mary Shelley's working-class readers would immediately have grasped 'the horrors' alluded to by Victor Frankenstein as he describes his 'secret toils' dabbling 'among the unhallowed damps of the grave'. In an era in which anatomy had become a flashpoint of conflict over commodification in life and death, this fictional account of proletarian bodies being stolen, dismembered, and monstrously reassembled would have carried a potent charge. It is fitting, then, that Shelley brought out a revised edition of her great work in 1831, the year in which the Anatomy Act gave surgeons the right to all unclaimed bodies of paupers who died in the poorhouse. As 'the classic fictional account of the bodysnatch-ing era', *Frankenstein* imaginatively grasped and enacted the horrors of corpo-real commodification that daily haunted working-class people.[236] Consistent with this, the first illustration to accompany *Frankenstein*, from the 1831 edi-tion brought out by Bentley's Standard Novels, portrays the Creature awak-ening to consciousness amidst a collection of human and animal body-parts (Figure 3).

To the idea of an enormous body constructed from dissected human and non-human parts, Shelley added the crucial idea that Frankenstein's crea-ture should be animated by electricity. This was more than mere authorial

---

235. Shelley 1996b, p. 280.
236. Marshall 1995, p. 14. In many respects, however, the 1831 edition is less politi-cally radical than the original. On this point see Baldick 1987, pp. 61–2; and O'Flinn 1983, pp. 201–2. There is a danger of overstating this political shift, however, as Bennett (1998) rightly points out.

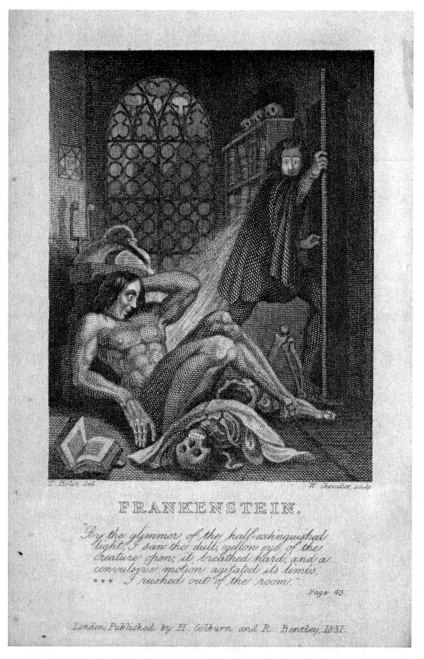

Figure 3   Frontispiece to the revised edition of *Frankenstein* by Mary Shelley,
published by Colburn and Bentley, London 1831

fantasy. During highly publicised experiments in the 1790s, the Italian scientist Luigi Galvini had moved nerves and muscles of dead animals via electrical currents. In the next decade, Galvini's nephew, Luigi Aldini, extended such experiments to the corpses of recently executed criminals by wiring them to a large copper-and-zinc battery. These 'scientific' demonstrations rehearsed the punitive class-politics of anatomy: even in death, the bodies of the poor were not free from direction, regulation and inscription by the ruling class. Indeed, as if to flaunt the politics of class-humiliation, Aldini would attach his wires to the head and anus of the plebeian corpses he reanimated. More than this, however, his experiments recast these politics in the framework of *industrial* capitalism. Where Rembrandt's Nicolas Tulp had mimicked proto-capitalist manufacture by applying a tool to a pauper-body, Aldini mimicked the industrial factory system by attaching a mechanical power source to the criminalised body. Mary Shelley was well aware of these experiments with bodies and electricity; in the Introduction to the second edition of her classic, she listed 'Galvinism' as part of the stock of ideas from which she had drawn in composing her novel.[237] Equally significant, in the context of the repression of Luddite opposition to displacement of labour by power-driven machinery, she would also have known that the relationship between proletarian bodies and industrial power was a contested one – in both life and death.

As if to warn the British ruling classes of the dire consequences that awaited them should they persist in so abusing proletarian bodies and minds, Mary Shelley made Ingolstadt in southeast Germany the site of the monster's birth. Again, the significance of this would not have escaped astute readers. In his four-volume *Memoirs of Jacobinism*, Abbé Barruel had identified Ingolstadt as the birthplace of a secret society, the Illuminati, a band of revolutionary conspirators deemed responsible for the French Revolution. Percy Shelley was particularly fascinated by Barruel's work, and he, Mary Shelley, and others regularly read it aloud together.[238] A number of anti-Jacobin novels also linked Godwin to the Illuminati, and the author of *Political Justice* had himself chosen a site near Ingolstadt as the location of the philosopher's stone in his novel *St. Leon*. In addressing herself to the semi-paranoid anxieties of

---

237. On Aldini's experiments and Mary Shelley's knowledge of Galvinism, see Hitchcock 2007, pp. 33–4.

238. On Barruel's work and its reception by Percy and Mary Shelley see McNiece 1969, pp. 22–3, and St. Clair 1989, pp. 213, 437, 539 n. 5.

Britain's rulers, Mary Shelley presents them with a Jacobin-monster run amok, a microcosm of mass-plebeian upheaval, as the inevitable consequence of their system of oppression.

More than this, she renders the Creature's killing spree, directed at Frankenstein's relatives and friends, as his creator's responsibility – indeed, as an expression of the very essence of the latter's own being. In a moment of rare lucidity, after the Creature's first murder, Frankenstein recognises as much: 'I considered the being I had cast among mankind, and endowed with the will and power to effect purposes of horror…nearly in the light of my own vampire, my own spirit let loose from the grave, and forced to destroy all that was dear to me.'[239] Here, Shelley brilliantly depicts the Creature as Frankenstein's double, an alter ego that embodies his essence. The Creature's destructive rampage is just the other side of Frankenstein's self-destructive character. 'I am thy creature,' the monster reminds his creator in a fateful scene,[240] and, as the murders proliferate and the corpses pile up, Frankenstein bemoans that he is condemned to carry 'about with me my eternal hell'.[241] What awaits Britain's rulers, the novel instructs, is a never-ending hell of conflict, violence and death – the inevitable byproducts of the split society of which the Luddite uprisings were merely a premonition. The labouring masses would soon, Shelley cautioned, seethe for bloody revenge. As the Creature warns Frankenstein,

> Are you to be happy while I grovel in the intensity of my wretchedness? You can blast my other passions, but revenge remains…I may die, but first you, my tyrant and tormenter, shall curse the sun that gazes on your misery. Beware; for I am fearless, and therefore powerful.[242]

Yet, Victor Frankenstein, like Britain's rulers, seems incapable of heeding these warnings. But even as he appears driven by fate to run toward his doom in his reckless, vengeful pursuit of his monster, Mary Shelley lets it be known that other outcomes are possible. She does so by letting the Creature speak.

---

239. Shelley 1999, v. 1, Ch. 6, p. 104.
240. Shelley 1999, v. 2, Ch. 2, p. 126.
241. Shelley 1999, v. 3, Ch. 7, p. 225.
242. Shelley 1999, v. 3, Ch. 3, p. 192.

This is a move that deserves the closest attention. After all, contrary to most film-versions, in which the Creature is typically a mute brute, Shelley portrays him as an intelligent being with linguistic capacities.[243] This decision highlights the monster's humanity and radically demarcates him from zombies. Indeed, in one of the most celebrated film-versions, the most famous Hollywood actor to play the Creature, Boris Karloff, deliberately *zombified* him. Karloff gave the Creature the shuffling gait we associate with zombies and vigorously opposed letting the monster speak. 'If he spoke, he would seem more human', he protested.[244] Yet, this is precisely Shelley's intent. As grotesque and horrifying as the Creature might be, his capacity for speech is a fundamental marker of his humanity, of the fact that proletarians are intelligent and articulate members of humankind – i.e. *not* zombies. Indeed, conferring speech on the Creature is essential to the central hinge of the novel, a lengthy speech in which the monster narrates his life-experience and stakes his claim for justice. 'The decision to give the monster an articulate voice is Mary Shelley's most important subversion of the category of monstrosity', one commentator rightly notes.[245] Yet, it is not just the capacity for language that subverts, but the actual content of the decisive speech in which the Creature sets forth a radical analysis of its own plight. Echoing Paine and Godwin, the Creature's oral treatise constitutes a veritable *Declaration of the Rights of Monsters*.

'Hear my tale', the monster exclaims.[246] And, for six chapters that comprise over twenty per cent of the text, we do just that. Abandoned by Frankenstein, 'I was a poor, helpless, miserable wretch', the Creature explains. In order to procure the means of survival, his first acts involved searching for drink, warmth, food, and shelter. Settling into a 'hovel' adjacent to the cottage of a poor rural family, the De Laceys, he observes their loves and labours. Desirous of helping them, the monster works at night in order to provide the family with food and fuel, left surreptitiously under cover of darkness. Here, Mary Shelley offers her own radical economics. While mainstream political economy emphasised the magic of the market, regulated by Adam Smith's famous

---

243. On film-versions of Frankenstein see O'Flinn 1983; Hitchcock 2007; and Milner 1996, pp. 161–7.
244. As quoted by Hitchcock 2007, p. 173.
245. Baldick 1987, p. 45.
246. Shelley 1999, v. 2, Ch. 2, p. 127.

'invisible hand', Shelley foregrounds the *invisible labours* that sustain economic life. She delineates the surplus-labour, work above and beyond that required for his own subsistence, through which the Creature aids his neighbours. In what can only have been a deliberate reply to bourgeois economics, she parodies Adam Smith's metaphor in having the monster explain, 'I afterwards found that these labours, performed by an invisible hand, greatly astonished' the De Laceys.[247] This striking formulation materialises the unseen labour of the invisible hands that sustain the capitalist economy, thereby enacting a critique of political economy from the standpoint of labour, one that rehearses Byron's insistence in his maiden-speech that it is the reviled mob 'that labour in your field, serve in your houses'.

But, in addition to sustaining society through its work, these labouring monsters are also rational, communicative beings. Observing the family, the Creature teaches himself to speak and to read, yet more evidence that he is not a mindless zombie. He finds and studies works by Plutarch, Milton and Goethe. But his political education is most decisively formed by overhearing the text of a classic of the radical Left, C.F. Volney's *Ruins of Empire*, read with commentary by the young man of the family to his lover, a Christianised Arab feminist, whose presence and life-story raise interesting anticolonial themes in the text.[248] Mary Shelley's choice of Volney's *Ruins* represents an inspired political statement. Long a favourite of her husband, *Ruins* was a staple of the revolutionary movement. Published in France in 1791, just as the revolution was intensifying, it was translated quickly into English and German. The book was embraced by radical organisations like the London Corresponding Society and the United Irishman, and was even found in Brazil in the possession of a mulatto engaged in a multiracial conspiracy.[249] Volney was a determined critic of the patriarchal family, an opponent of slavery (whose abolition he voted for in the revolutionary Assembly in France), and a proponent of the anti-Eurocentric view that human civilisation, along with the arts

---

247. Shelley 1999, v. 2, Ch. 4, p. 140.

248. Among works which have explored the anti colonial implications of this aspect of *Frankenstein*, see Bohls 1994, pp. 23–36; and Bush 1998. For an interesting but somewhat more ambivalent evaluation of *Frankenstein* in this regard see Spivak 1985, pp. 254–9.

249. Linebaugh and Rediker 2000, p. 342. In an often interesting article, Anca Vlasopolos fails to grasp the significance of Volney, mistakenly arguing that the Creature receives an education in the 'aesthetic prejudices' and 'language' of the upper class. See Vlasopolos 1983, p. 127.

and the sciences, originated in Africa. He was also an unrelenting opponent of private property, exploitation and class-inequality. The slavery of individuals derived, he argued, from the 'abusive right of property', which in turn produced 'an intestine war in which the citizens, divided into contending corps of orders, classes, families, unremittingly struggled to appropriate to themselves, under the name of *supreme power*, the ability to plunder everything'. Society was thus 'divided into a group of wealthy drones, and a multitude of mercenary poor', and these two classes, 'essentially opposite and hostile', entered into a recurring contest of the sort Mary Shelley depicts in *Frankenstein*. Volney too portrayed the ruling class as rushing to its own destruction: 'the day approaches when this colossus of power shall be crushed and crumbled under its own mass'.[250]

The Creature's enlightenment via Volney is a case-study in radical education. Hearing *Ruins* recited, he recounts, he wept over the destruction of the aboriginal peoples of the Americas and 'heard of the division of property, of immense wealth and squalid poverty'. He learned that the individual is valued according to 'descent united with riches', i.e. according to everything the Creature lacks. 'And what was I?...I knew that I possessed no money, no friends, no kind of property.... Was I then a monster, a blot upon the earth, from which all men fled, and whom all men disowned?'[251] A being without kin, friends, property or wealth, the monster represents the negation of bourgeois distinction. He is the inhuman human, a violation of the social order who is nonetheless its product. He is capitalist society's dirty secret – one it must disavow in order to legitimate itself in its own eyes. The monster's very being is thus an offence to bourgeois sensibility. And, for this simple ontological fact – not for anything he has done – he must be destroyed.[252]

Rejected by society, and most painfully by his creator, the monster declares war on Frankenstein and the social order he represents. In so doing, he undertakes conscious action of the sort that would be impossible for zombies. He begins by turning on the De Lacey family – who appropriated the products of his surplus-labour only to violently reject his approaches – by using the

---

250. Volney 1990, pp. 33, 34, 35, 38, 51.
251. Shelley 1999, v. 2, Ch. 5, pp. 145–6.
252. This is a recurring theme throughout *Frankenstein*. In addition to the Creature, Justine Moritz, the De Lacey family, and Safie's father are all punished for crimes they did not commit.

classic weapon of Promethean and plebeian insurgency: fire. 'I lighted the dry branch of a tree, and danced with fury around the devoted cottage…with a loud scream I fired the straw and heath and bushes I had collected…and the cottage was quickly enveloped by the flames.'[253] I noted above the use of fire as a tool of revolt: by the rebellious crowd which set parts of London ablaze during the Gordon Riots, and by Luddite protesters who torched the houses of manufacturers. Such associations would have been obvious to many of Mary Shelley's early nineteenth-century readers for whom fire, that Promethean force, was a time-honoured weapon of radical insurgency.

Pausing on the road of murderous revenge, the Creature searches out Frankenstein in hopes of averting further violence. What he needs, he urges, is for his creator to make him a female companion. Significantly, this demand for an elementary social relationship, a pair bond, is proffered in the language of Paineite radicalism: 'I demand it of you as a right.'[254] At the same time, it is couched as a plea for recognition as a fellow being: 'Let me see that I excite the sympathy of some existing thing; do not deny me my request!'[255] Shelley here merges the assertion of rights with an appeal for recognition: proletarian rebellion, she intimates, is fundamentally about the desire for recognition as equals, as full-fledged members of human society. In rebuffing demands for equal recognition, the ruling class instructs the oppressed that they are inferior, substandard members of a monstrous race. Indeed, it is in these terms that Frankenstein, having acceded to the Creature's demand and commenced work on a partner for him, subsequently reneges. Reflecting that the monstrous couple might propagate, he is horrified at the prospect that 'a race of devils' could be unleashed on humankind.[256] 'Trembling with passion,' he informs the reader, 'I…tore to pieces the thing on which I was engaged.'[257] In this pivotal scene, Shelley insightfully weaves together themes of gender, class and racial hatred. Frankenstein rehearses a powerful fear of females and their control of biological (as opposed to artificial) reproduction, consistent with his own withdrawal from women. At the same time, he enacts a venomous hostility toward the grotesque 'people of the body' who perform

---

253. Shelley 1999, v. 2, Ch. 8, p. 163.
254. Shelley 1999, v. 2, Ch. 9, p. 169.
255. Shelley 1999, v. 2, Ch. 9, p. 170.
256. Shelley 1999, v. 3, Ch. 3, p. 190.
257. Shelley 1999, v. 3, Ch. 3, p. 191.

the world's invisible labours. It is worth recalling in this regard that the original English meaning of proletariat refers to those whose only function is to produce children.[258] The term thus carries a double resonance, degrading the female labour of biological reproduction while also abasing the lives of all who are defined by physical toil. Construing proletarian monsters as a 'race of devils', of dangerous hyper-embodied beings, Frankenstein resorts to the ruling class's favoured means of punishment – dissection – by tearing the half-finished female Creature 'to pieces'. And the Creature responds in kind. He produces a string of corpses – the basic element of the anatomist's work – as if to incessantly remind Frankenstein of the barbaric dissections of which he is guilty: the bodies of those he dismembered to produce his monster; the severed corpse of the unfinished female; the dissection of the Creature from all social bonds and connections.

In becoming a provider of corpses, the Creature mimics Frankenstein's profession but with a dialectical inversion; rather than plebeian corpses, the bodies he snatches come from the anatomist's own family and social class.[259] This is one of many doublings that occur throughout the novel as each of the protagonists assumes a role (pursuer, mourner, anatomist, murderer) previously occupied by the other. These reversals open onto a remarkably insightful passage in which Frankenstein reflects on the horrible irony of working-class 'freedom' in modern society. Hoping to kill the Creature, he first remarks, 'If he were vanquished I would be a free man.' Yet, trapped as he is in the cycle of destruction, the paradox of his statement immediately strikes him. 'Alas! what freedom? such as the peasant enjoys when his family has been massacred before his eyes, his cottage burnt, his lands laid waste, and he is turned adrift, homeless, pennyless, and alone, but free.'[260] In the course of reflecting on the charade of freedom for one who has suffered dispossession and loss, Frankenstein perceives the irony of 'liberty' for the proletariat: to be, like the Creature, 'homeless, pennyless, and alone'. And it is this, Mary Shelley warns, the denial of social connection and belonging to the poor, which will rebound on the ruling class. The rage of the proletariat will ultimately consume everything – families and properties – in an inferno of riot and revenge, reducing all

---

258. Linebaugh and Rediker 2000, p. 93. On racialised people of the body, see Bannerji 1995, p. 33.
259. Marshall 1995, p. 215.
260. Shelley 1999, v. 3, Ch. 5, p. 211.

to the same pitiful state. In this vein, the book ends on the linked deaths of its doubled protagonists. A dying Frankenstein, rescued at sea, recounts his tale to Captain Walton, while the Creature, apprised of the death of his creator, announces that he will now take his own life – by lighting himself on fire in an act of inverted Prometheanism. On this note of mutual death and destruction, the novel ends, though with a certain ambiguity as to whether the Creature has died or merely disappeared.[261]

And, yet, a crucial scene precedes the novel's denouement and offers a potential escape from the cycle of death and destruction. Belying the claim that *Frankenstein* is purged of reference to collective movements, Mary Shelley stages a sailor's rebellion that averts a terrible calamity. As Captain Walton pushes ever further toward the North Pole, with the dying Frankenstein aboard, his crew grows increasingly alarmed by the dangerous polar ice the ship is encountering and by the extreme cold which has already cost several lives. Convinced that disaster lurks in further pursuing the voyage, the sailors threaten a mutiny. And they do so in profoundly democratic style, electing a 'deputation' to 'demand' that Walton turn back. Reluctantly and with great bitterness, Walton consents.[262] Unlike Victor Frankenstein, who failed to turn back from his voyage to disaster, Walton is compelled by collective action to change direction, thereby forestalling catastrophe.[263]

In sketching this scene, Shelley drew upon a rich tradition of popular rebellion among sailors. Subjected to some of the harshest forms of capitalist discipline aboard floating factories, sailors built a potent culture of resistance that included strikes, work-stoppages and structures of countervailing authority to that of the captain. When on land, they were among the most rebellious elements of the urban mob. Their most sustained confrontations at sea took the form of mutiny – an outright seizure of the ship and its command. And when they did take control of a ship, they typically administered it according to markedly democratic and egalitarian norms.[264] Mary Shelley's portrayal of the collective power of sailors curtailing the reckless autocracy of a

---

261. This ambiguity was sharper in Mary Shelley's original draft, prior to revisions by Percy Shelley. See Mellor 2003, pp. 15–16.

262. Shelley 1999, v. 3, Ch. 7, pp. 235, 237.

263. Mary Shelley may also have been trying to strike a gendered note here, as Walton's willingness to heed the sailors could be seen as a product of his ongoing dialogue (via letters) with a female voice, that of his sister.

264. See the marvellous study by Rediker 1987, especially Chapters 5 and 6.

master was both credible and, for ruling classes who feared plebeian mutinies, ominous. Yet, consistent with her Godwinian liberalism, she does not conjure up a sailor's rebellion to preach revolution but, rather, to recommend a new class-compromise in which the voices of the downtrodden are heeded rather than ignored.

To be sure, Godwinian liberalism was distinguished by its powerful critique of the prevailing system of property and power in British society. By attacking property-relations, the Godwin-Wollstonecraft school departed decisively from mainstream-liberalism, making tentative contact with plebeian radicalism. But in disowning collective movements in favour of individual writing and educative work, it took up a decidedly middle-class posture at odds with the radical workers' movement. The political outlook inherited by Mary Shelley was thus an *anxious radical liberalism*.[265] And this brings us to Mary Shelley's own horror over the mob. An 1817 letter to her husband epitomises this attitude. Commenting on a recent newsletter by the reformer William Cobbett she exclaims, 'he appears to be making out a list for a proscription – I actually shudder to read it – a revolution in this country would not be so *bloodless* if that man has any power in it…I fear he is a bad man. He encourages in the multitude the worst possible human passion *revenge*…'.[266] Revenge, of course, is precisely what fuels the monster's murder spree in *Frankenstein*. The Creature too makes Shelley anxious, and this allows her to tap into similar anxieties among her readers. Dedicated as she is to social reform – the urgency of which she hopes to persuade her readers – she deeply fears rebellion from below. Like her father, hers are a politics of enlightened gradualism driven by publicly spirited members of the middle class intent on mediating between the rulers and the mob. Discussing the oppression of the Italian people by Austria in the 1840s, for instance, she declares her sympathies with the subjugated, while similarly counselling against revolt. 'Peaceful mediation and a strong universal sense of justice' are to be enlisted 'instead of the cannon and the bayonet,' she advises.[267]

---

265. I see Mary Shelley's politics as something more than the 'anxious liberalism' described by Baldick (1987, p. 55). There is a more radical critique of property-relations animating her position than such a term implies. At the same time, I think Baldick is right to perceive deep-rooted anxieties about the crowd in Shelley's outlook.

266. ''Letter to Shelley' September 30, 1817', in Jones 1944, Letter 36.

267. Shelley 1996a, p. 68.

Mary Shelley largely shared this political stance with her husband, albeit with some qualifications. While the young Percy Shelley had undertaken political agitation, particularly among the Irish, his idol, William Godwin, sharply condemned such activism. Urging his pupil to eschew agitation, Godwin wrote that 'discussion, reading, enquiry, perpetual communication' were his favourite methods. 'But associations, organised societies, I firmly condemn', he declared.[268] Shelley soon capitulated, announcing his conversion to Godwin's position. Never again was he to engage in political activism. Yet, uncertain about the political efficacy of merely writing on behalf of reform, he regularly flirted with the idea that a great social upheaval might be necessary to change society. Never were these flirtations more serious than in 1819, the year after his wife published *Frankenstein*, when he explicitly reopened the question of insurrectionary politics. The impetus for this was the massacre on 16 August 1819 of peaceful working-class demonstrators at St. Peter's Field in Manchester. The huge demonstration of up to 120,000 people was called to demand electoral reform, particularly so that Manchester might have its own member (or members) of Parliament. Just as the first speaker commenced his oratory, mounted soldiers attacked the crowd. Leading the assault were the yeomen, 'the Manchester manufacturers, merchants, publicans, and shopkeepers on horseback',[269] who struck with a vengeance, killing 11, among them a child, and wounding over 400 others.[270] Peterloo, as the massacre was soon dubbed, provoked massive popular indignation. Amidst the outrage, Percy Shelley quickly penned *The Mask of Anarchy*, a seething response hailed as 'the greatest poem of political protest ever written in English'.[271]

More than this, however, Shelley determined to sort through the problem of political reform in the face of such class-violence. To this end, he laboured over an essay, 'A Philosophical View of Reform', which, after commencing on a remarkably timid footing, turns to the question of revolution. If the opening sections explore the prospects for peaceful, incremental change, a shift occurs halfway through the essay as he finally confronts the fundamental question raised by Peterloo: how to pursue social progress if the British autocracy violently resists all campaigns for reform. 'Let us hope,' he writes, that, faced

268. As quoted by St. Clair 1989, p. 325.
269. Thompson 1963, p. 686.
270. For a brief account see Kesteven 1967.
271. Holmes 1974, p. 532.

with peaceful mass-protest, 'the oppressors would feel their impotence' and grant reforms. If, however, they find 'civil war preferable to resigning any portion however small of their usurped authority,' he asserts, 'we possess a right of resistance.' More than this, 'the last resort of resistance is undoubtedly insurrection'.[272] Unlike some theorists of the right of revolution, such as John Locke, Shelley imagines that it is the mass of the oppressed, indeed of the working class, who possess this right of insurrection, not merely a coterie of propertied gentlemen.[273] Any doubts on this score are dispelled by a reading of his great poem, 'Prometheus Unbound', whose composition overlaps with that of 'A Philosophical View'.

The poem begins with the bondage of Prometheus, bound to a rock by order of Jupiter. Prometheus's lover, Asia, and her sister Panthea set out to liberate the confined god. To succeed, however, they must first make contact with the murky figure, Demogorgon, who resides in a cave.[274] The identity of Demogorgon has mystified many critics. But this is more a political failing than a strictly literary one, having to do with a refusal to acknowledge the radicalism that animated Shelley's writing.

Demogorgon is initially described as 'a tremendous gloom' and later as 'a mighty darkness'.[275] In Act 3, Jupiter denounces this creature as his 'detested prodigy',[276] echoing the terms in which Frankenstein describes his monster. Another set of clues is provided when, in seeking to commune with Demogorgon, Asia and Panthea hear the Song of the Spirits which repeatedly urges them to go 'Down, down!' in order to 'unloose through life's portal/The snake-like Doom coiled underneath' the throne of Jupiter.[277] Demogorgon is thus a dark, immensely powerful but still unformed being, the rejected offspring of Jupiter, who resides below the earth's surface. It takes little imagination to recognise 'him' as precisely what the Greek origin of 'his' name suggests: *demos-gorgon*, the people-monster.[278] It is especially significant in this regard that an

---

272. Shelley 1990, p. 81.
273. On Locke in this regard, see McNally 1989, pp. 17–40.
274. As in many of Shelley's poems, women are the key actors for liberation. Moreover, the name Asia also reflects a recurring theme in Shelley: the idea that the winds of change may originate in the East.
275. Shelley 1960, Act 1, line 207, p. 212; Act 2, Scene 4, line 2, p. 236.
276. Shelley 1960, III.i.62.
277. Shelley 1960, II.iv.96–7.
278. I use the male form here, as most commentators do, although it seems to me that this creature might well be read as non- or bi-gendered.

influential radical newspaper of the day, with which Shelley may have been familiar, was called the *Gorgon*.[279] Moreover, this publication was not alone in identifying the radical cause with ruling-class images of the monstrous rabble. In Greek legend, the gorgons consisted of three grotesque females only one of whom (Medusa) could see, albeit through just one eye. Tellingly, another radical broadsheet took the name *Medusa*. In invoking proletarian monstrosity in 'Prometheus Unbound', Percy Shelley thus improvised on a contemporary radical trope, one which also figures in *Frankenstein*. The difference here is that the monster's awakening is potentially regenerative of society, rather than merely destructive. But, because Demogorgon is not fully formed, Asia undertakes to educate him – specifically to free him from the spell of religion.[280] Once enlightened, he is ready to assume his revolutionary mission.

What follows in Act 3, Scene 1 is nothing less than an insurrectionary uprising, as Demogorgon dethrones Jupiter and propels him into the underworld. One of the more astute commentators on this poem notes that Shelley models this upheaval on the dramatic image of a volcanic eruption. 'A dispute which eclipses the sun and shakes the planets (possibly even the Milky Way)', he notes, can only imply a revolutionary insurgency.[281] And once the tyrant is banished by force, Shelley depicts a world transformed:

> The loathsome mask has fallen, the man remains
>
> Sceptreless, free, uncircumscribed, but man
>
> Equal, unclassed, tribeless, and nationless
>
> Exempt from awe, worship, degree, the king
>
> Over himself…[282]

Mary Shelley's *Frankenstein* does not offer us, except perhaps in its description of the sailors' revolt, prospects for a better world. But by figuring the creation of the proletariat in the idioms of grave-robbing and anatomy, it secured its place as, among other things, one of the great political-psychological portrayals of the monstrosities of the market. In so doing, it subtly deciphered the horrors of the 'lectures' read upon working-class bodies and minds by nascent capitalism. It was during this period, after all, that working people

---

279. Thompson 1963, p. 676. See also Foot 1984, pp. 195–6.
280. Shelley 1960, II.iv.1–128. See the excellent discussion in Foot 1984, pp. 197–9.
281. Matthews 1968, p. 184.
282. Shelley 1960, III.iv.193–7.

were increasingly described in terms of a body-part: hands.[283] Indeed, the very language of the day often further reduced these hands to physical extensions of the means of production, variously denoting them as farmhands, dockhands, machinehands, deckhands. In the latter case, that of sailors, when referred to collectively they became a mammoth-agglomeration of detached parts, summoned with the cry, 'all hands on deck.'

The dominant ideology both reified working people in this way, reducing them to abstracted body-parts, while denying their significance in the creation of wealth and society. In a classic process of mystification, the driving force of capitalism was detached from the actual hands of labour and attributed to the *invisible hand* of the market. By returning capitalism to the realities of the (grotesque) labouring body, *Frankenstein* fore-grounded the processes of social anatomisation by which people became 'hands', and through which the invisible hands of labour simultaneously generated the wealth of the ruling class. Despite this critical thrust, however, and despite rendering the proletarian monster as intelligent and articulate, as something other than a zombie, Mary Shelley, too recoiled from the ugliness of the proletarian monster that capitalism had created.[284] But working-class radicals, among them those who supported papers like *Gorgon* and *Medusa*, were already affirming proletarian monstrosity. In so doing, they shifted the dialectic of monstrosity in a direction that would be claimed by Marx.

283. As the *Oxford English Dictionary Online* (1989) documents, this usage appears to originate in the second half of the seventeenth century. For an insightful reading of the presence of the severed hands of labour in Gothic fiction see Rowe 1999, Chapter 4.

284. Indeed, Mary Shelley seems to want to insist on the reality of the monster's ugliness (2.4.139).

Chapter Two

Marx's Monsters: Vampire-Capital and the Nightmare-World of Late Capitalism

> 'Perseus wore a magic cap so that the monsters he hunted down might not see him. We draw the magic cap down over our eyes and ears so as to deny that there are any monsters'.
>
> – Karl Marx[1]

Capitalism is both monstrous and magical. Crucially, its magic consists in concealing the occult economy – the obscure transactions between human bodies and capital – on which it rests. Entranced by this sorcery, the equivalent of magic-caps pulled over our eyes and ears, bourgeois common sense vigorously denies the monsters in our midst. But, as with all anxious denials, what has disappeared performs a return of the repressed. Deprived of a palpable reality, vampires, werewolves and zombies nevertheless amble across movie- and television-screens and through the pages of pulp-fiction. To be sure, these are pale substitutes, faint and distorted after-images of the monsters we deny. Subjected to the ritual codes of a culture-industry, these are domesticated beasts, beings derived from the collective unconscious in order to produce harmless items of mass-consumption.

---

1. Marx 1976, p. 91.

Part of the genuine radicalism of Marx's critical theory resides in its insistence on tracking and naming the monsters of modernity. Where critical theory abdicates knowledge of the monstrous, it invariably reduces its agenda to amelioration, to polite suggestions for more civil communication. In so doing it renounces its own critical impulses.[2] It is only in staring horrors in the face and insisting on their systemic, not accidental, character that theory sustains radical commitments. This is why Marx's *Capital* overflows, as we shall see, with detailed narratives of the 'monstrous outrages' of capital: factories in which 'Dante would have found the worst horrors in his Inferno surpassed'; unrelenting 'traffic in human flesh'; the turning of 'children's blood' into capital; the 'crippling of body and mind' of the workers; 'the extirpation, enslavement and entombment in mines of the indigenous population' of the Americas; 'the conversion of Africa into a preserve for the commercial hunting of blackskins'; 'the vampire' that 'will not let go while there remains a single muscle, sinew or drop of blood to be exploited'.[3] To name these horrors is also to perform a counter-magic to the sorcery of capital. For capital's great powers of illusion lie in the way it invisibilises its own monstrous formation. In endeavouring to pull off the magic-cap of modernity, Marx sought a confrontation with monstrosity. He set out to reveal the legions of vampires and werewolves that inhere in capital so that they might be banished. Yet, across much ostensibly critical theory today, the beasts have fled the field – or, rather, they have given way to the ceremonial fiends of the culture-industries. Where this occurs, radical theory too enters into complicity with the monster-denial that marks modern consciousness.

Perhaps fittingly, it is in a novel by an indigenous writer of the Americas that we discover a uniquely perceptive treatment of Marx's monsters. Working in an imaginative space generated by the clash of native peoples in the Americas with capitalist modernity, Leslie Marmon Silko mines Marx's images of monstrosity for the work of remembering and resisting. To this end, her novel, *Almanac of the Dead*, traces the political awakening of an aboriginal woman, Angelita La Escapia, through her encounter with Marx's *Capital*:

---

2. As it does in the work of Jürgen Habermas, where it emerges as a warmed-over left liberalism. On this point see McNally 2001, pp. 108–9, and Morris 2001.

3. Marx 1976, pp. 356, 353, 379, 382, 484, 915.

Marx was the first white man La Escapia had ever heard call his own people vampires and monsters. But Marx had not stopped with accusations.
Marx caught the capitalists of the British empire with bloody hands. Marx
backed every assertion with evidence; coroner's reports with gruesome stories about giant spinning machines that consumed the limbs and lives of the
small children working in factories. On and on Marx went, describing the
tiny corpses of children who had been worked to death...

...Tribal people had had all the experience they would ever need to judge
whether Marx's stories told the truth. The Indians had seen generations of
themselves ground into bloody pulp under the wheels of ore cars in crum-
bling tunnels of gold mines. . .

...Marx had never forgotten the indigenous people of the Americas, or of
Africa. Marx had recited the crimes of slaughter and slavery committed by
the European colonials who had been sent by their capitalist slave masters to
secure the raw materials of capitalism – human flesh and blood.[4]

Silko reads Marx as a great storyteller. In search of the powers with which
to cure 'the suffering and evils of the world', Marx 'had understood stories
are alive with the energy words generate', she writes. 'Word by word, the
stories of suffering, injury and death...aroused the living with fierce passion and determination for justice'.[5] Marx's tarrying with monstrosity – with
werewolves and the mangled bodies of dead children, with vampires and the
slaughtered remains of indigenous peoples – functions, for Silko, as considerably more than rhetorical flourish. In her reading, it fulfills critical theory's
obligation to give voice to suffering.[6] With Marx, she asserts that the essence
of capitalist monstrosity is its transformation of human flesh and blood into
raw materials for the manic machinery of accumulation. Rather than merely
provocative metaphors, then, Marx's monsters are signs of horror, markers of
the real terrors of modern social life. All too often, this dimension of Marx's
thought has vanished from sight, along with the monsters he detailed.

Part of the problem is that Marx sought a new language, literary as well
as theoretical, a radical poetics through which to read capitalism. Legions of

---

4. Silko 1992, pp. 312, 315.
5. Silko 1992, pp. 316, 520.
6. 'The need to lend a voice to suffering is a condition of all truth' (Adorno 1973,
pp. 17–18).

commentators have failed to appreciate this, attempting instead to reduce Marx's language to prior conceptual orders – to the categories of classical political economy or German philosophy – or to those of subsequent philosophical perspectives, such as structuralism or poststructural linguistics. In so doing, they have exiled whatever does not fit these theoretical discourses, declaring it to be inconsistent, undeveloped, and unacceptable. Louis Althusser, for instance, famously claimed that the more historical and empirical sections of *Capital* – devoted to detailed analyses of capitalist industry, and to workers' struggles against machinery and over the length of the working day – obeyed a logic at odds with the theoretical sections of the text, an interpretation which has enjoyed a wide influence.[7] And even where they eschew such dualistic claims, numerous critics have simply assumed that, in deciphering the theoretical structure of *Capital*, they could safely ignore Marx's ethnography of working-class experience, illuminated as it is by extended historical discussions, literary references, copious empirical documentation, and explicitly dramatic constructions. Yet, all such interpretive strategies fall short. Far from textual adornment, Marx's literary stylistics and empirical analyses – the very places where we most often encounter monsters – are integral elements of his conceptual schema. Rather than marks of inconsistency or superfluous ornaments, Marx's persistent shifts in register and idiom, from complex theoretical mappings of the commodity to metaphorically charged descriptions of the crippling effects of capitalist production on workers' bodies, reflect deeply held views about his object of study, the capitalist mode of production, and about the adequate theoretical protocols for tracking and demystifying it. Because capitalism constitutes an alienated, topsy-turvy world, one in which phenomena regularly appear upside-down, the theoretical discourse that maps it needs to mimic the wild movement of things so as to better expose it. This is especially important, given the way that capitalist inversions become normalised for everyday thought and action. As a result, like Brecht, Marx seeks to estrange us from the familiar so that we might actually see it for what it is. To this end, he requires a dialectical language of doublings and reversals.

---

7. Althusser 1994; Read 2003, pp. 14, 30–4, 91.

Dialectics and the doubled life of the commodity

Amongst other things, dialectical thought is distinguished by the notion that theoretical analysis and exposition are not extrinsic to the object of knowledge. As opposed to 'external cognition', which imposes a predetermined method on what it seeks to understand, dialectics proceeds by way of immanent criticism, aspiring to trace the internal movement and structure of its object of study. Rather than bringing a phenomenon under its demands, dialectical investigations are shaped by the characteristics of the object being explored. This makes dialectical analyses literally phenomenological exercises in explicating the internal *logic of phenomena*.[8] An approach of this sort creates unique problems, however, where the object of investigation does not obey conventional logics. How, for instance, do we analyse a phenomenon that observes 'magical' transformations in which material things turn immaterial and vice versa? In grappling with such problems, Marx developed the multi-faceted strategy of exposition and presentation to which I have alluded.

To be sure, such strategies are not entirely unique to Marx. One commentator on Hegel's *Phenomenology of Spirit* remarks, for instance, that 'the book is filled with jokes, puns, wisecracks, sarcasm, parody, and all those ingredients which tend to make an academic work "not serious"'.[9] Such features are not mere idiosyncrasies of personal style. Instead, they are integral to the dialectical quest for a language and imagery with which to track the doublings and inversions of phenomena. Marx's *Capital*, too, as many critics have observed, overflows with symbolism, metaphors, ironic barbs, and a stunning range of allusions to world-literature.[10] Yet, whereas Hegel has been decried as 'a *horrible* writer', whose *Phenomenology* was composed in utter haste,[11] Marx was an exceptional stylist whose great work is a literary, as well as a theoretical and political, masterpiece. We should thus see his textual presentation as deeply considered, as a deliberate part of his theoretical strategy. More than this, Marx's need for a unique theoretical language was more pressing than was Hegel's. After all, Marx recognised that the doublings of capitalist

---

8. See Hegel 1977, pp. 32–40; and Marx and Engels, 'The Holy Family' (1975b, p. 35). I have briefly discussed procedures of immanent criticism in McNally 2004, pp. 152–3.
9. Solomon 1983, p. xii.
10. See Prawer 1976.
11. Solomon 1983, p. xi.

society are more than the stuff of irony – they are also the grounds of mystery (the 'mystery of commodities') and of horror, whose presence dominates his chapter on the working day and his analysis of the 'pre-history' or 'primitive accumulation' of capital.[12]

Even more than Hegel's *Phenomenology*, then, *Capital* overflows with features that 'tend to make an academic work "not serious"' – outrage, irony, sarcasm, moral condemnation, Gothic imagery, overtly dramatic constructions. Rather than stylistic ornamentations, these features are, I insist, essential aspects of Marx's text, integral means for the expression of his core theoretical arguments. Determined that his critique of political economy should form 'a dialectically articulated artistic whole',[13] Marx laboured painstakingly over its presentation. His surgically delivered irony, his references to werewolves and vampires, his deployment of Shakespeare, Dante, Cervantes, and Goethe were all deeply considered parts of his effort to divine the mysteries of capitalist social life.

While most commentators fail to grasp this point, a handful of critics have appreciated something of Marx's stylistic achievements. Reading *Capital* as a work of imagination, Edmund Wilson, for instance, argued that 'Marx is certainly the greatest ironist since Swift'. And, turning to the argumentative strategy at work in *Capital*, he observes:

> The meaning of the impersonal-looking formulas which Marx produces with so scientific an air is, he reminds us from time to time as if casually, pennies withheld from the worker's pocket, sweat squeezed out of his body, and natural enjoyments denied his soul. In competing with the pundits of economics, Marx has written something in the nature of a parody...

He then continues with respect to the structure of the text:

> In Marx the exposition of the theory – the dance of commodities, the cross-stitch of logic – is always followed by a documented picture of the capitalist laws at work, and these chapters, with their piling up of factory reports,

---

12. Note that for Marx this prehistory is regularly re-enacted throughout the 'repetition-compulsion' of capitalist accumulation. See, for instance, Marx 1971, Part 3, p. 272: 'Accumulation merely presents as a continuous process what in primitive accumulation appears as a distinct historical process...'

13. 'Marx to Engels, July 31 1865' in Marx and Engels 1987. In this translation, Marx's letter refers to his book as an 'artistic whole' that possesses a 'dialectical structure'.

their prosaic descriptions of misery and filth, their remorseless enumeration of the abnormal conditions to which the men, women and children of the working-class have had to try to adjust themselves... – these at last become intolerable. We feel that we have been taken for the first time through the real structure of our civilization and that it is the ugliest that has ever existed...[14]

Stanley Edgar Hyman, who also reads *Capital* as 'imaginative literature', notes that its 'poetic texture... is an amazing richness of image, symbol, and metaphor'. Arguing that the text's basic form is dramatic, Hyman too observes its doubled structure, remarking that 'the book's periodic descents into the horrors of capitalism are spaced so that each comes as a fresh shock, and each is followed by a deliberate flatness, what Stendahl called "benches for my readers to sit down on"'.[15] While less attentive to the alternating movements of the text, Ann Cvetkovich too argues for a dramatic reading of *Capital* as 'a sensation narrative', one that pivots on 'the aches and pains of the labouring worker's body'.[16]

These observations are replete with insights concerning Marx's power-ful use of parody, to the alternating structure of his text as it jolts back and forth between theoretical abstraction and detailed, often horrifying, empirical description, particularly of the torments of the labouring body. Yet, as much as they intuit something of its dramatic structure, these authors flounder badly with respect to the core theoretical arguments of *Capital*.[17] As a result, each severs the theoretical from the stylistic, choosing to assess Marx in predomi-nantly aesthetic terms. One of my objects in what follows is to read Marx's theory and his stylistics together, to show the inner connection between the method of exposition and his theoretical mapping of the commodity-form.[18]

---

14. Wilson 1973, pp. 340, 342, 343.
15. Hyman 1962, pp. 138, 133.
16. Cvetkovich 1992, p. 165.
17. Wilson (1973, p. 288) declares Marx's critique of political economy a piece of metaphysics; Hyman (1962, p. 128) has the most vulgar understanding of Marx's value-theory; and Cvetkovich (1992, pp. 189, 195) buys into utterly superficial notions of the postindustrial economy and the uncritical, postmodernist idea that commodification is socially and historically universal. For my critique of the latter view see McNally 2001, Chapter 2.
18. Robert Paul Wolff (1988, p. 20) attempts something similar in his marvellous book, *Moneybags Must Be So Lucky: On the Literary Structure of Capital*, where he rightly argues that 'Marx's literary style constitutes a deliberate attempt to find the philo-sophically appropriate language for expressing the ontological structure of the social

This involves attending to Marx's persistent use of body-imagery in his account of the commodity and to the dialectical reversals of the material and the immaterial that he locates at the very heart of value.

Tracing dialectical reversals, as I argue *Capital* does, requires a continual flow of metaphor. Again, this corresponds to the nature of the object of investigation, since Marx deciphered the ontology of capitalism as literally metaphorical, as constituting a social order in which some things regularly stand in for, substitute themselves for, other things. The term metaphor derives, of course, from the idea of transfer or translation.[19] Marx's use of the term reflects this meaning, as it does the Shakespearean deployment of metaphors as powerful rhetorical figures 'in which one thing, idea or action, is referred to by the name of another'.[20] Great lover of Shakespeare's texts that he was, Marx uses similar techniques to depict the behaviour of commodities in capitalist society. Capitalism, he argues, comprises a society in which commodities announce their value in and through something else (units of money); the particular value of a commodity is thus referred to 'by the name of another'. In this metaphorical structure of substitutions, where one thing (money) stands in for another (a specific commodity), there lies a social universe of alienation and exploitation. Indeed, there is an element of Gothic horror in these displacements, involving as they do a doubling process in which the truth of one thing or agent can only be arrived at through another which stands in opposition to it, much as Victor Frankenstein's truth is embodied in his hostile Creature. Marx's persistent use of metaphors, literary references and Gothic imagery are thus strategies for theorising the doublings and transpositions that occur in a world governed by capital.[21]

---

world'. Where I depart from Wolff is in my emphasis on the dialectical inversions of body and spirit that run through Marx's text.

19. Metaphor: 'a figure of speech in which a word or phrase literally denoting one kind of object or idea is used in place of another to suggest a likeness or analogy between them', *Merriam Webster Collegiate Dictionary* 1996, p. 730. On the etymology of the term see also *The Concise Oxford Dictionary of English Etymology* 1996.

20. See Dobson and Wells 2001.

21. The claim that Marx saw capitalism as metaphoric has nothing to do with the more giddy currents in postmodern theory, since the substitutions he describes are anything but random. There is, for Marx, a systematic, persistent, non-contingent *and distorting* character to these displacements, one governed by an inverted relation between bodies and value-inversions that constitute processes of *real abstraction*.

That such displacements and doublings are monstrous is hinted at in the first sentence of *Capital*, where Marx announces that the wealth of capitalist society first presents itself as an 'immense collection [*ungeheure Warensammlung*] of commodities'.[22] The English translation fails to capture the full import of Marx's formulation. For the word here translated as 'immense [*ungeheure*]' also means *monstrous*. And Marx would appear to be playing on these multiple meanings – preparing his readers for the idea that the wealth of capitalist society takes on a life of its own and comes, by an unsettling reversal, to dominate its creators. Precisely this is what he tells us in his notebooks for *Capital*, where he describes capitalist wealth as a 'monstrous objective power'.[23] But what does it mean to suggest that goods designed to satisfy human needs and desires can be monstrous? Such a statement is merely rhetorical unless commodities are something more than items for satisfying human wants. In analysing this 'something more', we begin to apprehend the doubled structure of the commodity.

There is nothing original in the observation that Marx describes the commodity as doubled. From the outset of *Capital*, he tells us that commodities are a contradictory unity of use-value and exchange-value. As use-values, commodities meet human needs. But, as exchange-values, they obey a different imperative, to procure other goods, or their universal representative – money – in order to augment the wealth of their owners.[24] Capitalism, as Marx demonstrates, is entirely about the latter process raised to the *nth* degree; it is about commodity-exchange for purposes of endlessly accumulating abstract universal wealth (money), as opposed to specific use-values. The pursuit of ever-expanding exchange-value – or, as Marx prefers, *value* – speaks to an invisible, immaterial quality of commodities. After all, no commodity can undertake an infinite physical expansion. Its material features (through which it satisfies specific human wants) are finite. No matter how many of these goods we might imagine, they still inhabit the world of material limits. But, taken as values, commodities are, in principle, infinitely expansive since there is

22. Marx 1976, p. 125.
23. Marx 1973, p. 831.
24. In introducing money at this stage of the discussion, I am not proceeding as methodically as does Marx, though I think this is not a problem for my purposes. For good reason, Marx comes explicitly to money only after a systematic discussion of non-monetary exchange of commodities.

no inherent limit to the monetary wealth their owner/seller might accumulate. It was in these terms that Aristotle distinguished unnatural acquisition of goods [*chrematistics*] from natural acquisition [*oikonomia*]. Whereas the latter, household-economy, acquires goods for their use (and thus observes natural limits), *chrematistics* drives beyond all limits, seeking an unlimited accumulation of wealth/money.[25] But, to do this, to push beyond all physical limits, capital must accumulate an aspect of the commodity that is immaterial, invisible and intangible. 'Not an atom of matter enters into the objectivity of commodities as values,' writes Marx. 'We may twist and turn a single commodity as we wish; it remains impossible to grasp it as a thing possessing value'.[26] And, here, we encounter the monstrously doubled form of the commodity that endows it with 'metaphysical subtleties and theological niceties'.

Let us take Marx's initial example of commodity-exchange, 20 yards of linen equals one coat. Here, he tells us, the value of a certain quantity of linen is expressed in something else, a coat. Yet, there is no property of 'coatness' that resides in linen. There must be an unseen similarity, a common property not accessible to the senses, which makes these commodities commensurable. We can see the nature of this problem more clearly if we expand the initial formula so as to express the value of linen in quantities of coats, or tea, or iron, or gold, or shoes, and so on. Then we get a formula like 20 yards of linen = 1 coat, 10 pounds of tea, 0.5 ton of iron, 2 ounces of gold, 1 pair of shoes... Here, it becomes clear that exchange-relations cannot possibly be based on the physical or natural properties of these goods, since the universe of all possible commodities is simply too diverse and variegated for all of them to share common material characteristics. Instead, what the coat expresses about the linen – its value – 'represents a supra-natural property',[27] something that 'transcends sensuousness'.[28] This invisible property constitutes the 'phantom-like objectivity' of value. And the supra-sensuous characteristic they share has to do with their being products of human labour in the abstract, labour considered in abstraction from everything that makes it concrete, discrete and individual.[29]

---

25. Aristotle 1981, Book 1, Chapters 9–10.
26. Marx 1976, p. 138.
27. Marx 1976, p. 149.
28. Marx 1976, p. 163.
29. There are important debates within Marxism as to the structure of the argument by which Marx moves from value to abstract labour. Most adherents of the Uno school (see, for example, the writings of Kozo Uno, Thomas Sekine and Makotoh Itoh) have

When we equate coats, linen and gold, therefore, we are equating weaving, spinning and mining – each of which is a qualitatively distinct work-process. We are saying that each of these unique labour-processes, however much they differ concretely as productive activities creating distinct use-values, have produced the same intangible thing: a certain quantity of value, measurable by money. The capitalist market must abstract, therefore, from all of the qualitative features of these work-processes in order to equate them as quantities of the same thing, homogeneous and interchangeable labour.[30] What capitalism does, therefore, is to construct the values of products of labour on the basis of an unseen and intangible property they share *as commodities* (but not as use-values), that of being general products of human labour abstracted from the concrete work-processes involved. The capitalist economy thus effects a *real abstraction* in which products become bearers of an invisible substance (value) and concrete labour becomes the bearer of labour in the abstract: 'indifference toward the specific content of labour is not only an abstraction made by us; it is also made by capital, and it belongs to its essential character'.[31]

But a system of abstract labour can only come into being if real concrete labourers are compelled to produce for the market, rather than for use. And this happens systematically only where the activity of labour has been alienated from the labourer, only where labour is controlled, regulated and directed by capitals that are obeying the dictates of the market (to produce at socially-necessary labour-times or faster). This is what it means to say that capitalism operates by way of a real abstraction: the very life-activity of workers is detached, or abstracted from them. In claiming that capitalism is organised on the basis of *abstract* labour, Marx would thus seem to have the literal sense of the word in mind. The Latin root of the verb to abstract (*abstrahere*) means 'to draw away', or literally to separate, detach, cut off.[32] And capitalism performs precisely this separating, dissecting and alienating operation when it abstracts from the concrete and specific individuals who perform unique productive acts, treating all work as effectively identical and interchangeable, as

---

problems with Marx's order of presentation in *Capital*, as does Arthur 2004, Chapter 5. While I cannot explore these debates here, I should note that I do not entirely accept these criticisms of Marx's procedure. In any event, the authors I have mentioned all arrive at the same conclusion as does Marx, albeit by different routes.

30. Marx 1976, pp. 135–6.
31. Marx, 'Economic Manuscript of 1861–63', in Marx and Engels 1988, p. 55.
32. See the quite useful discussion by Rader 1979, pp. 150–9.

quanta of the same undifferentiated abstract substance. Moreover, inherent in the operations of these processes of real abstraction is a whole structure of mystification.

To illustrate this structure, Marx takes the mundane example of a table. He notes that 'as a use-value, there is nothing mysterious' about a table, since it has observable properties that make it humanly useful. He continues:

> The form of wood, for instance, is altered if a table is made out of it. Nevertheless, the table continues to be wood, an ordinary, sensuous thing. But as soon as it emerges as a commodity [a good produced for purposes of exchange – D.M.], it changes into a thing that transcends sensuousness. It not only stands with its feet on the ground, but, in relation to all other commodities, it stands on its head, and evolves out of its wooden brain grotesque ideas, far more wonderful than if it were to begin dancing of its own free will.[33]

Closely attending to this remarkable passage, which has rarely been given the attention it deserves, allows us to grasp the 'metaphysical subtleties and theological niceties' with which the commodity abounds.[34] As a good produced for exchange rather than use, a commodity, says Marx, 'stands on its head'. As much as it may look and feel like a table, it is in fact something else: a repository of universal exchangeability, of human labour in the abstract, ultimately measurable in a quantum of money. Its sensuous qualities are in principle irrelevant to its function as a means to monetary accumulation.[35] In declaring itself as such, the table advances 'grotesque ideas,' i.e. monstrous thoughts. It proclaims itself to be something non-sensuous, something with universal properties (exchangeability with all other commodities), rather than finite, particular ones (such as those of wood fashioned into a table). Without this capacity to transcend sensuousness, the table could never be anything more than a use-value; it could not assume the doubled form of a commodity.

---

33. Marx 1976, pp. 163–4.

34. Jacques Derrida (1994, pp. 150–70) has discussed this passage at some length. Yet, his discussion is most unhelpful since, as I have argued elsewhere, Derrida uncritically naturalises capitalist relations so as to produce elementary confusions. See McNally 2001, Chapter 2.

35. I say in principle, because this is the dynamic of capitalism. In practice, a given use-value can fail to be met by market-demand – in which case, it realises no value and represents no actualised abstract labour.

If it is to enter into the world of commodity-exchange, it must shed its *table-ness* and re-emerge as a sum of money. And money is not any one thing – it is the means of having everything, tables, iron, tea, cotton, and so on; it is simultaneously all and therefore none. And every commodity must be capable of this transformation out of specificity (as a use-value) and into abstract generality (as a value in exchange, a sum of money). Upon entering a world in which commodities stand on their heads and evolve monstrous ideas, we thus move into the spectral world of value. The initially doubled form of the commodity as use-value and exchange-value now generates yet further doublings, as the following schema indicates:

	Commodity	
↓		↓
Use-value	↔	Exchange-value
Material	↔	Immaterial
Sensuous	↔	Non-sensuous
Visible	↔	Invisible
Concrete	↔	Abstract
Body	↔	Soul/Spirit

In order to make sense of all this – particularly the last of these doublings (body/soul), which has received remarkably little attention in the critical literature – let us return to Marx's famous value-equation, 20 yards of linen = 1 coat. When we equate the value of linen with that of a coat, says Marx, the coat counts only 'as the body of value [*Wertkorper*]'. Something immaterial and non-sensuous (value) is being expressed in and measured by something material (a specific use-value, such as a coat). Marx continues, 'The value of the linen is therefore expressed by the physical body of the commodity coat.' But, in recognising itself in the coat, the linen sees something other than its material, sensuous coatness. Instead, alongside its sensuous characteristics, it recognises the coat as 'a bearer of value'. Or, more dramatically, what the linen acknowledges in the coat is 'the soul of value [*Wertseele*]'.[36] Now, this is quite peculiar language. It is also far from haphazard. Turning subsequently to the problem of the measure of value, and using an analogy with weight, Marx chooses to illustrate his point with iron. Referring to 'the bodily form of the iron', he informs us that 'the iron counts as a body', and proceeds to

---

36. Marx 1976, p. 143.

link the roles played by 'the body of the iron' and 'the body of the coat'.[37] So deliberate is this language that we find it reproduced – e.g. *le corps d'une marchandise* – in the first French edition of *Capital* (1872), the only translation whose publication Marx oversaw.[38]

Having pushed this comparison, Marx abruptly declares the limits of his own analogy. Used as a measure of weight, 'iron represents a natural property', whereas the body of the coat, as a measure of value, 'represents a supra-natural property', what he has earlier described as the soul of value.[39] This strange language of body and soul is, I submit, both ironic and deeply serious. Marx urges that value, a spectral entity whose objectivity is 'phantom-like', can only express itself through the material bodies of commodities – including, as we shall see, the bodies of those who bear the commodity labour-power. Commodities thus inhabit a world of 'magic and necromancy' in which sensuous things (use-values) are mysteriously transformed into entities of an altogether different order (values), as if by alchemy. Through these reversals, material goods metamorphose into bearers of something ghostly. More sinister, the survival of people depends upon their worth in these ghostly terms. Since the capitalist form of wealth (value) is disembodied, a phantasmal entity that lives and grows only by taking possession of the bodies of commodities, 'individuals are now ruled by abstractions', says Marx.[40] It comes as little surprise, then, that the monstrous entity to which he most frequently likens capital is the vampire.[41] But, before pursuing this point, let us explore further the idea of value as something phantom-like, which returns us to Marx's theory of the fetishism of commodities.

The spectre of value and the fetishism of commodities

As I discuss further in the next chapter, the European discourse of the fetish emerged as a means of marking Africans as primitives who superstitiously attributed divine powers to brute things. Yet, in a powerfully ironic act of inversion, the young Marx turned the charge of fetish-worship back on the

---

37. Marx 1976, pp. 148, 149.
38. See Marx 1969, pp. 53, 54, 57, 58.
39. Marx 1976, p. 149.
40. Marx 1973, p. 164.
41. See Neocleous 2003, pp. 668–84.

European ruling class, declaring that it was they who bowed down before objects: gold, in the case of the Spanish colonisers of the Americas, and wood where the rulers of the Rhineland were concerned.[42] Rather than the rationalists they proclaim themselves to be, urged Marx, Europe's rulers in fact idolise things.[43] Worse, in their plundering mania for things, like gold and silver, their fetishism takes on murderous proportions. Much of the critical charge of this argument derives from its strategy of reversal, revealing the 'primitivism' attributed to Africans as a projection of European attitudes and behaviours. But, as he developed his systematic critique of political economy, Marx observed a further irony: more than a 'religion of sensuous desire', a fantastic devotion to things, commodity-fetishism at its deepest level is a religion of *non-sensuous* desire.[44] However much capitalists bow down before things, their true god is immaterial. Rather than desire things for their material properties, capitalists actually seek that invisible and immaterial property they share: value. After all, it is only their property as products of human labour in the abstract, labour stripped of all material specificity, which makes commodities commensurable and exchangeable with money. But this means that value, the entity worshipped by capitalists, is entirely invisible, intangible, an actual power whose objectivity is purely phantasmal. As Peter Stallybrass shows, there is a compelling irony at work in this line of argument. 'To fetishize commodities is, in one of Marx's least understood jokes', he writes, 'to reverse the whole history of fetishism. For it is to fetishize the invisible, the immaterial, the supra-sensible'.[45]

This observation underlines the originality of Marx's argument. Fetishism is typically understood as a form of object-worship. In the history of Protestantism, to fetishise is to worship mere things, such as icons or statues, rather than God. In liberal political philosophy, human subjects fetishise

---

42. Marx, 'The Leading Article in No. 179 of the *Kolnische Zeitung*' in Marx and Engels 1975a, p. 189; and Marx, 'Debates on the Law on Thefts of Wood', in Marx and Engels 1975a, pp. 262–3.

43. Here, Marx anticipates elements of the critique of the liberal Enlightenment later advanced by Theodor Adorno and Marx Horkheimer in *Dialectic of Enlightenment*: a rationalism that, mimicking the value-abstraction, aspires to a disembodied reason separated from the realm of labouring bodies, ultimately returns to the material world in vulgar fashion. I develop this point at more length below.

44. Marx quotes the term 'religion of sensuous desire' in 'The Leading Article in No. 179 of the *Kolnische Zeitung*', in Marx and Engels 1975a, p. 189.

45. Stallybrass 1998, p. 184.

when they abnegate their autonomy by obeying the 'dictates' of things, rather than acting as free moral subjects.[46] As he developed his critique of political economy, however, Marx turned his attention to the nature of the human subjects promoted by liberalism, arguing that they are, in fact, hollow vessels, ideal types without social content, abstracted from their actual social circumstances so that they might be equated with each other. Just as the capitalist market abstracts from the concrete character of the use-values that enter into exchange, liberalism abstracts from the real (and unequal) relations of society so as to endow each individual with a formal (hence empty) equality. Liberalism and German idealist philosophy thus enact a kind of idolatry even more preposterous than reverence of sensible things: worship of an abstraction, a 'subject' that lacks all content and substantiality. As he developed his critique of political economy, Marx came to extend this line of argument, constructed with respect to German idealism, to the value-relations that drive the world of commodities.

As we have seen, the value of commodities on capitalist markets has nothing to do with their sensible, material features. If it did, then radically dissimilar goods could not exchange with each other and could not be measured on the same scale (via money). Yet, despite their radical dissimilarities, any and all goods in a capitalist economy can have a monetary price, a marker of their universal exchangeability. Value must, therefore, be something immaterial, something all commodities share irrespective of their sensible differences. So, when we fetishise commodities, as Stallybrass observes, we attribute extraordinary powers to an *immaterial* substance. However much we may confuse the value of things with their material being (which results in the crude materialism typically associated with commodity-fetishism) we are, in fact, bowing down before something spectral, a practice infinitely more absurd than the worship of material things. Since value transcends sensuousness, its fetishisation results in the idealist/capitalist contempt for the concrete, the sensuous

---

46. As Immanuel Kant puts it in his *Critique of Judgement*, fetishism involves 'the substitution of a respect for the Object in place of one for the idea of humanity in our own self – the Subject'. See Kant 1952, Volume 1, p. 106. In this *Critique*, devoted to aesthetic judgement, Kant uses the term 'subreption'. But it is clear that this term maps onto the concept of fetishism, which he explicitly mobilises in *Religion within the Boundaries of Mere Reason* to describe the behaviour of the worshipper who 'is under the delusion of possessing an art of achieving a supernatural effect through entirely natural means' (Kant 1998, p. 172).

and the embodied. As in religion, so in capitalist society, the material world is subordinated to non-material powers, bodies subordinated to spirits, the body of value colonised by the soul of value. In this respect, value operates similarly to the way the theoretical concept behaves in idealist philosophy – as a universal abstraction that substitutes for the concrete particulars of life. Consider, for instance, a memorable passage from *The Holy Family* (1845). Attacking the speculative procedures of 'Critical Criticism', Marx parodies them as follows:

> If from real apples, pears, strawberries and almonds, I form the general idea 'Fruit', if I go further and *imagine* that my abstract idea 'Fruit', derived from real fruit, is an entity existing outside me, is indeed the *true* essence of the pear, apple, etc., then – in the *language of speculative philosophy* – I am declaring that 'Fruit' is the 'Substance' of the pear, apple, almond, etc. I am saying, therefore, that to be a pear is not essential to the pear, that to be an apple is not essential to the apple; that what is essential to all these things is not their real existence, perceptible to the senses, but the essence I have abstracted from them and then foisted on them, the essence of my idea – 'Fruit.' I therefore declare apples, pears almonds, etc., to be mere forms of existence, *modi*, of 'Fruit'...my speculative reason declares these sensuous differences inessential and irrelevant. It sees in the apple *the same* as the pear...[47]

By the time he wrote his mature critique of political economy, Marx had concluded that value actually operates the way idealist speculation reasons – by constantly abstracting from the concretely sensuous in order to endow abstractions with being, substance, reality. He thereby deciphered a homology between 'the language of speculative reason' and 'the language of commodities'. This is what makes it meaningful to describe the capitalist mode of production as a system of *real abstraction*, an inverted, topsy-turvy world. We see something of this homology between capital and speculative reason in a passage like the following:

> If I state that coats or boots stand in a relation to linen because the latter is the universal incarnation of abstract human labour, the absurdity [*die Verruktheit*] of the statement is self-evident. Nevertheless, when the producers of coats and boots bring these commodities into a relation with linen, or with

---

47. 'The Holy Family' in Marx and Engels 1975b, pp. 57–8.

> gold and silver (and this makes no difference here), as the universal equiva-
> lent, the relation between their own private labour, and the collective labour
> of society appears to them in exactly this absurd [*verruckt*] form.[48]

We once again encounter the limits of English translation here. The term
verrukt, translated as 'absurd' equally signifies crazy or deranged, while *die
Verrücktheit* implies craziness, lunacy. Indeed, an older English translation
of *Capital* used just these terms, rendering the words in the first sentence
quoted above as 'the craziness of the statement' and those in the last sentence
as 'the same deranged form'.[49] Marx clearly wants to suggest that there is
something crazy at work where coats, boots and linen are transformed into
repositories of an invisible substance, human labour in the abstract. And, by
viewing this displacement as deranged, Marx's critique of fetishism moves,
as we have seen, on a track quite different from the Protestant attack on
idolatry. In treating things and the products of human labour as artificial
and impure, Protestantism fetishises the immaterial (God). Capital observes
the same logic by substituting value/money as the real god. The result is
fetishisation of something spectral, non-sensuous, immaterial. Nevertheless,
crude materialism, a fetishisation of things *qua* things, re-emerges as a component part of the fetishism of commodities. After all, value can only exist
by 'inhabiting' or 'possessing' things (and bodies), since only actual concrete
goods can exchange with one another.[50] The result is a dialectical reversal
into vulgar materialism, a worship of objects. It is this aspect of commodity-
fetishism that is seized on exclusively in many accounts – accounts which
miss the more complex mapping of fetishism that Marx sketches. In his discussion of 'Critical Criticism', Marx traced a similar slippage, arguing that
it too eventually seeks 'some semblance of real content' by returning from
the abstraction '*Fruit*' to '*diverse*, ordinary real fruits', but that this return to
the real can only occur 'in a *speculative, mystical* fashion'.[51] And to mystify

---

48. Marx 1976, p. 169.
49. Marx 1967, p. 76.
50. It is worth noting here that 'concrete' need not mean tangible. A haircut, for
instance, is not itself palpable though its material transformations, or at least some of
them, are. The same applies for most ostensibly 'immaterial' services, a point which
has confused a variety of postmodern commentators on Marx.
51. Marx 1967, p. 58.

real objects is to fetishise them *qua* objects, to imagine value as an immediate product of nature.

This alternation between wild idealism and crude materialism was familiar to the young Marx from the time of his early critique (1842–3) of Hegel's political philosophy. Although intent on showing that the truth of existence lies on the side of thought, Hegel's idealism also seeks to explain the world as a whole. And this commitment to explaining the totality of existence forced him to return to nature and relations amongst material things and human agents. As with value in capitalist society, the flight from the real – from things, embodiment and human practice – cannot be sustained. As soon as it needs content, Hegel's philosophy has no option but to topple back to earth.[52] But, having tried to absorb the world of nature and human social practices into thought, this return to the real takes the form of a collapse. Rather than a dialectically-mediated relationship, it reverts to a crudely immediate one. Attempting to give some institutional ballast to the state – in order to supply its ideal form with some actual content – Hegel reverts to the crudest naturalism, rooting the state in inheritance of the throne through the blood line of the royal family. He thus surrenders, as Marx puts it, to 'zoology', leaving us with a theory where nature creates political rulers in the same fashion in which 'it creates eyes and noses'.[53] The idealist search for concreteness, for some actual living substance in which to ground the state, degenerates 'into the crassest materialism' in which 'nature takes revenge on Hegel for the contempt he has shown her'.[54]

Marx would subsequently locate the same alternation between wild idealism and crude materialism at the heart of commodity-fetishism. While capital insists that it is all, and that the material world of nature and humans counts for nothing, it ultimately reverses itself, fixating naturalistically and one-sidedly on the very objects it has scorned. To truly abandon the world of nature and human material practice would signal its death. Capital, as Marx explains, lives and expands only through purchase and sale of commodities. It thus undergoes a set of transformations (a circuit) in which a commodity is sold for money, which is then used to purchase further commodities. Marx figures

---

52. Marx 1975, p. 398.
53. Marx 1975, p. 174. Marx refers to zoology – with respect to the hereditary nobility – on p. 175 of this work.
54. Marx 1975, p. 174.

this circuit as M-C-M, where M denotes money and C commodities. Yet, this circuit only makes sense in capitalist terms if the second M has greater value than the initial one. With this in mind, Marx rewrites his formula as M-C-M', where M' is greater than M. Capital is thus continually in motion, says Marx, assuming at different moments the forms of commodities and money. It is not reducible to any one of these forms, however. Instead, it is their dynamic unity. Value, that immaterial stuff at the heart of capitalism, thus assumes successive material forms only to abandon them: 'in the circulation M-C-M both the money and the commodity function only as different modes of existence of value itself.... It is constantly changing from one form into the other, without becoming lost in this movement; it thus becomes transformed into an automatic subject'.[55] For all its ghostly objectivity, value flourishes only by attaching itself to, by temporarily possessing, entities whose objectivity is appreciably more palpable. But this attachment takes the form of a grotesque doubling, as the soul of value strives to capture the bodies of value, to possess them, and to evacuate them of all sensibility and concreteness, indeed to suck the life from them in the case of living labour.

Marx portrays this vampire-like possession as positively demonic. Its consequence is a nightmare-world in which the products of past labour come to dominate living labour. Vast agglomerations of factories and machines compose an automated system in perpetual motion, relentlessly sucking up surplus-labour, draining the life energies from labouring bodies. Capital, Marx intones, assumes the form of 'an animated monster' which begins to 'work', 'as if its body were by love possessed'.[56]

'As if by love possessed': vampire-capital and the labouring body

The phrase, 'as if by love possessed' comes from Goethe's *Faust*. There is little doubt that it captivated Marx. In addition to citing it in the first volume of *Capital*, he also deploys it in his preparatory notebooks and in the manuscripts that became *Capital*, Volume Three. Describing how capital seizes the surplus-labour of workers and transmutes it into gigantic systems of machinery designed for further exploitation of labour, he writes: 'Thus the

---

55. Marx 1976, p. 255.
56. Marx 1976, p. 302. See also p. 1007.

appropriation of labour by capital confronts the worker in a coarsely sensuous form; capital absorbs labour into itself – "as though its body were by love possessed"'.[57]

The words Marx cites come from the 'Auerbach's Cellar' chapter in Part One of Goethe's *Faust*, which recounts a wine-party in a basement-tavern. During the party, one of the revellers breaks into a drinking song about a cellar-rat which, poisoned by a cook, becomes sick and convulses with cramps, 'as if its body were by love possessed'.[58] It is hardly surprising that Marx, who could recite long sections of *Faust* from memory, should have compared capital's appropriation of the labouring body to possession (and poisoning) by an unseen power that induces physical convulsions. But the position of this chapter in Goethe's text is also suggestive, coming as it does right after a scene in which Faust signs a contract in blood with the devil Mephistopheles.[59] After all, not only does Marx too descend into a cellar of sorts – the underworld of work – he also reveals the wage-contract as no ordinary transaction, but rather one signed in the blood of the labourer.

Marx's descent into a cellar comes as part of a key strategic reversal at the end of Part Two of *Capital*, Volume One, where we leave 'the noisy sphere' of circulation in order to enter 'the hidden abode of production',[60] the underworld that harbours essential truths about capitalism. This move reverses the whole trajectory of Western philosophy which, since Plato, has sought truth by means of an ascent from the cave, a rising from darkness to light, metaphors which centrally informed Hegel's intellectual development.[61] In direct opposition, Marx argues for leaving the arena in which everything is visible, 'where everything takes place on the surface and in full view of everyone'.[62] He insists on entering the cave, the domain of darkness, the space of invisible

---

57. Marx 1973, p. 704.

58. The original German reads here: 'Als hatte sie Lieb im Leibe'. This line has also been translated into English by Walter Kaufmann (Goethe 1961, p. 215) as 'As if love gnawed his vitals' and by Philip Wayne as 'When love consumes their vitals' (Goethe 1949, p. 102). I have chosen to stick with the rendering provided by Marx's translator, Ben Fowkes, for reasons of consistency.

59. For an interesting discussion of this chapter of *Faust*, see Kemple 1995, pp. 30–42.

60. Marx 1976, p. 279.

61. Plato 1941, Chapter 25. For Hegel's use of similar metaphors, see Harris 1972.

62. Marx 1976, p. 279.

forces.[63] And, just as Plato's ascent is a move from the arena of bodies to that of forms, Marx's counter-move involves a journey from the sphere of form – value-form, to be precise – to the domain of bodies and their labours.

As if to underline the importance of this move, Marx enlists a series of dramatic devices. Informing us that we are now about to follow the buyer of labour-power (the capitalist) and its seller (the worker) 'into the hidden abode of production, he warns us that on its threshold 'there hangs the notice "No admittance except on business" '.[64] Marx here nods to Dante's *Inferno*, in which the poet, entering the threshold of hell, reads an inscription that ends with the words, 'Abandon Every Hope, All You Who Enter Here'.[65] Marx intends us to understand that in leaving the apparently heavenly sphere of exchange – 'the exclusive realm of Freedom, Equality, Property and Bentham' – we are descending into a hell, and that therein resides the fundamental truth of capitalism. As with Dante, so for Marx the voyage through the sufferings of hell is essential if we are to acquire genuine knowledge of our world. In this migration to the underworld, the main characters undergo decisive transformations finally to appear in their true light as unequals:

> When we leave this sphere of simple circulation…a certain change takes
> place, or so it appears, in the physiognomy of our *dramatis personae*. He who
> was previously the money-owner, now strides out in front as a capitalist; the
> possessor of labour-power now follows as his worker. The one smirks self
> importantly as if intent upon his business; the other is timid and holds back,
> like someone who has bought his own hide to market and now has nothing
> else to expect but – a tanning.[66]

With this strategic reversal, Marx returns to the problem of 'the body of value' set out in Parts One and Two. This is, I submit, the deep elaboration of his account of fetishism. Marx wants us to see that value is fundamentally about corporeality, about the labouring bodies without which the spectral and vampiric powers of capital cannot take flight. In order to defetishise capital's logic of abstraction and disembodiment, Marx's critical procedure

---

63. My analysis here is indebted to the insightful discussion of this theme in Wolff 1988, pp. 52–3. What I have added to Wolff's account is the move from form to bodies.
64. Marx 1976, p. 280.
65. Dante 1984, p. 89.
66. Marx 1976, p. 280.

involves disruptive strategies of re-embodiment – by way of reinstating the labouring bodies that are the precondition of value. *Marx thus de-fetishises by way of re-embodiment*. And this move, I urge further, is not extraneous to his value-theory; it is not something superfluous to the dialectic of capital.[67] In attending to labouring bodies, Marx is in fact inside the dialectic of capital, tracking with irony and horror the way it subverts and reverses itself. After we enter the hidden abode, the dark cave of capitalist production, we are submerged in the shadowy underworld of labouring bodies. As if to signal as much, in the last sentence of Part Two Marx suddenly shines the spotlight on the worker's body, instructing us that, rather than an ordinary commodity, the seller of labour-power has brought 'his own hide to market' and can now only expect 'a tanning'. Henceforth, he insistently brings the abused and exploited labouring body to the fore. Alongside the accumulation of capital, he accumulates reports on workers' bodies. As he graphically describes labour-processes, machineries, hours of work, wages, injuries, diseases, we feel the heat of the factory, the strain of bodies adapting to machines, the cramped quarters that distort the human frame, the industrial processes that make the body ill. Smallpox, tetanus, diphtheria and other diseases are painstakingly itemised and linked to industrial processes that attack the human corpus.[68]

Marx's corporeal turn in Part Three of *Capital* assists us in seeing the unseen. Amidst its noise and commotion, the sphere of exchange *invisibilises* the labouring body. By confining itself to the movement of commodities after they have left sites of production, the market conceals the labour-process, pushing it off stage, into an unlit space. In leading us into the underworld of the market, just as Ben Okri will do in his *Famished Road* series, Marx seeks to nurture night-vision, to help us see in the dark. Of course, classical political economy raised the problem of invisibility prior to Marx, most famously in Adam Smith's metaphor of the 'invisible hand' of the market. Smith uses this metaphor to suggest that individuals acting in their self-interest unwittingly

---

67. I am taking issue here with the highly suggestive notion of a dialectic of capital as a 'pure theory' of capitalism modelled on Hegel's *Logic*, an interpretation advanced by the so-called Uno school. See Uno 1977, and especially Appendix 1 by Sekine, 'An Essay on Uno's Dialectic of Capital'. See also Sekine 1997.

68. Marx 1976, pp. 593, 356, 847.

advance the general interest of society.[69] In a fully commercialised market-society, suggests Smith, an unseen mechanism co-ordinates and regulates the component-parts of the economic system in spite of the purely atomistic motives of individuals.[70] But, for Marx, these unseen forces are much more ominous. Crucially, they involve the 'invisible threads' that chain workers to a life of exploitation. Despite 'the legal fiction of a contract' between workers and capitalists, the former are, in fact, compelled (by their separation from means of production) to sell their labour. And, once they have made this sale, workers discover that it is their hides they have delivered to capital – and that it is a hiding they will receive. Rather than a free agent, then, the wage-labourer is subjected to an economic coercion every bit as real as the political coercion imposed on the slaves of antiquity. But, where the latter was entirely visible, encoded in public markings of inequality, the coercive bonds upon the modern worker are unseen: 'The Roman slave was held by chains; the wage-labourer is bound by invisible threads'.[71]

In order to make those threads visible, Marx descends to the sphere of the labouring body, exposing the sufferings to which it is subjected. He accents the body in pain, the body possessed and deformed by capital.[72] In so doing, he tells the tales of monstrous suffering underlined by Silko. Three passages in particular illustrate this strategy of representation. The first invokes Dante in its description of industrial horrors:

> The manufacture of matches...has brought with it tetanus, a disease which a Vienna doctor already discovered in 1845 to be peculiar to the makers of matches. Half the workers are children under 13 and young persons under 18.... Only the most miserable part of the working class, half-starved widows and so forth, deliver up their children to it, their 'ragged, half-

---

69. Smith 1969, p. 304; Smith 1976, Volume 1, p. 456. Smith used the metaphor in his earlier 'History of Astronomy' in a way that linked it intriguingly to superstition. See Lindgren 1967, p. 49.

70. This, of course, requires free markets and correct institutional arrangements, according to Smith. On this point, see McNally 1988, Chapters 4–5.

71. Marx 1976, p. 719. I grant Marx a certain poetic license here, since the picture of Roman slavery is often more complex than he suggests. On these issues, see Wood 1989, and de Ste Croix 1981. While Wood and de Ste Croix disagree on a number of issues, they concur in offering a much more complex picture of ancient slavery than does Marx. It is also crucial here that we not conflate ancient slavery with the horrors of slavery in the 'New World'.

72. For a much more extensive reading of Marx in this regard, see Scarry 1985, Chapter 4.

starved, untaught children'.... With a working day ranging from 12 to 14 or 15 hours, night-labour, irregular meal times, and meals mostly taken in the workrooms themselves, pestilent with phosphorous, Dante would have found the worst horrors in his Inferno surpassed in this industry.[73]

The next passage enumerates some of the diseases fostered by the 'slaughter houses' of capitalist industry:

> In the hardware manufactures of Birmingham and the neighbourhood, there are employed, mostly in very heavy work, 30,000 children and young persons, besides 10,000 women. They are to be found in a range of unhealthy jobs: in brass foundries, button factories, and enamelling, galvanizing and laquering works. Owing to the excessive labour performed by their workers, both adult and non-adult, certain London firms where newspapers and books are printed have gained for themselves the honourable name 'slaughter houses'. Similar excesses occur in book-binding, where the victims are chiefly women, girls and children; young persons have to do the heavy work in rope works, and night work in salt mines, candle factories and chemical works; young people are worked to death at turning the looms in silk weaving, when it is not carried on by machinery. One of the most shameful, dirtiest and worst paid jobs, a kind of labour on which women and young girls are by preference employed, is the sorting of rags. [There follows a detailed description of the global circuits of the trade – D.M.]...The rag-sorters are carriers for the spread of small-pox and other infectious diseases...[74]

The final passage prosaically describes the drawing of workers' blood (in this case that of children) and charges capital with 'blood sucking':

> Where lace-making ends in the counties of Buckingham and Bedford, straw-plaiting begins.... The children generally start to be instructed in straw-plaiting at the age of 4, often between 3 and 4. They get no education, of course. The children themselves call the elementary schools 'natural schools', distinguishing them in this way from these blood-sucking institutions...The straw cuts their mouths, with which they constantly moisten it, and their fingers.[75]

---

73. Marx 1976, p. 356.
74. Marx 1976, p. 592.
75. Marx 1976, p. 598.

As his reference to Dante intimates, across these passages Marx takes us on a journey through hell. And, here, he also finds a common ground with Gothic literature. It has been aptly remarked that Gothic tales owe much of their terror to their spatial settings: 'cellars, attics, chambers long closed off'. In the confines of such enclosed spaces, horror and death announce themselves. After all, what makes these claustrophobia-inducing spaces terrifying is that they are sealed off from life – from 'air, sunlight, human presence and care. They are repulsive in that they bespeak abandonment and unlife'.[76] And so it is with the capitalist factory, which 'steals the time required for the consumption of fresh air and sunlight', and engages in 'sheer robbery of every normal condition needed for working and living'.[77] If there is a Marxist Gothic, then, it is one that insists, amongst other things, on journeying through the night spaces of the capitalist underworld, on visiting the secret dungeons that harbour labouring bodies in pain.[78] Another shared feature with the Gothic is a fixation on corporeal vulnerability. Bodies are always imperilled in Gothic tales, threatened by invasion and dismemberment. And in a whole genre of the Victorian Gothic, severed hands that haunt the living serve as a reminder of what has been done to the labouring poor.[79] It comes as little surprise, then, to find Marx repeatedly mining Gothic imagery to depict capital's inscriptions on workers' bodies. Taking the example of the horrid sweatshops of the silk industry, he tells us that employers sought out children between 11 and 13 because of the size of their fingers and their lightness of touch. 'The children,' Marx charges, 'were quite simply slaughtered for the sake of their delicate fingers'.[80]

In these images of body-parts – fingers, mouths, blood – Marx limns the dismembering drives of capital. In so doing, he also underlines the corporeal realities of fetishisation.[81] For, if one aspect of fetishism is the substitution of

---

76. Morgan 1998, p. 73.

77. Marx 1976, pp. 375–6, 599.

78. Margaret Cohen has recommended a 'Gothic Marxism' that attends to the irrational. See Cohen 1993, pp. 1–2. She seems not to have figured Marx's voyages through the capitalist underworld into her account.

79. Rowe 1999, Chapter 5.

80. Marx 1976, p. 406.

81. Of course, there are also distinctively erotic modes of fetishisation of human body-parts. As Walter Benjamin intuited, however, these are not unrelated to capital's reification of the labouring body. On this point see McNally 2001, Chapter 5, and Leslie 1997, pp. 66–89.

a part for a whole, this is precisely what capital accomplishes, fragmenting workers and reducing them to mere parts of themselves. In dividing labour-processes into ever-smaller motions that can be repeated with ever-greater speed, capitalist manufacture anatomises the labouring body, fixating on specific organs, muscles and nerves. Capital 'mutilates the worker', writes Marx. Indeed, 'The individual himself is divided up and transformed into the automatic motor of a detail operation, thus realizing the absurd fable of Menenius Agrippa, which presents man as a mere fragment of his own body'.[82]

As we have seen in the previous chapter, the tale in question describes Menenius Agrippa, friend and confidante of Coriolanus, calming the rebellious Roman mob with the claim that if body-parts (including parts of the body-politic) rebel against the belly (which he compares to the Roman aristocracy), they imperil the very organ that nourishes and sustains them. While Marx might have relied upon a number of sources for this tale, amongst them the version that appears in Plutarch's *Lives*, it is likely that he was most recently familiar with the variant proffered in Shakespeare's *Coriolanus*.[83] And what is most striking about Shakespeare's rendition, as we have seen, is the way it employs tropes of dismemberment to illuminate social conflict. A Roman aristocrat and warrior who loathes the plebs, Coriolanus persistently insults the common people by comparing them to body-parts and afflictions – tongues, bosoms, scabs, measles. In a particularly revealing exchange, as we have seen, he even addresses them as 'you fragments',[84] as if to mark them as inherently dismembered. Drawing upon this play, as he seems to have done, in order to depict the fragmentation of proletarian bodies, Marx restaged social conflict in terms of corporeal fragmentation. But, while Shakespeare imagines social dismemberment as purely destructive, Marx pictures the dismemberment performed by capital as *destructively productive*. Rather than simply an exercise in mutual annihilation, the fragmentation of workers' bodies is productive – of capital, and of the 'collective worker' that might undo it.[85] Marx thus

---

82. Marx 1976, pp. 481–2.

83. As Nicolaievsky and Maenchen-Helfen (1973, pp. 258–9) remark, the Marx family observed a veritable Shakespeare-cult, with Marx regularly reciting long passages from Shakespeare by heart.

84. William Shakespeare, *Coriolanus*, I.1.222.

85. On the important concept of the collective workers see Marx 1976, pp. 464–9. I return to this concept in a different idiom in the Conclusion, where I discuss the *hopeful monster*, the revolutionary proletariat.

extends an insight that the Roman plebs transmit in Shakespeare's text when, protesting their hunger, they intone, 'the leanness that afflicts us, the object of our misery, is as an inventory to particularize their abundance; our sufferance is a gain to them'.[86] In offering up his own inventory of bodily suffering, Marx reveals it to be the means by which capital particularises *its* abundance.

The monster that best fits Marx's account of production via corporeal destruction is, of course, the vampire. Time and time again, he reminds us that capital, like the undead, attains life and power by consuming the energies of the living, by sucking their blood. So powerful is this imagery that Marx uses the vampire-metaphor three times in the course of *Capital*'s long chapter on the working day. 'Capital is dead labour which, vampire-like, lives only by sucking living labour', he first pronounces. Further into the chapter, he decries capital's 'vampire thirst for the living blood of labour.' And, in the last paragraph of the chapter, he warns that 'the vampire will not let go "while there remains a single muscle, sinew or drop of blood to be exploited"'.[87] Three interrelated claims are bound up with these uses of the vampire-metaphor. First is the argument for exploitation: the idea that capital feeds off living labour. Second is the idea of invisibility: like vampires, which are creatures of darkness and night, capital's bloodsucking is unseen. Third is the notion of alienation: the insistence that capitalism involves an inversion by which the dead (material objects of past labour, known as means of production) dominate the living (actual human labourers). The first of these ideas is familiar to readers of Marx and the second is one we have already touched on. But the third deserves some elaboration.

If the purpose of production is to create wealth with which to satisfy human needs, then the means of production – the tools, equipment, buildings, machineries and raw materials – serve as means to that end. But, in capitalist society, a peculiar inversion occurs: a means becomes an end – accumulation of *means* of production becomes the *end* to which living labour is subordinated. Capital accumulates wealth not to satisfy needs but in order to accumulate ever more: 'Accumulate, accumulate! That is Moses and the prophets', chortles Marx.[88] The dynamic of capital involves piling up ever

---

86. Shakespeare, *Coriolanus*, I.1.20–2.
87. Marx 1976, pp. 342, 357, 416.
88. Marx 1976, p. 742.

more means of production so that labour might be exploited more intensively and extensively – thus expanding the means of production and the machinery of profit-making, *ad infinitum*. Labour becomes thereby a means to an end, the expansion of the means of production. Or, to put it in Marx's preferred terminology, living labour (the concrete activity of productive humans) becomes a means of expanding dead labour (the means of production created by past activity): 'Living labour appears merely as a means to realize objectified, dead labour, to penetrate it with an animating soul while losing its own soul to it'.[89] It becomes the function of living labour to reanimate the products of past labour, to bring dead labour to life. As a result, claims Marx, echoing his reference to *Faust*, 'The product of labour...has been endowed by living labour with a soul of its own'.[90] Capitalism thus involves 'transubstantiation', a process in which a quality – in this case life – is transferred from one substance to another.[91] In awakening past labour, living labour raises it from the dead, makes it undead. Indeed, only the vital activity of labour keeps capital from lapsing into a death state: 'Living labour must seize on these things, awaken them from the dead'.[92] In so doing, living labour also alienates and deadens itself. 'All the powers of labour project themselves as powers of capital',[93] thus rendering workers appendages of the animated monster. In a perverse dialectical inversion, the very powers of labour that re-animate the dead also deaden the living, reifying them, reducing them to a zombie-state.

Zombie-labour and the 'monstrous outrages' of capital

Like zombies, living labour under capitalism becomes 'subservient to and led by an alien will and an alien intelligence'.[94] In tandem, the mass of machinery to which workers are subordinated in production assumes the form of an *'animated monster'*, a monstrosity endowed with a soul and intelligence of its own.[95] Factories, machines, assembly-lines, computerised production-systems all take on a life of their own, directing the movements of labour,

---

89. Marx 1973, p. 461.
90. Marx 1973, p. 454.
91. Marx 1973, p. 308.
92. Marx 1976, p. 289.
93. Marx 1976, p. 756.
94. Marx 1973, p. 454.
95. Marx 1976, p. 302.

controlling workers as if they were merely inorganic parts of a giant apparatus. As capital assumes the form of 'a mechanical monster whose body fills whole factories', workers become 'conscious organs of the automaton'.[96] This reference to workers as organs of capital, which we also find in other Marxian texts,[97] returns us to the theme of corporeal fragmentation. Labouring for capital, protests Marx, workers become mere appendages of this 'animated monster', dismembered body-parts activated by the motions of the grotesque corpus of capital.

The logic Marx captures was captured brilliantly in the twentieth-century context by Harry Braverman. In *Labor and Monopoly Capital*, Braverman showed how a series of technical innovations enabled capital to increasingly control and regulate acts of labour as if they were indeed just interchangeable parts of a continuous flow of capital's self-expansion. Motion-and-time studies in particular, in which every process of production is broken down into a succession of smallest possible human motions, each of which is timed, have served as a means for employers to calibrate any and every work-process. Machines, equipment, desks, chairs, assembly-lines, price-scanning equipment and so on are all modified to decrease the time required to complete a motion. In a *Guide to Office Clerical Time Standards*, used by many corporations, almost every imaginable office-activity is subjected to time-standards. Opening and closing drawers, stapling, typing, opening envelopes are all so calibrated. Swivelling a chair in order to turn to another task should take 0.009 minutes, for instance.[98] Abstract time, time measured and calibrated according to mathematical efficiencies, becomes the basis of concrete activity. As a result, humans become nothing but bearers of undifferentiated life-energies, dispensed in units of abstract time. In Marx's memorable phrase, 'Time is everything, man is nothing; he is at the most, time's carcase'.[99] What capital does to workers, therefore, is exactly what witches are said to do when they

---

96. Marx 1976, pp. 503, 544. As if to underline the monstrous dimensions of the automated capitalist factory, Marx makes reference to the ancient monster, Cyclops, four times in the course of two pages in his chapter on 'Machinery and Large-Scale Industry' in *Capital* (1976, pp. 506–7).

97. 'The different working individuals seem to be mere organs', Marx observes in *A Contribution to the Critique of Political Economy* (1970, p. 30).

98. Rinehart 1996, p. 85. In general see Braverman 1974.

99. Marx 1963, p. 54.

create a zombie: 'to reduce a person to body, to reduce behaviour to basic motor functions, to reduce social utility to raw labour', as one critic puts it.[100]

Perhaps now we can more fully grasp the poetic knowledge embedded in many zombie- and vampire-tales, such as those emanating from Sub-Saharan Africa today, which I explore in the next chapter. These fables dramatise some of the most fundamental features of capitalist modernity: its tendency to mortify living labour, to zombify workers in order to appropriate their life-energies in the interests of capital. If it is true that 'The only modern myth is the myth of zombies – mortified schizos, good for work,'[101] then it is in Sub-Saharan Africa that this truth has been most powerfully rendered. And this is fitting. It was West Africans who, after all, captured as commodities in order to fuel the capitalist plantation-economy, most fully experienced the mortifying tendencies of capitalism. Indeed, Fanon's argument that the racialised and colonised suffer a kind of ontological death could be said to apply with greatest force to the experience of enslaved Africans.[102] By reducing people – sentient, creative, passionate, loving, hating, desiring humans – to property, capitalist slavery imposed a death-in-life. Even after the abolition of slavery, anti-black racism continues to reproduce central aspects of this life-denying reification.[103] As the urban poor of postcolonial Africa struggle today to understand the forces of capitalist globalisation that wreak havoc on their lives, they are drawing upon and reworking experiential categories derived from the ontological deaths of slavery, racism and colonialism. In so doing, they disclose essential truths about capitalism. As Marx observed, when we turn our gaze from the 'respectable forms' of capitalism in its heartlands to observe 'the colonies', the 'inherent barbarism of bourgeois civilization lies unveiled before our eyes'.[104]

---

100. Dendle 2007, p. 48.
101. Deleuze and Guattari 1983, p. 335.
102. See Fanon 1967 and 1968. For a powerful rereading of Fanon's work which challenges a variety of postmodernist/postcolonial interpretations, see Sekyi-Otu 1996.
103. See Lewis R. Gordon 1997, and Gonzalez 1997.
104. Marx 1973a, p. 324. Many of Marx's published writings on India are deeply flawed by his European biases concerning Asian history and his somewhat teleological notion that, for all its crimes, British colonialism does the service of creating capitalist social forms in the colonies, thereby preparing them for social progress. At the same time, Marx denounces the terrible crimes committed by colonialism. For perceptive and nuanced assessments of Marx's views in this area see Habib 2002, and Ahmad 1992, pp. 221–42. The evidence also suggests that later in life Marx began to significantly revise his views of non-Western history, communal property, and family-

Marx intends his readers to understand this barbarism as real, not merely metaphorical. Capital commits 'monstrous outrages', he insists – from 'the extirpation, enslavement and entombment in mines of the indigenous population' of the Americas, 'the conversion of Africa into a preserve for the commercial hunting of blackskins' to profiting from 'the capitalized blood of children' in English mines and factories. Capital thus comes into the world 'dripping from head to toe, from every pore, with blood and dirt'.[105] This is the point grasped with such acuity by Silko when she writes that

> Marx caught the capitalists of the British empire with bloody hands.... Marx had never forgotten the indigenous people of the Americas, or of Africa. Marx had recited the crimes of slaughter and slavery committed by the European colonials who had been sent by their capitalist slave masters to secure the raw materials of capitalism – human flesh and blood.

In returning us to blood and flesh, witchcraft-tales from Sub-Saharan Africa and elsewhere disclose hidden truths about the capitalist mode of production.

As we shall see in the next chapter, the most potent aspect of these tales is their rendering of zombies as *forced* labourers, workers compelled to produce for others. Not only do such tales capture the idea of alienated labour performed at the behest of others; equally significant, they also interrogate the invisibility of the process, its mysterious and elusive character, which enables it to escape sensory detection. In non-capitalist class-societies, such appropriation is entirely evident, with peasants and others directly handing over part of their labour, their product, or the money equivalent to the ruling class in the form of rent and taxes. But, in bourgeois society, it is capitalists who pay workers, offering them wages as payment for their labour. Yet, this visible exchange conceals the invisible *counter-exchange* from which capital profits. For, once they purchase labour-power as a commodity, capitalists can squeeze more from it than the value of the wages paid. They do so by obliging labourers to work longer than the time required to produce the value of their wages. Everything beyond this constitutes *surplus-labour*, to use Marx's termi-

---

and state-formation. On these points see Smith 2002, pp. 73–84, and Anderson 2002, pp. 84–96.

105. Marx 1976, pp. 353, 915, 920, 926.

nology, a *surplus-value* above and beyond the capitalist's costs of production. As ever-expanding value, writes Marx, capital 'has acquired the occult ability to add value to itself'.[106] But, as African vampire-tales intuit, this occult ability turns on monstrous exploitation of living labour, on capital's 'werewolf-like hunger for surplus labour'.[107] Yet, because all of this happens in the darkness of the hidden abode of production – not in the noisy daylight-world where all other commodities are exchanged – it is unseen. No wonder, then, that Mary Shelley shows Frankenstein's Creature performing unseen labours at night to feed the De Laceys, or that African vampire-tales depict exploitation as a secret night-time ritual. To grasp the invisible powers of capitalist exploitation and accumulation requires the night-vision made possible by a dialectical optics.

Marx's general formula for capital (M-C-M′), as I have intimated, is designed to map this invisible world. For once our eyes are able to see inside the dark underworld of production, we can grasp the circuit of capital as in fact having the following dimensions: M-C...(LP + MP)...C′-M′, where LP denotes labour-power and MP means of production. The secret of capitalist profit (surplus-value) is derived, in short, from the purchase of labour-power and means of production which the capitalist brings together in the hidden abode of production in order to exploit living labour. And it is this secret that *Frankenstein* and African zombie-stories seek to unravel with their tales of nocturnal labours. Marx tells a similar tale of transfiguration. It is one in which the free worker metamorphoses into the forced labourer – and in which the figure of the vampire reappears:

> It must be acknowledged that our worker emerges from the process of production looking different from when he entered it. In the market, as owner of the commodity 'labour-power', he stood face to face with other owners of commodities, one owner against another owner. The contract by which he sold his labour-power to the capitalist proved in black and white, so to speak, that he was free to dispose of himself. But when the transaction was concluded, it was discovered that he was no 'free agent', that the period of time for which he is free to sell his labour-power is the period of time for

---

106. Marx 1976, p. 255.
107. Marx 1976, p. 353.

which he forced to sell it, that in fact the vampire will not let go 'while there remains a single muscle, sinew or drop of blood to be exploited'.[108]

It is time now to turn to that commodity – labour-power – that gives vampire-capital access to the muscles, sinews and blood of living labourers. It is, after all, a peculiar one. From the standpoint of the circulation of commodities, labour-power appears like any other good that exchanges for money. But the peculiarity of this commodity is that, rather than a thing, it is a living power, an energy, a *potentia*, consumed in the hidden abode of production. Moreover, its consumption by the capitalist is simultaneously an act of production, generating goods, surplus-value and capital. Thus, the more rapaciously the capitalist 'consumes' it, the more blood he sucks from it, the more wealth labour-power generates for him. What the labourer sells, in other words, is her life-energies; and those energies (and its bearer, the worker) are subjected to the tyranny of capital for the contracted life of the act of consumption/ production. By a perverse dialectical reversal, the worker discovers she is not at all the free agent she appeared in the realm of exchange. Instead, her life-activity is appropriated by capital for alien purposes – and the world of commodity-exchange suddenly takes on a nightmarish guise. Rather than an expression of freedom, the exchange of labour with capital turns out to be life- denying:

> …the exercise of labour-power, labour is the worker's own life-activity, the manifestation of his own life. And this life-activity he sells to another person in order to secure the necessary means of subsistence. Thus his life-activity is for him only a means to enable him to exist. He works in order to live. He does not even reckon labour as part of his life; it is rather a sacrifice of his life. It is a commodity which he has made over to another…life begins for him where this activity ceases, at table, in the public house, in bed.[109]

On the capitalist market, human creative energies are transformed into things (commodities) that are sold like any other. True, the wage-labourer herself is not treated as a thing to be purchased once and for all, as is a slave. Nonetheless, she is compelled to treat her life-energies and her time – the

---

108. Marx 1976, pp. 415–16.
109. Marx 1952, p. 20.

space of human development, as Marx calls it – as a collection of things. The worker

> sells himself piecemeal. He sells at auction eight, ten, twelve, fifteen hours of his life, day after day, to the highest bidder...to the capitalist. The worker belongs neither to the owner nor to the land, but eight, ten, twelve, fifteen hours of his daily life belong to him who buys them.[110]

Wage-labour thus obliges workers to treat their creative, corporeal energies as divisible bits to be auctioned off. And this shapes and distorts the worker's sense of self. As Georg Lukács pointed out, commodification re-organises the very forms of human experience, the ways in which we perceive and understand ourselves and our capacities. Commodification both reshapes the world around us and penetrates into the psyche of the human individuals involved: 'Objectively a world of objects and relations between things springs into being (a world of commodities and their movements on the market). Subjectively – where the market-economy has been fully developed – a man's activity becomes estranged from himself'. Labour-commodification thereby 'stamps its imprint upon the whole consciousness of man; his qualities and abilities are no longer an organic part of his personality, they are things which he can "own" or "dispose of" like the various objects of the external world'.[111]

The commodification of labour-power, the transformation of human creative energies into commodities, thus daily realises 'the absurd tale of Menenius Agrippa' in which human beings relate to their life-energies as alienable fragments of personhood, as dead things that can be sold off. The secret of capitalism resides in this fragmentation of the labouring self, in the way that wage-labourers turn over their *bodies of value* to capital in incremental bits over a lifetime. The time workers give over to capital is 'dead time', time separate from their 'real' lives, a sort of death-in-life. No wonder, then, that images of the living dead proliferate so widely in the capitalist culture-industry. And no wonder too that workers newly subjected to the pressures of commodification find this death-in-life anything but normal. Typically, they encounter it as positively demonic – an unnatural and depraved theft of their life-energies. In

---

110. Marx 1952, p. 21.
111. Lukács 1971b, pp. 89, 100.

Britain, as we saw in Chapter One, before workers became habituated to looking upon the requirements of capitalism 'as self-evident natural laws',[112] the horror of fragmented personhood was registered in riots against the anatomists. And *Frankenstein* gave literary expression to these plebeian anxieties about the processes of dissection and dismemberment central to the rise of capitalism.

We find something similar at work in the vampire-tales emanating from Sub-Saharan Africa in the era of neoliberal globalisation. But these African narratives, as we shall see, are no mere repetitions. Emerging in the context of postcolonial experiences of capitalist globalisation, these portrayals of occult transactions between money and body-parts also probe the alchemy of finance-capital, thus tackling a fundamental feature of capitalism in the age of neoliberal globalisation.

Money: capitalism's second nature

Before turning to some of the specific forms of money and 'financialisation' in late capitalism, we need first to remind ourselves of the uniqueness of a fully monetary economy, of a society in which money invades virtually all the socio-economic transactions amongst people.

The utter uniqueness, some would say perversion, of capitalist society consists in the way money replaces nature as the essential condition of human life. In all other forms of society, it is interaction with nature – with land, water, animals and vegetation in particular – that guarantees survival. Of course, people's relations with land and nature in non-capitalist societies have often been governed and constrained by lop-sided and exploitative property-relations. Ownership of land has been distributed in grossly unequal ways and the majority has laboured on behalf of others. Nevertheless, throughout human history, most labourers have had some sort of consistent possession of land. Working as peasants on small tracts of land, they have had access to the most basic means of life. Although typically obliged to pay rent to landlords and taxes to the state, and constrained in terms of where they could live, who they could marry, and so on, they nonetheless had land (both personal and communal) on which to grow crops and raise animals. A defining feature of

---

112. Marx 1976, p. 899.

capitalism, as we have seen in Chapter One, is that it breaks this access to land by dispossessing people and throwing them onto the labour-market. Indeed, we have now reached the point, for the first time in history, in which the majority of humans no longer live on the land.

In depriving most people of land – and the foodstuffs, fuel and housing materials that come with it – capitalism fundamentally restructures our relation to the natural and social environments. No longer is basic subsistence underwritten by direct access to one's own plot or via communal rights to land. Instead, it is money and money alone, generally acquired through the sale of labour-power, which provides the necessities of life. Without money, there is no access to the use-values generated by the interaction of human labour and the natural environment.[113] This, of course, is what it means to inhabit a world governed by exchange-value. In seeking to subsume every possible item under its logic, capital increasingly commodifies and *monetises* more and more domains of social life. No longer are goods essential to life considered entitlements – indeed, neoliberalism has been for thirty years re-fighting the battle against all such notions. Instead, capitalist society, particularly one 'cleansed' of social rights, dictates that access to the necessities of life shall depend upon money – and sufficient quantities of it at that.

Money thus constitutes the basic form of the *second nature* that develops with capitalism, that set of social conditions that makes up the indispensable foundation of human life and that makes possible interaction with nature and, thereby, human survival itself.[114] In such circumstances, it increasingly appears natural that money should operate as the universal mediator between people and between humans and nature. By constituting a second nature, money does indeed govern essential processes of naturo-social life. As a result, the exchange abstraction – the social process by which people and things become equatable with one another and expressible in money –

---

113. Of course, as we have seen in Chapter 2, people may poach and squat on privatised land. Similarly, states or charitable organisations may provide for provision of basic needs. But these are all non-capitalist strategies, insofar as they short-circuit the market.

114. The concept of second nature was developed, with a nod to Hegel, by the Hungarian philosopher Georg Lukács in his *Theory of the Novel* (1971a, p. 64). Lukács then reworked the concept in relation to Marx's notion of fetishism in his classic work, *History and Class Consciousness* (1971b). The idea had a powerful impact on both Theodor Adorno and Walter Benjamin and was used explicitly by Alfred Sohn-Rethel in his *Intellectual and Manual Labour: A Critique of Epistemology* (1978, pp. 60–1).

is normalised, albeit only after long social and cultural struggles and transformations, as we have seen. As it imposes its form of social synthesis on society, capital refashions the experience of space and time, quantifying and abstracting each.[115] The monetised logic of capital thus ruptures the human sensorium, substituting quantitative relations (monetary values) for qualitative ones based on the unique sensible features of goods. As Georg Simmel noted, the money-relation 'hollows out the core of things, their peculiarities, their specific values and their uniqueness.... They all rest on the same level and are distinguished only by their amounts'.[116]

And the same applies to human beings; they too are largely distinguished by the quantities of money they represent. Indeed, the monetisation of a society typically ushers in frightening and disorienting confusions between persons and things, as money becomes animated with powers of life and death and persons increasingly sell themselves, as if they were things. Tracking the semantic and cultural disruptions attendant on the monetisation of everyday-life in eighteenth-century England, Margot Finn observes 'a constant slippage between the category of the person and the category of the thing'.[117] Indeed, money that talked, that assumed humanlike personality, was a recurrent theme of English fiction throughout this era,[118] just as it is in some African folklore today. Conferring identity, power and social location, money in capitalist society truly is the regulating social power. In addition to governing my survival, the possession or absence of money also powerfully determines my relations to others. By constituting my relation to the market, money locates me socially. And the means by which I procure it positions me in a system of class-relations. Money both holds society together – it is the common basis for social life, the mechanism of social synthesis – at the same time that it separates social agents into antagonistic classes. As the young Marx put it, money 'is the true agent of separation and the true cementing agent, it is the chemical power of society'.[119] A thing, something deposited in a bank, carried in a pocket or digitally accessed via a debit-card, structures our relations with other humans. More than this, individuals acquire their social being in and

---

115. See Sohn-Rethel 1978, pp. 5, 46–8.
116. Simmel 1997, p. 340.
117. Finn 2003, p. 34.
118. Lynch 1998, and Valenze 2006, Chapter 2.
119. 'Economic and Philosophic Manuscripts' in Marx 1975, p. 377.

through money; without it they effectively exist outside modern social life, as does Frankenstein's Creature. It follows that in our society 'the individual carries his social power, as well as his bond with society, in his pocket'.[120] The monetised social relations of capitalism thus simultaneously compel and privatise; they enforce a method of survival in which people, stripped of communal entitlements, sell their individual assets (mainly labour-powers) on the market.

Yet, money also appears to be the great equaliser. Everyone wants it, gets it, spends it. In the grocery-store, my dollar is as good as that of the store-owner. As much as money fragments and divides, it also unites all participants in the market-economy in a network of interdependence and interaction. This is one reason why the source of profit and class-inequality is so elusive. And it is also a reason why Marx's decoding of commodity-exchange as a cryptic process of monetary accumulation is so indispensable to critical knowledge of our world. In undertaking this decoding, Marx deciphered the occult properties of money *as capital*. Today, however, money has become more awesome and more cryptic than ever before – and prone to great convulsions which reap monstrous havoc on the lives of millions.

'Self-birthing' capital and the alchemy of money

Money has thus always exercised grotesque powers in capitalist society, literally capable of determining who shall live and who shall die. In late capitalism, these awesome powers assume ever more mysterious and elusive forms. Much of this has to do with the processes of *financialisation*, which have greatly expanded the range of interest-bearing activities by capital, and whose basis I shall explore shortly. But as financialisation pivots on the intrusion of credit, debt and interest-payments into ever more spheres of social reproduction, we need first to interrogate the phenomenon of interest-bearing capital itself.[121]

As we have seen, Marx's analysis of capital pivots on the critical insight that the formula M-C-M' conceals material transformations that occur in the

---

120. Marx 1973, p. 159.
121. I have explored the roots of financialisation in McNally 2009, pp. 35–83 and at more length in McNally 2010.

hidden abode of production. To capture the esoteric movement of capital, he advances the expanded formula, M-C. . .MP+LP. . .C'-M'. This allows him to show how, beneath the sphere of circulation of commodities and money (M-C-M'), capital expands by exploiting labour, appropriating surplus-value, and reinvesting much of it in new forces of production. But Marx was well aware that not all capitalists profit through purchasing means of production in order to produce commodities (and the surplus-value they contain). In the complex structure of capitalism, some capitals confine themselves to purely financial transactions. Take banks, for instance, which are specialised institutions that pool and store financial savings and lend them at interest.[122] Banks do not organise the production of commodities and they do not oversee the creation of surplus-value; but they do make a profit. This profit, based largely on interest from loans, derives either from workers' wages (when loans are made to wage-earners) or from surplus-value on productive capital. In the latter case, a capitalist takes out a loan to finance machinery, equipment or buildings and then pays back interest and principal out of the surplus-value generated by exploiting labour-power that works with these means of production. Thus, even though the source of interest is the surplus-value generated by living labour, it is the case for money-lending capital that it can make a profit simply through the circuit M-M', by lending out money and receiving more in repayment.

From the standpoint of the system as a whole, the circuit of financial capital thus mystifies the inner logic of capital. This is why interest-bearing capital is such 'a godsend' for bourgeois ideology, according to Marx, since it mystifies the real social process by accruing profit without passing through the underworld of production. Appearing to generate profit without the mediation of labour, interest-bearing capital comprises an 'automatic fetish,' money that seems capable of breeding more money from itself. Self-expansion appears here as an inherent property of money: 'Like the generation of trees so the generation of money...seems a property of capital in this form of money capital'. The actual social relation without which capital cannot subsist (wage-labour) is occluded; it thus appears as if 'the *thing* (money, commodity, value) is now

---

122. Banks, particularly in an era of decommodified money, also have significant means of creating credit-money, a process I leave to the side for the moment.

already capital simply as a thing'.[123] In this pure fetish of money-capital, based on the circuit M-M', we encounter a fantastic bourgeois utopia where capital endlessly gives birth to itself without entering the mundane world of labour and material production.

It is striking that Marx returns in this context to his favourite line from *Faust*. For in the course of his discussion of interest-bearing capital he intones that 'the money's body is now by love possessed. As soon as it is lent...interest accrues to it no matter whether it is asleep or awake, at home or abroad, by day and by night'.[124] Money, here, seems to participate in alchemy, the magical transformation of one material into another, particularly the translation of base-metals into gold. Paper-assets – not only bank-loans (which are assets for banks because they draw interest), but stocks, bonds, promissory notes or any other form of *fictitious capital* – look as if they possess an inherent capacity to metamorphose into material assets. In truth, fictitious capitals merely represent 'future claims on surplus value and profit',[125] claims which become literally fanciful should the borrower default in the event of failure to generate adequate profits.

Let us take the most elementary case of a fictitious capital, a share, a piece of paper that entitles its owner to a tiny portion of a company's future profits – *if* they ever materialise. Now, in principle, these stocks are backed up by material assets (means of production, stocks of goods, bank-holdings). And these, when joined to labour, can generate commodities which, if sold in adequate numbers at sufficient prices, will yield profits. Should all this happen, paper-claims on potential wealth can be realised as actual wealth. But, in the world of finance and speculation, as Marx noted, these certificates 'can also become duplicates that can themselves be exchanged as commodities'. In this case, a paper-asset with only a potential value begins to operate as if it were a commodity (a repository of abstract labour). As prices for these paper-titles to future wealth rise, a whole structure of hyper-fetishism arises in which people frantically believe in the magical properties of paper-assets

---

123. Marx 1981, pp. 516, 517, 516.
124. Marx 1981, pp. 517–18.
125. Marx 1981, p. 362. On fictitious capital see Marx 1981, pp. 595–601. It should be added that fictitious capitals can be composed of claims on shares of future working-class incomes, as in the shape of mortgage or credit-card debt that is securitised, i.e. sold as a financial asset.

to become ever more valuable. Rather than bearing a definite proportion to the value of the underlying real assets of a firm, paper-assets seem to take on a life of their own, inflating without reference to anything 'real.' This, as we shall see, has also given rise to absurd claims for a postmodern economy of speculation in which distinctions between the real and the fictitious no longer apply. Yet, as the crisis that broke in 2007–8 revealed, just like every great crisis of capital before it, when such paper-claims 'circulate as capital values, they are illusory, and their values can rise and fall quite independently of the actual capital to which they are titles'.[126] Eventually, the fictions will be exposed, the bubbles will be burst. Throughout the course of 2008, for instance, as something like $50 trillion in nominal wealth evaporated from the world's stock- and credit-markets, a financial cataclysm drove home the persisting difference between 'real' and fictitious assets. This is not to say that fictitious capitals do not sometimes assist actual accumulation and that they do not have real social-economic effects. It is to insist, however, that claims on future wealth are just that – claims that may, or may not, be realised.

It is interesting, in this regard, that crucial parts of *Faust* deal with the magic of paper-currency. When Faust and Mephistopheles visit the Emperor of a fictive kingdom, they instruct him (and his Lord-Treasurer) in the new alchemy of money. Thanks to the 'magic powers' of Mephistopheles, 'paper-wealth' is substituted for commodities ('pearls or gold') and, not being subject to the material limits of the latter, it acquires the capacity for infinite accumulation. Enchanted by the fantastic powers of paper-money, the Lord-Treasurer proclaims, 'I gladly take as colleague the magician'.[127] In these crucial sections of his text, Goethe depicts the system of national paper-money as a modern form of alchemy.[128] It is clear that Marx intends something similar with his analysis of money and fictitious capital. While much clearer about the capacities of state-issued currencies and credit-monies to drive a capitalist economy, Marx also recognised that, in the realm of apparently free-floating paper-assets, the line between truth and fiction, real capital and fictitious capital, seems to dissolve – particularly in the late-capitalist world of proliferating financial instruments. Yet, to take this as the truth, as the whole story, is to collude

126. Marx 1981, p. 608.
127. Goethe 1959, Act One, pp. 68–73.
128. Binswanger 1994, p. 33.

with the hyper-fetishism that obscures all connection of wealth to the world of labour, to the hidden abode of production.

Now, we can see the superficiality of the political economy of postmodernism advanced by theorists such as Jean Baudrillard and Jacques Derrida. As I have shown at length elsewhere,[129] these postmodern thinkers take precisely these fetishes of financial capital at face-value and imagine capitalism entirely in terms of self-birthing, self-expanding money. 'Money is the only genuine artificial satellite', writes Baudrillard. 'A pure artifact, it enjoys a truly astral mobility...it rises and sets like some artificial sun.' Indeed, this pure artifact, this new solar centre of the economy, involves 'a sort of ecstasy of value, utterly detached from production and its conditions; a pure empty form'.[130] Entranced by the seeming dematerialisation of money and the increasingly esoteric operations of finance-capital, a slew of postmodernist commentators have sealed their complicity with the fetishism of commodities by conjuring away the labouring bodies upon which the circuits of capital rest. A trendy 'anti-foundationalism' thus becomes the frame for an account of (post)modern society as a world without bodies, one in which we no longer need a critical theory of value to illuminate the hidden recesses of capitalist social life. Baudrillard shrinks from none of these conclusions, proclaiming 'The end of labour. The end of production. The end of political economy' and announcing that we have arrived at 'the end of the scene of the body'.[131] Postmodernist theory of this sort thus mimics late capital's own narrative, in which sweatshops and bodies in pain have been erased by the digitised circuits of the so-called age of information.[132] In so doing, it utterly fails as a critical theory, entirely unable to account for traumatic global financial meltdowns, of the sort that started in the summer of 2007, and the very real suffering, ruin and death they spread. In forfeiting a hermeneutics of suspicion in the face of the preposterous self-representations of late capitalism, in refusing to see contradiction and crisis at the heart of capitalism and its financial forms, such postmodern theory exposes itself as mere apologetics, as uncritical theory.[133]

---

129. See McNally 2001, Chapter 2.

130. Baudrillard 1993, pp. 33, 35.

131. Baudrillard 1993, p. 34, and 1990, p. 25. Baudrillard first articulated his confused break from value-theory in *For a Critique of the Political Economy of the Sign* (1981). I have explicated Baudrillard's many confusions in this area in McNally 2001, pp. 63–70.

132. See McNally 1998, pp. 99–106.

133. A term applied by Christopher Norris to Baudrillard, with respect to the latter's view on the First Gulf War. See Norris 1992, especially Chapter 1 and Postscript.

This is not to deny that there are new forms of finance-capital, to which I turn shortly, unique to the era of neoliberal globalisation. It is to insist, however, that these urgently require the sort of decoding performed by Marx. And it is to remind ourselves again that the great virtue of a major genre of monster-stories, from *Frankenstein* to the urban vampire-tales flourishing throughout the African subcontinent, is their obsessive tracking of the human bodies and unseen labours that feed the machinery of accumulation. More than this, in insisting that something monstrous is at work, and in warning of the risks global financial circuits pose to human bodies, these fables can equip us with a form of night-vision that illuminates the neoliberal world of wild money.

Wild money: the occult economies of late-capitalist globalisation

Late capitalism is a conjurer's realm of wild money. So demonically out of control is financial wealth that, like an apparition, it appears able to materialise in monstrous concentrations only to melt away just as quickly. Take, for instance, the December 2001 collapse of Enron, a company ranked months earlier as the seventh largest in the United States. A mere year before, as it generated over $100 billion in revenues, Enron was publicly valued at $65 billion. Then, as if at a wizard's command, all that wealth simply vanished. Sold some weeks after declaring bankruptcy, *Fortune* magazine's five-time 'most innovative company in America' went for nothing, literally *nothing*. Or consider the even more staggering collapse of venerable investment-firm Lehman Brothers in the fall of 2008, which shattered confidence in global markets. Prior to its crash, Lehman was valued at more than $690 billion. It too went for almost nothing.

If we seek to understand the occult economy of late capitalism, and its cryptic world of enchanted wealth, it would be hard to find better case-studies than Enron and Lehman Brothers. For here we encounter, in pristine form, the bizarre workings of capital today. Yet, to truly grasp these debacles, we must move beyond the mainstream-tale of corporate greed and corruption. However much Enron or Lehman offer paradigmatic examples of fraud and deceit, what brought them down goes much deeper than that. Their pathologies were systemic, not idiosyncratic. Even one mainstream-journalist has observed that the Enron tale is 'the story of how American capitalism worked at the close of the twentieth century'.[134] And that larger story, to which I return shortly, is also the tale of the 2008 disintegration of all five Wall-Street investment-banks, none of which can be divined outside an analysis of what has happened to global capitalism, and how world money has transmuted, since about 1970.

* * *

Capitalism has always been prone to wild financial speculation followed by great crashes.[135] But there is something unique about the forms taken by speculative bubbles throughout the recent history of capitalism: their inherence in new forms of world-money. In this regard, a crucial metamorphosis occurred in the 1970s.

Throughout capitalist history, money has typically had some connection to a tangible commodity, usually a precious metal. It is not true, however, that precious metals have constituted the predominant money-forms. Instead, paper-monies – and, since the eighteenth century, usually state-regulated national currencies – have generally served as the immediate means of exchange. These *credit-monies* are effectively IOUs that circulate from hand to hand, through one market-transaction after another, based on the belief that they are backed by real economic assets. But as credit-monies – so named because they are issued as credits against the assets (and ability to pay) of their issuer – they are not themselves intrinsically valuable. A US dollar-bill, for instance, costs about three cents to produce, as does a $100 bill. Unlike commodity-monies, such as precious metals, whose value is related to the socially-necessary labour they represent, credit-monies circulate based on estimates of the credit-worthiness of those who offer them. When we carry paper-money in our wallets, or store it on a bank-card, we effectively accept that the central bank that issued this money can guarantee its value; we trust that, thanks to its economic might, we can get real goods in exchange for the paper- (or digital) currency it issues. Most of the time, this is a safe bet. But, where state-currency undergoes a crisis – as happened in Argentina in 2001 –

---

134. Fox 2003, p. 7.
135. See, for instance, Kindelberger 1978.

the credit-worthiness of the national money evaporates, inducing a rush to convert it into commodities or more stable currencies.

The predominant form of credit-money is that issued by central banks, known as *fiat-money*. These have usually been loosely tied to the value of a commodity, most often gold, or to the world's dominant currency, such as the British pound and the US-dollar, which itself usually maintained a metallic link. Such ties have often been fragile – witness the suspension of convertibility of currencies into gold during the Great Depression of the 1930s. But the idea that the world-financial and monetary system can operate indefinitely without any established connection to a commodity is of recent vintage. Even during the era of the so-called Bretton-Woods system (1945–73), the world-economy was regulated by a dollar-gold standard.[136] While the US-dollar was the basic world-money used for settling international transactions, it was legally tied to gold (each dollar being convertible for one thirty-fifth of an ounce of gold). And, since they were valued in terms of dollars, all other currencies were simultaneously priced in gold as well. Of course, most of the time, convertible currencies will circulate without anyone bothering to cash them in for precious metal. By the late 1960s, however, things changed in the case of the dollar-gold standard. As foreign holdings of dollars built up (due to US balance-of-payments deficits), investors and banks began to cash in their dollars. In response, the American government chose to honour dollar-gold convertibility only for central banks. Then, in August 1971, with the American gold-stock having fallen by $6.7 billion in the first half of the year, US President Richard Nixon closed 'the gold window', declaring that even central banks could no longer convert dollars into gold.[137] It soon became clear that this abandonment was more than temporary. The world had entered into an era of *decommodified* money, a global currency-régime lacking any tie to an underlying commodity.

With Nixon's declaration, the world of money changed radically. The global financial system lost any anchorage in gold (or any other commodity) and became a pure and simple national credit-money system (or fiat-money system). All other currencies, which had been tied to the dollar, similarly became

136. For an overview of the Bretton-Woods system see Eichengreen 1996, Chapter 4, and Panic 1995, pp. 37–54.
137. For an excellent overview of these developments, see Robinson 1973, pp. 397–450.

unhinged and began to 'float' in value, often swinging wildly in the course of a day. A new and volatile global environment emerged in which it became increasingly difficult for firms, particularly those operating multinationally and thus utilising multiple currencies, to predict the costs of investments, or the scale of their earnings. The world-economy entered an epoch of exchange-rate volatility – of sharp fluctuations in the relative values of currencies – of the very sort that the Bretton-Woods planners had sought to avoid. As a result, currency-trading quickly became the world's largest market by far.

As monetary instability became the order of the day, so did 'risk-management'. After all, firms that operated multinationally confronted the risk that profits made in a particular national market might be wiped out by devaluation of the local currency. A German multinational, for instance, that made a $50 million profit on its US sales and operations could find itself booking merely a $40 million gain at its home-office if the dollar declined by 20 per cent against the mark (or the euro today). Global businesses thus began to search for 'hedges' against currency-fluctuations, turning to complex finan-cial instruments known as *derivatives*, which are meant to provide protection from financial and currency-volatility. Indeed, the timing here could not be clearer: trade in derivatives, known as financial futures, began in 1972 when the Chicago Mercantile Exchange created the International Money Market; business in currency-futures (purchase of currencies at a certain rate at some future point in time) commenced the next year. During the 1980s, options on currencies were also introduced on the London Stock Exchange and the Lon-don International Financial Futures exchange. And, as much as derivatives have now been extended to a vast array of financial 'assets', their dramatic growth since 1972 has been driven by currency-hedging.[138]

The combined effect of floating currencies, financial instabilities, risk-management instruments and currency-speculation was an explosive growth in the market for foreign exchange (known as the forex-market). Forex, the global business in currency-trading, has become far and away the world larg-est market, and one that continues to grow spectacularly. As Table 2.1 indi-cates, the daily turnover in foreign-exchange markets amounted to $15 billion in 1973, just as we entered the new world of decommodified money. Twelve years later, the daily forex-turnover had jumped ten times to $150 billion,

---

138. For a more detailed analysis of this issue see McNally 2010.

Table 2.1   Daily turnover in foreign-exchange markets, selected years 1973–2004

Year	Amount
1973	$15 billion
1985	$150 billion
1995	$1.1 trillion
2004	$1.9 trillion
2007	$3.2 trillion

Source: Bank for International Settlements

a figure that shocked many commentators at the time. Another ten years on, even that amount looked paltry as daily forex-trading soared to $1.1 trillion. Yet, the steep rise in currency-trading was far from over; by 2004 the daily volume hit nearly $2 trillion, and, by 2007, it had surpassed $3.2 trillion.[139]

These numbers make little sense until we recognise that most currency-trading is speculative in nature. To be sure, businesses operating multinationally need to regularly buy and sell currencies, in order to make foreign investments or to conduct basic operations. But the bulk of forex-trading bears no relation to the actual movement of goods or investment-capital. By the mid-1990s, in fact, the *daily* volume of currency-trading was equal to the average *monthly* volume of trade in goods and services. And, by the late 1990s, the global forex-trade was more than ten times larger than the world's annual Gross Domestic Product.[140] So, while currency-trading became vitally important in an era of heightened monetary instability, it also became an end in itself, a site of tremendous speculative activities. If traders could accurately predict which currencies were likely to rise and which to fall, they could reap enormous profits without ever undertaking the long-term risks associated with building factories, buying machines, hiring workers, constructing supply- and distribution-chains, and so on. Currency-markets thus seemed to offer the capitalist utopia in which money breeds money; it just became a question as to guessing which monies would be winners and which losers. The extraordinary growth of forex-trading thus drove those processes frequently understood as the *financialisation* of late capitalism. And, here, derivatives feature prominently.

---

139. These figures are taken from multiple issues of the *Triennial Central Bank Survey* published by the Bank for International Settlements.
140. Akyuz 1995, p. 70; Singh 2000, p. 16.

Financial derivatives took off from the early 1970s on because they make it possible for the US-office of the same German multinational we have described to purchase a contract giving it an *option* to sell US-dollars at a set rate to the German mark, thus preventing a loss of profits in the event that the dollar should fall. In the event of the dollar rising or staying steady, the firm could choose not to exercise that option, and merely pay the cost of the contract – thus giving a straight profit to the option-seller. But, if the dollar were to fall, the German company would have protected its US-profits for a relatively small price. Similarly, a firm that expected interest-rates to fall in one country and rise in another could purchase a *swap*-contract by which it literally swapped the (higher) interest-rate it expected to pay in one country for the (lower) rate it anticipated elsewhere, and vice versa in the case of interest-bearing securities.

As for the term 'derivative', it simply refers to a financial contract whose price is said to be *derived* from some underlying asset. But, in fact, most of the underlying prices are themselves predictions as to future value. Derivatives, or at least their proliferation in late capitalism, thus reflect a profound transformation in the form of money, in which currencies are no longer linked to past labour (embodied in gold), but largely to future labour, to acts of production and exchange that are as yet unperformed. In this sense, they express a decisive mutation in the form of money in late capitalism.[141] Of course, derivatives in raw commodities, particularly agricultural goods like wheat, have been around for a long time. But the dramatic growth of markets in *financial* derivatives began, as we have seen, in the early 1970s. Indeed, derivatives-markets quickly eclipsed those in stocks and bonds. In 2006, for instance, more than $450 trillion in derivative-contracts were sold. That compares with $40 trillion for global stock-markets, and about $65 trillion of world bond-markets in the same year.[142]

As we have seen, the explosive growth of derivatives was a response to a world-economy characterised by heightened uncertainty about the capacity of money to measure values (particularly prices and profits). Through futures-contracts, options, swaps and other instruments, all meant to minimise risk by locking in an exchange-rate or a rate of interest in a given market, investors

141. McNally 2009, pp. 56–9.
142. See Lucchetti 2007.

sought to overcome financial uncertainties. But the rise of these instruments also created tools with which companies could shift from conservative tactics of *risk-management* (entering currency- and financial markets simply to protect their business-operations) toward aggressive strategies of speculation which actually increase risk – as the world-financial crisis that broke out in 2007 graphically demonstrates. In addition to allowing firms to hedge risk, by buying contracts that protect them from sharp fluctuations in currencies, interest-rates or the value of various assets, derivatives also created new platforms for speculation, by way of bets as to the movements of future prices for virtually anything. The immense speculative (and hence destabilising) possibilities of derivatives reside in the way in which they monetise temporal shifts.[143] As we have observed, like all fictitious capitals, derivatives involve bets as to *future* values – of currencies, interest-rates, stocks, bonds, etc. In this respect, they mirror the new world of global money. If, previously, money had some tie to values based on past labour (embodied in gold, which was stockpiled in central-bank reserves) today it is largely linked to fictitious capitals, such as the US federal debt, denominated in bills and bonds sold by the US-Treasury. As a result, capitalists now try to price money and other paper-assets in terms of future values, by calculating their anticipated prices at some point down the road – a day, a week, a month, and so on. Increased financial volatility is inherent in such a situation, and if predictive models fail to capture their complex dynamics, then not only does their 'whole intellectual edifice' collapse, as former US Federal-Reserve chairman Alan Greenspan conceded during the crisis of 2008, but so can global markets.[144]

The tremendous instability in derivatives-markets, and the immense flaws in the mathematical efforts to model them, is a product of a contradiction at the heart of capitalism. While survival for a capitalist firm pivots on the successful (i.e. profitable) translation of concrete labours into (socially-necessary) abstract labour-times, the fact that contending companies compete over the capture of values means that this translation is always precarious. And an

---

143. Something of this is grasped by Pryke and Alleyn 2000 (pp. 264–84). Unfortunately, their postmodernist leanings lead them to muddle crucial issues by supposing that values can now literally invent themselves. That fictitious capitals ultimately collide with the world of value-relations – witness Enron, WorldCom, or the financial meltdown of 2007–8 – completely eludes them.

144. Alan Greenspan, Testimony to the House Committee on Oversight and Government Reform, 23 October 2008.

accumulation of failures to realise values can generate a systemic crisis. The same occurs at a more rarefied level in derivatives-markets. After all, derivative-pricing models, which guide investors decisions, require that all concrete risks – climatological, political, monetary, and more – be measured on a single metric. It is essential to derivatives-pricing that the relative riskiness of early snow in Florida (and the associated damage to the orange-crop) be measurable against the risk of the yen rising against the dollar, or of the Bolivian government nationalising the hydrocarbons-industry. Derivatives-markets must, in other words, be able to translate concrete risks into quantities of *abstract risk*.[145] And they can no more do this in a reliable way than can firms invariably realise concrete labours as value (abstract labour), and certainly not at levels that guarantee profitability. While the global financial crisis brought that reality home with a crash in 2007–8, the writing had been on the wall since the collapse of Enron in 2000, at the time the biggest bankruptcy in history.

Enron: case-study in the occult economy of late capitalism

Perhaps no corporation better embodied the obscure practices of neoliberal speculative finance or the new forms of hyper-fetishism than Enron, whose spectacular collapse was a portent of the crash of 2007–9.

Launched in 1985 as a natural-gas pipeline-company, Enron underwent a stark metamorphosis in the 1990s. Not only did it evolve increasingly into an online-bank and derivatives-trader, the company's growth was also astronomical. Annual revenues of $4.6 billion in 1990 exploded to $101 billion ten years later, making the firm larger than Sony or IBM. Riding such growth, the company's stock soared to $90 a share. Then came the implosion. By the time it was over, more than $60 billion in shareholder-value had been annihilated. From one of the most valued equities in America, Enron became a penny-stock, trading at a laughable 36 cents a share. Explaining this colossal corporate collapse, most commentators have pointed to fraud and corruption. Both of these vices were certainly in abundance. Yet, there is something too easy about this narrative, focusing as it does on aberrance rather than systemic mutations in millennial capitalism. For the Enron story was simply

---

145. See Puma and Lee 2004, pp. 143–50.

not possible outside the context of the system of wild money established since the 1970s.

That Enron was the product of a *Zeitgeist*, part of a unique moment in economic history, can be gleaned by looking at its wider reception and perception. For five years, after all, *Fortune* magazine lauded the firm, rating it 'the most innovative' in America. Even as the company's crisis was about to break, the magazine ranked Enron amongst its '10 Stocks to Last the Decade'. And the prestigious business-magazine was not alone. Nobel prize-winning economist Myron Scholes, co-author of the formula for pricing derivatives, singled out two corporations as financial innovators of unique scope and power: General Electric and Enron.[146] While his underlying analysis was clearly absurd – joining therein the derivatives-pricing models he co-designed and which imploded in 2007 – Scholes did point to the metamorphosis of these firms from industrial into financial corporations.

In the case of Enron, this metamorphosis conformed to the 'postindustrial' and 'postmodern' model that was all the rage in the 1990s. Under the direction of Jeffrey Skilling, who headed its financial-services division and rose to become president and CEO, Enron sought to shed hard assets in the US – in 1999, for instance, it sold its oil- and gas-producing facilities and its regulated electric-utility – in favour of ostensibly intangible ones. Seduced by nonsense about 'virtual' corporations, Skilling proclaimed that the energy-company of the future 'won't be based on pipes and wires and generating facilities; it will be based on intellectual capital'. So, when entering into the fibre-optics business, Enron officials mocked companies like AT&T for building actual telecommunication-networks. Instead, Enron simply bought access to the networks of others, short-circuiting the development of actual infrastructure.[147] With its soaring revenues and stock-price, Enron looked like proof positive that, in the virtual economy of late capitalism, 'immaterial' assets – brand-names, logos, smart trading networks – are the key to profits, not labour linked to real means of production. Before long, this bit of hyper-fetishism would wreak havoc.

---

146. See Partnoy 2003, p. 303.
147. Excerpts from Jeffrey Skilling's speech at the Arthur Andersen Oil and Gas Symposium, 6 December 1995, as quoted by Fox 2003, p. 76; Partnoy 2003, p. 358.

As the company transmuted into a 'postindustrial' corporation, derivatives-trading assumed an ever-larger role. The rush to derivatives came with Enron's decision to remake itself as, first, an energy-trading firm and, secondly, a bank – and increasingly an internet-bank – that extended credit to those with whom it traded. This strategy was premised on the neoliberal drive to deregulate prices. So long as the government regulated energy-prices, volatility was limited, as was the space for profiting on price-fluctuations. Yet, as anyone who drives a car knows, energy-prices are highly unpredictable. With governments de-regulating prices, Enron rushed into this volatile market, signing contracts to deliver energy at a fixed set of prices over time. In the process, it effectively became a derivatives-trading firm.

Price-deregulation produces volatility in the same way the move into a world of floating exchange-rates did. And, since energy-prices are inherently unpredictable – susceptible as they are to influence by war in the Middle East, a hurricane on the US Gulf-coast, sabotage of oilfields in Nigeria, an especially hot summer or cold winter in North America – they are a prime target of speculation. Correctly guessing the direction of events allows investors to monetise temporal shifts, i.e. to profit from accurately predicting future states. And guessing wrong can spell disaster. Salivating over prospects for the latter in a deregulated energy-industry, Enron jumped into a series of hedge-deals. One of the earliest involved an aluminium-company in Louisiana which bought its gas in local markets but paid a set price to Enron. Note here something crucial: Enron was not providing the gas, it was only guaranteeing a price. The aluminium-firm continued to obtain its physical supplies of gas locally. But, rather than pay a fluctuating price to local providers, it paid a fixed price to Enron (who assumed the fluctuating local costs). This deal is a classic *swap*. Nothing physical was being traded, only two sets of prices, one fixed, the other fluctuating. In its pursuit of price-stability, the Louisiana company bought a contract for a fixed price, while Enron sought to profit from gaps between the fixed (selling) price and fluctuating (buying) prices. Because the underlying prices were derived from gas-prices, a swap like this constitutes a classical derivative. And, once it figured out how to make a profit on contracts like these, Enron quickly branched out into other hedge-markets. It was soon doing billions of dollars in pulp- and paper-derivatives – essentially trading pulp- and paper-prices in the same way it sold gas-prices. Next came derivatives in the weather.

While the idea of the weather as an underlying asset seems a bit far-fetched, it is easy to see how trading a volatile price could lead to 'commodifying' the weather. After all, there are many companies whose prices and profits are dramatically affected by weather-patterns. A hot summer in California, for instance, raises the price of electricity required to cool homes and factories, while a cold winter in Florida, to use an earlier example, adversely affects the orange-crop, thereby raising orange-prices. Governments, consumers and manufacturers thus want protection against soaring heat (and energy-costs), while the energy-firm fears an abnormally cool summer – and the lower prices and profits it brings. Similarly, an orange-juice firm dreads a cold winter in Florida, and the higher prices for oranges a poor crop entails, and would happily buy protection (in the form of a weather-derivative). And, so, hedges were bought and sold on the weather – a form of fictitious capital if ever there was one – as Enron moved into the global casino in every conceivable sort of derivative-contract. Indeed, as one analyst rightly notes, after 2000 'Enron was, in reality, a derivatives-trading firm, not an energy firm'.[148] And as it barrelled into online-trading, its metamorphosis accelerated, especially when, with the launch of EnronOnline, the company added chemicals, aluminium, and copper-derivatives to its operations.

Online-trading quickly became the centre of Enron's activity; indeed, within eight months of its launch, internet-trading dominated the corporation's daily business, with deals hitting $2.5 billion per day.[149] Having struck on derivatives as its cash-cow, the company sought out ever newer markets, establishing EnronCredit.com in 2000 in order to trade credit-derivatives, wagers as to the creditworthiness of a particular company. In this new and rapidly expanding sphere for derivatives, Enron would bet on a firm it considered sound by offering a reasonably priced credit-derivative on it (effectively betting that it would not default – and paying up if it did). If it thought otherwise, it would bet against it, by trying to get another trader to assume the risk (which might involve a complex set of derivatives-trades). A derivative of this sort is typically known as a Credit-Default Swap (CDS). But note two things again. First, no tangible asset is being traded here, just bets as to future states (in this case, solvency or bankruptcy). Secondly, all of these wagers involve high degrees

---

148. Partnoy 2003, p. 297.
149. Fox 2003, p. 234.

of uncertainty. And, given their sizes and the amount of leverage involved, a number of bad bets could quickly trigger a financial meltdown, of the sort that took place at the insurance giant AIG in 2008 when, after it had defaulted on a mere $14 billion of the $1 trillion in CDS-contracts it had sold, traumatising the market, the US-government bailed out the firm.[150]

Like AIG, Enron too made a number of 'bad bets'. The effects of these were amplified by its creative (and often illegal) use of shell-companies to take on huge debts related to its derivatives trades. Known as Special-Purpose Entities (SPEs), such shell-companies are trusts created to hold some of a company's assets against which it borrows. Most importantly, a parent-firm can move large amounts of debt off its books by transferring it to SPEs, thereby protecting its credit-rating and stock-price. It is as if, as a borrower, I could create an alter ego who buys houses and cars on credit, yet without my credit-rating (and the rate of interest at which I can borrow) being affected. More than this, it is as if I could then borrow from my alter ego, offering IOUs in return. By the time it disintegrated, Enron had set up an extraordinary 2,800 offshore-units. By comparison, telecommunications-giant AT&T had merely thirty-six at the time. But it was not just the proliferation of SPEs which was the issue; it was also their structure. Many of them extended the parent-company credit in exchange for Enron stock, valued at a certain price. In effect, then, Enron was borrowing from itself and offering IOUs (Enron stock) in return. But, if Enron stock ever plummeted, then the parent-company would have to assume this debt or extend ever more stock (since more collateral would be required to back up its loans), something investors could be expected to notice. And this, in turn, would spark a downward spiral in the stock-price, in turn worsening the debt-picture and requiring that yet more depreciating stock be issued, or the debt assumed by the parent-company. All of this would lead to further sell-offs *ad infinitum* – infinity being measured here by the zero-point of corporate collapse. And this is precisely what happened once the company's nosedive commenced. With speculators playing Enron's own game – but now by betting against *Fortune*'s beloved firm – Enron stock fell, more debt came onto its books and, investors now betting against its future, the stock tumbled further and further.[151] In short, the very structure that allowed the

---

150. Cox 2008; see also Philips 2008.
151. For a more detailed account see Fox 2003, pp. 230–66.

company to expand via accumulation of fictitious capitals was also biased toward implosion as soon as financial opinion moved against it in a big way. To their chagrin, Enron executives were instructed in the most basic rule of fictitious capital: bubbles eventually deflate. Like a reversing river, the very momentum that had swept Enron to superstar-status now propelled its astonishing collapse.

Yet, to end the story here is to miss another key element in the Enron saga: its implication in the imperialist practices of 'primitive accumulation'. In the age of neoliberal empire, primitive accumulation is often accomplished by using the debt of nations in the South as a lever to expropriate land, natural resources and industrial assets. These forms of 'accumulation by dispossession', to use David Harvey's apposite term, entail the exercise of enormous economic pressures by global banks, Western governments, and neoliberal agencies (like the IMF and the World Bank) that press agents in the South into offering up public assets and natural resources to global creditors.[152]

Not surprisingly, this process took off in the 1970s, as institutions holding dollars that could not be converted into gold sought out borrowers – and found many of them in governments of Third-World nations. In the decade after 1973, more than $480 billion was loaned to countries in the South, quintupling total Third-World debt in a mere ten years. Then, at the end of the decade, these Third-World borrowers were cruelly hammered by soaring interest-rates on these loans. And as the world-economy staggered into another recession (1980–2), many debtor-nations teetered on the brink of insolvency. Indeed, after Mexico announced in August 1982 that it was broke and could not repay its loans, some thirty countries lined up to refinance more than $400 billion in foreign debt.[153] Rather than treat this as a crisis, Western bankers and bureaucrats saw it as an opportunity. The desperate need for debt-refinancing was fashioned into a whip with which to impose neoliberal structural-adjustment programmes of privatisation, deep cuts to social-service spending, and financial liberalisation as conditions of new loan-arrangements. Budgets, investment-laws, economic policy and the like were all effectively re-written so as

---

152. See Harvey 2003, Chapter 4. Harvey's description of a number of predatory practices within late capitalism is quite salient. However, there are a number of ambiguities in his use of the Marxian idea of 'primitive accumulation', as Ellen Meiksins Wood (2006, pp. 9–34) points out.

153. Gwynne 1986, pp. 19–21.

to further open the human and natural resources of the South to ever more intensive exploitation by capital from the North. Inevitably, none of these concessions lowered the debt-burden. In fact, in the two decades after 1980, the external debt of Third-World countries more than quadrupled – from $586 billion to over $2.5 trillion by 2000.[154] And this only gave Western capital more stimulus to accumulate via dispossession.

In addition to structural-adjustment programmes, which opened up national economies to extensive foreign ownership, capitalists from the North used debt for equity-swaps, forgiving loans in return for assets (factories, mines, water-systems, offices, hotels, pipelines and more), thereby dispossessing local states and capitalists of their property. While this tactic was used aggressively throughout Latin America in the 1980s, it acquired especially ominous dimensions during the East-Asian crisis that erupted in 1997. Not only did pressures from the IMF force the governments of these nations to open their banking, insurance- and securities-markets to foreign firms, but the devaluation of local assets (as a result of the collapse of currency values) enabled foreign capital to buy them up on the cheap. Indeed, some analysts suggest that the invasion of American and Japanese capital into the region may have precipitated 'the biggest peacetime transfer of assets in the past fifty years anywhere in the world'.[155]

It is in this context of systematic bullying and domination of indebted nations in the Global South that Enron entered the stage of global predation. Over the years, Enron acquired rights to build a huge power-plant in Dabhol, India, about 100 miles south of Bombay; to construct similar plants in Turkey, and one on an island off the coast of China; to develop a nearly 2,000 mile-long gas-pipeline from Bolivia to Brazil, described by the *Washington Post* as 'Enron's scar on South America' for the damage it would wreak in Amazonian forests; to operate water- and sewage-systems in Cancun, Mexico and in two regions of Argentina; to run an electrical utility in Sao Paulo, Brazil; and to build a power-plant in Indonesia. All these initiatives were part of a process of commodifying precious resources (Enron also moved aggressively into the global water-business) in order to profit from control over resources and/or the means to generate and transport them, such as power-plants and

---

154. World Bank 2001a, p. 248.
155. Wade and Veneroso 1998, p. 20.

gas-pipelines. Enron thus figured centrally as one of the 'new enclosers' of the global commons.[156] But enclosure of the global commons, by dispossessing Third-World peoples of natural resources and the means of distributing them, frequently pivots on pressure from imperial states and their associated 'multilateral' agencies, like the World Bank and the IMF. And Enron was well connected in this regard, closely associated with the Bush clan, which gave it access to two state-governors (George W. in Texas and Jeb in Florida) and two presidents (George the first and George the second).[157] On multiple occasions, White-House officials intervened with foreign governments in countries like Mozambique, whose oil-supplies were in the line of fire, or Argentina, where Enron wanted a share of the country's newly-privatised gas-company. The Argentine deal brought over 4,000 miles of natural-gas pipeline into Enron's hands, giving it effective control over gas-transport in the region's Southern Cone. Enron also moved into Argentina's energy-market in a big way – and its machinations there contributed to the economic catastrophe that ripped through the country in 2001.[158]

Through these practices, Enron sought to dispossess people in the Global South of land, water, pipelines and water-systems. And it was not above using violence to achieve these ends, as it did in India during the 1990s when it procured a contract to build a massive power-plant in the state of Maharashtra, a contract so preposterously lucrative that even the World Bank twice concluded that it was utterly 'one-sided' in Enron's favour.[159] In addition to its extortionate contract, Enron also displaced poor Indians so that it could build storage-tankers for liquid natural gas – an absolutely classic example of accumulation by dispossession. In response, anti-Enron protests escalated – and so did the company's tactics. According to Human Rights Watch, Enron colluded with police who beat and jailed protesters.[160] Yet, as costs of the project rose and as anti-Enron protests mounted, the state-government tried to wriggle out of the contract. In a typical act of neocolonial arrogance, Enron declared that it

---

156. See McNally 2002, pp. 66–70; Harvey 2003, p. 148. It is interesting to note here that actual material assets were indeed pursued in the Global South while merely virtual assets became the norm for Enron's US-operations.

157. See Prashad 2003, pp. 48–62.

158. See Prashad 2003, pp. 97–9.

159. Prashad 2003, p. 100.

160. Fox 2003, p. 55; Prashad 2003, p. 111.

would use contractual guarantees to begin selling off government-properties in order to get its money. Nevertheless, imperial bullying, even when buttressed by interventions by the likes of US Vice-President Dick Cheney and Secretary of State Colin Powell, could not break the opposition. Social movements kept up the pressure and the dispute wound its way through the courts until, shortly before its collapse, Enron effectively abandoned the project.

'Capital comes into the world dripping in blood from every pore'

The Enron case is instructive in part because, critically probed, it provides a key to understanding the occult economy of late capitalism: beneath the esoteric circuits of finance lie material practices of plunder of the world's resources and its labourers. As much as Enron tried to remake itself in America as a financial-services firm specialising in derivatives, its operations always remained tethered to predatory practices in the Global South. As Marx insisted in the crucial Part Eight of his life's work, capital comes into the world 'dripping from head to toe, from every pore, with blood and dirt'.[161] Performing his work of detection, Marx catches the world's rulers with 'bloody hands' as Silko puts it; he exposes their 'crimes of slaughter and slavery'. And so, revealing capital to be a vampire, Marx charges it with sucking the life-blood out of the workers of the world. And this imagery, transposed into the African present, animates the tales of vampires and zombie-labourers that proliferate throughout Sub-Saharan Africa today. Yet, however specific the tales we shall examine may be to their African context, they are not unique to that region. As Latin America too has endured the march of the predators, so it has produced similar fables of modernity.

On the heels of its debt-crisis of the 1980s, Latin America was subjected to asset-raiding on a colossal scale. Between the mid-1980s and the mid-1990s, as much as three-quarters of all foreign direct investment in the region went not to finance new investment, but simply to buy up privatised public firms or financially troubled private ones, i.e. to take over existing assets, usually

---

161. Marx 1976, p. 926.

on the cheap.[162] Yet, at the end of all that looting and pillaging, the region was more indebted than ever. And the people were poorer. In the short space of two years, from 1998 to 2000, twenty million more people fell into poverty, according to the UN Economic Commission for Latin America and the Caribbean. That brought the number of impoverished Latin Americans to 223 million, almost 44 per cent of the population. Throughout the region, close to half the population toils in the so-called informal sector, working for meagre wages without any form of health care, pension-plan or unemployment-insurance.[163] Little surprise, then, that stories of rapacious monsters hunting for body-parts have found a new resonance, particularly amongst the poorest and the most disenfranchised. Such tales have flourished, for example, throughout the indigenous territories of Chipaya, which traverse parts of Peru, Bolivia and Chile. During the 1980s, rumours circulated of human fat being extracted from bodies and exported to the United States to lubricate cars, aeroplanes, computers and other machines. In 1987 came legends of a special army of 5,000 slaughterers, authorised by the president of Peru, seeking human fat as payment for the country's foreign debt. Then, the following year, stories were disseminated about machine gun-toting gringos invading schools and kidnapping children whose extracted eyes and organs were sold abroad.[164]

As the wealth and people of whole regions of the world are consumed by vampire-capital from the North, as hunger and destitution haunt the lives of millions, it is hard to dismiss such fables as fantastic. Or, better perhaps, it is difficult to regard them as merely fantastic. For they comprise a genre of *fantastic realism* that illuminates the way human bodies are systematically ground up by the gears of global capitalism, a genre which is dialectically elaborated in Marx's theory of vampire-capital. It is in this light that we need to ponder China Miéville's observation that 'The fantastic might be a mode peculiarly suited to and resonant with the forms of modernity'.[165] This is certainly true of Shelley's *Frankenstein* and of the vampire- and zombie-tales to which I shortly turn, as it is of key sections of Marx's *Capital*, where tables and chairs dance, commodities stand on their legs and speak, and vampire-capital

162. Petras and Veltmeyer 2001, p. 80.
163. Petras and Veltmeyer 2003, pp. 6–7.
164. Wachtel 1994, pp. 82–5.
165. Miéville 2002, p. 42.

sucks the blood of living labour. Like their African counterparts, these recent Latin-American tales are fables of monstrosity that map the contemporary devastations of global capital. And like their nineteenth-century predecessors, they also hint at the discontent of the rebel-monsters that comprise the hopeful underside of global capital's depredations.

Chapter Three
African Vampires in the Age of Globalisation

From various parts of Sub-Saharan Africa today come unsettling tales of vampires and zombies and of extraordinary intercourse between the living and the dead. A whole slew of folktales, spanning oral culture, videos and pulp-fiction, depicts processes of magical accumulation that traverse the world of the occult. In Nigeria, newspapers carry reports of passengers on motorcycle-taxis, who, once helmets are placed on their heads, transform into zombies and begin to spew money from their mouths, as if they had become human ATMs.[1] In Cameroon, rumours abound of zombie-labourers toiling on invisible plantations in an obscure night-time economy. Similar stories of possessed workforces emanate from South Africa and Tanzania, including tales of part-time zombies, captured during their sleeping hours, only to wake up exhausted after their nocturnal exploitation.[2] While labour is seen as possessed, money too is said to be enchanted. Congolese stories, for instance, tell of 'bitter' dollars, secreted within their possessors' homes, whose sudden and uncontrolled growth crushes their entrapped owner. Commodities too partake in these bizarre powers of

1. Drohan 2000. The comparison of these zombies with ATMs is made in this article by Professor Misty Bastian, whose work is frequently cited below.
2. Comaroff and Comaroff 1999b, p. 289. On zombies in Tanzania, see Sanders 2001.

expansion; tales flourish in southwestern Congo, for instance, of people being possessed and devoured by diamonds.[3] Similar accounts of extraordinary transactions between money and human bodies thrive in film and video. In Ghana, a popular 1990s video-film called *Diablo* depicts a man who transforms himself into a python, enters a prostitute's vagina and, after metamorphosing back into human form, collects the banknotes she vomits forth – thereby harnessing female reproductive powers for purposes of economic accumulation.[4] More recently, a widely popular Nigerian video-film, *Living in Bondage* (1992–3) – which launched 'Nollywood', today the world's third largest film-industry – portrayed a man who acquires riches after sacrificing his wife and drinking her blood. Literally hundreds of video-films have followed its path, expanding the immensely popular genre of 'voodoo-horror'.[5] All of these examples merely scratch the surface of a rich and expansive popular genre.

As much as Nigerian mass-culture is a focal point for the dissemination of these images, such folktales emanate, with unique local inflections, from one part of the African subcontinent to another, telling of credit-cards that provide instant commodities without registering debt, of magical coins that turn people into zombies, and of enchanted currencies that leave cash-registers and return to their owners after every purchase.[6] Most striking perhaps is the epidemic of stories of dismemberment and murder for the harvesting of body parts that bring riches, either as commodities for sale or as ingredients in magic-potions.[7] In Tanzania, for instance, legends proliferate concerning the murder of children whose skins are sold (at prices of around $5,000) for occult purposes. And among miners involved in the illicit diamond-trade between Angola and Congo, workers maintain that, when digging is unsuccessful, it is

---

3. De Boeck 1999, pp. 198, 187, 188. Since 1997, the former Zaire has been known as the Democratic Republic of the Congo. Like many commentators, I will denote it as Congo, distinguishing it from the small state of Congo-Brazzaville.

4. Meyer 1995, pp. 241–2. Meyer showed parts of this video during a lecture at the European Social Sciences History Conference, Amsterdam, May 2000.

5. See Daniel 2004, pp. 110, 116. On Nigerias video-industry; see McCall 2004, pp. 98–109. See also Haynes 2005, and, on the 'voodoo-horror' genre in Nigeria see Saro-Wiwa 2009, pp. 17–26.

6. Geschière 1997, pp. 148, 152–5, 165. See also Fisiy and Geschière 1991, pp. 261, 264–6; and Geschière 1999, pp. 221–2. See also Comaroff and Comaroff 1999b, p. 291.

7. On Nigeria see Drohan 2000; for South Africa, see Comaroff and Comaroff 1999b, p. 290.

necessary to sacrifice either male sperm or a body-part – a finger or an eye – in order to lift a curse that restricts productivity.[8] Not surprisingly, blood figures prominently in a whole slew of vampire-type stories. In Malawi in late 2002 and early 2003, for instance, government-leaders were widely denounced, and occasionally attacked, for their alleged participation in a blood-theft ring that was purported to trade blood to international agencies in exchange for food-aid. While Malawi's president repudiated these accusations, proclaiming that 'No government can go about sucking the blood of its own people – that's thuggery',[9] such protestations find little traction with people who have seen infant mortality-rates soar and life expectancies plummet in an era of globalising capital.

These Malawian tales are instructive for the ways they situate human bodies in the vampire-like circuits of international capital. This too is a recurrent feature of recent witchcraft-legends. In Cameroon, for example, a host of stories depict local mafias that export zombified labourers to Europe.[10] In another set of narratives from Malawi, youths describe aeroplanes, the essential means of transportation in the age of globalisation, which are built from human bones and fuelled by human blood. Similar occult dialectics of the local and the global are enacted in Ghana, where a young Akan priest promotes his anti-witchcraft shrine by claiming to 'understand market wars' – the better to offer lucrative 'international opportunities' – while another pronounces that 'the god who possesses me...has travelled to London and Frankfurt...he can decide the cocoa price if he wishes'.[11]

As we have seen, perhaps nowhere are legends of enrichment through disembodiment more widespread and compelling than in Nigeria. Popular Yoruba theatre, for instance, rehearses stories of child-stealers who, after abducting their young prey, trap them in secret rooms and use their blood to make medicines which, in combination with the correct utterances, cause money to pour into a calabash set upon the children's heads.[12] In Akinbolu Babirinsa's novel, *Anything for Money*, a Fulani herdsman in northern Nigeria discovers a metal-box containing a human head used for purposes of 'money

8. De Boeck 1998, p. 47.
9. *BBC News World Edition* 2002 and *New York Times* 2003.
10. Ciekawy and Geschière 1998, pp. 3–4.
11. Van Dijk 2001, pp. 106–7; Parish 2001, pp. 121, 130.
12. Barber 1997, p. 94.

magic'. Employed properly, it churns out wads of crisp twenty naira banknotes. But it is in the video-industry that such tales have proliferated most promiscuously. Churning out up to 1500 films annually, Nollywood's most popular genre is 'juju' or voodoo-horror, 'supernatural thrillers involving spirits, vampires and ghosts', meant to 'provide emotionally-satisfying explanations for wealth inequalities of injustices that abound in Nigeria'.[13]

Like all fables of modernity, these legends are more than the stuff of oral culture, literature, video and film. The fears, anxieties and values they express permeate everyday life, defining and shaping social perceptions and political action as much as the domains of folklore, literature and film. One example may be enough to illustrate this point, that of the 'Otokoto Riots' of 1996 in the Nigerian city of Owerri, when rumours of witchcraft sparked a local uprising.

The prelude to the riots was the disappearance on 19 September of that year of a young boy, Anthony Ikechukwu Okonkwo, one of a number of the city's children who had disappeared or been abducted since 1994.[14] Three days later, an employee of the Owerri Otokoto Hotel, Innocent Ekeanyanwu, was apprehended transporting the missing boy's head, wrapped in plastic in the trunk of a rented car. TV-stations widely broadcast clips of the accused abductor holding the boy's head. Within hours of the first reports, hundreds of men gathered in the city's central market and proceeded to attack houses and cars of Owerri's *nouveaux riches*, along with three buildings that housed two 'new breed' evangelical churches and one ashram. On 23 September, the day after his apprehension, Innocent Ekeanyanwu died in police-custody, arousing suspicions he had been murdered to protect his wealthy employers. The next day, police dug up the headless body of the murdered child in the compound of the Otokoto Hotel. A crowd again gathered and commenced to burn the hotel, a nearby department-store that catered to the rich, and a number of select stores, hotels and businesses connected with '419 men', wealthy speculators whose riches are associated with fraud and corruption. On 25 September, rioting and burning resumed, sparked by the alleged discovery of a roasted human corpse at the residence of one of Owerri's young millionaires,

---

13. Saro-Wiwa 2009, p. 22.
14. My account of these events is indebted to Bastian 2003, pp. 65–91; Smith 2001a, pp. 587–613; and Smith 2001b, pp. 803–26.

and of human skulls and 'human pepper-pot soup' purportedly found in the Overcomers' Christian Mission, a pentecostal church where the rich man worshipped. The rioters also targeted suspected traffickers in human body-parts, including Vincent Duru, owner of the Otokoto Hotel, who was alleged to have kept a huge cache of body-parts in a freezer in his village-home.[15] By the time the riots ended, more than twenty-five buildings and dozens of vehicles had gone up in flames.

Several features of these events are especially noteworthy. Not only did the riots target 419 men, the embodiments of illegitimate wealth; they also appear to have been hugely popular.[16] Equally significant, the eleven year-old victim came from a poor family and had been out hawking boiled peanuts for his guardians the day he went missing. The passions incited by his abduction and murder clearly resonated with anxieties about the market as a space that endangers bodily integrity, particularly for the young. Perhaps most instructive is the specific set of exaggerations that animated public accounts of the criminal investigation:

> Rumours, stories and media reports widely exaggerated the number of bodies unearthed at Otokoto Hotel. Newspapers carried reports of 8, 9, 11 and 18 bodies dug up. A front page story in a national daily reported two days after the riots that 'over 20 human heads have been discovered at various spots in the town by angry demonstrators' (*Daily Times* 1996:1). One of the more sensational newspapers led with an article saying that 200 human male organs were found in a goats belly stored in a freezer in Otokotos (Vincent Durus) village house (*Rising Sun* 1996:3).[17]

That the exaggerations should focus on corpses and detached body-parts is, I submit, anything but accidental. Moreover, if we care for the truth-value of exaggerations, to paraphrase Adorno, then we ought to attend to their deep significance as markers of capitalist modernity, as clues to the texture of everyday-life in Nigeria in the age of globalisation. We might approach this deep meaning via an apparently unrelated newspaper-article, published

---

15. Bastian 2003, p. 78.
16. Smith 2001a, pp. 596–8, 609, 604.
17. Smith 2001b, p. 816. There are clearly anxieties about imperiled masculinity at work here, a theme to which I return below.

almost a year and a half after the Otokoto Riots, in which an editorialist with the *Post Express Wired* writes of Nigeria's largest city:

> Our major expressways, within the city of Lagos, have become dumping grounds for corpses…victims of ritual killings.… People are being abducted to make money. While there is wailing and great sorrow in one home over a member of the family that is missing, there is joy and great gladness in some other because the missing man has become a money-machine to enrich it.[18]

Note here the way in which a human corpse becomes a modern 'money-machine' and in which ritual-killings and disappearances are means of enrichment for the perpetrators. It is as if capital-accumulation in Lagos, a 'dumping ground for corpses', traverses a cadaverous economy. While it is true that sorcery is not explicitly invoked in this editorial, the passage bears all the marks of the current genre of tales of bewitched accumulation. As one commentator on the Otokoto events observes, 'stories of child kidnappings, ritual killings, trade in body-parts, and other magical practices form part of a dynamic cultural complex for which witchcraft serves as a crude but widely recognized label'.[19] The author continues by reading tales of kidnapping and murder as phenomena that symbolically 'stand for the violence and polarization that increasingly undergird the structure of inequality in contemporary Nigeria.'[20] Yet, this is to radically under-theorise these events. To be sure, these are stories about the violence of inequality and social polarisation. But they are stories organised according to specific tropes, which pivot on images of dissection, corporeal fragmentation and disembodiment. And the specificities of such imagery require explanation. Consider, as cases in point, the claims for a pepper-pot soup full of human body-parts that is central to the Otokoto events, or the rumour that 200 human male organs were found in a goat's belly at Vincent Duru's village-house. If the popular imagination simply seeks fantastic depictions of inequality, it is not clear why it should turn so persistently to images of dissection, to the chopping up of human bodies.[21]

---

18. Zebulon Agomuo, 'The Era of Killings', *Post Express Wired*, 25 January 1998, as cited by Bastian 2003, p. 84.

19. Smith 2001a, p. 592.

20. Smith 2001b, p. 805; see also p. 817.

21. There are also crucial issues with respect to castration and emasculation, to which I return briefly below.

It is precisely this – the persistence of images of corporeal fragmentation and disembodiment – that I seek to scrutinise. There is no doubt that all such imaginings are multivalent, weaving together diverse strands of human experience – histories of race, gender, class, and kinship; memories of slavery, colonialism and war; experiences of marketised and monetised social relations; the savage consequences of structural adjustment-programmes; the corruption of postcolonial élites; the devastation wreaked by an AIDS-pandemic – into coherent local discourses.[22] There is also little doubt that these images have a multitude of local determinations that frequently elude even the most sensitive ethnographer. But, pulsating through the multifarious local moments of these aesthetics of horror, we find recurring images of accumulation via corporeal dismemberment and possession. And it is this strand – these powerful depictions of enrichment through disembodiment – that I wish to explore as explanatory markers of life in late capitalism. I make no claim for the comprehensiveness of this account. It is inherent in the phenomena under investigation that they overflow with localised meanings. But, unless we are content to adopt a cult of the local, unless we are prepared to ignore the general social phenomena at work at the micro-level, then it is imperative that we take up 'the challenge of linking small acts to wider processes', as one analyst of agrarian change and class-formation in Africa has put it.[23] Of course, to dialectically locate the global within the local involves recognising that the 'macro' itself exists only in and through the concrete particulars that compose it. But the reverse is true as well; the particular exists only in and through its interrelations with other particular moments and experiences. Together, these constitute a concrete totality, a rich complex of 'many determinations and relations', 'the unity of the diverse'.[24] The concepts 'local' and 'global' do not refer, therefore, to actually existing entities or domains of life which the critic must then connect to one another. Even when analytically isolated by the critic, they are always lived together in their dialectical unity. What these terms capture are aspects or *moments* of the rich, complex, diverse and many-sided phenomena that constitute everyday life in the age of globalising capitalism. But, because

---

22. On the ways in which witchcraft-tales remember and rework experiences of the slave-trade, see Shaw 2002; and Shaw 2001, pp. 50–70. On AIDS and witchcraft, see Yamba 1997, pp. 200–23.

23. Peters 2004, p. 306; see also p. 279.

24. Marx 1973, p. 101.

a concrete totality is always internally differentiated, a 'unity of the diverse', we can tease out that diversity by attending to regional spaces within the world-system and the *regional imaginaries* which there arise.

Regions are comprised of complex, differentiated spaces within the world-order, constituted in and through shared histories, distinct patterns of capital-accumulation, and unique socio-cultural and class-formations. By attending to such regional locations in the capitalist world-system, we enter into mediations that constitute the intricate dialectic of the local/global. And these locations can be sites for distinct kinds of social imaginings about the modern world. Such imaginings may indeed be as old as modernity itself.[25] But the 'cognitive mappings' of the whole that characterise globalising capitalism of the early twenty-first century have highly distinct characteristics, frequently pivoting on images of possessive money and possessed bodies.[26] It is typical of the cognitive cartography through which we map the space of global capitalism today that they deploy geographical metaphors: 'South' and 'North' being perhaps the two most significant of such spatial similes. While there are dangers in thinking of social relations in strictly spatial terms – among other things, social differences *within* those spaces can all too easily be elided – the truth embedded in these terms has to do with the reality of differentiated regional locations within the circuits of global accumulation. So, once we begin to identify regions in these terms, we are compelled to recognise the multiple scales on which they operate. As Henri Lefebvre remarked, social space is always *hyper-complex*, a combination of distinct, intersecting, overlapping and contradictory patterns of spatial organisation of human life.[27] The space of my community, for instance, is simultaneously a location for the material and social reproduction of individuals living in a diverse set of household-units, a site for the global reproduction of capital (formed in and through specific regionally-organised industries), a space of local and national jurisdictions for purposes of state-administration, a site of multiple languages (English, Cantonese and Vietnamese predominate in the case of my neighbourhood,

---

25. See Lazarus 1999, pp. 24–6.

26. I borrow the term 'cognitive mapping' from Fredric Jameson 1991, pp. 44–5, 51–4. But, whereas Jameson locates this problem in terms of grasping the 'alarming disjunction between the body and its built environment' due to the presence of 'the great global multinational and decentered communication network' (p. 44), my analysis focuses instead on the relation of the body/self to process of global accumulation.

27. Lefebvre 1991.

for example) and cultural practices. When we speak of regions within a world-system, then, we are referring to locations of specific patterns of life and labour, from infant mortality-rates and life-spans to the predominance of resource-extraction or 'informal' work. At another level, we are thinking of imaginative spaces for the production of meanings. And, as we have seen, however much they mobilise local languages and idioms, regional imaginaries in the world of modern capitalism also aspire to a regional cartography of *global* processes in the spheres of culture, economy and politics.

One of the reasons that local grammars and vocabularies are so powerfully resonant is that capital, contrary to a too-simple picture, does not extinguish the local, however much it works to impose its social logic on pre-existing forms of social life. Despite its absolutising pretensions, global capitalism operates by systematically *re-organising* existing social formations – disarticulating and rearticulating property, labour, authority, gender, sexual norms, family and community – so as to facilitate the accumulation of capital. Rather than literally invent a world in its image, capitalism exhibits a unique dialectic of incorporation, in which it accommodates the particular at the very moment it absorbs and refashions it. As a result, local cultural idioms are replete with knowledge of the global.

Narrating experiences of incorporation into the circuits of capitalism, local idioms subtend the cacophonous language of capitalist modernity. Rather than expressing 'traditional' values and meanings outside of modernity, these idioms capture the concrete enactment of the global at the level of lived experience, as well as the counter-narratives that probe the prospects for other histories, for social projects outside the logics of global capital. To be sure, all such regional imaginaries are formed through the differences – of class, gender, sexuality, ethnicity and more – that comprise the dialectic of the local and the global. As a result, circuiting across and between these locations is a network of contested meanings. And the matrix of flows and counter-flows of meanings includes narratives from the 'peripheries', as well as the centres of economic and cultural accumulation. From the start, modernity has been crucially formed in and through the cultural experiences of Africa and the African diaspora.[28] It follows that capitalist modernity is a world-process, not a

---

28. A point made powerfully by Gilroy 1993. Some of the significant shortcomings of Gilroy's important argument have been underlined by Lazarus 1999, pp. 51–67, and Chrisman 1997, pp. 51–64.

merely regional one, however much it unfolds through global hierarchies and subordinations.[29] Indeed, as we shall see shortly, one of the central images of the monstrosity of the market – the zombie – is a product of the African experience that was reworked first in Haiti, then discovered and adapted by Hollywood, only to be transformed again in recent African folktales. In the figure of the zombie-labourer, a key marker of modernity, we find traces of global circuits of capital and its others, and of the ways in which the latter imagined a new world of experience.

Zombie-tales, like contemporary witchcraft-stories in Sub-Saharan Africa, are thus *fables of modernity*.[30] To treat them as such, however, is to challenge the notion that, since modernity 'disenchants' the world by ridding it of spirits, witchcraft-tales can only be expressions of 'traditional' or 'premodern' values and beliefs in opposition to the norms of modernity.[31] Not only does such a view reproduce the colonialist illusion that Africans are prehistorical, peoples outside of history – precisely the racialised image mobilised by Hegel, which I shall discuss below; it also ignores the extent to which the emergence of modernist notions of space and time had to do intimately with the colonial relation, with the attempt to relate different spatio-temporal orders, such as those encountered in Africa, to that of Europe.[32] Africa and Africans were present at the birth of modernity, however much they are differentially implicated in it. More than this, notions of Africa as a premodern space also serve a deeply apologetic and ideological function, placing the enduring production of global poverty and social exclusion, of *global apartheid*, outside the dynamics of world-capitalism.[33]

In what follows, I shall insist on reading African witchcraft-tales as markers of and challenges to capitalist modernity. In so doing, I have the good fortune of building on some compelling work in critical anthropology, which has insisted that urban witchcraft-legends in Africa constitute, as Luise White

---

29. On this point see Lazarus 2002, pp. 43–64.
30. See Brown 2001.
31. The classic argument is, of course, that of Max Weber. The enduring retort from critical theory comes from Horkheimer and Adorno 1972. For an important gendering of the Adorno-Horkheimer analysis see Geyer-Ryan 1994, Chapter 14.
32. See, for example, Osborne 1995, pp. 16–21. For the implication of Africa in the modern world, see also Mbembe 2001, p. 8.
33. For one incisive analysis of global apartheid in South Africa see Bond 2003.

writes about African vampire-stories, 'new imaginings for new relationships.'[34] Drawing upon older imageries, these folktales endeavour to map the archaeology of the visible and the invisible that characterises a society governed by the commodity-form. As a result, the central preoccupations of these stories register decisive shifts in social experience. To put it baldly, if earlier forms of sorcery dealt predominantly with fissures and fractures among kin, the new occult deals with the life-threatening dangers of an *impersonal* mania for the accumulation of wealth.[35] Where the older sorcery was wielded by and against family-members and neighbours, the new form is typically inflicted on and by strangers. New modalities of witchcraft have thus largely abandoned the economy of the family for that of the market. As a number of commentators have noted, the use of occult power to create labouring zombies appears to be a quite recent and novel innovation within the repertoire of African sorcery.[36] Moreover, so much has the new occult come to inhabit the impersonal sphere of market-relations that, in some cases, witchcraft itself has become a commodity – a power that, no longer inherited or learned, can simply be purchased on the market.[37]

Rather than expressions of traditional values in opposition to the forces of capitalist modernity, recent urban discourses of bewitchment in Sub-Saharan Africa thus comprise complex, multilayered readings of the changing circumstances of social life in the age of globalising capitalism. Certainly, older idioms and orders of meaning are drawn upon in the elaboration of modern cultural semantics. But this is merely to note that meanings are always historical, that they do not conform to formalist principles of structural typology but, instead, involve never-ending re-workings of earlier modes of social thought and perception accompanied by the incorporation of new idioms

---

34. White 2000, p. 22.

35. For an excellent treatment of older witchcraft-practices and beliefs as embedded in kinship-relations see Geschière 1997, Chapters 2, 3.

36. See Fisiy and Geschière 1991, pp. 255, 261, 264, 265–6; Geschière 1997, pp. 139, 147–9, 156, 165; Rowlands and Warnier 1988, p. 129; Comaroff and Comaroff 1999a. For an interesting discussion of similar trends in Papua New Guinea, see Lattas 1993, pp. 52, 59. Peter Delius (2001, p. 443) who challenges the notion that zombies are new phenomena within African witchcraft-beliefs fails to mount any significant case in my view. Indeed, I read his account as *confirming* the position of those scholars who see zombies as new. Ultimately, however, the key question is the added resonance of images of *zombie-labourers* and their connections with money and global markets.

37. See Schmoll 1993, p. 204; and Sanders 2001, pp. 174–7.

of thought and feeling. New ways of imagining thus emerge out of hybrid-configurations of old and new, indigenous and 'foreign' systems of meaning.[38] To take a single example, there seems little doubt that new rituals and structures of belief regarding witchcraft 'accompanied the incorporation of rural African communities into colonial capitalist labour markets'.[39] While employing older idioms, novel and urgent problems of social life demanded new discursive forms, new grammars of experience.

My concern here is with a recent genre of urban African witchcraft-tales – one that speaks to the occult economies of globalising capitalism. These stories emerge according to unique patterns during the last quarter of the twentieth century, the classic era of 'globalisation', and persist into the new one, as a principally urban genre. They take root in a soil in which older kinship-patterns and forms of rural economy have been significantly eroded; they flourish in the increasingly anonymous and commodified spaces of large cities. While they are preceded by other semantic shifts in the folk-lore of witchcraft, particularly alterations that occur in the period between the World-Wars, there is something highly distinctive about the way these tales articulate troubling relations involving money, global markets, zombie-labour and human body-parts. At its heart, this genre of witchcraft-stories seeks to apprehend and evaluate the social practices and social ontology of capitalism – the acquisitive, accumulative, individualist modes of behaviour and the unique processes of abstraction and disembodiment characteristic of an economy organised by value-relations and money. At the same time, it also registers semantic shifts that highlight the intensification of commodified relations and the growing financialisation of contemporary capitalism.

Kinship and accumulation: from the old witchcraft to the new

Before we proceed, a word is needed about terminology. Since Western constructions of African witchcraft have been deeply inscribed by colonialist

---

38. For illuminating studies of these material processes of hybridisation in parts of Latin America, see Gruzinski 1988, particularly the discussion of 'colonial magic', pp. 257–9; Gruzinski 2001 and 2002. See also Rowe and Schelling 1991. For general reflections on these processes, based on case-studies that include Nigeria, see Pred and Watts 1992.

39. Auslander 1993, p. 177. On this point, see also White 2000.

imaginings of 'the primitive', it is tempting simply to forsake the term. This temptation is heightened by the fact that Western sensibility typically identifies witchcraft with evil, thereby obscuring its much more fluid meanings in many African contexts. The local words translated as 'witchcraft', or *sorcellerie* in French, do not carry a universally pejorative charge. In many African cultures, the terms employed refer to extraordinary powers that can be used for either social or anti-social purposes. In addition to this linguistic complication, matters are made worse by the long Western history of exoticising African peoples by reference to witchcraft. Constructing witchcraft-beliefs as 'primitive' and 'irrational', Western commentators have treated Africans as curious objects of amusement, or of 'study' by academic tourists from the global North. Notwithstanding these reservations, in tandem with some of the best work in critical anthropology, I will retain the term, in large measure because this is the language Africans themselves employ to describe occult power.[40] But, more than the issue of terminology, it is the question of meaning that is crucial. For newer urban grammars of witchcraft in Sub-Saharan Africa capture something lost in the *commodo-normative*[41] discourses of the West: a sense of the genuinely monstrous dynamics of a society subordinated to the commodity-form. Turned back on the 'developed' centres of world-capitalism, as well as critically deployed at home, African vampire-tales carry a powerful de-fetishising charge, one that de-naturalises commodified relations by presenting them as both bizarre and mysterious.

Turning now to the semantic shifts within African witchcraft-tales in the age of globalisation, let us begin with an overview of earlier genres. And, here, some qualifications are in order. There is no way of knowing what these practices and discourses looked like before they became objects of study and analysis – a process inseparable from Western contact and colonisation. The travel-histories, memoirs of Christian missionaries and colonial officials, and early work in Western anthropology from which the first accounts of African witchcraft are drawn were bound up with historical processes that dramatically transformed many aspects of African social life. More than this, in a common dialectic of modernity, Africans borrowed bits and pieces from Western

---

40. Geschière 1997, p. 14. For some useful reminders of the exoticising proclivities of Western treatments of African witchcraft see Pels 1998, pp. 193–209.

41. I borrow the term 'commodo-normative' from my friend Ben Maddison (2006, pp. 114–37).

religions, cosmologies and narratives in order to make sense of new structures of experience, many of them formed in and through colonial relations. What we get from these early literatures, then, are particular descriptions of African practices as they appeared to (usually ethnocentric) outsiders in the flux of colonial encounters. Yet, these literatures can be and have been read against the grain in order to cull real and sometimes subversive knowledge from these sources, not only about the biases and blindness of their authors, but also about aspects of African cultural practices. Such readings can be especially instructive where they mesh with later work in critical ethnography and anthropology.

Drawing on such work, older witchcraft-idioms, rooted in rural communities organised around family-farming, appear to have focused on the threats posed by private accumulation to the unity and solidarity of kin-groups and wider communities. Consequently, African communities typically mobilised ethics of reciprocity and redistribution to counter the solvent force of individual accumulation. To be sure, relations of reciprocity were entangled with exploitation and inequality.[42] Nevertheless, such modes of exploitation did not rest on notions of unfettered individual accumulation. In fact, inequality and exploitation were frequently hemmed in by social ethics that discouraged, indeed pathologised, excessive accumulation. For the Igbo in rural communities in Nigeria, for example, wealth that is stored up without being redistributed is regarded as highly dangerous, since it creates 'an unhealthy psychic heat' that can lead to death and disaster. Heat generated by individual accumulation can only be relieved (cooled), it is said, through the redistributive practices of healthy communal life. The witch who seeks to accumulate is, accordingly, perceived as an 'introvert', one whose inwardness involves turning away from the social group.[43] An enclosed self is thus inherently dangerous, since possessive individualists separate themselves off as private accumulators, thereby disavowing communal obligations.

Many African societies thus counterposed private accumulation to social unity, picturing them as fundamentally antagonistic forces. In this worldview, witches are *internal* threats to social cohesion, not ominous outsiders. Even

---

42. Sahlins 1972, pp. 133–4.
43. Bastian 1993, pp. 141, 148. On such notions in Congo/Zaire see De Boeck 1999, p. 190.

when their precise identities are unknown, it is taken as given that witches are members of the local community, people disposed to attack their neighbours and relatives. This stark counterposition between selfish acquisition and communal obligations also explains why many African societies saw the peculiar obsession of white colonialists with personal riches as signalling their incapacity for kinship. This sensibility is captured beautifully in a proverb associated with the Tsonga of the Transvaal lowveld:

> White people have no kin/nation
>
> their kin/nation is money[44]

To use the terminology developed by Karl Polanyi, which is not without its difficulties, most African societies, like non-capitalist societies elsewhere, embedded economic relations within a larger communal ethos (and social rituals corresponding to it) that governed social life. Rather than an independent force that could be counted on to regulate itself, as in market ideology, individual economic behaviour was ordered according to social-ethical norms.[45] For most African societies, the disembedding of economics, the privileging of the forces of private accumulation as ends in themselves, represented an unleashing of demonic energies that, by rupturing the social fabric, turned kin against kin and stimulated an orgy of violent individualism in which people would literally devour others. Like many non-capitalist moral economies elsewhere (which are today reconfigured in contradictory relations with capitalist forms of life), those in Africa have typically seen the economic cosmos in zero-sum terms: since wealth and resources are finite, one person's gain is another's loss. So, when witches disrupt the balance of things by engaging in non-communal appropriation, they invariably hurt others. In the idiom of the Ihanzu of north-central Tanzania, 'What the witch gains, others lose'.[46] Witches thus consume the sources of life itself, rather than recirculate them. Among the Igbo of Nigeria, 'the witch is an improper accumulator, an eater of blood, rather than a redistributor of wealth...she attempts to gain control over what should be communal wealth in order to enrich and prolong her

---

44. H. Junod and J. Jaques, *The Wisdom of the Tsonga-Shangaan People* (Cleveland, Transvaal: Central Mission Press, 1939), p. 78, as cited by Niehaus 1995, p. 532.

45. Polanyi 1968 and 1957. For critical reflections on Polanyi's notion of reciprocity see Sahlins 1972, p. 134.

46. Sanders 1999, p. 122 – see also, p. 125.

individual life'.[47] The witchcraft of personal acquisition – which co-exists, as we shall see, with the witchcraft of levelling – clearly expresses a powerful ambivalence. On the one hand, people fear the destructive forces of unfettered personal acquisition while, on the other hand, they often desire more personal wealth and resent the redistributive duties required of them. This frequently involves a dualistic perspective of the sort one finds among the people of the Bamenda Grasslands in Cameroon, for whom the zero-sum economy of everyday life contrasts with the invisible, enchanted and beautiful world of *Msa*, accessible only to 'cunning' individuals. *Msa* is a realm of abundance and infinite, rather than zero-sum, possibilities. Organised as a market in which 'the only currency is human beings', it is populated by devils, pure possessive individualists and accumulators who respect no social obligations and obey no codes of reciprocity.[48] Such notions of bewitched transactions in invisible markets have long been common to many African witchcraft-discourses, as have ideas of humans as currency, and both notions have been reworked in more recent idioms. In Ghana today, traders associated with pentecostalist churches sometimes imagine that, alongside the visible one, there is also an invisible market in which dealings are conducted in meat taken spiritually from humans who are eventually 'eaten up by witches until they become sick or die'.[49]

Whatever the attractions of individual acquisition, then, it is viewed as both a threat to others and a source of potential self-destruction. As a caution about the dangers involved, many older grammars of witchcraft warn that private accumulation elicits the rage witches feel toward displays of wealth. Among the Ibibio of Nigeria, witches are portrayed as jealous levellers intent on harming those who accumulate and exhibit wealth. Similarly, in the folklore of the Ihanzu of north-central Tanzania, 'modern' witches dislike development, progress and modernity and are inclined to destroy wealth. They too are levelling enforcers of 'nightmare egalitarianism'.[50] Not only do redistributive practices, such as potlatch-ceremonies, preserve group solidarity; by reducing

---

47. Bastian 1993, p. 138. As this passage indicates, many older witchcraft-beliefs are highly gendered, treating women as the group from which witches emanate. This is much less true of the new discourses of witchcraft to be discussed below.

48. Nyamnjoh 2001, pp. 44–5. See also Rowlands and Warnier 1988, pp. 118–32.

49. See Meyer 1999, p. 163.

50. Sanders 2003, pp. 164–5.

accumulated wealth, they protect the relatively prosperous individual from grievous attacks by sorcerers.[51]

Yet, as if to remind us of the ambivalence involved, of the way in which personal enrichment is something both illicit and desired, witches are also said to be greedy. Among the Ihanzu, a predominantly agricultural people grappling with increasing commercialisation, witches have typically been those who reap wealth disproportionate to their land and labour.[52] Thus, as much as witchcraft represents a warning about the harm that may come to those who seek personal wealth, it also expresses a powerful, if illicit, longing for 'magical' accumulation, for acquisition and enjoyment of riches without the performance of arduous labour.[53]

The more fully people are inserted into capitalist relations, the more intense this ambivalence toward individual enrichment seems to become. As much as individuals might disavow personal accumulation, after all, the imperatives of capitalism reward it. For peasants in systems of rural farming, commodification dictates that production for the market, and maximisation of income, are the keys to the survival of the family-farm. Yet deep tensions are involved in resorting to market-logics to preserve domestic farming. In Niger, for instance, many Mawri parents send their sons off as migrant labourers in hopes that their earnings might sustain the family-economy. In so doing, however, parents sever the kin-unit in order to preserve it. The family thereby undergoes a sort of amputation, a dissection which often foreshadows its death – particularly when children do not return. The monstrosities of the market manifest themselves here in a wrenchingly ominous form: as children are sent into the labour-market in an effort to preserve the family-unit, they are frequently 'devoured' by it, disappearing from the lives of their kin. It comes as little surprise that 'tales of death and dismemberment' figure prominently in the rumours of bewitchment that haunt the Mawri imagination.[54]

If capitalist markets disrupt kinship-relations, they are also held to distort the biology of human reproduction. Since hoarding is conceived as obstructing the natural flow of wealth (its perpetual circulation throughout local society), it is viewed as blocking up the sources of life. Indeed, sorcerers are often said

---

51. Offiong 1991, pp. 127–33; Fisiy and Geschière 1991, p. 254.
52. Sanders 1999, p. 118; Sanders 2003, pp. 161–2.
53. Fisiy and Geschière 1991, pp. 253, 260; Sanders 1999, p. 118.
54. Masquelier 2000, pp. 87, 111.

to appropriate the energies of human bio-reproduction for purposes of private acquisition. This, too, resonates with the notion of a zero-sum universe: if wealth is to be augmented and accumulated in unnatural (and anti-social) ways, this can only occur through the appropriation of reproductive energies from the domain to which they 'properly' belong, human procreation. Thus, while witches sometimes kill, their greed also drives them to steal the reproductive powers of others, or to divert their own.[55] The case of the West-African Mami Wata (or Mami Water), intriguing hybrid-creations, is instructive in this regard. Mermaid-like creatures that seduce humans into becoming their spouses, the Mami Wata endow their human partners with riches derived from the ocean-floor – if they renounce human marriage and reproduction. The sexuality of Mami Wata and their spouses is thus redirected from biological reproduction to the production of wealth.[56] By diverting reproductive energies into the dangerous and sterile process of individual acquisition of money and commodities, the witchcraft of accumulation undermines female biological reproduction. Yet, where women are concerned, this raises profound contradictions. After all, while threatening their normal socio-cultural role in a patriarchal society, witchcraft also opens the possibility that women might pursue both sex and wealth for individual purposes rather than for the reproduction of the community.

As women enter capitalist markets in greater numbers, one frequently encounters throughout Africa arresting imagery haunted by the idea of monstrous female sexuality run amok. In Nigeria, for example, young female witches [obanje] are said to manifest 'overwhelming sexuality and satanic avarice'.[57] In southern Niger, people warn of female spirits known as Marias, married women whose insatiable appetite for sex and candy leads them to prostitution, and who are said to often harm and occasionally kill the objects of their seduction.[58] Commodification of social life thus activates fears that

---

55. See Sanders 1999, p. 123; Bastian 1993, pp. 138–9; Meyer 1999, pp. 163–4.

56. See Masquelier 1992, pp. 62–4; Bastian 1997, pp. 123–6, 130–1; Meyer 1999, pp. 164–5. In some variants, Mami Wata are also male (see Meyer), while in others they also have children, 'but rarely have large families' (Bastian, p. 125).

57. Bastian 2001, p. 88. It should be noted that in many African societies women have been the principal market-traders. But their insertion into increasingly urbanised and globalised capitalist markets involves new social relations and dynamics.

58. Masquelier 1992, p. 56.

market-society can wickedly empower women, who symbolically castrate and emasculate men.

But we are now straying into discussion of the new witchcraft of market-accumulation. Before proceeding further in this direction, let me briefly summarise. The older languages of witchcraft posited, as we have seen, a zero-sum economy threatened by the personal greed of anti-social spirits. The envy of witches – both their unnatural passion for acquisition and their hostility to the accumulative practices of others – announced itself in attacks on neighbours and kin. Quite often, this was seen (and sometimes still is) as involving the appropriation of human procreative energies for purposes of accumulation. While providing gripping images of greed and possessive individualism, these languages of witchcraft have been unable to account for many novel features of globalising capitalism. As a result, discourses of sorcery have been reworked in remarkably inventive ways, particularly in urban Sub-Saharan Africa, where the impact of global capitalism has been especially devastating.

Zombies, vampires, and spectres of capital: the new occult economies of globalising capitalism

The dynamics of capitalist accumulation pose a fundamental challenge to bewitched economies based upon the zero-sum image. The apparently infinite capacity of capitalism to expand is simply not explicable in terms of this imaginary. As capitalist globalisation has imposed market-logics ever more directly on millions of African people, older withcrafts have bumped up against their explanatory limits. The Ihanzu, for example, understand that no amount of local theft could possibly account for the vast array of goods they see today in stores and in the hands of the wealthy. As a result, they now speak of something that exceeds traditional witchcraft, a new mode of occult accumulation driven by 'business witches' who do not need to devour and destroy in order to acquire.[59] Magically transcending the limits of the zero-sum game, this new sorcery is capable of potentially infinite wealth-creation, imagined in terms of great mountains of commodities and money.[60] For the

---

59. Sanders 2003, pp. 164–6.
60. Sanders (1999, p. 17) suggests that the Ihanzu find the new economic witchcraft 'incomprehensible'. This seems to me to go too far. To be sure, there is something

Temne of Sierra Leone, the new 'economic witchcraft' pivots on invisible transactions that move money from people's pockets to those of witches, or store it in an invisible 'witch-city', a place of skyscrapers, luxury-cars, airports, VCRs, and street vendors who sell human meat on a stick.[61]

Similarly, novel economies of witchcraft have emerged in Cameroon. Many older modes of sorcery among the Maka of East Cameroon exhibited the anti-accumulative, levelling qualities detailed above. For the Maka, *djambe* has long been wielded by the weak against richer kin. Hostility to modernist plans for local economic 'development' also informs a witchcraft called *gbati*, which originated in the late 1960s. Even more recently, however, new bewitched economies have emerged in Cameroon – known as '*ekong* in Doula, *nyongou* around Mt. Cameroon, *famla* or *kupe* in the West and North West, *kong* in the forests of Central and East Cameroon' – all of which revolve around 'a witchcraft of labour'.[62] These new modes of sorcery speak, among other things, to the practices of *feymen*, successful young entrepreneurs, whose wealth is both magical and global in operation. Among the Bakweri, the practitioners of the new forms of sorcery, *nyongo* witches kill their victims, as do the older-style witches, but, rather than eating them, they convert them into zombie-labourers. Similar ideas are found among many different peoples in Cameroon.[63] Particularly interesting is *ekong* among the Douala (or Doula), a new urban magic in which people are sold rather than eaten. The profits from these zombie-labourers are said to be credited directly to the witches' bank-accounts.[64] Despite their many differences of imagery and nuance, all these new notions of witchcraft share the assumption 'that witches no longer see their fellow men as meat to be eaten...but rather as labourers to be exploited'.[65]

In a similar vein, the Haya of the Kagera region of northwest Tanzania draw a distinction between sorcery and blood-stealing. Sorcerers, who have a level-

---

deeply mysterious and perplexing about it, but the new witchcraft nonetheless represents precisely an attempt to comprehend it.

61. Shaw 1997, pp. 859, 856.

62. Fisiy and Geschière 2001, pp. 232–3, 241, 242.

63. Fisiy and Geschière 1991, pp. 255, 260–2. The authors note (p. 256) that *nyongo* accusations took off in 1955, the period, as I argue in Chapter 4, which represents the emergence of the new forms of imperialism that laid the basis for the era of capitalist globalisation.

64. Rowlands and Warnier 1988, p. 129. See also Fisiy and Geschière 1991, p. 255.

65. Geschière 1999, p. 232.

ling propensity, seek to consume their victims. Blood-stealers, on the other hand, decompose the body into its constituent-parts converting it into 'transactable units' for sale.[66] We witness here a shift from use-value to exchange-value: rather than employing sorcery for immediate consumption, modern economic witches instead harness the productive capacities of victims for purposes of accumulation. In all these cases, bodies are not absorbed *into* the other, but transformed into *extensions* of the other – into forces of production (zombie-labourers) or commodities for exchange. The expansive dynamic of capitalism intrudes here into the very grammar of witchcraft. No longer does demonic greed revolve around the simple appropriation and consumption of finite social wealth. At the same time that African economies are being ruthlessly subordinated to the neoliberal logic of capital, through the combination of structural adjustment-programmes and world-market pressures, witchcraft in urban Sub-Saharan Africa has now entered the limitless circuits inscribed by the globalising logic of capitalism.

One sees aspects of this at work in rural settings as well, particularly in the growing number of regions in which land is being enclosed, privatised and commodified. As these phenomena occur – massively accelerated by capitalist demand for primary products (cotton, coffee, oil, rubber, cocoa, copper and the like) amid rising costs for food and fuel and a curtailing of credit for the rural poor – ownership of and access to land becomes increasingly precarious for the poor, while wealthier groups accumulate at their expense. In such circumstances, conflicts, often violent ones, over land, cattle, crops, and so on frequently provoke allegations of witchcraft. Central to such developments is the erosion of kinship by market-relations, as networks of reciprocity contract, and kin are converted into 'strangers'.[67]

With personal obligations being displaced by market-relations, witchcraft itself takes on impersonal characteristics. Just as capital does not care about the identities of those who make a commodity, but merely about its profitability, so the new witchcraft transcends relations among neighbours and kin, and subtends a novel anonymity. Tracking these changes, people in south-western Congo differentiate between 'the elders' sorcery [*ulaj wa amaleemb*]' and a new 'wild sorcery [*ulaj wa chisakasak*]'. Whereas the former involves

---

66. See Weiss 1999, pp. 188–92.
67. See Peters 2004, pp. 269–314; on witchcraft-allegations in this context, see p. 303; Peters 2002, pp. 155–78; and Woodhouse et al. 2001.

violations of the solidarity and reciprocity appropriate to kin-relations, the latter entails misfortunes in which a person 'may become the victim of a total stranger's evil intentions or greed', evidence of the impersonal pressures of market-based appropriation and accumulation.[68] This impersonal quality is also characteristic of the ritual murder that triggered the Otokoto Riots in Owerri, Nigeria in September 1996. As one analyst notes, 'the *lack* of related-ness between the young millionaires and their alleged victims is one of the most striking aspects of the stories of child kidnapping and ritual murder that circulated in the wake of the Owerri riots'.[69] However horrifying, evil deeds among kin are nonetheless explicable in terms of longstanding con-ceptions of the dangers that threaten communal life. One can at least plan for self-protection if names and faces are attached to those (neighbours or kin) who might threaten you. But if kidnapping, murder and dismemberment become an impersonal business, then the dimensions of horror start to burst the boundaries of the known. In the impersonal tumult of the urban market-place and the modern city, where evil is 'business, nothing personal,' horror enters a terrifying machinery of random violence.

No commentator has more insightfully examined such transformations in the African popular occult, and their interrelation with cultural and economic change, than historian Luise White. In a rich and nuanced analysis, White argues that vampires emerged in the African imaginary only in the twenti-eth century, when the increasing penetration of capitalist imperatives pro-voked new ways of comprehending and portraying the dangers of everyday life. Indeed, she argues compellingly that vampire-stories involved complex efforts to penetrate the mysteries of capitalist labour-processes.

White points out that many of the African terms that denote vampires derive from words used for specific groups who performed highly regimented work-routines. The Swahili word *wazimamoto* derives from the term for firemen, for example, while the word for vampires in colonial Northern Rhodesia, *ban-yama* (*munyama* in the singular) originally applied to game-rangers.[70] Most

---

68. De Boeck 1999, pp. 190–1. An astute commentator has also suggested that 'an impersonal quality is creeping into Nigerian witchcraft'. See Bastian 1993, p. 134, citing Emefie Ikenga Metuh, *God and Man in African Religion: A Case Study of the Igbo of Nigeria* (London: Chapman, 1981).

69. Smith 2001a, p. 595.

70. White 2000, pp. 11–12.

of these terms took on connotations of bloodsucking only in the twenty-five years after the First World-War. They are, in short, early twentieth-century expressions, strictly demarcated from older vocabularies of witchcraft. For this reason, White treats vampire-tales as entirely distinct from witchcraft-stories. I have chosen a different tack, preferring to locate vampires within the vocabulary of witchcraft, while distinguishing among various genres of sorcery. Notwithstanding this difference, the distinctions that White draws are highly illuminating for my purposes:

> African vampires…were a synthetic image, a new idiom for new times.… Witches and vampires were different because they operated in different historical contexts. Vampires were a discursive contradiction – firmly embedded in local beliefs and constructions but named in such a way that their outsidedness was foregrounded. Unlike witches, vampires were not rooted in local society; they did not fly or travel on familiars, but had mechanized mobility. Bloodsucking fireman had none of the personal malice of witches; it was a job. As such, it did not imperil people in tense relationships, it imperiled everyone. Firemen and their agents were not evil but in need of money.… Vampires were outside the social context that witches inhabited in East and Central Africa; they were seen to be internationalized, professionalized, supervised, and commodifying.[71]

This description traces semantic shifts that preceded, but conditioned, those I am describing. In insisting on the novelty of vampires in twentieth-century Africa, White highlights the ways in which new, and increasingly capitalist, social relations called forth new configurations of the popular imaginary. Twentieth-century folktales about vampires and bloodsucking provided, in turn, many of the discursive resources for the more recent spate of rumours and stories – which pivot on the image of the zombie-labourer – with which I am concerned. Over the last thirty years or so, I submit, vampires – or the witches who appropriate human bodies and energies for purposes of incessant accumulation – have become less foreign, particularly in urban settings in Sub-Saharan Africa. While they may be enmeshed in mysterious global networks, they are typically Africans located in the impersonal tumult of economic life in large cities, such as Lagos, as well as considerably smaller

---

71. White 2000, p. 29.

cities and towns, like Owerri. To be sure, the new sorcery is anonymous and businesslike; it is a professional rather than a personal affair. But those who engage in it are increasingly inside-outsiders, Africans who have dangerous connections with the occult forces of global markets and enterprises. Moreover, their victims await a new and highly specific fate: transformation into zombie-labourers.

Let us return, however, to White's appraisal of the emergence of African vampires in the first half of the twentieth century.[72] In a detailed and compelling analysis, she suggests that many African vampire-stories grappled with the bizarre characteristics of capitalist labour-processes and time-discipline, struggling to find hidden meaning within activities that appeared meaningless. She points out, for instance, that firefighters in Nairobi during the 1930s were expected to drill and polish their equipment nine and a half hours a day, while the night-watchman had to make reports every fifteen minutes. For this work, they were well paid by comparison with casual labourers.[73] That such ostensibly pointless activities could garner regular wages was in itself a mystery requiring explanation. More than simply mysterious, however, there was something traumatic involved in subordination to a régime of wage-labour. As E.P. Thompson pointed out in the case of the working class in eighteenth-century England, capitalist time-discipline is often experienced as a brutal assault on the social rhythms of precapitalist life, which are governed less by the abstract time of clocks and calendars divided into quantitative segments (seconds, minutes, hours, days, months) than by qualitative fluctuations having to do with seasons, weather, light and darkness, and the routines of labour, festivity and celebration. The insistence that workers are to report to work at a set time and are to work an unvarying number of hours, day after day, month after month, irrespective of the season, the weather, darkness, or festival-dates – all this involves a rupture in the qualitative patterns of concrete, lived time in societies undergoing conquest by capital. Consequently, workers newly subjected to régimes of abstract, quantitative time – to bells, whistles, stopwatches and punch-clocks – typically find the

---

72. Understandably, White avoids precise dating. She sees African vampires as emerging between 1918 and 1925 (2000, p. 16), then moving across much of colonial Africa during the next two decades.
73. White 2000, p. 133.

experience deeply disturbing, as did African slaves in the plantation-economy of the United States.[74]

In the African context, these upheavals in the character of lived time have often been experienced as painful ruptures in the very foundations of experience.[75] Rather than merely a set of technical changes in the way in which goods are produced and distributed, capitalist wage-labour entails radical disruptions in the fabric of everyday life – of space, time, body and self. The 'spatialisation' of time, its transformation into quantitative units that lose their unique qualities, figures as a dramatic rupture in the texture of the social world. This is especially so once labour becomes regimented by the pace of machine-production. Under these circumstances, not only are human beings treated like labouring machines, they are in fact compared to, measured against and subordinated to the 'superior' productive capacities of machines. Inserted into increasingly mechanised production-processes, human productive activity is treated as a measurable thing-like entity – labour in the abstract, stripped of all its unique features and characteristics. As human activity loses its significance within the automated operations of machine-driven production, it also loses its foundational properties. Rather than the animating power of the production-process, labour is now eclipsed by machines. This 'disappearance' of concrete labour within a mechanised production-process typically imperils conventional understandings of identity. The penetration of the self by machines comprises a monstrous threat to personhood, as if demonic forces are sucking the life from individuals. We should not be surprised to learn, then, that, in the mines of colonial Katanga, accusations of bloodsucking became especially persistent when mine-owners tested mechanised shovels as an alternative to pick-and-shovel men.[76] More recently, the quantification of time has assumed a prominent place in the witchcraft-narratives that have emerged alongside the integration of the Mawri of Niger into migrant labour-markets.[77]

As I have noted, the forms of work and temporality characteristic of capitalism often appear deeply mysterious and threatening to those raised within

---

74. On the British case, see Thompson 1991, and on slave-resistance to clock-time, see Smith 1997, pp. 133–50.
75. On this point see, for example, Auslander 1993, p. 175.
76. Higginson 1988, pp. 101–2.
77. Masquelier 2000, pp. 106–7.

alternative orders of experience. In a number of African vampire-tales, as we have seen, it is taken for granted that something hidden and illicit is at work when firemen, for example, endlessly conduct drills and polish their machines and equipment. The apparently senseless repetition of physical movements and the deeply intrusive forms of work-supervision are assigned enigmatic meanings drawn from the grammars of witchcraft. During the period between the World-Wars, police-recruits in Kampala, for example, often believed that their highly regimented, hierarchical and supervised work-processes disguised a régime of bloodsucking. Vampire-pits so hidden that they escaped the observation of most recruits were said to exist beneath station-floors – a theme repeated in similar contexts in other parts of Africa.[78]

The structure of these tales delineates a cardinal feature of capitalism: the elusive purpose of the complex apparatus of capitalist production, supervision, and the perpetual motion of disciplined labour that drives it. The animating goal – the exploitation of labour and the production of surplus-value for capital – remains obscure. As much as workers can feel its effects, they cannot see or touch the exploitation that marks their lives. Moreover, the same disciplinary régimes are imposed on those – police, firefighters, nurses, and so on – who are not engaged in commodity-production, and their rationale is, if anything, even more perplexing. By contrast, peasants forced to pay rents to a landowner have a hard and fast grasp of what is at stake; they know precisely the amount of product, money or hours of labour they turn over to their immediate rulers. However much it may be resented, their exploitation is anything but mysterious. In capitalist society, on the other hand, an inherent mystery pervades work-processes. Workers appear to be paid the value of their labour (wages) according to principles of free and fair exchange, yet an invisible process of exploitation transpires all the same, one that fuels the accumulation of capital. These obscure techniques of accumulation become even more puzzling in the era of capitalist globalisation with the rise of remarkably complex, enigmatic forms of financial accumulation discussed in Chapter Two.

Whatever else they may do, the vampire-tales analysed by Luise White endeavour to probe the mysteries of wage-relations and capitalist labour-processes. Convinced that something more is going on than what meets the

---

78. White 2000, pp. 138, and 133–46 passim.

eye, these stories seek to map an archaeology of the invisible in capitalist modernity. This is doubly so for the more recent witchcraft-narratives, which interrogate the occult powers that turn people into labouring zombies and human ATMs. In their hunt for the bodies that are being harmed and the blood that is being sucked, these stories seek out traces of the corporeal powers upon which capital feeds. Searching out the hidden processes by which embodied powers are appropriated and exploited, tracing the outlines of an occult economy that subsists on the energies of labouring bodies, the new genre of African witchcraft refuses the bourgeois narratives in which capitalist wealth gives birth to itself through a self-reproducing machinery that knows neither victims nor losers.

In their insistence that something not-quite-real is at work within global capitalism, some occult process of exploitation that conceals itself, these tales carry a *defetishising* charge. Across these stories, real bodies are implicated and at risk: they perform unseen zombie-labour; they are possessed by evil spirits that turn them into money-machines; they are dissected for marketable parts. A hermeneutics of suspicion animates these folktales, a thoroughgoing mistrust of the claim, popular among postmodern theorists of the so-called informational economy, that we have transcended the economics of materiality. For all their involvement with witches and spirits, these stories are driven by a materialist impulse to search out the sites where labouring bodies are at risk. And, in seeking out those bodies, these African discourses of witchcraft detail the ways in which they are enmeshed in dangerous logics of exploitation and accumulation – nowhere more life-threatening than in Sub-Saharan Africa itself.

African fetishes and the fetishism of commodities

Having dared to raise the issue of fetishism, we are obliged to interrupt our story. For to invoke the fetish is to enter a territory shaped by the colonialist imaginary. The Western discourse of fetishism emerged, after all, in the early-modern period when European traders and colonisers sought to regulate their shock over the ostensibly perverse, non-market values to which Africans subscribed. Deeply unsettled by the refusal of Africans to part with certain goods irrespective of what was offered in return, even substantial amounts of gold, European merchants invented the African fetish, a term derived from the Portuguese *feitiço*, which was adapted in turn from the Latin *facere* (to make or produce) and *facticius* (manufactured, artificial).[79] As this derivation indicates, fetishes were regarded as entirely artificial entities. Rather than conforming to the natural (market-) laws of the economic cosmos, they represented strange and unsettling human evaluations of things. These valuations were disturbing insofar as they substituted human conventions for the 'proper' relations among things (exchange-values) ostensibly ordained by God. They hinted at a world of chaos and caprice, beyond the rule-governedness of science, religion and the market. By treating the sacred items Africans would not trade as fetish-objects, as expressions of bizarre and 'primitive' human customs, European merchants simultaneously construed their own marketised value relations as part of the natural order of things, while positing African customs and practices as outrageous violations of all that is decent and proper. This was the interpretation advanced by the Dutch writer Willem Bosman whose book, *A New and Accurate Account of the Guinea Coast* – published in 1703, issued in English and French translations by 1705, and released in German in 1706 – decisively shaped the 'enlightened' European discourse of fetishism. Both Newton and Locke owned Bosman's book, and the text was cited by Adam Smith in his *Lectures on Jurisprudence*.

The concept of fetishism received its most protracted eighteenth-century treatment in Charles De Brosses's *Du culte des dieux fétiches* (1760), a text that drew the attention of the young Marx. In opposition to those who saw fetishes as allegorical (as had many early-modern analysts of ancient Egypt), De Brosses was a literalist who read the attribution of extraordinary powers to animals and things as pure and simple idolatry. Moreover, he universalised fetishism; rather than a uniquely African phenomenon, he saw it as natural to all childish, primitive, uncultivated, pre-rational minds, as an aberration born of fear and madness.[80]

Let us now submit this analysis to a dialectical reversal. By interrogating the fetish as a product of the fears of the Europeans who constructed it, rather than of those upon whom it was projected, we can discern the anxious premonition the concept was meant to contain: in insisting that certain goods not

---

79. See Pietz 1985, p. 5, and Brantlinger 1996, p. 42. See also the remarks by Mudimbe 1988, pp. 9–10.
80. Manuel 1967, pp. 203–4.

be commodified, after all, Africans were exposing as fictive all claims for the universality and naturalness of the European market-economy.[81] In a revealing passage in a book published four years before *Du culte des dieux fétiches*, De Brosses claims of 'primitive peoples', for example, 'Almost everywhere they have been found in a state of ferocious stupidity, perfidious and unapproachable. In some places they have even appeared to lack a taste for commerce and for the novelties which have been shown to them. They have maintained an obstinate silence'.[82] This obstinate silence represents the refusal to name a price, the unwillingness to agree that every object must have a market-value. For Europeans imbued with the commercial mentality, with the idea that the market-economy corresponds to the natural order of things, this silence before the gods of the market, was nothing less than heresy, a perverse refusal of one's natural duty. The idea that some things transcended the laws of value and exchange and could not be priced amounted to the claim that these laws were not natural, invariable and transhistorical. If, in fact, every human had a 'natural propensity to truck, barter and exchange one thing for another', as Adam Smith urged, then how could it be that Africans and others lacked 'a taste for commerce?' The only reassuring answers were that Africans had undergone some perversion from the natural course of things, or that their nature was not entirely human. In the face of the anxieties aroused by the non-market values of African peoples, Europeans constructed a marker of African primitiveness and perversion: the fetish. This construct tamed the anxieties brought on by observation of peoples who shunned the logic of the market. As in Freud's account of sexual fetishism, the fetishist is reassured by the creation of an object that covers over a frightening absence.[83] But, instead of the absent female phallus, European traders and writers invented the fetish in order to mask the absence of market-values among Africans. In their case too, a frightening discovery – that market-logic is by no means universal – was denied. After all, the only real alternative to constructing the discourse of the

---

81. On this phenomenon, see Guyer 1998, p. 250. I should point out that my reference to European market-economy does not imply that the whole of Europe was fully capitalist at this time. While only England had traversed the road to capitalism, marketised relations had developed a sustained significance within most European economies at the time.

82. De Brosses 1756, p. 44.

83. See Freud 1997, pp. 351–7. For a summary of Freud's analysis see McNally 2001, p. 71.

fetish – and its mapping of the natural versus the perverse – would have been to acknowledge the historicity of European market-relations, to recognise that the system was anything but natural and universal. And this would have been to contribute to a *defetishising* critique of capitalism itself. In an interesting passage in *Capital*, Marx suggests: 'The whole mystery of commodities, all the magic and necromancy that surrounds the products of labour on the basis of commodity production vanishes...as soon as we come to other forms of production'.[84] He forgot to add, however, that this mystery will not vanish if, in the face of other forms of production, people imbued with market-rationality manufacture the idea of the fetish. As a defensive reaction-formation, a structure of denial about the historicity of capitalism, the fetish preserved the ostensible universality of capitalism. Or, to put it somewhat differently, the European creation of the African fetish closed off defetishising knowledge of capitalism itself.

If this was the function of the fetish for Europeans unsettled by the non-market values of African peoples, what can we say of its content, of the actual properties Europeans attributed to fetishes? As William Pietz observes, the African fetish as constructed by the European Enlightenment is irreducibly material and singular.[85] Rather than seeing every entity as partaking of a universal category – or, in the case of the capitalist economy, seeing every good in terms of a general property (value) that makes it exchangeable with any and every other – Africans ostensibly held to the idea that some things were radically unique, not commensurable with others. Uncritically accepting this view of the African mind, Hegel proceeded to deny reason and history to Africa. The attribution of divine power to singular objects demonstrates, he argued, that Africans lack the category of universality, the basis of human rational thought. Rather than a world organised in terms of universal relations (which are the stuff of scientific knowledge), Africans inhabit, according to Hegel, a fantastic world of fetish-objects that simply reflect 'the arbitrary choice' of those who made them.[86]

---

84. Marx 1976, p. 169.
85. Pietz 1985, pp. 7–10. That this radical singularity was not the truth of 'fetishes' for Africans is argued by McCarthy 1994, pp. 126–7.
86. Hegel 1991, p. 94. For an absolutely path-breaking reading of Hegel in relation to colonialism, slavery and anticolonial struggles see Buck-Morss 2009.

One discerns in Hegel's analysis, which rehearses a racist anthropology of the civilised and the barbaric, the presence of repressed colonial desires. After all, the insistence that Africans are attached to the irreducible singularity of material things is easily read as containing a secret urge to escape the abstracting circuits of the commodity-form. In returning to the material uniqueness of things, in attending to what makes entities different to sensate bodies, African fetish-objects, as imagined by Europeans, carried a powerful erotic charge.[87] It is interesting in this regard that, for Africans, many of these fetishes are objects of the body, devoted to its health, biological reproduction, and the well-being of embodied social organisation, the body-politic. 'Fetishes' are thus directed to the types of corporeal needs and desires that are systematically suppressed in the abstracting logic of commodification.

The young Marx may have intimated something of this when he seized on one European characterisation of fetishism as 'the religion of sensuous desire'. Initially, however, Marx simply used a strategy of reversal, turning the charge of fetishism back against the ruling classes of Europe, insisting that it was they who bowed down before objects: gold in the case of the Spanish colonisers of the Americas, and wood where the rulers of the Rhineland were concerned.[88] Rather than the rationalists they believe themselves to be, claimed the young Marx, the European ruling classes in fact idolise things, they engage in fetish-worship. Clearly, there is much to this argument. Consider, for example, the map published with the first English edition (1705) of Bosman's *New and Accurate Account of the Guinea Coast, Divided into the Gold, the Slave and the Ivory Coasts*, where, as the title suggests, coastal spaces are identified with commodities. One encounters here a *geography of commodities*, with the West-African coast mapped in terms of commercial goods sought by Europeans. In a mania of reductionism, the Guinea coast is divided into four commodified segments, thus inscribing the totalising logic of the commodity-form into the land itself, and reducing the rich diversity of Africa, including its people, to a list of commodities.

Marx's ironic attack on the European ruling classes as idolaters, as people who worship things, finds its vindication in a map such as this. But, as he

---

87. See Pietz 1988, pp. 111–12.
88. Marx, 'The Leading Article in No. 179 of the *Kölnische Zeitung*', in Marx and Engels 1975a, p. 189; and Marx, 'Debates on the Law on Thefts of Wood' in Marx and Engels 1975a, pp. 262–3.

developed his systematic critique of political economy, Marx observed an even greater irony: that commodity-fetishism is also a religion of *non-sensuous* desire. However much capitalist fetishism bows down before things, its true god is entirely immaterial. After all, it does not want these things for their material properties; rather, it seeks that common (invisible and immaterial) property they all contain – value. This is the great insight of Peter Stallybrass, who grasped the powerful irony that drives Marx's defetishising critique. 'To fetishize commodities is, in one of Marx's least understood jokes', he writes, 'to reverse the whole history of fetishism. For it is to fetishize the invisible, the immaterial, the supra-sensible'.[89]

The value of commodities on capitalist markets has nothing to do, after all, with their sensible, material features. If it did, then radically dissimilar goods – from grain to gold, iron to digital information, coffee-beans to the act of copulation – could not exchange with each other and could not be measured on the same scale (via money). Yet, despite their radical dissimilarities, any and all goods in a capitalist economy (and this includes 'services') can enter into exchange with the whole world of commodities. Every conceivable good can have a price, a marker of its universal exchangeability. This can only mean, however, that the commensurability of goods, their capacity to operate as repositories of value in a world of commodity-exchange, does not reside in any of their material properties – if it did, then they could not exchange with those that lacked these properties. Value must, as we have seen, be something immaterial, something all commodities share irrespective of their sensible differences. It is only their property as products of human labour in the abstract, labour stripped of all material specificity, which makes commodities commensurable. But this means that value, the driving force that generates the manic activity of capital, is entirely invisible, intangible, an objectively effective power that operates by means of a 'phantom-like objectivity.'[90]

When we fetishise commodities, therefore, we attribute extraordinary powers to an *immaterial* substance. However much we may confuse the value of things with their material being (which results in the crude materialism associated with commodity-fetishism) we are, in practice, bowing down before something 'phantom-like', something supra-sensible. This allows us

89. Stallybrass 1998, p. 184.
90. Marx 1976, p. 128.

to appreciate the cleverness of what Stallybrass describes as 'one of Marx's least understood jokes'. For, if Africans are alleged to have worshipped the irreducible materiality of things, to have participated in a 'religion of sensuous desire', the commodity-fetishist practices an even more bizarre religion of non-sensuousness, a fantastic desire for the merely spectral form of things.

Many commentators miss the significance of this critical move, in part because they trace the theory of commodity-fetishism to the Protestant critique of idolatry. This interpretation sees Marx's concept as heir to a religious critique of practices that substitute human artefacts and customs for nature. The central error of this heresy is said to be that it dignifies human labour in place of God's work, contributing thereby 'to a fetishisation of the merely human'.[91] Yet, to read the theory of commodity-fetishism in these terms is, as we noted in Chapter Two, to miss a central thrust of Marx's historical materialism, in which it is the elevation of the gods of value and capital above human agents that is the problem. Marx thus significantly reverses the Lutheran criticism, which is fundamental to all idealism/spiritualism, by locating fetishism in devaluations and dislocations of human activity, in the denigration of the 'merely human' that results when people become subordinated to things and powers of their own making. Thus, while there is a crude materialism associated with commodity-fetishism – its misattribution of value to the material properties of things – there is, equally, and, in some respects, more crucially, a wild spiritualism: the worship of the phantom-like objectivity of value, the elevation of abstractions above people and objects. Since value (and its most appropriate formal expression, money) seeks to transcend sensuousness, its fetishisation results in the idealist/capitalist contempt for the concrete, the sensuous and the embodied. As in religion, so in capitalist society the material world is subordinated to non-material powers. In treating things and the products of human labour as artificial and impure, Protestantism fetishises the immaterial (God). For this reason, it is the most appropriate religion to capitalism. Yet, value can only exist by 'inhabiting' or 'possessing' things (and bodies) since only actual concrete goods can exchange with one another. This produces that vulgar materialism, the worship of objects, which is *one side* of commodity-fetishism, the side that is seized on exclusively in many accounts.

---

91. Hawkes 2001, p. 5. A similar interpretation is offered by Brantlinger (1996, p. 125) who argues that Marx saw fetishism as 'a sort of primitive materialism'.

After all, as much as capital insists that it is everything, and that the material world of nature and humans counts for nothing, it inevitably fixates on the very natural objects it has scorned. To truly abandon the world of nature and human material practice would signal its death. For all its ghostly objectivity, value flourishes only by attaching itself to entities whose objectivity is appreciably more palpable. Value needs, as Marx puts it, things and persons which will act as its 'bearers'.[92]

And this returns us to the fetishes that haunt Sub-Saharan Africa today. After all, Africa continues to be plundered for the products of nature: ivory, rubber, diamonds, cocoa, cotton, gold, oil. Digging, cutting and pumping, slashing through forest and jungle, blasting great holes into the earth, capitalism in Africa seems intent on nothing less than a veritable war against nature. And, with each manic effort to seize their continent's natural wealth, Africans have been captured, whipped, beaten, worked to death, structurally adjusted – all so that nature might be despoiled, people might be downtrodden, and capital might accumulate. The fury directed against nature and labourers has swelled into a monstrous system of violence and mayhem: private militias, state- and colonial armies have marauded across the continent, insuring that the natural resources ripped from the earth stay in the hands of the richest and most powerful.[93] Goethe's *Faust*, the momentous tragedy whose theme is the manic energies unleashed by emergent capitalism, would have found an appropriate setting in Africa:

> Daily they would vainly storm
> Pick and shovel stroke for stroke:
> Where the flames would nightly swarm
> Was a dam when we awoke
> Human sacrifices bled,
> Tortured screams would pierce the night,
> And where blazes seaward spread
> A canal would greet the light[94]

When the African explorer-adventurer Henry Morton Stanley oversaw construction, on behalf of King Leopold of Belgium, of a 400 kilometre-long road

---

92. Marx 1976, pp. 293, 295.
93. For one astute overview of capitalism and violence in Africa, see Drohan 2003.
94. Goethe 1961, pp. 253–4.

from the mouth of the Congo to what is now Kinshasa, his crews blasted their way through mountains and hills. This frenetic creative-destruction earned him the moniker *Bula Matari*, 'breaker of rocks', a term that, in later years, the people of the Congo would use to describe the machinery of the state. There is a marvellous poetic wisdom contained in this description. Intuitively, the Congolese people discerned that colonial and postcolonial states embody the same wild energies that brought their continent into the orbit of European colonialism – and unleashed a torrent of murder, a breaking of rocks and skulls, whose end is not in sight. In *Faust*, that profound fable of capitalist modernity, Goethe figured these same wild energies as diabolical powers portending immense suffering and destruction. And in the tales of vampires and witches stalking Sub-Saharan Africa today, these energies are imagined as monstrous forces that capture bodies, dissect them and sell their parts, or turn them into money-generating zombie-labourers.

These African tales carry a defetishising charge in their insistence that something strange and mysterious, something that threatens the bodily and moral foundations of social life, is at work in the global circuits of capital-accumulation. This premonition has nothing to do with trade and market-exchange being foreign to African history. Many precolonial African societies were extensively familiar with markets and trade.[95] But they were not societies which subordinated all aspects of socio-economic life to regulation by the market, which is why non-commodifiable goods ('fetishes' to Europeans) were a permanent feature of social life. It is a token of just how reified everyday-life has become in the West that most of us no longer find global capitalist processes bizarre and perplexing. So natural have commodified market-relations become for us, so normalised the esoteric transactions of capital, that we rarely find anything unsettling about it all. As a result, our mode of perception dulls, our critical energies atrophy. Unable to see the tracks of the invisible, we deny existence to whatever eludes our optical gaze; we lose touch with the hermeneutics of suspicion that animates much African folklore. These popular genres, however, remain attentive to the mysteries and sorceries of capital.

---

95. The literature in this area is too extensive to seriously discuss here. For a basic introduction see Fage 2002; for an impressive synthesis of the evidence for Sub-Saharan Africa see Coquery-Vidrovitch 1988. Good overviews of centuries of African commerce with European are provided by Thornton 1992, and Cooper 1993. See also Wallerstein 1985.

The fetishes they describe – vampires and economic witches – are thus tokens of defetishisation. To be sure, these tokens retain the limits inherent in all folk-tales: they inadequately map global processes, too often mobilising volatile anxieties and desires. If their critical insights are to be cultivated, these stories must be refracted through a dialectical optics. As we shall see, some extraordinary works of African literature manage to do just this.

But, before turning to these issues, we need to consider the figure which accompanies the vampire in African witchcraft-tales in the age of globalisation: the zombie.

The living dead: zombie-labourers in the age of globalisation

Observing the proliferation of zombie-stories coming out of South Africa today, one radical commentator suggests, 'The images of zombies in these stories are not derived from traditional South African folklore, but are rather taken full-blown from American horror films'.[96] There is a failure of dialectical imagination in such a claim, one that fails to grasp the flows and counter-flows of meaning through which figures of horror are constituted in late capitalism. To begin with, Hollywood's zombies are themselves adapted directly from the experience of enslaved Africans and their descendants in the former colony of Haiti. To the degree to which American horror-film transmits zombie-images to Africa, it reworks a cultural product of the African diasporic experience. So, when zombies populate the African cultural imaginary today, they carry deep charges that run through the modern African historical experience. More than this, what distinguishes the African stories we have tracked is the specific imagery of the zombie-labourer. And precisely this figure is glaringly absent in American horror-film of the neoliberal era. Hollywood's zombies today are creatures of *consumption*, brazenly mobbing stores and malls and consuming human flesh, not living-dead producers of wealth for others.[97] Rather than engaging in 'a sort of reverse exoticism' in

96. Shaviro 2002, p. 289.
97. See especially George Romero's film *Dawn of the Dead* (1978), the bulk of which takes place in a shopping mall, a site to which zombies are instinctively drawn. It is interesting to observe, however, that at the time of his first film in this genre, *Night of the Living Dead* (1968), Romero considered his monsters to be 'ghouls', not zombies.

which it 'appropriates the mythologies of the imperial centre',[98] therefore, African popular culture has produced a highly distinctive trope, one that builds on Haitian images of zombies, in order to track the unseen labourers of a global imperial economic order. Let us consider the history of the zombie-image in this light.

The earliest known origins of the zombie can be traced to West Africa, specifically the region of the lower Congo, where religious idioms identified the *nzambi* god or spirit. The *nzambi* was embedded in West-African belief-systems which held that the dead can return to visit their families, bringing either assistance or harm.[99] But, in Haiti, where, by 1789, half a million slaves toiled on French plantations in conditions approximating industrial labour,[100] the idea of the dead moving among the living was transmuted into the notion of the *living dead*, people lacking all aspects of human personality, save the bodily capacity for mindless toil. In the Haitian context, the zombie became a figure of extreme reification – a living labourer capable of drudgery on behalf of others, but entirely lacking in memory, self-consciousness, identity and agency, the very qualities we associate with personhood. It is particularly revealing that zombie-legends acquired a unique resonance during the period of American occupation of Haiti (1915–34), when US-marines used forced labour to build roads and other infrastructure. It was during this period that one of the most influential English-language depictions of the zombie appeared, William Seabrook's *The Magic Island* (1929), written after the author spent a year with a Haitian family that allegedly initiated him into the practices of voodoo. While his book is chock full of ethnocentric stereotypes, Seabrook manages to offer a highly poetic account of zombies, one that reverberated throughout Depression-era America and formed the basis for the creatures' earliest filmic representations. In a significant chapter entitled 'Dead Men Walking in the Cane Fields', Seabrook recounts a friends response to a question about 'zombie superstition' in Haiti with the following remarks:

> Alas these things – and other evil practices connected with the dead – exist. They exist to such an extent that you whites do not dream of, though evidences are everywhere under your eyes....

98. Shaviro 2002, p. 289.
99. Laroche 1976, pp. 46–8. See also Boon 2007, p. 36.
100. Dubois 2004, p. 30.

> At this very moment, in the moonlight, there are *zombies* working on this island.... If you will ride with me tomorrow night, yes, I will show you dead men working in the cane fields.

The friend proceeds to describe a group of zombies as 'a band of ragged creatures who [shuffle] along...staring dumbly, like people walking in a daze. [They are] vacant-eyed like cattle, [and make] no reply when asked to give their names'. Intriguingly, Seabrook's friend alleges that zombies work in the fields of the Haitian-American Sugar Company, a firm whose main plant is described, in terms reminiscent of Marx, as 'an immense factory plant, dominated by a huge chimney, with clanging machinery, steam whistles, freight cars'.[101]

Finally, when he takes the author to witness the creatures for himself, Seabrook writes that he observed

> three supposed zombies, who continued dumbly at work...there was something about them unnatural and strange. They were plodding like brutes, automatons. Without stooping down, I could not fully see their faces, which were bent expressionless over their work.... The eyes were the worst.... They were in truth like the eyes of a dead man, not blind, not staring, unfocused, unseeing. The whole face, for that matter, was bad enough. It was vacant, as if there was nothing behind it. It seemed not only expressionless, but incapable of expression.[102]

Whatever we make of these claims, Seabrook's account became the point of reference for the earliest depictions of zombies in American literature and film. Moreover, the central features of his rendition mesh with those found in another influential portrayal, by Alfred Metraux in his book, *Le Vaudou Haitien* (1957):

> The zombie remains in that grey area separating life and death. He moves, eats, hears, even speaks, but has no memory and is not aware of his condition. The zombie is a beast of burden exploited mercilessly by his master who forces him to toil in his fields, crushes him with work, and whips him at the slightest of pretexts...The life of the zombie, on the mythical level, is similar to that of the old slaves of Santo Domingo...

---

101. Seabrook 1929, pp. 94–95.
102. Seabrook 1929, p. 101.

> Zombies can be recognized by their vague look, their dull almost glazed eyes.[103]

It is this view of zombies – as mindless labourers – that entered the American culture-industry in the 1930s and 1940s, a point to which I return in the Conclusion. But, as I show there, the idea of the zombie as a living-dead labourer was displaced in American cultural production in the late 1960s by that of the ghoulish consumer. While this is an intriguing cultural shift, it moved the image away from those features that are particularly resonant in the African context in the neoliberal era. To put it plainly, if Hollywood's zombies today are largely mindless consumers, in Africa they are mindless workers. This is why, as one of the most sensitive commentators on Haitian zombies has put it, the zombie is a 'mythic symbol of alienation: of a spiritual as well as physical alienation; of the dispossession of the self through *the reduction of the self to a mere source of labour*'.[104] Those passingly familiar with Marx's accounts of alienated labour and reification will recognise profound intersections between those texts and this image of the zombie, the very imagery that has been reactivated across so much of the African subcontinent today. I shall return to these intersections in the Conclusion, where I will also explore the notion of zombie-rebels. But, for the moment, we ought to appreciate that, rather than mere rehearsals of Hollywood's mythologies, contemporary African zombie-legends carry a much more powerfully critical charge – one that brings us back to the question of labouring bodies in the age of capitalist globalisation.

Vampire-capitalism in Sub-Saharan Africa

Let us now return to metaphors of vampire-accumulation in Sub-Saharan Africa today, and the soil out of which they grow. This will assist us in grasping the complex association of violence with cryptic accumulation that forms the basis for popular African imaginings of late capitalism. To be sure, Sub-Saharan Africa represents a complex, highly differentiated subcontinent. The distinctions between, say, Togo and Nigeria are manifold. Nevertheless, as we have seen, shared histories and structural positions make it possible

---

103. Métraux 1957, pp. 250–1.
104. Laroche 1976, p. 56, my emphasis.

to map the location of specific *regions* in the world-system.[105] The following account of crucial historical processes and social relations is inevitably a stylised one. But this has certain advantages for our purpose – the critical analysis of folkloric understandings of the occult economies of late capitalism – as it highlights key registers in which late capitalism is experienced across the African sub-continent. The nine themes sketched out below thus comprise axes of experience that inform the regional imaginary.

i.) *A legacy of colonial violence*

Africa's insertion into the European world-economy was inseparable from colonial wars and the trade in human beings. Insisting on these processes as integral to the origin of world-capitalism, Marx memorably pronounced that capital comes into the world 'dripping from head to toe, from every pore, with blood and dirt'.[106] To be sure, a few countries on the subcontinent were never colonised, and a number of societies were never directly incorporated into the slave-trade. But the connection of the region to global circuits of capital was nonetheless built on these foundations.

And these global circuits did indeed run through blood and dirt, as millions were uprooted and sold, to perish *en route* to plantations in the Americas or to perform forced labour for white overseers armed with whips and guns, and deploying rape, kidnapping and multiple forms of physical, social and psychic violence.[107] On top of this, perhaps a quarter of the people of West Africa were enslaved at home, forced to work in the textile- or palm-oil industries, among others. The end of the slave-trade by no means reduced the scale of violence. The insatiable appetite of the colonisers for the natural wealth of the

---

105. As Manthia Diawara suggests, it is arguable that, as a result of shared locations and bonds of history, these regions also have shared imaginaries. See Diawara 1998, pp. 103–24. However, in rightly pointing to the significance of markets as sites of unofficial imaginaries, Diawara tends to flatten out their contradictions.

106. Marx 1976, p. 926. My own view, contrary to theorists such as Immanuel Wallerstein, is that the European world-economy of the sixteenth century was dominated by the dynamics of crisis-ridden feudalism. Only later, with the ascendancy of England, the first truly capitalist nation, does the European world-economy become subordinated to capitalist imperatives. By the height of the Atlantic slave-trade, capitalist imperatives are clearly dominant in Europe and America.

107. The literature in this area is voluminous. For a few of the works that have influenced my thinking about these issues see Davis 2006; Patterson 1998; Rediker 2007; Lovejoy 1986; Harms 2002; Berlin 2003; Davis 1981; Genovese 1976; Joyner 1984.

continent – gold, diamonds, rubber, palm oil, copper, ivory, coffee – invariably spelled conflict, abetted by the collusion of local élites. As emergent colonial capitalism came fully into its own in Africa after about 1880, the scale of the violence grew ominously. 'I intend to treat them like dogs', announced Leander Starr Jameson, high commissioner for Cecil Rhodes's southern-African settlement. In this spirit, African compounds were burned, caves full of Shona fighters dynamited, lands stolen, thousands murdered.[108] In King Leopold's Belgian colony of the Congo, millions were killed – perhaps as many as 10 million – in a campaign of forced labour, kidnapping of whole villages, forcible dislocation, and systematic executions. African communities often resisted the colonial violence with extraordinary determination. But the brutality of the colonisers was unrelenting. When Africans resisted forced labour in the rubber-trade, their hands would be chopped off by Belgian troops, who left the victims to die while mounting the severed hands on stakes as a warning to others.[109] As European colonialism dispossessed people of their land, drove them into forced labour, imposed taxes and conscripted African men into their armies, they drowned one revolt after another in blood. In the Maji Maji uprising in southern Tanganyika (1905–7), a rebellion against both forced labour on cotton-plantations and the taxes extracted by German colonialism, the colonisers responded by killing at least 12,000 Africans. Forty-five years later, British troops wiped out similar numbers while repressing the Mau Mau revolt in Kenya.

In Africa, global capitalism keeps rehearsing these origins in accumulation through violence and war, and this has been formative for the regional imaginary. Ben Okri captures something of this in his novel, *Infinite Riches*, where he portrays the dreams of a colonial Governor-General of an African nation on the eve of its independence:

> .... the Governor-General then dreamt of a luxurious road over the ocean, a road that was fed from all parts of Africa. A macadam road of fine crushed diamonds and sprinkled silver and laminated topaz. A road that gave off the sweet songs of mermaids and nereids. Beneath this marvellous road there were dead children and barbarous fetishes, savage masks and broken spines, threaded veins and matted brains, decayed men and embalmed women. It

---

108. See Drohan 2003, pp. 25–33.
109. See Hochschild 1999.

was a road made from the teeth and skulls of slaves, made from their flesh
and woven intestines.[110]

ii.) *Colonialism, dispossession, and the forcible imposition of monetised relations*

During the period of full-fledged colonial rule (roughly 1880–1960), the
European powers worked systematically at subjecting Africans to market-
economics. They largely remained cautious, however, about creating a black
urban working class. As a result, while avoiding a full-fledged proletarianisation of Africans, they imposed monetary taxes to press the colonised into commercialised farming, sometimes supplemented by wage-labour.[111] By forcing
Africans into monetary relations, such taxes, which encountered widespread
resistance, lead to an intrusion of market-imperatives and to the semi- or full
proletarianisation of many who were unable to pay. And, in some parts of
the sub-continent, notably southern Africa, Kenya and the Rhodesias, taxes
were sometimes deployed in order to drive large numbers of people off their
lands, leaving them with little option but to seek paid labour in order to
survive.[112] There are few clearer indicators of the purposes of these policies
than the fact that, in many cases, there was one way for Africans to win relief
from taxes – by proving that they had worked a sufficient number of days
for Europeans during the previous year.[113] Colonial taxation, frequently in
the form of hut- or poll-taxes, was thus a deliberate instrument for heightened commercialisation of economic life and the semi-proletarianisation
of many Africans.[114] A case in point is the British South Africa Company,
which imposed taxes of ten shillings per year so that indigenous peoples
would be forced into market-relations (and in this case into labour-markets) in order to raise the means of payment. The Governor of the British
Protectorate of Kenya in 1913 articulated this practice as a cornerstone of
colonial policy:

---

110. Okri 1998, p. 204.
111. See Cowen and Shenton 1991, pp. 143–74; and Idahosa and Shenton 2004, pp.
81–4.
112. For some general considerations, see Cohen 1985, pp. 181–97. For an interesting
discussion of Nigeria in this regard, see Iyayi 1986, pp. 27–39.
113. See Forstater 2005, p. 60.
114. Davies 1966, p. 35. See also Viinikka 2009, p. 124.

> We consider that the only natural and automatic method of securing a
> constant labour supply is to ensure that there will be competition among
> labourers for hire and among employers for labourers; such competition can
> be brought about only by a rise in the cost of living for the native, and this
> can be produced only by an increase in the tax.[115]

Contrary to the governor, there was nothing natural about it. Colonialism
aimed at the deliberate construction of market-relations and, in some circumstances, at forcing Africans into markets as sellers of their labour-power. This
meant using coercive means – taxes backed up by military force (the Maji
Maji revolt, after all, was in part a rebellion against colonial taxes). From the
start, nascent capitalist social relations were thus experienced as *unnatural*, as
a foreign imposition designed to destroy customary ways of life.

iii.) *Colonial and postcolonial states as bodies of armed men*

If capitalist states always involve a shifting balance between coercion and
consent, between the use of force and strategies of legitimation, as Gramsci
suggested, colonial capitalism tends to tip decisively in the former direction.[116]
Here, more than anywhere else, states resemble bodies of armed men, to
employ Engels's metaphor. And postcolonial states have largely persisted
in this pattern, for a number of compelling reasons.

First, subordination to the capitalist world-economy has meant that all postcolonial states in Africa, even those that sought an 'African socialism', found
themselves, sooner or later and to differing degrees, recolonised by the world-
market. Sometimes eagerly, sometimes through incremental but grinding
pressures of the world-market and international financial institutions, local
élites were fashioned into homegrown personifications of capital, prepared to
operate as the privileged local gendarmes of the world-system. Inevitably, the
imperatives of capitalist accumulation exacerbated social inequalities, deepening the stratifications and class-divisions in African societies, and inducing
cycles of resistance which have been countered by brute force.

---

115. As quoted by Bernstein 1992, p. 7.
116. Gramsci's account of the complex, shifting character of consent in ruling-class
domination is set out in *Selections from the Prison Notebooks* (1971, pp. 257–64).

Secondly, postcolonial states inherited spatial-administrative structures (often binding together hundreds of ethnic groups) that lacked organic social unity. While a radical political project might have generated new solidarities, official processes of decolonisation were frequently hastened in order to deprive radical movements of time to build a mass-base with which to contest elections.[117] Having tried to abort the emergence of militant mass-movements, or crush them where they did emerge (the Belgian Congo, for instance), colonialists would oversee the installation of conservative elements into state-office. Once in control of the state-machinery, these forces typically used patronage and spoils to construct an élite-coalition, often drawn from specific ethnic groups, which dominated state and economy. This set in motion a truncated dialectic in which opposition-parties and movements in turn appealed to the excluded on grounds of ethnicity, not class. The result has been a pattern of 'ethnic conflict' – in fact the product of élite class-projects linked to imperial power, not something inherent in cultural differences – that has reinforced violence and state coercion.

Related to this, thirdly, is the frailty of local processes of capital-accumulation. Since African capitalism is decidedly weak (with manufacturing and finance confined to local markets), marginalised in world-markets, and foreign-dominated, rarely have these societies undergone processes of sustained and diversified accumulation of the sort that took place in Europe and North America, parts of Latin America, and more recently in East Asia. As a consequence, indigenous ruling classes generally lack viable bourgeois national projects that could rally the support of considerable social strata whose members see themselves as beneficiaries of a growing and developing national economy. African ruling classes thus lack national accumulation-strategies that can provide the social-material foundation for ruling-class hegemonies that tip more to consent than coercion.

The combined effect of these processes is the persistence of state-forms that rest upon and reproduce social and political violence. And, as economic crisis has accompanied neoliberal globalisation, these tendencies have been intensified in a context of declining living standards and conditions of life.

---

117. Allen 1995, p. 304.

iv.) *Neoliberalism, structural adjustment and mass-impoverishment*

While the neoliberal programmes of structural adjustment promoted by the World Bank and International Monetary Fund (IMF) have as one of their ostensible aims the rooting out of 'corruption' from African régimes, these programmes of mass-impoverishment have, in fact, merely reshaped the terrain for swindling and looting. Structural adjustment, usually required by Western governments, the World Bank and the IMF as a condition for urgently needed loans, involves a package of 'reforms' with the following features: massive cuts in public spending (leading to mass layoffs, the closing of schools and hospitals); the elimination of state-subsidies on basic commodities consumed by the poor, such as grains, flour and heating oil; privatisation of state-enterprises (mines, trading companies, public utilities, water-systems); devaluation of the local currency, which pushes up the prices for imported goods consumed by the population and cheapens exports (thus impoverishing millions of agricultural producers while bringing in less to the national treasury and driving up the trade deficit); opening up the national economy to foreign ownership; liberalisation of the financial system, which relaxes conditions for new banks and other lending institutions to form, encourages Western banks to set up shop, and frequently breeds shady financial practices.[118]

One African nation after another has heeded the prescriptions of the Western international financial institutions (IFIs). The results have been catastrophic. While Sub-Saharan Africa exports a much higher share of its gross domestic product than do countries in North America, Europe or Latin America – exactly the route the IFIs proclaim as the road to prosperity – the vast majority are in an economic free fall. Across the 1980s, as structural adjustment was implemented, national output per capita persistently *contracted* in one African nation after another: for the continent as a whole, the average decline was about two per cent per annum. The most serious drop (4.6 per cent annually) occurred in Côte d'Ivoire, the World Bank's poster-boy for neoliberal economics.[119] Indeed, despite its adherence to neoliberal dogma, Africa as a whole continues to attract less and less foreign direct investment

---

118. See the discussion in McNally 2006, pp. 163–4. For more detailed treatment, see Bond 2006.

119. Simon 1997, p. 92.

(FDI). The continent's share of the FDI flowing to 'developing regions' fell from 13.8 per cent in the mid-1980s to 5.3 per cent by the early 1990s. Put in global terms, Africa attracts less than one per cent of world FDI.[120] Meanwhile, manufacturing industries are collapsing and unemployment is soaring as, courtesy of trade-liberalisation, imports flood local markets. By the early 1990s, for example, the industrial sector in Lagos, Nigeria's largest city and the site of much of the country's manufacturing industry, was operating at a mere 36 per cent of capacity, as factories closed or cut back under the impact of global competition.[121]

Hammered by declining foreign investment, disintegrating manufacturing industries, and plummeting prices for primary products – cocoa, cotton, palm-oil, minerals, coffee, and the like – African nations have had no option, if they are to obey the rules of the game, but to go begging to international lenders in an effort to keep their economies afloat. The accompanying devaluation of local currencies directed by the IFIs then drives up the costs of borrowing – which affects all economic agents who must devote a larger share of incomes to debt-repayment. By the early 1990s, Africa as a whole had accumulated foreign debts equal to 70 per cent of total annual output. This combined debt represents four times the value of everything the continent exports in a year. The consequences are staggering. By 2000, Sub-Saharan Africa was sending $337 million per day to the West in debt-repayment.[122] Through these global circuits of debt and structural adjustment, as one African political economist argues, the continent is being subjected to a systematic 'recolonisation'.[123] Little wonder folklore and mass-culture imagine global corporations to be sucking the blood of the subcontinent.[124]

---

120. Hoogvelt 2002, p. 17.

121. Abiodun 1997, p. 201. For general analysis of the dynamics that underpin this crisis see Bond 2003 as well as Bond 2006. See also Bush 2004, pp. 173–202.

122. Data from Radoki 1997 and McNally 2006, p. 48.

123. Onimode 1988, p. 280.

124. These trends should be sufficient evidence that those analyses that focus overwhelmingly on 'internal' explanations of Africa's crisis are theoretically and politically impoverished. For an example of the 'internalist' approach which drops issues of global capitalism entirely from the equation, see Chabal and Daloz 1999. Of course, the corruption and violence of African élites must be analysed and condemned. But these phenomena must also be *explained*, which requires starting from Sub–Saharan Africa's relation to the system of global capitalism and attendant class-formations.

Perhaps the most staggering statistic in this regard comes from the World Bank itself: between 1987 and 2000, per capita incomes in Sub-Saharan Africa contracted by fully 25 per cent.[125] Yet even that statistic is too rosy: currency-devaluations required by the IFIs have sent the costs of basic goods like bread and heating oil soaring, while the speculation induced by financial liberalisation has driven rents and housing costs astronomically higher. Meanwhile, collapsing prices for agricultural products force millions to abandon the land and head for already overcrowded cities lacking adequate housing, sanitation and running water. Lagos alone, to which I return shortly, receives 300,000 new entrants each year.

The human toll is shocking. Countries like the Ivory Coast, Nigeria and Congo-Brazzaville, once classified as 'medium-income countries', have experienced a horrifying regression. Seventy per cent of the people live below the poverty-threshold (earning a dollar or less per day), and life-expectancy, which was 58 in 1950, fell to 51 by 2000. Indeed, Zambia, Zimbabwe, the Ivory Coast and Kenya have life-expectancies below 50, and moving toward 45, as falling standards for nutrition and rising disease-rates ravage the population. All told, indices of human development are regressing in 14 countries on the African sub-continent.[126] Taking the African continent as a whole, the production and availability of food, industrial output, education, per capita income and life expectancy are all plummeting.[127]

v.) *Accumulation by violence: militarised predator-capitalism and struggles to control resource-extraction*

In a context of staggering regression, the economies of Sub-Saharan Africa have been thrown back onto primary commodities, derived from agriculture or mining, as their only substantial asset on the world-market. Across the subcontinent, involvement in the world-economy pivots on the extraction of natural resources. In 1965, fully 93 per cent of Sub-Saharan Africa's merchandise-exports consisted of natural resources, or 'primary commodities'. Despite rhetorics of development, this reliance on raw materials remains

---

125. World Bank 2001b. It is these developments, and their intellectual underpinnings, that Ben Fine characterises as 'zombieconomics.' See Fine 2009, pp. 885–904.
126. Nanga 2003.
127. Hoogvelt 2002, pp. 15–16.

effectively unchanged.[128] Worse, the terms of trade have consistently shifted to the disadvantage of primary producers, as prices of precious metals and agricultural goods have fallen relative to those of manufactured goods. Between 1980 and 2000, for instance, cotton-prices dropped by 47 per cent, those for coffee by 64 per cent, while cocoa and sugar lost three-quarters of their market-value. These catastrophes have locked most of Africa into a devastating cycle of impoverishment.

For many élites on the African subcontinent – though South Africa is a significant *partial* exception – the only viable strategy for accumulation is to use the national state, or to seize control over a resource-rich territory within the nation-state, in order to reap the 'rents' (the taxes that can be demanded of multinational firms mining for diamonds, copper, gold, cobalt, magnesium and the like) that accrue to those who can claim ownership or control of the natural resources of the nation – its land, its minerals, its agricultural products, its oil. The result is a *rentier*-style capitalism, in which local élites live off rents rather than the profits generated by capitalist industry. Multinational corporations looking to exploit these resources are only too happy to collaborate in the business of taxes, bribes and armed thuggery, if it allows them to monopolise access to scarce resources.[129] As a result, much competition for capital and power takes the form of bitter struggles to control the state, or to fracture it by seizing sub-national territories rich in primary commodities. These methods of accumulation by violence, reminiscent of the strategies deployed by the colonialists, are at the heart of a number of the civil wars gripping Sub-Saharan Africa today.[130] However much these may express themselves in ethnic form, at issue is a contest to control natural resources in order to accumulate on the basis of the rents derived from them. Even a study by World-Bank analysts found that it is not longstanding ethnic grievances but economic conflict which is the key to understanding African civil wars since 1965.[131] The

---

128. Radoki 1997.
129. See Drohan 2003.
130. Cases in point are the recent civil war in ex-Zaire, that in Liberia, or the current civil war in Sierra Leone. On Liberia, see Outram 1997, pp. 355–71. On Sierra Leone see Zack-Williams 1999, pp. 143–62. For an insightful general analysis (albeit one vitiated by Weberian assumptions) based on four case-studies, see Reno 1998. A powerful interpretation of civil war in Sudan, and its gendered implications, in these terms has been advanced by El Jack 2007, pp. 61–81.
131. Collier et al. 2003.

upshot is a militarised form of capitalism in which contending fractions of the ruling classes appear as predators, using force to monopolise the natural wealth of whole nations, or parts thereof.

vi.) *Vampire-capitalism run amok: the road to social disintegration*

Because so much of Sub-Saharan Africa lacks any viable basis for sustained projects of capitalist development, predatory methods of accumulation described above predominate. As these involve little more than securing the technological and military means to rip resources from the ground, little of which will be re-invested in local industries, a form of parasitism readily emerges in which fortunes accrue to those who control the state (or subnational territories and military forces). State-power and the exercise of violence tend in these circumstances to become grotesquely individualised, manifest in the personal dictatorships of the likes of Joseph Mobutu Sese Seko, who ruled Zaire and siphoned off between four and six billion US dollars before being overthrown in 1997; General Mohammed Siad Barre, who dominated Somalia from 1969 to 1991; General Maryam Babangida who managed to loot perhaps $12 billion from the Nigerian treasury during his rule (1985–93), or his successor, General Sani Abacha, who is believed have pilfered $4 billion in a mere five years as head of state.[132]

These political phenomena inhere in the very forms of postcolonial capitalism in much of Sub-Saharan Africa. In turn, predatory accumulation tends to undermine the very bases of the domestic economy, making strategies of national development even more precarious. Mobutu's Zaire is an extreme case in point. As one commentator has put it, 'To visit Zaire in the last years of Mobutu's era was to enter a world of cannibal capitalism.' Despite being rich in diamonds and minerals, the Zairean economy contracted by more than 40 per cent from 1988 to 1995 while gross domestic product per capita plummeted by 65 per cent in the quarter-century after 1958.[133] Taken to their end point, these cannibal-tendencies induce sustained social disintegration whose inevitable result is social and ethnic fragmentation, political collapse at the national centre and a proclivity to civil war. Yet, local rulers and

---

132. Abacha became Babangidas 'successor', however, only by overthrowing the individual, Ernest Shonekan, who Babingida had picked to succeed himself.
133. Collins 1997, p. 592.

multinational corporations often continue to profit handsomely in these circumstances.[134] While parasitism does not always reach this extreme, it inheres
as a tendency embedded in the trajectories of many postcolonial states in Sub-
Saharan Africa. In the case of Nigeria, for instance, which has oscillated since
independence between civilian and military rule, the siphoning of national
wealth (based on oil) by ruling élites has produced a nation in which per
capita income, at $260 US in 2003, is lower than it was at independence forty
years ago.[135]

vii.) *Struggle on the land: enclosure, social inequality and the crisis of kinship*

One oft-ignored aspect of neoliberalisation is the escalation of conflicts over
land. Yet, as most agrarian incomes contract, at the same time as handsome
prospects open up for a few – particularly where land can be used for eco-
tourism, safari-hunting, timber, oil or mineral extraction – much of rural
Africa has been wracked by rural displacement, private enclosure, disputes
over ownership-rights (including battles over squatting) and increased class-
differentiation in the countryside. Such trends have been well documented for
a diverse range of countries and regions that includes Niger, the Ivory Coast,
Botswana, Ghana, Rwanda, Burundi, Kenya, Northern Nigeria, Mozambique,
North-West Cameroon, Southern Somalia, N.E. Tanzania, Malawi, Zimbabwe
and Burkino-Faso.[136] As the poor fall into debt, and are forced to sell off and
vacate their land, the better-off can in turn buy up, consolidate and enclose
the soil. The resulting class-differentiation is in turn sharply accelerated by the
intensified market-pressures of the neoliberal era – from reductions on subsi-
dies for foodstuffs and fuel to newly restricted access to credit for the poor.
With landlessness growing at one pole alongside concentrated ownership at
another, older village-structures and obligations are eroded by competitive
market-relations. The result, as one analyst notes, is 'not only intensifying

134. On this point see Reno 1998.
135. World Bank 2003.
136. Reynault 1998, pp. 221–42; Bassett 1993, pp. 131–54; Peters 1984, pp. 29–49;
Amanor 1999; Amanor 2001; Peters 2004; Myers 1994, pp. 603–32; Gohhen 1998, pp.
280–308; Besteman and Cassanelli 1996; Peters 2002; Nyambara 2001, pp. 534–49; Hammar 2001, pp. 550–74. I have benefited greatly from Pauline Peters's writings on this
question and the comprehensive survey to be found in her 2004 article cited above.
Also instructive are the case-studies gathered in Woodhouse et al. 2001.

competition over land but deepening social differentiation…new social divisions that, in sum, can be seen as class formation'.[137]

With such social differentiation comes a transformation in senses of self and community. An 'enclosed self', a private accumulator and appropriator, one who increasingly treats economic resources as strictly private property, and tends to withdraw from obligations to others. Consequently, responsibility for others declines and notions of community undergo a 'narrowing in the definition of belonging'.[138] Decreasingly able to appeal to practices of reciprocity, the poor find their choices are migration to urban centres or 'theft' and squatting. In response, the wealthy and government-authorities wage campaigns against 'squatters' and prosecutions of the poor for taking formerly common goods, such as forest-wood. In a context of intensifying conflicts over land, and demonisation of one social group by another, witchcraft-accusations flourish.[139]

viii.) *Squatter-cities and the struggle for survival*

As agriculture collapses and rural poverty mounts, as civil war and organised displacement sweep a number of countries, Africa's major cities are growing at a phenomenal rate. Notwithstanding efforts by colonialists to limit urbanisation of Africans and keep them away from their administrative centres, African cities grew massively throughout the postcolonial period. Today, the continent has the highest rate of urbanisation in the world.[140]

From the start, much African labour in these cities was concentrated in the 'informal sector'.[141] This awkward and somewhat misleading term describes a set of social-economic practices outside of the standardised relations generally associated with large businesses or public service and their regularised hours, wages and conditions of work. Street-hawking, scavenging, petty production in the home, and the provision of services ranging from sex to

---

137. Peters 2004, p. 279.
138. Peters 2004, p. 204. See also Nyambara 2001, pp. 535, 544–6, and Peters 2002, pp. 160–1, 166, 174, 178.
139. See Nyambara 2001, pp. 539, 544, 546; Myers 1994, p. 613; Hammar 2001, pp. 552, 561–2; Peters 2004, p. 303.
140. Saro-Wiwa 2009, p. 21.
141. See Lugalla 1997, pp. 430–3. For general background see Coquery-Vidrovitch 1988.

transportation constitute the principal activities in this sector. And as manu-facturing industries collapse and structural adjustment-programmes displace thousands of nurses, teachers and civil-service workers, as thousands pour into the cities from the countryside, and as unemployment mounts, this sec-tor is growing exponentially, comprising the last hope for millions.[142] Indeed, the United Nations estimates that fully 90 per cent of Africa's new 'jobs' of the early twenty-first century will be generated in the informal sphere.[143] In important respects, urban evolution across Africa thus conforms to Mike Davis's incisive description of the emerging 'planet of slums' in which we now live: a world where the majority of humankind resides in cities, not on the land, huge numbers eking out a bare existence in the informal economy, in the midst of squatter-camps and sprawling ghettoes awash with poverty. Rather than products of industrialisation, as were many nineteenth-century cities in Western Europe, observes Davis, Third-World cities frequently resemble nineteenth-century Dublin, a city built largely on rural dislocation and poverty, not industrial growth.[144] And, while pulverised by the effects of global capitalism – falling commodity-prices, rural depopulation, declin-ing living standards and life-expectancies, proliferation of urban slums – the majority so affected is not pulled into formalised wage-labour. At the same time, and in opposition to unilinear tendencies in Davis's argument, these processes are inscribed within the making and remaking of African working classes, complexly organised communities in which individuals and their kin combine wage-labour, 'informal' activities and more in order to reproduce themselves.[145]

Unable to afford adequate housing, huge numbers of people across urban Africa crowd into substandard dwellings, or squat on unoccupied land on the fringes or in the interstices of cities, where they erect makeshift-structures that offer minimal protection from the elements and that lack adequate sanitation or running water. There they combine with poor, working-class communi-ties with distinct patterns of survival and resistance. The cumulative result of these movements in one part of the continent after another is momentous.

---

142. Rogerson 1997, p. 346.
143. Global Observatory 2003, p. 104.
144. Davis 2004, p. 10.
145. On this point, including telling criticisms of some of Davis's theses, see Zeilig and Seddon 2009, pp. 14–19.

Looking across Africa, Davis notes the emergence of a 'shanty-town corridor of 70 million people that stretches from Abidjan to Ibadan: probably the biggest continuous footprint of urban poverty on earth'.[146]

ix.) *Financialisation, corruption and magical capitalism*

In the midst of appalling poverty, enormous fortunes continue to accumulate, particularly in the hands of new financial élites that have exploited the era of structural adjustment. We can trace some of the key processes involved by tracking financial liberalisation in Nigeria. Beginning in the mid-1980s, Nigerian governments, newly committed to structural adjustment, eased access to the financial sector (making it much simpler to set up banks and lending institutions), while raising interest-rates. The results were virtually instantaneous: the number of banks tripled between 1986 and 1992, three hundred finance-companies emerged in 1992–3 alone, while the number of mortgage-firms increased more than tenfold, from twenty-three in 1991 to 252 two years later.[147] This untrammelled proliferation of financial institutions reflected the emergence of new accumulation-strategies in the context of neoliberal restructuring. As one commentator notes, under structural adjustment, 'the financial circuit develops autonomously from the productive one...as new fields of valorization are opened up to finance new government debt, imports of luxuries, as a result of trade liberalization, luxury housing, as a result of increased income inequality, and a multitude of speculative investments'.[148]

But, as in all contexts where speculation runs rampant, many investors crossed the line into financial manipulation and fraud, especially as government retreated from regulating financial transactions. Military élites in Nigeria, long accustomed to breaking the rules and looting institutions, moved quickly into finance, bringing with them political connections and exceptional proficiency at fraud. By the early 1990s, 'pyramid schemes, check kiting, duplicate bookkeeping, bribery and unembellished swindles were endemic in

---

146. Davis 2004, p. 15.
147. Lewis and Stein 1997, pp. 7–9.
148. Carmody 1998, p. 29. As I have noted in Chapter Two, however, financial capital can never entirely break free of the dynamics of accumulation in the commodity-producing sector.

the financial system'.[149] In some cases, the assets of banks were simply looted through fictitious transactions.[150] Inevitably, financial institutions began to collapse; by 1995, Nigeria's financial sector was in the midst of a full-blown meltdown of the sort that creates opportunities for even more massive fraud. Not that Nigerian banks were unique in these respects. A 1993, US-Senate investigation revealed that the Western-based Bank of Credit and Commerce International (BCCI), which operated in many African countries, engaged in multiple forms of fraud and deception, among them arranging fabricated loans to the government of Cameroon, using state-funds for illicit financial transactions, under- and over-invoicing imports and exports, depositing profits of fraud in overseas-banks, laundering dirty money, and falsifying government-accounts. BCCI was no isolated case; in 1994, American Express Bank was found guilty of deceiving the World Bank and the IMF by falsifying the accounts of the Kenyan government.[151] And, as we have learned throughout the global financial crisis that broke in 2008, Western banks and lending institutions, up to and including major investment-banks like Lehman Brothers, were experts in dubious financial practices.

But, while exercises in swindling are by no means unique to Africa, they assume greater economic and cultural weight where productive methods of capital-formation (investment in factories and equipment in particular) are few and far between. Financial transactions, intricate fraud, and speculation have been the principal means of constructing new fortunes in Africa during the era of structural adjustment. It thus comes as little surprise that throughout much of the continent, 'money is seen as something having a magical and mysterious quality, which bears no relation to work and effort'[152] – as, in short, an enchanted power.

Bewitched accumulation, famished roads, and the endless toilers of the Earth

It is little surprise as well that the urban centres of Sub-Saharan Africa today are breeding grounds of the fantastic. These hectic conglomerations of

149. Lewis and Stein 1997, p. 13.
150. See Reno 1998, 190–4.
151. Bayart, Ellis, and Hibou 1999, pp. 76–9.
152. Bayart, Ellis, and Hibou 1999, p. 112.

teeming ghettoes, labyrinthine markets, dirt-streets, squatter-encampments, congested roadways, ramshackle sweatshops, and segregated quarters for the rich pulsate with high-voltage energy and conflict. Take the following (exoticised) description of Lagos, whose more than 10 million people make it the largest city in Nigeria, and one of the world's 'mega-cities':

> Its rush hour near the stadium in Lagos where Nigeria has just lost a foot-ball match.... Girls balancing bags of water on their heads edge their way through the traffic to vend their wares. Toilet brushes, cutting shears, smoked fish, hankies, inflatable globes, and even a steering wheel are sold by boys as the coil of traffic becomes more ensnared....
>
> It's difficult to find the centre, let along the logic, of this city reputed to be the most dangerous in Africa. Three bridges connect about 3,500 square kilo-metres of lagoon, island, swamps and the mainland, where unlit highways run past canyons of smouldering garbage before giving way to dirt streets weaving through 200 slums, their sewers running with waste. So much of the city is a mystery.[153]

Whirling through this perpetual motion of people and things is a chaos of commodities. Market-transactions occur everywhere. As street-hawking becomes the survival-strategy of ever-growing armies of women and young people, the sacred and the profane rub together in improbable conjugations:

> Routinely on sale are racks of cigarettes, orange drinks of uncertain origin in plastic bags, the Bible, the Koran, traditional hats, key chains, black market cassettes and CDs, pocket calculators, a Tummy Trimmer exercise machine in a cardboard box that boasts a busty blond in a bathing suit, tomatoes, onions, countless pairs of shoes, car seat cushions, steering wheel grips, fan belts, sunglasses by the dozens, newspapers, magazines....[154]

To this mania of the market we can add the systematic relations of violence and corruption that have dominated political-economic life since colonial-ism – manifest in the everyday coercion of police who demand bribes, in rampant political thuggery, regular episodes of military rule, and the constant looting of government revenues by state-élites. Next, factor in the psychic,

---

153. Otchet 1999.
154. Maier 2002, p. 25.

cultural and social effects of untrammelled marketisation in the age of neoliberalism and structural adjustment: crushing poverty; the decline of people's immune systems as diets deteriorate and illness spreads; the soaring rents that force the poor into ever more substandard housing; the endless proliferation of street-hawking as a means of bare survival. Then contrast all of this with the fabulous new fortunes made through financial manipulations and state-contracting, and with the ever more opulent lifestyles of the rich who, ensconced on two barricaded islands, isolate themselves from the legions of the impoverished, whose ranks swell by 300,000 newcomers each year. As segregation between these two groups grows, conflicts proliferate. Almost as quickly as new slum-settlements emerge, as did roughly 200 between the late 1980s and the late 1990s, the authorities clear out whole districts inhabited by poor Lagosians, often transforming them into sites of real-estate speculation, as occurred in the Maroko area, where the homes of some 300,000 people were wiped out.[155]

In the midst of their precarious lives, the poor cultivate a morbid humour. The overcrowded and accident-prone mini-buses and jitneys they use to move about the city are referred to as 'flying coffins' and 'moving morgues', examples of a plebeian wit that simultaneously mocks and condemns the desperate circumstances of their daily lives.

Now, imagine a young writer trying to give literary expression to the dialectic of dreams and despair, violence and love, destitution and wealth, riot and resignation that animate this city. His earliest novels undertake these dialectical investigations by way of a fairly straightforward social realism. The first, *Flowers and Shadows*, written at nineteen years of age, explores the corruptions associated with the worship of money and personal power. In one potent scene, the capitalist of the novel, a factory-owner, sacrifices a chicken while praying before a carved image that holds 'a small cutlass in one hand and a ten Naira note in the other'.[156] A second novel, *Landscapes Within* struggles with the dilemma of how to observe moral responsibility in a corrupt society.

Then a shift occurs – in both form and style. The writer moves from the novel to the short story while experimenting with fantastic modes of

---

155. Gandy 2005. This article is an important account of the history of Lagos, particularly during the neoliberal period.
156. Okri 1980, p. 123.

representation. He begins to draw upon the resources of local oral traditions, particularly notions of the spirit-world and of transactions between the visible and the invisible. Two stories in a volume entitled *Stars of the New Curfew* map a strikingly original aesthetic trajectory. 'In the City of Red Dust' chronicles the travails of two ghetto-dwellers during a day of fiftieth birthday celebrations for their country's military governor. While fighter-jets thunder overhead and dancers gyrate to military music, the pair head off for the local hospital, hoping to sell their blood in order to make a few naira with which to buy food and drink. The polyvalent trope of blood-peddling captures the desperate reality of people forced to sell their bodily powers, their very life-energies, in order to survive. More than this, however, it gestures to a society that is bleeding profusely, one where everything is drenched in the blood of the poor. The trope also highlights the obscure causal relations at work in society: as the locals sell themselves to make ends meet, the governor is honoured with 'gold necklaces from secret societies and multinational concerns'.[157] The dialectic of blood and gold is further referenced at the story's end, as one of the blood-sellers flips through books that speak to the sorcery of accumulation. 'There were books on magic, alchemy, letter-writing, books on fortune-telling, on how to communicate with spirits, a complete guide to palmistry, and the sixteen lessons of a correspondence course called *Turning Experience Into Gold*'.[158]

These concerns with magic and reification (the turning of experience into gold), and with the cryptic connections between wealth and the bodies of the poor, take on greater aesthetic power in the story from which the volume takes its name, 'Stars of the New Curfew'. As the tale begins, the narrator is describing his career peddling useless (and sometimes harmful) medicines to poor Lagosians. Obsessed by selling, he will deal in anything, 'from empty matchboxes to burnt-out candles'.[159] Remarkably, he finds buyers for these too. Soon, however, he is visited by nightmares in which the stars in the sky are being auctioned – and paid for 'either with huge sums of money, a special part of the human anatomy, or the decapitated heads of newly-dead children'. This dream scene is followed by one in which the salesman himself is

---

157. 'In the City of Red Dust', in Okri 1988, p. 55.
158. 'In the City of Red Dust', in Okri 1988, p. 78.
159. 'Stars of the New Curfew', in Okri 1988, p. 84.

on the auction-block, as 'money-men' proffer large sums of cash, animals, or human body-parts for his head. Troubled by the nightmare, he proceeds 'like all sensible and secret Lagosians...to consult with herbalists and sorcerers'.[160] Then, when his sales of a new medicine contribute to seven deaths, the narrator returns to W, his home-city, 'a town with a history of slave-trading, a town of bad dreams, surrounded by creeks and forests of palm-trees and rubber plantations. It had become a centre of excitement only on account of its oil wells'.[161] In this short passage, our author, Ben Okri, both gestures to his own home town, Warri, and to the devastating downward-spirals of colonial and postcolonial capitalism. Tracing capital's circuits through people, palm-oil, rubber and oil, Okri grounds the contemporary violence of market-relations in the anatomisation of human bodies. Back in W, the townspeople prepare for the annual 'public display of wealth', a violent contest between its two wealthiest families. At the heart of the competition is the fact that each of the leaders of the rich, warring families needs 'blood for his elixir'.[162] As the contest unfolds, the salesman apprehends an awakening of destructive and horrific ancient spirits:

> I began, I think, to hallucinate.... I passed the town's graveyard and saw the dead rising and screaming for children. It seemed as if the unleashing of ritual forces had released trapped spirits. Nightmares, riding on two-headed dogs, their faces worm-eaten, rampaged through the town, destroying cars and buildings. They attacked the roads, they created pits at the ends of streets for unwary drivers to sink into.[163]

Here, devices associated with the idioms of African witchcraft are deployed as ways of portraying the blood lust, ritual killing, and tribal war that animate postcolonial capitalism.

The day of the ritual contest arrives. Around a platform, on which large portraits of the two millionaires hang, gather the 'ordinary inhabitants of the town – the touts, beggars, carpenters, bar-owners, prostitutes, managers of pool shops, clerks, oil rig workers, petty bureaucrats, people with odd afflic-

---

160. 'Stars of the New Curfew', in Okri 1988, pp. 93, 94, 95.
161. 'Stars of the New Curfew', in Okri 1988, p. 111.
162. 'Stars of the New Curfew', in Okri 1988, p. 128.
163. 'Stars of the New Curfew', in Okri 1988, p. 129.

tions, an old man without an eyelid, a young man on crutches'.[164] All had come to catch money. 'We needed modern miracles' the salesman observes. 'We were, all of us, hungry'. And the miracle they had gathered to witness 'was that of the multiplying currency. We had come to be fed by the great magicians of money, masters of our age'.[165] The linkages here come fast and furious: millionaires; manufacturers of terror; magicians of money. And as the people fight and scramble, scratch and claw for the money that is thrown to the crowd by each side, the salesman comes to the revelation that modern society offers a single choice – 'to be on the block or a buyer'.[166]

With 'Stars of the New Curfew', Okri mines the imaginative resources with which he will create the fecund world of his *Famished Road* cycle. From the reservoirs of African folklore, much of it rooted in Yoruba literature and theatre, he rallies conceptions of an esoteric world, invisible to ordinary perception, a realm of spirits, dreams, and ghostly powers, with which to illuminate the dynamic forces tearing at postcolonial capitalism.[167] Yet, like all great writers, Okri is reworking traditional forms, transforming the older idioms with which he works in order to create a new aesthetic language of immense power.

There is, of course, nothing new about writers using the discourses and tropes of folklore to enrich literary production. As Mikhail Bakhtin powerfully demonstrated, François Rabelais's great Renaissance-novel, *Gargantua and Pantagruel*, gave literary form to the bawdy, festive, carnivalesque language of the late-medieval/early-modern marketplace. Rabelais's greatness, for Bakhtin, consists in having generated a new language drenched in the defiant laughter of the market-crowd, one which mocks the dreary, pompous seriousness of official culture. In so doing, however, Rabelais did not merely chronicle the discourse of popular culture. Instead, he leavened literature with folklore, transforming each in order to create a language that was neither conventionally literary nor simply folkloric. The result, in Bakhtin's words,

---

164. 'Stars of the New Curfew', in Okri 1988, p. 135.
165. 'Stars of the New Curfew', in Okri 1988, p. 136.
166. 'Stars of the New Curfew', in Okri 1988, p. 143.
167. It is important to recognise that Yoruba 'tradition' is immensely fluid and porous and has itself been made over and rewritten in the course of its mobilisation for literary purposes. For some considerations on the interpretive problems posed by this, see Quayson 1997, pp. 10–14. I also agree fully with Quayson when he asserts (p. 13) that Okri draws on Yoruba writers 'as a means of expressing a sense of identity embracing *all* available indigenous resources' (my emphasis).

was a 'new consciousness', one born 'at the intersection of many languages'.[168] The same could be said of Shakespeare, for whom popular vernaculars inter- sect with poetry of tremendous force. Something analogous takes place, in Okri's *Famished Road* cycle.[169] Okri turns to the folklore of the postcolonial African city, particularly its resonant discourses of spirits and sorcery, in order to probe the catastrophic cycle of poverty, violence and betrayal that has entrapped its peoples. He, too, translates these discourses into a new liter- ary language, a 'new consciousness' designed to restore hope and renew Afri- can and world-history. Yet, there is a crucial strategic difference between the two operations. At times, Bakhtin treats early-modern popular culture as an utterly self-sufficient domain, impervious to the effects of the official culture, ever-ready to dislodge the dominant order.[170] While far from insensitive to the resources of popular laughter (see *Infinite Riches*, Book Six, Chapter Nine, 'The Forgotten Power of Laughter'), Okri also grasps the narcotic attractions of power and money to the poor, as well as the debilitating weight of fear. Whereas Bakhtin seems at times to read Rabelais's task merely as marshaling the powers of carnivalesque laughter to smash the brittle structures of official culture, Okri perceives a dialectic of terror and power to be undone, one that feeds off the people's nightmares and divisions. He imagines that the strategic centre of any struggle for liberation is the minds of the oppressed themselves.[171] And this requires that he renovate the language of sorcery and enchantment, all the while endeavouring to unleash its imaginative powers.

Okri is not unique in reworking the resources of African oral tradition for literary purposes. He had a powerful – and acknowledged – predecessor in Amos Tutuola, author, most famously, of *The Palm-Wine Drinkard* (1953) and *My Life in the Bush of Ghosts* (1954).[172] Tutuola's works are seminal for their

---

168. Bakhtin 1984, p. 471.
169. Okri has identified three novels in this cycle: *The Famished Road* (1992a), *Songs of Enchantment* (1993) and *Infinite Riches* (1998). It is intriguing that Okri's novel-cycle emerges at exactly the same time as does Nollywood.
170. For more on this point see McNally 2001, Chapter 4.
171. 'The real quarrel of the oppressed is not with the oppressors. It is with them- selves' (Okri 1997, p. 133). This dynamic of Okri's work has been attacked, and mislead- ingly lumped in with postmodernism, by Andrew Smith (2005, pp. 8–9). In my view, Okri is not reducing the crisis of postcolonial society to the failures of the oppressed; instead, he resists fatalism by pointing out that the oppressed have (and have had throughout the postcolonial period) the power to make things otherwise.
172. Both now published in a single volume: *The Palm-Wine Drinkard and My Life in the Bush of Ghosts* (Tutuola 1984). Okri makes many gestures to Tutuola across his texts,

unique rendering of Yoruba folklore, and for the way in which they highlight the element of the grotesque. References to slavery, debt, money and wage-labour frame key moments in these texts, and markets are frequently linked with forests, the traditional dwelling place of dangerous spirits. Crucially, images of corporeal distortion and dismemberment loom large. Tutuola reworks, for example, a widespread folktale about a girl who refuses marriage and ends up falling into the clutches of 'a complete gentleman' – in fact a disembodied skull who has assembled himself into human form by renting body-parts from forest-dwellers. It is especially striking that the girl first encounters the 'complete gentleman' in a marketplace and that the narrator estimates that, were he to be sold, the gentleman would go for a price of at least two thousand pounds.[173] Running throughout Tutuola's version of this tale is a series of flows between body-parts, markets, and money: body-parts are rented; the assembled creature is evaluated in terms of monetary value; and the initial contact between the girl and the manufactured creature takes place in a market. The transactions of an increasingly commercialised society are being modelled here, first, in terms of the buying and selling of detached human bits and, secondly, in terms of the enchantments of commodities – in this case, the desired complete gentleman, composed of commodified parts, whose market-value is judged to be extremely high.

Tutuola does not, however, probe the monstrosities of the market in terms of the unique space of the urban economy.[174] In making the modern African city, such as Lagos, a living character of sorts in his stories and attributing to it mysterious, magical, and ominous qualities, Okri revolutionises the literary language of folklore. He urbanises it, immersing it in the fabulous and frightening transactions of contemporary urban space. In so doing, he brings the forest, the traditional site of evil spirits, into the city, remapping the urban as

---

none more explicit than the story 'What the Tapster Saw' in *Stars of the New Curfew* (1988). Even there, however, Okri pays tribute through transformation, not repetition. An apparently multinational oil-company, Delta Oil, is at the heart of the story and figures as a marker of capitalist modernity throughout.

173. Tutuola 1984, p. 202.

174. While Tutuola does move his protagonists through many towns, there is nothing in his texts that resembles the huge urban conglomerations that are at the centre of Okri's novels and stories.

a site of contestation among animal and spirit forces. The result, as one commentator notes, is 'the spiritualization of modern urban space'.[175]

The Famished Road begins on the eve of independence for a nation like Nigeria with the voice of a narrator who is a spirit child or *abiku*. It is widely believed, particularly in southern Nigeria, that because such children, part-human/part-spirit, are drawn back to the spirit-world, they die early, leaving grieving parents behind.[176] But spirit-children are also attracted to the world of humans, resulting in a cycle of births, premature deaths and rebirths. Indeed, some variants suggest that it is the responsibility of parents to offer spirit children a life worth living, one which makes them desire to stay in the realm of humans. Okri clearly imagines Nigeria as an *abiku* nation, one that regularly dies with the betrayal of its hopes, only to be reborn again – each time, thus far, into the same dismal circumstances.[177] Tellingly, he names his narrator Azaro, from Lazarus who, in Biblical lore, rose from the dead. In expounding a story in which Azaro's parents try to draw their *abiku* child fully into the human world, Okri reminds the people of Nigeria that they have yet to offer their child-nation, the country dreamed of at Independence, reason to stay. But hope lives in the cycle of rebirth. And rebirth is a task for all humanity, not merely one nation.[178]

In offering an imaginative account of what ails Nigeria, among other nations, Okri exploits the grammar of witchcraft to dramatise *why* the country keeps dying. Looming large here are a set of interconnected themes having to do with roads, markets, power, accumulation, spirits, money, fear, history and dreams. While both building upon folklore and refashioning it, Okri creates a double alienation effect. On the one hand, he uses folklore to render the everyday world strange, depicting it as a startling realm of invisible, bewitched powers. At the same time, rather than simply affirm indigenous belief-systems, he transfigures them, disrupting popular beliefs so as to challenge the people of Nigeria/Africa/the world to become something

175. Fraser 2002, p. 84.

176. While spirit-children are known as *abiku* among the Yorubas and Ijos, the Igbos use the term *ogbaanje* to refer to them. See Bastian 1997, pp. 116–23, and Bastian 2002, pp. 59–67. Spirit-children also figure as '*ogbanje*' in Chinua Achebe's classic *Things Fall Apart* (1959, pp. 74–8).

177. Okri 1992a, pp. 487, 494. See also the poem, 'Political Abiku' in Okri 1992b, pp. 71–5.

178. Okri 1992a, p. 494.

other than what they are. 'In an atmosphere of chaos art *has* to disturb some-thing…you have to liberate it from old kinds of perception', he has argued.[179] And the monstrously enchanted world he creates initiates us into a disorient-ing realm of perception and cognition.

A key Okri strategy is to de-familiarise urban markets, rendering them dan-gerous and bizarre. In the third chapter of *The Famished Road*, he likens them to forests: 'I noticed that the forest swarmed with unearthly beings. It was like an overcrowded marketplace'.[180] The next chapter depicts Azaro wander-ing through the streets of the city. Having slept under a truck, he awakens hungry and strolls through the marketplace, where he is drawn to the sights and smells of food. But the peddlers of the market drive the child away, a reminder that the market satisfies monetary demand, not need. Only some-one abnormal, perhaps non-human, offers him food: a man with four fingers. Then follows a dizzying description of the marketplace, one of many found in *The Famished Road*:

> I watched crowds of people pour into the marketplace. I watched the chaotic movements and the wild exchanges and the load-carriers staggering under their sacks. It seemed as if the whole world was there. I saw people of all shapes and sizes, mountainous women with faces of iroko, midgets with faces of stone, reedy women with twins strapped to their backs, thick-set men with bulging shoulder muscles. After a while I felt a sort of vertigo just looking at anything that moved. Stray dogs, chickens flapping in cages, goats with listless eyes, hurt me to look at them. I shut my eyes and when I opened them again I saw people who walked backwards, a dwarf who got about on two fingers, men upside-down with baskets of fish, women who had breasts on their backs, babies strapped to their chests, and beautiful children with three arms.… That was the first time I realised it wasn't just humans who came to the marketplaces of the world. Spirits and other beings come there too. They buy and sell, browse and investigate.[181]

The notion that markets are populated by invisible spirit-forces is common to much African folklore. But Okri suggests that these forces are perceptible – if we can develop new ways of seeing. For Azaro, this involves shutting his

---

179. Wilkinson 1990, p. 81.
180. Okri 1992a, p. 12.
181. Okri 1992a, pp. 14–15.

eyes and re-opening them, as if to see anew. Then things begin to emerge in astonishing shapes and forms. Mobilising the folkloric grotesque, Okri dwells on human corporeal distortion, describing a dwarf who moves about on two fingers, women with breasts on their backs, upside-down men (all of whom have their analogues in figures seen before Azaro shuts his eyes). While these are familiar tropes of the sort we find in Tutuola's novels, the shift from forest to marketplace is decisive, as it takes shape as an urban forest, a realm of hidden dangers. A subsequent episode in the novel highlights these.

In this later sequence, Azaro has gone in search of his mother, who is a small trader in the market. Initially, he is overwhelmed by the sheer number of female hawkers, 'all of them selling identical things'. There follows a detailed description of the many kinds of foods that abound there. 'And', he continues, 'just as there were many smells, so there were many voices, loud and clashing voices which were indistinguishable from the unholy fecundity of objects'. A further detailed description accents the improbable combinations, the wild variety, 'the unholy fecundity' of the world of commodities.

> Women with trays of big juicy tomatoes, basins of garri, or corn, or melon seeds, women who sold trinkets and plastic buckets and dyed cloth, men who sold choral charms and wooden combs and turtle doves and string vests and cotton trousers and slippers, women who sold mosquito coils and magic love mirrors and hurricane lamps and tobacco leaves, with stalls of patterned cloths next to those of fresh-fish traders, jostled everywhere, filled the roadside, sprawled in fantastic confusion.[182]

Next, this phantasmagoria of commodities is contrasted with the conflictual relations of market-capitalism: 'There was much bickering in the air and rent-collectors hassled the women...'. In the midst of the confusion, Azaro becomes dizzy and disoriented, unable to locate his mother. Then, as in the scene where he shuts his eyes only to see differently, his perception is altered as he weeps 'without any tears'. He encounters an old man at a stall and receives food and water from him. Azaro then lies down and sees and hears fantastic things and voices, including a conversation among the spirits of the marketplace. After discussing the poverty and violence that will afflict the country in the postcolonial period, the voices drift away and darkness sets

---

182. Okri 1992a, p. 161.

in. In the darkness, Azaro can now find his way: 'Spirits of the dead moved through the dense smells and the solid darkness. And then suddenly the confusing paths became clear. My feet were solid on the earth'. The strategic moves here are deeply significant. Once again, acute perception begins where Azaro can see or hear spirits, where he can discern the invisible forces of market life. Despite darkness, indeed because of it, he can now find his way.

Throughout these passages, as throughout much of *The Famished Road*, real perception occurs at night, in darkness. In terms of the co-ordinates of much folklore, this is noteworthy. Night and darkness, after all, are the archetypal times and spaces of evil and transgression.[183] If it is only in darkness that Azaro can find his way through the marketplace, hints Okri, this is because the market is a night-space, a site of violence and danger. The daylight-world of ordinary perception obscures the true nature of the forces that inhabit the market. But, for those able to see in the dark, the market emerges as what it truly is, a forest-world dominated by malevolent spirits of the night. Behind the confusing carnival of commodities, Azaro now beholds confinement, turbulence and brutality:

> I followed the waning brightness of the path and came to a place where white chickens fluttered and crackled noisily in large bamboo cages. The whole place stank profoundly of the chickens and I watched them fussing and beating their wings, banging into one another, unable to fly, unable to escape the cage. Soon their fluttering, their entrapment became everything and the turbulence of the market seemed to be happening in a big black cage. Further on, deeper into the night, I saw three men in dark glasses pushing over a woman's flimsy stall of provisions.[184]

Moving through the darkness, armed with a sort of night vision, Azaro perceives thugs, affiliated with the Party of the Rich, toppling the stall of a female hawker. Each time she sets her stall back up, they knock it over again. The woman re-appears with a machete and sends the thugs fleeing. After they have gone, a lamplight illuminates the face of the woman – and Azaro is shocked to recognise his mother. Not only is this a case of delayed recognition, a recurring theme in Okri, it again involves the dialectic of darkness

---

183. For some interesting (largely Western) cross-cultural comparisons in this regard see Palmer 2000.

184. Okri 1992a, p. 168.

and light.[185] Unlike the monsters of the market – evil spirits and thugs – his mother, one of millions of poor and oppressed female traders in the market, can only be recognised in the light.

Darkness and night also figure centrally in Azaro's descriptions of the main site of capitalist accumulation in *The Famished Road* and its successor novels, the bar belonging to Madame Koto, the dominant character of *The Famished Road* cycle after Azaro and his parents. Arguably, one of the least appreciated aspects of this cycle of novels is the way Okri maps the transformative effects of capital-accumulation on this female bar-owner, who becomes the richest and most politically powerful person in the locale.

The local people regularly describe Madame Koto as a witch.[186] In one lengthy passage, Azaro summarises how the locals resort to witchcraft-tropes to make sense of her ever growing wealth and power:

> The most extraordinary things were happening in Madame Koto's bar. The first unusual thing was that cables connected to her rooftop now brought electricity....
>
> Madame Koto, much too shrewd not to make the most of everyone's bewilderment, increased the price of her palm-wine and peppersoup.... In the midst of all this Madame Koto grew bigger and fatter until she couldn't get in through the back door. The door had to be broken down and widened. We saw her in fantastic dresses of silk and lace, edged with turquoise filigree, white gowns, and yellow hats, waving a fan of blue feathers, with expensive bangles of gold and silver weighing her arms, and necklaces of pearl and jade around her neck....
>
> People came to believe that Madame Koto had exceeded herself in witchcraft. People glared at her hatefully when she went past. They said she wore the hair of animals and human beings on her head. The rumours got so wild that it was hinted that her cult made sacrifices of human beings and that she ate children. They said she had been drinking human blood to lengthen her life and that she was more than a hundred years old. They said the teeth in her mouth were not hers, that her eyes belonged to a jackal, and that her foot was getting rotten because it belonged to someone who was trying to dance

---

185. On delayed recognition in Okri see Fraser 2002, pp. 77–8.
186. Okri 1992a, pp. 91, 100, 281.

in their grave. She became, in the collective eyes of the people, a fabulous and monstrous creation.[187]

Okri clearly delights here in comparing capitalists to animals who subsist on the corporeal energies of the poor and appropriate parts of their bodies. But note how he begins with the social-material dynamics of accumulation itself: the connection of electrical cables to the bar. The processes which transmute accumulators into 'fabulous and monstrous' creations have their roots in transformations of the human environment (Okri returns us repeatedly to the manic felling of trees). All of these material changes transfigure the individuals involved. In an especially noteworthy scene, as he observes the wealthy clientele in the bar, it dawns on Azaro 'that many of the customers were not human beings.... They seemed a confused assortment of different human parts. It occurred to me that they were spirits who had borrowed bits of human beings to partake of human reality.'[188] Azaro becomes convinced that these beings are attracted to a fetish that hangs on the wall of Madame Koto's bar. He proceeds to steal the fetish and bury it in the forest, the symbolic site of malevolent powers. Here, I would suggest, Okri is linking Madame Koto's new fetish – money/power – to longer-standing fetish-practices. He insinuates that urban capitalism harnesses demonic energies to the new fetishism of commodities, money and capital. He portrays a system inhabited by creatures who borrow 'bits of human beings' – just as the capitalist 'borrows' the life-energies of human labour-power – in order to 'partake of human reality'.

Okri's movement between commodity-fetishism and older witchcraft beliefs involves reworking the latter at the same time as he deepens the former. Rather than portray Madame Koto as inherently demonic, he offers us a highly ambiguous character, one capable, particularly in the early parts of the cycle, of great kindness and generosity. Instead of someone saturated by primordial evil, he portrays the evil of circumstances, depicting the methodical transformation of an individual by conditions she tries in vain to shape. In this sense, the capitalist is a creature of fate, someone who ultimately acquiesces to an inevitable destiny (greed and corruption). It is not that Okri absolves members of the dominant class of personal responsibility – far from it. It is the

---

187. Okri 1992a, p. 374.
188. Okri 1992a, p. 136.

choice which is fateful; other choices would not bring the same imperatives, the same fate. But while insisting on responsibility, he highlights the ways in which the drive to escape poverty and to earn respect on capital's terms entails imperatives – the requirement to endlessly accumulate and participate in brutal relations of power – that turn people into something quite other than what they intend. In one scene, Azaro notices wealthy men and thugs of the Party of the Rich pouring into the bar. He now sees the proprietress in a new light. 'Madame Koto, who seemed to me afraid of nothing under the heavens, moved with such alacrity it appeared she was afraid of incurring their displeasure.'[189] This too constitutes a revelation. Azaro senses that, contrary to local belief, Madame Koto is far from all-powerful. Nor is she unique: 'She was not the only one; they were legion'.[190] In the hierarchy of capitalist power Madame Koto, all-powerful to the locals, submits to those richer and more powerful than she. Azaro observes one of the rich men offending Madame Koto while dancing with her. She comes at him with a broom, but he merely laughs, intoning that if she marries him she will 'sleep on a bed of money'. He proceeds to use his singular source of power – money – to tame her.

> …[H]e brought out a crisp packet of pound notes and proceeded to plaster note after note on her sweating forehead. She responded with amazing dexterity and, as if she were some sort of desperate magician, made the money disappear into her brassiere. She danced all the while. He seemed very amused by her greed…. And then quite suddenly he put away his packet of money, and danced away from Madame Koto, his faced glistening with the ecstasy of power.[191]

This passage captures the systemic character of what ails Madame Koto, her immersion in a force-field in which money is the new god, the ultimate fetish, the source of fantastic wealth and power. Madame Koto is an exemplar of the doctrine of unintended consequences. She, like all those who succeed in the fierce turbulence of the market, inevitably metamorphoses into something vampire-like, into a monstrous and fabulous creature that lives off the exploitation of others.

---

189. Okri 1992a, p. 221.
190. Okri 1992a, p. 495.
191. Okri 1992a, p. 223.

As if to emphasise the ruptural processes involved, Okri repeatedly utilises images of material-physical transmutation – like the attachment of electrical cables to the bar – to highlight the social and material processes of accumulation that animate these personal metamorphoses.[192] Throughout *The Famished Road*, Madame Koto's bar regularly undergoes material improvement and expansion: a new counter is constructed, 'almanacs of the Party of the Rich' are placed on its walls, a gramophone is purchased, the bar is wired for electricity, an extension is built onto the bar.[193] In noting many of these changes, Azaro remarks that Madame Koto is, in archetypically capitalist fashion, 'experimenting with efficiency'.[194] Soon, a single bar is not enough. She opens another in a different part of the city and adds 'a mighty stall in the big market'.[195] As she accumulates and expands her business, the proprietress also hires labourers: prostitutes, a driver for her car (a decisive marker of her wealth), servants. She even hires Azaro's mother for a while as a cook. These accumulative strategies induce both physical and personality changes. Madame Koto's body grows enormously fat; her disposition becomes nasty and vicious. But these changes are clearly linked to accumulation of money and new means of production. Several crucial scenes in Chapter 11, Book Three of *The Famished Road* capture these dynamics:

> The bar was silent. Then I made out someone chuckling.... I made out the form of a head bent over, of a person rapt in a secret ritual.... I tiptoed to the counter and saw Madame Koto counting money. She was so engrossed in the counting that she didn't notice my entry. Her face shone and sweat ran down from her hairline, down her cheeks and ears, down her neck, into her great yellow blouse. She would count a bundle of notes and then laugh. It was a strange kind of laughter. It sounded like vengeance.[196]

When she becomes aware of Azaro's presence, Madame Koto is angry and begins to boast: 'Things are going to change, you hear? You think this area

192. While recognising that Okri's depiction of Madame Koto is highly ambivalent, Quayson (1997, p. 146) contends that the author legitimates 'the worst popular suspicions about her' as a witch. As should be clear, I think this is to miss one of the crucial ways in which Okri is reworking popular folklore, using its imaginative powers to construct a more comprehensive picture of the dynamics of accumulation.

193. Okri 1992a, pp. 239, 214, 272, 373; and Okri 1993, p. 36.

194. Okri 1992a, p. 214.

195. Okri 1992a, p. 374.

196. Okri 1992a, p. 249.

will stay like this forever? You think I am going to be doing everything alone? No! Soon I am going to get some young women to serve for me. I am going to get one or two men to carry heavy things and run messages'.[197] Azaro comments, 'For the first time I began to dislike her.... She had changed completely from the person I used to know'. Still, Madame Koto is not done. 'You think I don't want to build a house,' she continues, 'to drive a car, you think I don't want servants, you think I don't want money and power, eh? I want respect. I am not going to run a bar forever. As you see me – now I am here, tomorrow I am gone.'[198]

The manic, Faustian energies of capitalist accumulation are starkly drawn here. The process of unending 'creative destruction,'[199] the demonic impulse requiring that everything solid should melt into air – all this is starkly encapsulated in Madame Koto's statement, 'Now I am here, tomorrow I am gone'. *The Famished Road* cycle highlights the modes in which capitalist power draws upon terrifying energies of self-interest and self-advancement, frenetic drives to expand. The repeated remaking of Madame Koto's bar, which Azaro describes as its 'cyclical transformations',[200] is designed to figure these frenzied imperatives. In calling up animal-spirits, manic accumulation breeds wickedness, which in turn feeds off Madame Koto's 'craven volcanic desire' and her 'greedy rage'.[201] Okri portrays a machinery that breeds malevolent appropriators, one often gestured at in urban folktales or Nollywood's voodoo-horror: a global system of occult transactions between money and human bodies.

More than this, in a potent de-mythifying move, Okri intimates that the vampire-powers of the rich are nourished by the nightmares of the poor and the divisions among them. In the supercharged final chapter of *The Famished Road*,[202] where fear and hope battle for the future of the country, Azaro explains that 'we had bad dreams about one another while Madame Koto...extended her powers over the ghetto and sent her secret emissaries into our bodies. Our fantasies fed her'.[203] Okri touches a crucial theme here, one missed by

197. Okri 1992a, p. 250.
198. Okri 1992a, pp. 250–1.
199. Schumpeter 1950, pp. 81–6.
200. Okri 1993, p. 99.
201. Okri 1993, p. 140.
202. Significantly, this chapter also constitutes the whole of the Book Eight and Section Three of the novel.
203. Okri 1992a, p. 496.

many commentators.[204] The mythology of power propagated by the rich can only survive, he intimates, if it is sustained by the dreams of the poor. In *The Famished Road* and *Infinite Riches* Azaro's father and mother are successively seduced by dreams of fame and influence – in the first case, when his father's boxing exploits become legendary, in the second case, after his mother leads an uprising of local women and is pictured on the front page of a newspaper. Depicting the growing arrogance and self-importance of each of Azaro's parents, Okri reminds his readers that they too are implicated in the fetishisms and mythologies of power; their fantasies of fame and fortune are the negative energies off which the powerful feed. These energies also fuel bitterness and division among the poor ('we had bad dreams about one another'). 'Poverty,' warns Azaro's father, 'makes people strange, it makes their eyes bitter, it turns good people into witches and wizards'.[205] Here is a key to the transformations of Madame Koto. But more than this, here is a caution as to the unintended consequences of trying to escape poverty on the terms of the market.

Let us now return to that market and to another critical Okrian move that deserves our attention. Recall the first passage about Azaro's experience of the market that I quoted above. Azaro tells us 'I watched crowds of people pour into the marketplace. I watched chaotic movements, wild exchanges and the load-carriers staggering under sacks'.[206] In a series of deft transitions, Okri takes us through the tumult of the crowd and the wild circuits of commercial exchange to briefly observe the labourers who move these commodities about. Just as quickly he moves on. But a hint has been dropped, a seed planted. He repeatedly returns from the transactions of the market to the toil without which exchange would not be possible. While drawing our eyes to labour, Okri also underlines its invisibility in capitalist market-society, the way in which labour disappears in the circuits of exchange, concealed in

---

204. This dimension of Okri's remapping of the discourse of witchcraft, one that implicates the divisions among the poor and their fantasies of achieving power on its terms certainly does not represent a legitimation of 'the worst popular suspicions' about Madame Koto (see footnote 192 above). It is also a much more subtle reading of the position of the oppressed than that suggested by Smith (2005).

205. Okri 1993, p. 121. See also the statement of the capitalist of *Flowers and Shadows* (1980, p. 14), '*My son, poverty is a curse...*' The novel then demonstrates the terrible price this individual pays for attempting to escape poverty through the worship of money and the exploitation of others.

206. Okri 1992a, p. 15.

Marx's famous 'hidden abode of production.' The following passage subtly explores just this invisibility:

> For a while Dad disappeared from my life. I woke up and he wouldn't be there. I went to sleep and he wouldn't have returned. He worked very hard and when I saw him on Sundays he seemed to be in agony. His back always hurt...Dad worked very hard carrying loads at the garage and the market-places and he earned very little money. Out of what he earned he paid the creditors...And out of what was left we could barely manage to pay the rent and eat. After some days of not seeing Dad I asked Mum what had happened to him.
>
> He's working for our food, she said.[207]

This intriguing passage is replete with insights. Dad has disappeared. As a labourer in a world dominated by frenetic market-activity, he is invisible. When Dad is physically present, he carries the traces left by work on his aching body. Something unseen, the bodily pain of the worker, serves as a stubborn reminder as to what drives the market-economy. At multiple points throughout the first novel in the cycle, Okri returns to the site of the body in pain. 'Too much load. My back is breaking', Dad tells his son.[208] But rendering labour visible is itself painful, disquieting. A series of remarkable scenes occur in this regard when Azaro again takes to wandering through the city.

> In my wanderings I left our area altogether, with its jumbled profusion of shacks and huts and bungalows, and followed the route of the buses that took workers to the city centre.
>
> ...I went on walking and saw a lot of men carrying loads, carrying monstrous sacks, as if they were damned, or as if they were working out an abysmal slavery. They staggered under the absurd weight of salt bags, cement bags, garri sacks. The weights crushed their heads, compressed their necks, and the veins of their faces were swollen to bursting point. Their expressions were so contorted that they almost seemed inhuman.[209]

Then Azaro reaches the garage, which, echoing his earlier experience of the marketplace, he experiences as 'the most confusing place I'd ever seen'. He

---

207. Okri 1992a, p. 78.
208. Okri 1992a, p. 126.
209. Okri 1992a, p. 144.

observes people and vehicles hurtling back and forth in a teeming chaos of objects. In a further echo of his first trip to the market, he announces that 'I became dizzy, hungry and confused'.[210] He sees grandfathers, fathers and young children all straining under the weight of massive loads. Then he hears 'the protestations of a familiar voice.' In a moment of shock, he recognises his father among the load-carriers: 'He looked completely different. His hair was white and his face was mask-like with engrained cement.... They loaded two bags of salt on his head and he cried GOD SAVE ME! and he wobbled and the bag on top fell back into the lorry. The men loading him insulted his ancestry, wounding me...'. Azaro eventually calls out to his father, who breaks into tears of shame and hurriedly moves away, only to trip and collapse in the mud. 'Dad stayed on the ground, covered in mud, not moving, as if dead, while his blood trickled from his back and mixed with the rubbish of the earth'. Azaro's wanderings in the city are no longer innocent. Exposed to the dirty secret that the basis of modern society lies in the blood of labour, which mixes with the rubbish of the earth, he intones, 'My wanderings had at last betrayed me, because for the first time in my life I had seen one of the secret sources of my father's misery'.[211]

Dad's body serves as a marker for the irreducibility of labour. Later in the novel, Azaro remarks of his father that 'His neck ached all the time. He developed sores on his feet. The skin around his shoulders, the back of his ears, his neck, and all along his spine began to peel away. His skin turned a greyish colour because of the salt and cement that spilled on him from the loads he carried'.[212] The labouring body is here colonised by commodities, transfigured as a beast of burden. In a particularly poignant passage, Azaro observes his father awakening and hints at the relationship between labour and corporeal pain: 'The dried surface of his wounds came off on the sheets. His pain was reopened. He went to work as usual.'[213] And by doing so, by dragging his ailing body to work, Dad sustains the world of commodity-exchange. In a voice resonant with despair, he informs Azaro, 'I have been carrying the world on my head today.'[214]

---

210. Okri 1992a, p. 147.
211. Okri 1992a, p. 149.
212. Okri 1992a, p. 187.
213. Okri 1992a, p. 284.
214. Okri 1992a, p. 60.

While much of Okri's strategy for instating the forgotten world of labour pivots on images of Azaro's father and his massive, aching body, he also regularly portrays the invisible domestic labours of the protagonist's mother: preparing food; pouring palm-wine; washing sheets; making up beds. But it is her endless days in the 'informal economy', hawking goods, enduring the violence of thugs, and her labour in Madame Koto's bar that figure decisively. Mum regularly returns home having sold next to nothing, her face registering the grinding hardship of their poverty and her unseen labours. 'My life is like a pit,' she intones in a moment of despair. 'I dig it and it stays the same. I fill it and it empties'.[215] This passage links to Azaro's early observations on the women of the marketplace. There were so many female hawkers, he noted, 'all of them selling identical things, that I wondered just how Mum sold anything at all in this world of relentless dust and sunlight.'[216] After further wanderings in the market he intuits that his mother's situation is not unique: 'I saw that her tiredness and sacrifice were not her's alone but were suffered by all women, all women of the marketplace.'[217] On another of his rambles, he comes across 'the industrious women of the city', carrying basins of food on their heads.[218] Finally, in *Infinite Riches*, he encounters a horde of women, some of whom he recognises, and he remarks of their world-building labours, 'They were the endless toilers of the earth, the strong-willed market women, the women who worked all life long in salt marshes...the hawkers who trod the endless dream of their roads ...'.[219]

Yet, this observation is not a passage to melancholy. For hope resides in that endless dream of the endless toilers of the earth, a hope which, in the final volume of the *Famished Road* cycle, finds voice in the whispered word, *revolution*.[220] As if to underline this meaning, Okri assigns the boxing moniker Black Tyger to Azaro's father. The name motions, first, to William Blake and his poem, 'The Tyger' written in 1793 and inspired in part by the great uprising of the Paris poor that toppled the French monarchy.[221] But more than this, Blake had also drawn inspiration from the struggles of maroons –

---

215. Okri 1992a, p. 443.
216. Okri 1992a, p. 161.
217. Okri 1992a, p. 162.
218. Okri 1992a, p. 114.
219. Okri 1998, p. 254.
220. Okri 1998, pp. 199–200.
221. 'The Tyger' in Blake 1988, pp. 24–5.

self-liberated former slaves from Africa – in the Americas. And this theme features potently in his poem 'America' with its memorable line, 'Thou art the image of God who dwells in darkness of Africa'.[222] Okri amplifies the sound of Blake's subversive call by bestowing the nickname Black Tyger on Azaro's father. Freedom Road, that elusive path of hope and human redemption, runs through Africa, these two visionary poet-agitators remind us. As if to cement this link to Blake, Okri has also published a volume of poems, *Mental Fight*, which takes its title from Blake's revolutionary dictum:

> I will not cease from Mental Fight
> Nor shall my Sword sleep in my hand
> Till we have built Jerusalem[223]

But Black Tyger is not the singular symbol of the oppressed. As we have seen, 'the industrious women of the city' also take the stage, nowhere more dramatically than in the chapters of *Infinite Riches* that recount an uprising of the local women, led by Mum, who raid a police station and free its prisoners.[224] As the women meet, organise and mobilise, 'the word politics took on a warmer meeting', notes Azaro.[225] But, uttering a warning as to the dangers of the postcolonial period, Okri details how the rising of the women was soon taken over by 'new women, with beautiful dresses and polished manners', 'elite women' who try to 'lead the original women in another direction, quieting their urge to rebel, their desire to raid stations, descend on law courts and hospitals'.[226] The demobilisation of poor women, the refashioning of their movement by women of the dominant classes, once again leaves the people treading the endless road of their dreams. The famished road of freedom can be satiated, hints Okri, only through the means envisioned by Blake in 1793 – the propulsive self-liberation of the oppressed, an emancipation-movement through which they remake themselves and their world.

---

222. 'America a Prophecy', in Blake 1988, p. 52. On the inspiration Blake derived from maroon-struggles, see Linebaugh and Rediker 2000, pp. 344–51. Among the best works on Blake and his radicalism are Thompson 1993 and Erdman 1991.
223. Okri 1999. There is also an interesting exchange in *Infinite Riches* (1998, p. 268) which refers to Blake's claim that the soul of a black boy is white, i.e. pure. Blake's poem, 'The Little Black Boy' can be found in Blake 1988, p. 9.
224. Okri 1998, p. 33.
225. Okri 1998, p. 34.
226. Okri 1998, p. 37.

With this move into the sphere of historical action, Okri's subtle deployment of the imagery of witchcraft transcends the domain of folklore while preserving its essential ingredients. To paraphrase Walter Benjamin, Okri dissolves folklore into the space of history.[227] By enlisting witchcraft-idioms in the service of a radical aesthetics, a dialectical optics that estranges the modes of perception and cognition associated with commodified life, Okri tethers images of bewitched accumulation to a defetishising impulse. His initial move involves strategies of de-familiarisation that render the transactions of the capitalist market strange and bewildering. Like contemporary urban folklore, Okri attends to the anonymity of sorcery, to the sheer randomness of violence in market-society. This strategy pries open the space for new modes of experiencing capitalist relations – as when Azaro closes his eyes and, reopening them, sees immaterial beings in the market. This displacement of ordinary perception enables us to apprehend 'magicians of money' as part-animal, part-spirit-creatures who borrow 'bits of human beings to partake of reality'. Okri thus draws upon popular rhetorics of enrichment through disembodiment to construct an intricate image of capital as a vampire-power seizing the labouring bodies of the poor – even colonising them, as salt and cement do with Dad's skin – in order to feed the demonic appetites of accumulation. Crucially, this accumulation does not merely fatten the oppressors (though it certainly does that); more significantly, it steadily expands their material power, the means of production and the labourers at their command, as we see with the 'cyclical transformations' of Madame Koto's bar.

But, just as there is no accumulated wealth without the labour of the poor, so there can be no vampires without the blood of the living. And, in the sheer, stubborn survival of the poor, their persistent struggle for a better life, hope resides.[228] As much as capital possesses them, invading their bodies and spirits, the world's labouring poor, 'the endless toilers of the earth', can never be fully colonised. They are relentlessly driven by a hunger – of both the body and the spirit – to remake the world. But, in order to do so, they must re-dream it. And this means awakening from the nightmare-world of everyday-life in

---

227. '…[H]ere it is a question of the dissolution of mythology into the space of history' (Benjamin 1999, Notebook N, p. 458).

228. On the significance of survival to Okri see Fraser 2002, p. 47. See also in this regard his comment about the Mum-figure from *The Famished Road* in Wilkinson 1990, p. 85.

order to activate dreams of justice and hope. As Black Tyger tells Azaro, 'We must take an interest in politics. We must become spies on behalf of justice.... We must look at the world with new eyes. We must look at ourselves differently.... We haven't begun to live yet'.[229]

If we have not begun to live yet, this is because we inhabit a vampiric night-world, a zombie-economy of the living dead. Okri's accomplishment is to have opened doors onto this world by disrupting ordinary modes of perception. Reworking popular hermeneutics of suspicion, he helps us see what eludes everyday experience in bourgeois society: grotesque market-forces that colonise human bodies and spirits. Giving these monsters and their effects a fantastic perceptibility, he portrays the world in which we live as an occult economy of terrifying transactions between bodies and money. But, in that space, he also locates the 'spies on behalf of justice' who compose the *hopeful monster* of popular revolt from below.

---

229. Okri 1992a, p. 498.

Conclusion

Ugly Beauty: Monstrous Dreams of Utopia

Capitalist market-society overflows with monsters. But no grotesque species so command the modern imagination as the vampire and the zombie. In fact, these two creatures need to be thought conjointly, as interconnected moments of the monstrous dialectic of modernity. Like Victor Frankenstein and his Creature, the vampire and the zombie are doubles, linked poles of the split society. If vampires are the dreaded beings who might possess us and turn us into their docile servants, zombies represent our haunted self-image, warning us that we might already be lifeless, disempowered agents of alien powers. 'Under the hegemony of the spirit world of capital,' writes Chris Arthur, 'we exist for each other only as capital's zombies, its "personifications", "masks", "supports", to use Marx's terms'.[1] In the image of the zombie lurks a troubled apprehension that capitalist society really is a night of the living dead.

Arthur's insight returns us to the salient image that proliferates throughout Sub-Saharan Africa today: the zombie-labourer. Having emerged in Haiti in the early twentieth-century, the earliest zombies were indeed 'dead men working', unthinking body-machines, lacking identity, memory and consciousness – possessing only the physical capacity

---

1. Arthur 2004, p. 172.

for labour. Unlike flesh-eating ghouls, who have come to stand in for them in the culture-industries of late capitalism, these zombies harbour the hidden secret of capitalism, its dependence on the bondage and exploitation of human labourers. However, because they are the *living* dead, zombies possess the capacity to awaken, to throw off their bonds, to reclaim life amid the morbid ruins of late capitalism. As much as they move slowly and clumsily through the routinised motions of deadened life, zombies also possess startling capacities for revelry and revolt, latent energies that can erupt in riotous nights of the living dead. Bursting across movie-screens and the pages of pulp-fiction, such zombie-festivals contain moments of carnivalesque insurgency, horrifying disruptions of the ordered and predictable patterns of everyday-life. Without warning, a rupture in the fabric of the normal transforms the living dead into hyper-active marauders. The maimed and disfigured seize the streets and invade shopping malls; authority collapses; anarchy is unleashed. Part of the attraction of such displays, and of much of the horror-genre generally, resides, of course, in its capacity to gratify as much as to frighten. As viewers, we (or at least many of us) derive a deep pleasure from images of fantastic beings wreaking havoc upon polite citizens of well-ordered society. And, here, we can locate part of the utopian charge animating zombie rebellions.

As Bakhtin reminds us, utopia often comes bathed in the grotesque. It does so in reaction to the anti-sensuous, anti-corporeal striving of official cultures to tame bodies and desires, enclose property and personality, regulate labour and recreation, control festivity and sexuality. Against the dreary and anti-corporeal seriousness of sanctioned modes of life, oppositional cultures engage in parody by way of inversion. They elevate the degraded and debased – outcasts, freaks, the simple-minded, and the hideously deformed. And they often do so by celebrating the bizarre, fractured and over-sized human body, deploying a *grotesque realism* that mocks dreary officialdom and inverts its values and symbolic orders. The utopian register of grotesque realism moves via a dialectic of inversion; the degraded now do the degrading, bringing low that which official culture has elevated, uplifting what has been suppressed. Yet, the utopian impulse highlights rebirth as much as degradation. 'To degrade is to bury, to sow and to kill simultaneously, in order to bring forth something more and better', writes Bakhtin. 'To degrade also means to concern oneself with the lower stratum of the body, the life of the belly and the reproductive organs...'. Contrary to the defined and enclosed heroic

body of the bourgeois/aristocratic male, then, the grotesque body 'is unfinished, outgrows itself, transgresses its own limits. The stress is laid on those
parts of the body that are open to the outside world...the open mouth, the
genital organs, the breast, the phallus, the potbelly, the nose'.[2] And, with
respect to the zombie-genre, we should add: the cut, the sore, the dangling
limb, all of them reminders of the corporeal fragmentation at the heart of capitalism, and of the open wounds that join wage-labourers into a monstrous
collectivity.

To be sure, the culture industries seize on, sanitise and repackage these
carnivalesque images, endeavouring to cathect riotous energies into the
consumption of commodities. Such commodification of the carnivalesque
proceeds by reifying its elements, replacing regenerating laughter with
mere irony.[3] And yet, the process of taming subversive impulses is never
total; something always exceeds and resists its grasp. After all, the very de-
radicalising effects of mass-culture are achieved only by awakening precisely
the desires meant to be sublimated. It follows that 'a process of compensatory
exchange must be involved here', as Fredric Jameson observes.

> If the ideological function of mass culture is understood as a process
> whereby otherwise dangerous and protopolitical impulses are 'managed'
> and defused, rechanneled and offered spurious objects, then some prelimi-
> nary step must be theorized in which these same impulses – the raw mate-
> rial upon which the process works – are awakened within the very texts that
> seek to still them.[4]

And it is these utopian energies that animate the nightmares of the ruling
classes, the bad dreams that surface in characters like Jack Cade; in Azaro's
father as he grows monstrously large and vanquishes the thugs of the Party
of the Rich; in the many-headed hydra of the rebellious mob; in the riotous
women of *Infinite Riches*; in Frankenstein's Creature; in Marx's image of the
insurgent global proletariat.

---

2. Bakhtin 1984, pp. 21, 26. Bakhtin's brilliant study is not without its limitations.
I address some of these in McNally 2001, Chapter 4. For one particularly interesting attempt to rework Bakhtin in terms of gender and race, see O'Connor 1991, pp.
199–217.

3. See Bakhtin's comments (1984, pp. 386–8) on Lucian. The culture-industries,
I contend, merely exacerbate these same tendencies.

4. Jameson 1981, p. 287.

One of the decisive things about the many-headed monster and Frankenstein's Creature is that they are multiplicities that comprise a unity. The hydra-mob's many heads connect to a common body, just as the corporeal bits of Frankenstein's creature, made up of animal and human parts, cohere into a living, breathing, speaking colossus. The ascription of the latter attribute – speech – is, as we have seen, amongst the most subversive aspects of Mary Shelley's story, perhaps why it is omitted in most film-adaptations. It is bad enough, after all, that a creature assembled from fragmented parts might actually assume a human form, however distorted. But, with speech, it becomes exponentially more threatening, capable of association with others of its ilk. In Shelley's tale, of course, the Creature is isolated and forlorn, desperately seeking a companion. It speaks only to its oppressors and tormenters. But, traversing her novel lurks the anxiety that the Creature might not forever be alone, that it might acquire a companion, reproduce, and form a monstrous social collectivity – and this prospect is hinted at in the sailors' rebellion that hurries the novel to its close.

Collective rebellion by labourers signals the course imagined by Marx, who is said to have enjoyed the story of *Frankenstein*.[5] In his call for associated action and organisation, Marx imagines that the 'crippled monstrosity'[6] of the working class might reassemble itself, find its voice, and begin to move to a new rhythm, not that of capital's machines, but one of its own making. In this dance of the grave-diggers, Marx identifies monstrous forces of redemption and regeneration. He envisions the multiplicity that is the collective worker acquiring a new consciousness and identity, a new praxis. There is no loss of individuality here; on the contrary, a new mode of individuality is generated in the act of revolutionary re-assemblage. In this spirit, Marx projects the emancipation of the collective worker in terms of the creation of a new 'organic social body wherein people reproduce themselves as individuals, but as social individuals'.[7] In so doing, he envisions proletarian liberation as a dance of the *concrete universal*, to borrow a term from Hegel, a dynamic totalisation that affirms identity and difference, or what Marx calls elsewhere, a 'unity of the diverse'.[8] While Marx himself may not always have envisioned

---

5. See Wheen 1999, p. 72.
6. Marx 1976, p. 481.
7. Marx 1973, p. 832.
8. Marx 1973, p. 101.

this collective agent in all its potential diversity, this is the direction in which the logic of his position tends.[9]

It is suggestive in this regard that Britain's sailors, the group responsible for collective revolt in *Frankenstein*, were just such a unity of the diverse, 'multi-racial – Irish, English, African,' as two historians note. So much was this the case that 'by the end of the Napoleonic wars, roughly one-quarter of the Royal Navy was black'.[10] Assembled from multiple groups of the dispossessed, the deep-sea proletariat rose to moments of exceptional militancy and solidarity. It seized ships in mutinous insurgencies; it challenged the rule of state and capital; and it transgressed the enclosures amongst nationalities and ethno-racial groups, acquiring a heightened grotesquerie in its violations of the emerging categories of race.

* * *

Proletarian monsters are, by definition, monsters of the body. Not only do their corporeal powers become the life force of capital, enabling the latter's vampire-like expansion; more than this, their emancipatory struggles entail monstrous claims of the body against the abstracting powers of capital. Marx's dance of the grave-diggers – a festive zombie-riot – involves a victory of the sensuous over the non-sensuous, the material over the abstractly ideal. Bodies loom large, grotesquely so, in this narrative of liberation and their monstrous presence reverberates across stories of zombies on the march.

This is the point at which Marx's communist vision rejoins the great plebeian tradition excavated by Bakhtin, in which 'the immortal labouring people constitute the world's body', in the words of one commentator.[11] It is also the point at which it converges with that *anthropological materialism*, to use

---

9. I have addressed some of these issues in 'Unity of the Diverse: Global Labor in the Age of Global Capital', paper presented to the first North-American *Historical Materialism* conference, York University, Toronto, April 27–9, 2008. It is also worth noting that the late Marx returned to some of these questions, writing tens of thousands of words on ethnicity and gender. See Smith 2002, pp. 73–84, and Anderson 2002, pp. 84–96. But, as Susan Buck-Morss has powerfully and provocatively noted, recording the true diversity of plebeian insurgence also means rewriting the story of freedom (and slavery) in terms of the suppressed record of the world-historical Haitian Revolution. See Buck-Morss 2009.

10. Linebaugh and Rediker 2000, pp. 132, 311.

11. Suvin 1982, p. 113.

Walter Benjamin's designation, whose pivot is the emancipation of the flesh.[12] In affirming its concrete embodiment as a living collectivity, the insurgent working class rescues labouring bodies from their near-death, their function as mere automata that enable capital's valorisation.

This moment of rebellion is also one of recuperation. The zombies awake, and in doing so reclaim their very corporeality from the abstracting powers of capital, establishing the ontological precondition for the recovery of memory, identity and history. So shattering is a zombie-awakening, so disruptive of the molecular structure of bourgeois life that it is typically figured as a frenzied upheaval of nature itself. After all, the monstrous collective body of labour inevitably appears as an elementally natural force in a society that has abstracted it from history and the social. Okri grasps precisely this naturalisation of the labouring body when, in portraying Azaro's father at work, he tells us that 'his blood trickled from his back and mixed with the rubbish of the earth'.[13] The idiom of horror remains the only genre for registering the insurgency of a monstrous body joined to the very earth itself. Take Dickens's description from *Barnaby Rudge*. He begins with three ringleaders of the Gordon Riots, whom he describes as 'covered with soot and dirt, and dust, and lime; their garments torn to rags; their hair hanging wildly about them; their hands and faces jagged and bleeding with the wounds of rusty nails'. Behind them is 'a dense throng' of insurgents, offering 'a vision of coarse faces...a dream of demon heads and savage eyes, and sticks and iron bars uplifted in the air'. This 'bewildering horror', Dickens writes, pulsed with 'many phantoms, not to be forgotten all through life'.[14]

There is a horrified poetics of class and gender at work here. The mob is simultaneously animalised and feminised. Its femininity does not, of course, partake of genteel passivity; rather, it consists of crazed, transgressive, plebeian womanhood. The riotous rabble is defined by blood and dirt, by huge, all-consuming passions, by the life-swallowing powers of 'mother-earth'. The female grotesque thus features centrally in the construction of the monstrous mob.[15] So do the categories of race.

---

12. Benjamin 1999, pp. 591, 633.
13. Okri 1992a, p. 149.
14. Dickens 2003, Chapter 50, p. 419.
15. See generally Russo 1994. The postmodernist tenor of this text means, unfortunately, that the thematics of class are largely eclipsed. See also Sipple 1991, pp. 135–54, where internal relations of class and gender are perceptively posed. An outstand-

The extent to which the European working classes were 'racialised' in the discourse of emergent industrial capitalism is rarely appreciated today. Yet, during the epoch in which scientific racism emerged in order to rationalise the oppression of Africans and colonised peoples, its categories were sufficiently pliable to racialise the labouring poor of Europe as well. Granier de Cassagnac, for instance, in his *Histoire des classes ouvrières et des classes bourgeoises* (1838) asserted that proletarians were a subhuman race formed through the interbreeding of prostitutes and thieves. In a similar register, Henry Mayhew's *London Labour and the London Poor* (1861) divided humanity into two distinct races: the civilised and the wanderers. The latter, including the labouring poor of Britain, were defined by their ostensible incapacity to transcend the body and its desires.[16] Similar processes can be observed in Sweden, where proletarians were represented as 'another race', as 'crude' and 'coarse', as 'a seething mass, a formless...rabble', partaking in the realm of 'the primitive, the animal'.[17] Central to this racialisation and feminisation of the working classes was the attribution of a grotesque corporeality.

It is this stuff of hyper-embodiment that is frequently celebrated in popular culture, including the horror-genre. When the zombies strike back, it is their huge, awkward, oozing bodies that appear most prominently. As in Marx or Bakhtin, there is a plebeian poetics at work here, an ugly beauty of the grotesque body of the oppressed.

* * *

Here is something lacking, however, in the zombie-revolts that emerge in popular culture today. And that something is what has been lost in the transition from Haitian to Hollywood zombies – and the very thing that has been recuperated in zombie-tales emanating today from Sub-Saharan Africa. Haitian zombies, as we have seen, are mindless labourers, people reanimated from the dead who lack everything – identity, consciousness, memory, language – save the brute capacity for labour. They are physical bearers of labour-power and nothing more. This feature figured prominently in American popular

---

ing historical treatment of these dialectics of class, race and gender is presented by McClintock 1995.

16. See McNally 2001, p. 4. On the construction of scientific racism see McNally 2002, Chapter 4.

17. Frykman and Lofgren 1987, p. 129.

appropriations of zombies in the era of the Great Depression. As we have seen, in William Seabrook's *The Magic Island* (1929) zombies are portrayed as 'dead men working in the cane fields', as 'automatons...bent expressionless over their work'.[18] And, throughout the Depression-era, the image of the zombie as a living-dead labourer was never lost in Hollywood-horror. In the film *White Zombie* (1932), for instance, Bela Lugosi plays Murder Legendre, bewitched sinister factory-owner in Haiti who raises the dead to toil in his sugar-mill. As one critic of the film remarks, 'The gaunt, sinewy workers with sunken eyes shuffle in production assembly lines and around the large, central milling vat. They are reifications of despair and hopelessness, no more than cogs in the mighty machine themselves'.[19] This image of alienated, crushing, mindless labour in capitalist society resonated powerfully in a US wracked by unemployment, poverty and class-resentment. But it was largely lost with the revival of the zombie in American culture during the radical upsurges of the 1960s, a revival which owes much to George Romero's pioneering films beginning with *Night of the Living Dead* (1968). For Hollywood's rediscovery of the zombie was, in fact, a revision, one that short-circuited the figure of the zombie-labourer. Interestingly, as previously noted, although he used the term 'living dead', Romero initially imagined his monsters as flesh-eating ghouls, not zombies, and it is that construction – as flesh-eating monsters – that now defines 'zombies' within mass-culture in North America and Europe.[20] This emphasis on consumption, on eating flesh, was central to the displacement of the zombie-labourer. By repositioning zombies as crazed consumers, rather than producers, recent Hollywood horror-films tend to offer biting criticism of the hyper-consumptionist ethos of an American capitalism characterised by excess. But this deployment comes at the cost of invisibilising the hidden world of labour and the disparities of class that make all this consumption

---

18. Seabrook 1929, pp. 94, 101.

19. Dendle 2007, p. 47. *White Zombie* has produced a wide range of reactions amongst critics. Its racist stereotypes of Haitians have been rightly deplored. At the same time, some critics have seen in the film a (perhaps unconscious) critique of US-imperialism in Haiti. For a sampling of positions see Rhodes 2001; Williams 1983; Lowry and deCordova 2004, pp. 173–211; and Bishop 2008, pp. 141–52. As Dendle (2007, pp. 48–9) notes, *White Zombie* also registers deep gender-anxieties about the growing independence of American women during the War.

20. See Dendle 2001, p. 121, who points out that the word zombie never appears in the film, only 'ghoul' and 'flesh-eating ghoul'. On the remaking of the zombie as ghoul over the past forty years, see Boon 2007, p. 38.

possible. As a result, contemporary zombie-films, at their best, tend to offer a critique of consumerism, not capitalism – one that fails to probe the life-destroying, zombifying processes of work in bourgeois society.

The occlusion of the zombie-labourer also de-radicalises images of zombie-revolt. During World-War Two, a period of race-, gender- and class-upheaval in America, zombies emerged as figures of rebellion. A whole series of 1940s zombie-movies in fact 'denied the possibility of complete containment',[21] locating horror in zombie-*awakening*, rather than in their passive, controlled state. Rarely, however, was the zombie-idiom used as subversively as it was in Jacques Tournier's haunting film, *I Walked with a Zombie* (1943). Celebrated as 'one of the finest of all American horror films',[22] *I Walked with a Zombie* depicts the decline of colonial capitalism in the form of a dysfunctional white family, descended from slave-owners, as it sinks slowly into decay and self-destruction on a small Caribbean island. Deploying a problematically gendered trope, a white woman comes to stand in for a dying colonialism. Characters in the film remark of her, as of her class as a whole, that 'she was dead in her own life' and 'dead in the selfishness of her spirit'.[23] In a dramatic reversal, zombies now take shape as creatures from the imperial metropole, not the colonial hinterland, as the living dead of a morbid colonialism, passively waiting to be washed away by the tides of history. Fittingly, the film ends with the deceased 'white zombie' and her lover disappearing into the sea, as the voice of a black character intones, 'forgive them who are dead and give peace and happiness to the living'.

At the historical moment *I Walked with a Zombie* was offering its cultural critique of empire, a new and innovative 'zombie-music' was emerging to give expression to rebellious counter-currents amongst African-Americans. The very year the film appeared (1943) the so-called 'Harlem Riot' erupted following the shooting of a black soldier by a white cop.[24] The Harlem uprising came amidst a growing radicalisation of African-Americans in unions,

---

21. Dendle 2007, p. 49.
22. Wood 2004, p. 126.
23. A clear gender-theme runs through *I Walked with a Zombie*, suggesting that anxiety about female independence functions as a trope for exploring anxieties about the death of colonialism.
24. See 'The Harlem Outbreak' in James, Breitman, Keemer et al. 1980, pp. 281–7, and Capeci 1977.

the military, and burgeoning civil-rights organisations. As new practices and cultures of resistance formed, music became a key register for expressing discontent with racism, menial jobs, unemployment, poor wages, and military conscription.[25] In after-hours clubs and apartments, a young, defiant generation of jazz-musicians forged a radically new musical language, soon known as *bebop*, as an aesthetic idiom for new structures of feeling – anger, pride, non-conformity with white America, hostility to racism and privilege.[26] Bebop was a complex, musically sophisticated, emotionally expressive protest-music. It required exceptional musicianship and creativity and enormous facility at improvisation. In and through it, the new jazz-revolutionaries produced a music of dissonance, of jarring contrasts and poly-rhythms as they turned chord-progressions around, played against a tune's underlying harmony, and shifted tempos – all in an effort to create a visionary African-American aesthetic that spoke to a world in disarray while pulsating with the rhythms of zombie-rebellion.

One of the geniuses at the heart of this artistic revolution was pianist Thelonious Monk (1917–82) who created a series of remarkable jazz-compositions built around his singularly angular phrasing, highlighted by unusual intervals, dissonance and displaced notes.[27] Amongst fellow jazz-artists, Monk's musical language was sometimes known as *zombie-music*. Pianist Mary Lou Williams explains: 'Why "Zombie music"? Because the screwy chords reminded us of music from *Frankenstein* or any horror film'.[28] In Monk's music, 'screwy chords' express the rhythms of a world out of joint, a space of reification in which people are reduced to things – and in which they vio-

---

25. For a treatment of the overall social and cultural context, see also Kelley 1996, Chapter 7.

26. Jones 1963, pp. 171–211, remains amongst the best treatments of the social and musical foundations of the bebop-revolution. Also worth consulting, even if less insightful, are Giola 1977, Chapter 6; Gitler 1985; Hobsbawm 1989, pp. 54, 82–4. Russell 1973 has intimations of the political content of many of the bebop-rebel's musical innovations. Saul 2003, Part 1, is also helpful. I should add here that my claim for bebop as an African-American protest-music does not mean that it is an exclusively black cultural phenomenon. Like all great aesthetic movements, it has a universalising dynamic, a capacity to express a wide range of cultural experiences; but its social, cultural and political roots are African-American.

27. At long last, we now have the biography Monk deserves in Robin D.G. Kelley's outstanding work, *Thelonious Monk: The Life and Times of an American Original* (2009). Appendix A, 'A Technical Note on Monk's Music', outlines Monk's signature-musical innovations.

28. Williams 1954. See also Stearns 1958, p. 222.

lently awaken from their frozen state. This is an aesthetic of disharmony, of a broken world whose bits can never be entirely reassembled. There is a stark and unsettling beauty here, one comprised of 'frozen sounds,' as Williams puts it. Monk's tunes insert us into a world in which things come to life – in which, to reprise Marx, tables begin to dance and evolve 'grotesque ideas' out of their wooden brains.[29] But, in Monk's compositions, we hear not only the jarring sounds of things coming to life; more than this, we heed the rhythms of zombie-movement, the ferocious sounds of the dance of the living dead. It is now widely recognised that the entire African-American experience is bathed in living death, in the 'double consciousness' of being both person and thing.[30] And Monk's music captures this in the monstrously beautiful cadences of the banging, smashing, crashing chords of an emerging African-American protest-music, one that gave a new urban cadence to 'the rhythmic cry of the slave', to use Du Bois's apt expression.[31]

The music of the enslaved – both song of sorrow and cry of freedom – is, like all horror idioms, a language of doubling. Across these musical landscapes, freedom and bondage clash, producing that jarring dissonance in which pursued and pursuer reverse positions, each chasing and fleeing the other. Only a music of poly-rhythms, shifting tempos, and displaced notes could begin to capture the 'ugly beauty' of this experience, to invoke the title of one of Monk's compositions.[32] After all, enunciating the wounds and scars of oppression, the beauty of zombie-music can only be ugly. In giving voice to bodies in pain, it howls these wounds, names them, explores them, accents them. For this reason, horror must remain one of its idioms. And yet, in its very artistic production, it defiantly asserts the enduring beauty of survival and resistance – and of the pursuit of freedom. For, as Monk's preeminent biographer states, 'Thelonious Monk's music is essentially about freedom',

---

29. Marx 1976, pp. 163–4.
30. The foundational text here is W.E.B. Du Bois, *The Souls of Black Folk* (1994 [1903]). On the history of this pioneering text see Lewis 1993, pp. 277–96. Du Bois's concept of 'double consciousness' has influenced generations of social theorists. For important discussions, see Allen 1997, pp. 49–67, and Lewis R. Gordon 1997, pp. 69–79. A crucial text in extending the range of application of Du Bois's concept is Paul Gilroy, *The Black Atlantic: Modernity and Double Consciousness* (1993). For an important critical response to Gilroy's text, see Chrisman 1997.
31. Du Bois 1994 [1903], p. 156.
32. Monk's tune, 'Ugly Beauty', first appeared on his album *Underground* (Columbia Records, 1968).

and this contributes to its haunting beauty.[33] Like Frankenstein's Creature, the crippled monsters of labour, the descendants of African slaves, speak – and sing, dance and create world-moving art. Through this zombie-music, the living dead come to life, dance across a landscape of corpses and ruin, and affirm the irreducible beauty of their freedom-song.

Today, modern jazz no longer occupies its central position as protest-music, even if its influences can be detected in genres as diverse as hip-hop and Afrobeat. Interestingly, a new zombie-music of sorts, carrying a jazz-influence, emerged in Nigeria during the 1970s, just as neoliberal globalisation was setting in and provoking the spate of vampire and zombie-tales we have explored. In Fela Kuti's hit-album *Zombie* (1977), the image of the living dead is re-deployed in a searing attack on the Nigerian army, whose members (and their political masters) figure as zombified monsters preying on the people. A churning mix of black power, socialism and pan-Africanism, Kuti's Afrobeat-music both reflected and inspired social protest and opposition (including riots in Accra during a 1978 performance of 'Zombie').[34] As in *I Walked with a Zombie*, Kuti's famous tune reverses the metaphor, portraying the ruling classes and their troops as the true zombies, not those who labour for capital.

Like the Gothic novel, Kuti's tune rehearses a dialectical reversal whose classic formulation is to be found in Hegel's drama of master and slave. In his *Phenomenology of Spirit*, Hegel takes us through a role reversal in which the master, in his dependence on the labour of the slave, becomes a passive, lifeless being, bereft of historical initiative, while the slave discovers in labour her life-generating, world-building capacities.[35] The dialectic thus undergoes a boomerang-effect, zombifying society's rulers and awakening the oppressed to their historical capacity to extend the realm of human freedom. If, in the Hegelian dialectic, 'Progress in the realization of Freedom can be carried out only by the slave',[36] historical reversal toward freedom comes for Marx by way of the insurgence of the global proletariat. But, here, Marx's knowledge

---

33. Kelley 2009, p. 2.
34. It must be acknowledged, however, that Fela Kuti's music and life also embody elements of misogyny in his efforts to uphold 'traditional' practices of male polygamy.
35. Hegel 1977, pp. 117–18.
36. Kojève 1969, p. 50.

was deficient, as he too did not grasp the extent to which an actual revolution made by African slaves – the Haitian Revolution (1794–1805) – figured directly in Hegel's view that the freedom of slaves must be won through their own emancipatory struggle in a revolutionary 'trial by death'. But Susan Buck-Morss's path-breaking research in this area suggests persuasively that Hegel not only followed Haitian events, but that 'he used the sensational events of Haiti as the linchpin in his argument in the *Phenomenology of Spirit*'.[37] In so doing, she reinstates the dialectic of race and class that is constitutive of capitalist modernity, while demonstrating that a revolutionary movement of black slaves was the high point of freedom-struggles in 'the age of revolution'.[38]

Rethinking the history of bourgeois modernity in this way requires that we read the post-Hegelian treatment of the master-slave relation through Fanon as much as Marx.[39] Indeed, doing so renders more powerful Marx's reversal of the zombie-dialectic. After all, Marx depicts capitalists too as prisoners of reification, as systematically zombified. 'The capitalist', he writes, 'functions only as *personified* capital, capital as person, just as the worker is no more than *labour* personified.' In strictly economic terms, it is capital that rules, not capitalists; the latter are mere bearers of capital's imperatives. Because they are merely things personified, 'the rule of the capitalist over the worker is the rule of things over man, of dead labour over the living'. As a result, capitalists too function as the living dead. Colonised and directed by things, they live hollowed out lives, spiritually poor for all their plenty. Yet, reified though they are, capitalists do not have an interest in or capacity for de-reification. Instead, they 'find absolute satisfaction' in this 'process of alienation', whereas the

---

37. Buck-Morss 2009, p. 59.

38. This is the title of a major historical work by Eric Hobsbawm (1962), a book that barely registers the Haitian Revolution. For a key historical study that corrected the record see the classic work by C.L.R. James, *The Black Jacobins* (1963). See also Blackburn 1988, Chapter 6, and Dubois 2004.

39. The key text here is Frantz Fanon, *The Wretched of the Earth* (1968). Fanon's dialogue with Hegel is well known, though often poorly theorised. Fortunately, Ato Sekyi-Otu's powerful work, *Fanon's Dialectic of Experience* (1996) provides us with a philosophically rich reading of Fanon in this regard. Feminist deployments of the master-slave dialectic have often operated within a psychoanalytical frame in which slavery is treated as a metaphor for domination, rather than an actual social-historical relation. See, for example, Jessica Benjamin's important work, *The Bonds of Love: Psychoanalysis, Feminism, and the Problem of Recognition* (1988).

worker 'confronts it as a rebel and experiences it as a process of enslavement'.[40] While capitalists can only remain in their zombie-state, workers are impelled toward a dialectical awakening.[41]

And, yet, there are blockages here, which perpetuate the sleep-like state and postpone the moment of awakening. And the danger is that the moment of awakening might be missed, to paraphrase Adorno.[42] Put differently, there is a danger that the proletariat might not be monstrous enough, that its internal separations, the ultimate key to capital's power over it,[43] might leave it too unco-ordinated to perform its zombie-dance. Because internal division is the secret to the zombie-sleep in labour's relation to capital, to its submissiveness and subordination to an alien will, Marx saw the key to unions and workers' organisation not in their strictly material achievements but, rather, in the spirit of opposition they cultivated. Without struggle, resistance and international organisation, he argued, workers risked becoming 'apathetic, thoughtless, more or less well-fed instruments of production'[44] – in short, zombies who cannot awaken. Until that awakening, monstrous utopia lives on in stories, dreams, music, art, and moments of resistance that prefigure the grotesque movements through which the collective labourer throws off its zombified state in favour of something new, frightening and beautiful.

* * *

And this returns us to the emancipation of the body, to the liberation of monstrous corporeality and sensuous existence from the abstracting circuits of capital. But it should also serve to remind us that there is no emancipation of the body short of a radical transformation of the relations between persons and things, short of the liberation of all our 'relations to the world – seeing, hearing, tasting, feeling, thinking, contemplating, sensing, wanting, acting, loving'.[45] It is the essence of any materialist phenomenology that humans

---

40. Marx, 'Results of the Immediate Process of Production' in Marx 1976, pp. 989–90.
41. On dialectics of awakening in Walter Benjamin, see McNally 2001, pp. 211–19.
42. Adorno 1973, p. 3. While the profundity of Adorno's point ought never to be understated, he comes perilously close to de-dialecticising the historical moment of working-class failure. See McNally 2001, pp. 216–19.
43. A point made powerfully by Lebowitz 1992, pp. 66–83.
44. Marx, ' "Chartism", July 1, 1853' in Marx and Engels 1979, p. 169.
45. Marx, 'Economic and Philosophic Manuscripts', in Marx 1975, p. 351.

are enmeshed in an object-world shaped in and through their practical activity – clothes, dwellings, beds, chairs, tables, cups, plates, tools, toys, books and more comprise the social-material and meaningful nexus of all lived experience. Yet capitalism inserts the market as forced mediator in our relations to such things. It wraps objects in the straight-jacket of the capitalist value-form. And, in so doing, it empties them of their concrete, sensible features, turning them into mere repositories of exchange-value. 'Warmth is ebbing from things', observed Walter Benjamin, in a reflection on the hollowing out of things into mere vessels of phantom-objectivity (value).[46] As Stallybrass brilliantly reminds us, these dynamics of reification and abstraction touched so personal an item for Marx as his own overcoat, whose circuits in and out of the pawn-shop he gloomily tracked. Ironically, an overcoat figured crucially in the actual life and death of Aris Kindt, the anatomised subject of Rembrandt's *The Anatomy of Dr. Nicolaas Tulp*. Unable to procure the money with which to buy one, Kindt resorted to a non-market solution: theft. For that, he was convicted, executed and dissected. It is such struggles between life and death, bound up with our relations to things, that Marx tracks throughout *Capital*. The overcoming of the rule of the market thus also means a restoration of the world of concrete objectivity, so that objects might become things 'that are touched and loved and worn'.[47] The liberation of people from the dictates of the market entails, for Marx, their reconnection with things in their concrete, sensuous, textured particularities. Dialectical reversal means not only the political victory of the oppressed; it also means de-reification, the reanimation of the relations amongst things and persons via the liberation of things, as well as persons, from circuits of abstraction.

It seems particularly significant that such a drama of reconnection with things appear prominently in a series of stories that Marx created for his daughter, Eleanor. Centred on a down-on-his-luck magician named Hans Rockle, who kept a toy-shop, Marx spun these stories for his daughter over several months. Rockle, explained Eleanor Marx,

> ...was always 'hard up.' His shop was full of the most wonderful things –
> of wooden men and women, giants and dwarfs, kings and queens, workmen

---

46. Benjamin 1996, p. 453.
47. Stallybrass 1998, p. 186.

and masters, animals and birds as numerous as Noah got into the Arc, tables
and chairs, carriages, boxes of all sorts and sizes. And though he was a magician, Hans could never meet his obligations either to the devil or the butcher,
and was therefore – much against the grain – constantly obliged to sell his
toys to the devil. These then went through wonderful adventures – always
ending in a return to Hans Rockle's shop.[48]

Here, we observe the dialectic of loss and recovery, as Hans Rockle's toys
are alienated (in payment to the devil), disappear into commodity-circuits
where they undergo great adventures, only to return to his shop. And, in
this return, resides the dream of utopia. In their reversion to use-value and
their dis-alienation, in their exit from the circuits of market-exchange, things
are recuperated, their ebbing warmth restored.

There is a magic at work in liberation, then, one that brings persons and
things back to life and breaks the spell of zombieism. That magic resides
often in stories today, just as it did in Marx's tales for his daughter. Lurking in such stories, observes Silko, are 'relentless forces, powerful spirits,
vengeful, restlessly seeking justice'. In *Almanac of the Dead*, she thus imagines
'Marx as a storyteller who worked feverishly to gather together a magical
assembly of stories to cure the suffering and evils of the world...'.[49] Ultimately, as Marx well knew, magical stories press to be taken up by 'magic
hands', to borrow Fanon's term. Rather than the detached 'hands' to which
capital tries to reduce them, the world-proletariat needs to become a many-
headed and many-handed monster, like Shelley's Demogorgon (the people-
monster), capable of shaking the very planets and upending Jupiter's throne.
We glimpse something of these possibilities in Jack Cade's ramblings, in the
battles of Black Tiger, in the mobs that smash the locks and burn down the
prisons in *Barnaby Rudge*, in the 'industrious women of the city' who storm
government-offices and police-stations in *Infinite Riches*. Too often, however,
these insurgent crowds stop short, seeking liberation at the hands of others.
This is why everything rests, as Fanon saw, on the oppressed realising

> ...that everything depends on them...that there is no such thing as a demi-
> urge, that there is no famous man who will take the responsibility for every-

48. Eleanor Marx 1973, p. 147.
49. Silko 1992, p. 316.

thing, but that the demiurge is the people themselves and the magic hands are finally only the hands of the people.[50]

It is those magic hands that possess the power to slay the monsters of the market. Until such time, the endless toilers of the earth will continue to nurture monstrous desires for utopia as they walk 'the endless dream of their roads'.

---

50. Fanon 1968, p. 197.

References

Abiodun, Josephine Olu 1997, 'The Challenge of Growth and Development in Metropolitan Lagos', in Radoki (ed.) 1997.

Achebe, Chinua 1959, *Things Fall Apart*, Greenwich: Fawcett.

Adelman, Janet 1980, '"Anger's My Meat": Feeding, Dependency and Aggression in *Coriolanus*', in *Representing Shakespeare: New Psychoanalytic Essays*, edited by Murray M. Schwartz and Coppelia Kahn, Baltimore: Johns Hopkins University Press.

Adorno, Theodor 1973, *Negative Dialectics*, trans. E.B. Ashton, New York: Seabury Press.

—— 1974, *Minima Moralia*, trans. E.F.N. Jepcott, London: Verso.

Ahmad, Aijaz 1992, *In Theory: Classes, Nations, Literatures*, London: Verso Books.

Akyuz, Yilmaz 1995, 'Taming International Finance', in Michie and Smith (eds.) 1995.

Allen, Chris 1995, 'Understanding African Politics', *Review of African Political Economy*, 65: 301–20.

Allen, Ernest, Jr. 1997, 'On the Reading of Riddles: Rethinking Du Boisian "Double Consciousness"', in Gordon (ed.) 1997.

Allen, Robert C. 1992, *Enclosure and the Yeoman*, Oxford: Clarendon Press.

Althusser, Louis 1994, 'Marx dans ses limites', in *Ecrits philosophiques et politiques*, Volume 1, Paris: Stock/IMEC.

Amanor, Kojo S. 1999, *Global Restructuring and Land Rights in Ghana: Forest Food Chains, Timber and Rural Livelihoods*, Uppsala: Nordiska Afrikainsititutet Research Report n. 108.

—— 2001, *Land, Labour and the Family in Southern Ghana: A Critique of Land Policy Under Neoliberalism*, Uppsala: Nordiska Afrikainsititutet Research Report n. 116.

Anderson, Kevin B. 2002, 'Marx's Writings on Non-Western Societies', *Rethinking Marxism*, 14, 4: 84–96.

Andrews, Lori and Dorothy Nelkin 2001, *Body Bazaar: The Market for Human Tissue in the Biotechnology Age*, New York: Crown Publishers.

Aries, Philippe 1981, *The Hour of Our Death*, trans. Helen Weaver, New York: Knopf.

Aristotle 1981, *The Politics*, trans. T.A. Sinclair and Trevor J. Saunders, Harmondsworth: Penguin Books.

Arthur, Chris 2004, *The New Dialectic and Marx's 'Capital'*, Historical Materialism Book Series, Leiden: Brill.

Ashraf, P.M. 1983, *The Life and Times of Thomas Spence*, Newcastle upon Tyne: Frank Graham.

Aston, T.H. and C.H.E. Philpin (eds.) 1985, *The Brenner Debate*, Cambridge: Cambridge University Press.

Auslander, Mark 1993, '"Open the Wombs!": The Symbolic Politics of Modern Ngoni Witchfinding', in Comaroff and Comaroff (eds.) 1993.

Austen, Jane and Seth Grahame-Smith 2009, *Pride and Prejudice and Zombies*, Philadelphia: Quirk Books.

Austin, Greta 2002, 'Marvelous Peoples or Marvelous Races: Race and the Anglo-Saxon *Wonders of the East*', in Jones and Sprunger (eds.) 2002.

Bacon, Francis 1870, *Works*, Volume 6, edited by James Spedding et al, London: Longmans.

Bakhtin, Mikhail 1981, *The Dialogic Imagination*, edited by Michael Holquist, Austin: University of Texas Press.
—— 1984, *Rabelais and His World*, trans. Helene Iswolsky, Bloomington: Indiana University Press.
Baldick, Chris 1987, *In Frankenstein's Shadow: Myth, Monstrosity and Nineteenth Century Writing*, Oxford: Clarendon Press.
Baldwin, Edward [William Godwin] 1806, *The Pantheon: Or Ancient History of the Gods of Greece and Rome*, London: Thomas Hodgkins.
Bannerji, Himani 1995, *Thinking Through: Essays on Feminisms, Marxism, and Anti-Racism*, Toronto: Women's Press.
Barber, Karin 1997, 'Popular Reactions to the Petro-Naira', in *Readings in African Popular Culture*, edited by Karin Barber, Bloomington: Indiana University Press.
Bassett, Thomas 1993, 'Land Use Conflicts in Pastoral Development in Northern Cote d'Ivoire', in *Land in African Agrarian Systems*, edited by T.J. Basset and D.E. Crumney, Madison: University of Wisconsin Press.
Bastian, Misty L. 1993, '"Bloodhounds Who Have No Friends": Witchcraft and Locality in the Nigerian Popular Press', in Comaroff and Comaroff (eds.) 1993.
—— 1997, 'Married in the Water: Spirit Kin and Other Afflictions of Modernity in Southeastern Nigeria', *Journal of Religion in Africa*, 27, 2: 116–34.
—— 2001, 'Vulture Men, Campus Cultists and Teenaged Witches: Modern Magics in Nigerian Popular Media', in Moore and Sanders (eds.) 2001.
—— 2002, 'Irregular Visitors: Narratives About *Ogbaanje* (Spirit Children) in Southern Nigerian Popular Writing', in *Readings in African Popular Fiction*, edited by Stephanie Newell, Bloomington: Indiana University Press.
—— 2003, '"Diabolical Realities": Narratives of Conspiracy, Transparency, and "Ritual Murder" in the Nigerian Popular Print and Electronic Media', in *Transparency and Conspiracy*, edited by Harry G. West and Todd Sanders, Durham, NC.: Duke University Press.
Baudrillard, Jean 1981, *For a Critique of the Political Economy of the Sign*, trans. Charles Levin, St. Louis: Telos Press.
—— 1990, *Fatal Strategies*, trans. Philip Beitchman and W.G.J. Niesluchowski, New York and London: Semiotext(e)/Pluto.
—— 1993, *The Transparency of Evil: Essays on Extreme Phenomena*, trans. James Benedict, London: Verso Books.
Bayart, Jean-François, Stephen Ellis and Beatrice Hibou 1999, *The Criminalization of the State in Africa*, Oxford: James Currey.
BBC News World Edition 2002, "Vampires' Strike Malawi Villages", 23 December.
Becket, J.V. 1991, 'The Disappearance of the Cottager and the Squatter from the English Countryside: The Hammonds Revisited', in *Land, Labour and Agriculture, 1700-1920*, edited by B.A. Holderness and Michael Turner, London: Hambledon Press.
Beier, A.L. 1985, *Masterless Men: The Vagrancy Problem in England, 1560–1640*, London: Methuen.
Benjamin, Jessica 1988, *The Bonds of Love: Psychoanalysis, Feminism, and the Problem of Recognition*, New York: Pantheon Books.
Benjamin, Walter 1973, *Understanding Brecht*, trans. Anna Bostock, London: New Left Books.
—— 1996, 'One-Way Street', in *Selected Writings, Volume 1: 1913–1926*, edited by Marcus Bullock and Michael W. Jennings, Cambridge, MA.: Belknap Press.
—— 1999, *The Arcades Project*, trans. Howard Eiland and Kevin McLaughlin, Cambridge, MA.: Belknap/Harvard University Press.
Bennett, Betty T. 1998, *Mary Wollstonecraft Shelley: An Introduction*, Baltimore: Johns Hopkins University Press.
Berlin, Ira 2003, *Generations of Captivity: A History of African-American Slaves*, Cambridge, MA.: Harvard University Press.
Bernstein, Henry 1992, 'Agrarian Structures and Change: Sub-Saharan Africa', in *Rural Livelihood: Crisis and Response*, London: Oxford University Press.

Besteman, Catherine and Lee V. Cassanelli (eds.) 1996, *The Struggle for Land in Southern Somalia: the War Behind the War*, Boulder: Westview Press.

Bildhauer, Bettina and Robert Mills (eds.) 2003, *The Monstrous Middle Ages*, Toronto: University of Toronto Press.

Billing, Christian 2004, 'Modelling the Anatomy Theatre and the Indoor Hall Theatre: Dissection on the Stages of Early Modern London', *Early Modern Literary Studies*, 13, April: 1–17.

Bilson, Anne 2009, 'March of the Zombie', *Guardian*, 1 June.

Binswanger, Hans Christoph 1994, *Money and Magic: A Critique of the Modern Economy in Light of Goethe's Faust*, trans. J.E. Harrison, Chicago: University of Chicago Press.

Bishop, Kyle 2008, 'The Sub-Subaltern Monster: Imperialist Hegemony and the Cinematic Voodoo Zombie', *The Journal of American Culture*, 31, 2: 141–52.

Blackburn, Robin 1988, *The Overthrow of Colonial Slavery 1776–1848*, London: Verso Books.

Blake, William 1988, *The Complete Poetry and Prose of William Blake*, newly revised edition, edited by David V. Erdman, New York: Anchor Books.

Bohls, Elizabeth 1994, 'Standards of Taste, Discourses of "Race," and the Aesthetic Education of a Monster: Critique of Empire in *Frankenstein*', *Eighteenth Century Life*, 18, 3: 23–36.

Bond, Patrick 2003, *Against Global Apartheid: South Africa Meets the World Bank, IMF and International Finance*, 2nd edition, Cape Town: University of Cape Town Press.

—— 2006, *Looting Africa: The Economics of Exploitation*, London: Zed Books.

Boon, Kevin Alexander 2007, 'Ontological Anxiety Made Flesh: The Zombie in Literature, Film and Culture', in *Monsters and the Monstrous: Myths and Metaphors of Enduring Evil*, edited by Niall Scott, Amsterdam, NY.: Rodopi.

Brammall, Kathryn M. 1996, 'Monstrous Metamorphosis: Nature, Morality and the Rhetoric of Monstrosity in Tudor England', *The Sixteenth Century Journal*, 27, 1, Spring: 3–21.

Brantlinger, Patrick 1996, *Fictions of State: Culture and Credit in Britain 1694–1994*, Ithaca: Cornell University Press.

Braverman, Harry 1974, *Labor and Monopoly Capital: The Degradation of Labor in the Twentieth Century*, New York: Monthly Review Press.

Brecht, Bertolt 1964, *Brecht on Theatre: Development of an Aesthetic*, edited by John Willett, London: Methuen.

Brenner, Robert 2001, 'The Low Countries in the Transition to Capitalism', *Journal of Agrarian Change*, 1, 2: 169–241.

Brockbank, Philip (ed.) 1976, 'Introduction', in *Coriolanus*, London: Arden.

Brockbank, William 1968, 'Old Anatomical Theatres and What Took Place Therein', *Medical History*, 12, 4: 371–84.

Brown, Elizabeth A.R. 1981, 'Death and the Human Body in the Later Middle Ages: The Legislation of Boniface VIII on the Division of the Corpse', *Viator*, 12: 221–70.

Brown, Laura 2001, *Fables of Modernity: Literature and Culture in the English Eighteenth Century*, Ithaca: Cornell University Press.

Buck-Morss, Susan 1989, *The Dialectics of Seeing*, Cambridge, MA.: MIT Press.

—— 2009, *Hegel, Haiti and Universal History*, Pittsburgh: University of Pittsburgh Press.

Burke, Edmund 1986, *Reflections on the Revolution in France*, Harmondsworth: Penguin Books.

—— 1991, 'Letter to a Noble Lord', in *The Writings and Speeches of Edmund Burke*, Volume 9, edited by R.B. McDowell, Oxford: Clarendon Press.

Burn, Richard 1755, *Justice of the Peace and Parish Officer*, Volume 2, 1st edition, London.

Burnett, Mark Thornton 2002, *Constructing 'Monsters' in Shakespearean Drama and Early Modern Culture*, New York: Palgrave Macmillan.

Burns, William E. 1999, 'The King's Two Monstrous Bodies: John Bulwer and the English Revolution', in Peter G. Platt (ed.) 1999.

Bush, Ray 2004, 'Undermining Africa', *Historical Materialism*, 12, 4: 173–202.

Bush, Ronald 1998, 'Monstrosity and Representation in the Postcolonial Diaspora: *The Satanic Verses, Ulysses, and Frankenstein*', in *Borders, Exiles, Diasporas*, edited by Elazar Barkan and Marie-Denise Shelton, Stanford: Stanford University Press.

Butlin, R.A. 1979, 'The Enclosure of Open Fields and the Extinction of Common Rights in England, circa 1600–1750: A Review', in *Change in the Countryside: Essays on Rural England 1500–1900*, London: Institute of British Geographers.

Byres, Terence J. 2006, 'Differentiation of the Peasantry Under Feudalism and the Transition to Capitalism: In Defence of Rodney Hilton', *Journal of Agrarian Change*, 6, 1: 17–68.

Byron, George 1991, *The Complete Miscellaneous Prose*, edited by A. Nicholson, Oxford: Oxford University Press.

Capeci, Dominic J. Jr. 1977, *The Harlem Riot of 1943*, Philadelphia: Temple University Press.

Carmody, Padraig 1998, 'Constructing Alternatives to Structural Adjustment in Africa', *Review of African Political Economy*, 75: 25–46.

Carroll, William C. 1994, '"The Nursery of Beggary": Enclosure, Vagrancy, and Sedition in the Tudor-Stuart Period', in *Enclosure Acts: Sexuality, Property and Culture in Early Modern England*, edited by Richard Burt and John Michael Archer, Ithaca: Cornell University Press.

Cartelli, Thomas 1994, 'Jack Cade in the Garden: Class Consciousness and Class Conflict in 2 *Henry VI*', in *Enclosure Acts: Sexuality, Property and Culture in Early Modern England*, edited by Richard Burt and John Michael Archer, Ithaca: Cornell University Press.

Césaire, Aimé 1996, 'Poetry and Knowledge', in *Refusal of the Shadow: Surrealism and the Caribbean*, edited by Michael Richardson, London: Verso.

—— 2000, *Discourse on Colonialism*, New York: Monthly Review Press.

Chabal, Patrick and Jean-Pascal Daloz 1999, *Africa Works: Disorder as Political Instrument*, Oxford: James Currey.

Charlesworth, Andrew 1983, *An Atlas of Rural Protest in Britain 1548–1900*, Philadelphia: University of Pennsylvania Press.

Chase, Malcolm 1988, *'The People's Farm': English Radical Agrarianism 1775–1840*, Oxford: Clarendon Press.

Chrisman, Laura 1997, 'Journeying to Death: Gilroy's *Black Atlantic*', *Race and Class*, 39, 2: 51–64.

Ciekawy, Diane and Peter Geschière 1998, 'Containing Witchcraft: Conflicting Scenarios in Postcolonial Africa', *African Studies Review*, 41, 3: 1–14.

Clark, Kenneth 1988, *An Introduction to Rembrandt*, London: John Murray/Readers Union.

Clemit, Pamela 2003, '*Frankenstein, Matilda* and the legacies of Godwin and Wollstonecraft' in Schor (ed.) 2003.

Cobban, Alfred and Robert A. Smith (eds.) 1967, *The Correspondence of Edmund Burke*, Volume 6, Cambridge: Cambridge University Press.

Cohen, Margaret 1993, *Profane Illuminations: Walter Benjamin and the Paris of Surrealist Revolution*, Berkeley: University of California Press.

Cohen, Robin 1985, 'From Peasants to Workers in Africa', in *The Political Economy of Contemporary Africa*, edited by Peter C.W. Gutkind and Immanuel Wallerstein, Beverley Hills: Sage.

Collier, Paul et al. 2003, *Breaking the Conflict Trap: Civil War and Development Policy*, Washington: World Bank.

Collins, Carole J. L. 1997, 'Reconstructing the Congo', *Review of African Political Economy*, 74: 591–600.

Comaroff, Jean 1997, 'Consuming Passions: Child Abuse, Fetishism and "The New World Order"', *Culture*, 17: 7–25.

Comaroff, Jean and John Comaroff 1999a, 'Alien-Nation: Zombies, Immigrants, and Millennial Capitalism', *Codesria Bulletin*, 3/4: 17–26.

—— 1999b, 'Occult Economies and the Violence of Abstraction: Notes from the South African Postcolony', *American Ethnologist*, 26, 2: 279–303.

—— (eds.) 1993, *Modernity and its Malcontents: Ritual and Power in Postcolonial Africa*, Chicago: University of Chicago Press.

Connor, Steven 1996, 'Space, Place and the Body of Riot in *Barnaby Rudge*', in *Charles Dickens: Longmans Critical Readers*, edited by Steven Connor, London: Longman.

Cooper, Frederick 1993, 'Africa and the World Economy', in *Confronting Historical Paradigms*, edited by Frederick Cooper et al., Madison: University of Wisconsin Press.

Coquery-Vidrovitch, Catherine 1988, *Africa: Endurance and Change South of the Sahara*, trans. David Maisel, Berkeley: University of California Press.

Cowen, Michael and Robert Shenton 1991, 'The Origin and Course of Fabian Colonialism in Africa', *Journal of Historical Sociology*, 4, 2: 143–74.

Cox, Christopher 2008, 'Swapping Secrecy for Transparency', *New York Times*, 19 October.

Craig, William J. (ed.) 1914, *The Complete Works of William Shakespeare*, Oxford: Oxford University Press.

Creegan, Kate 2008, 'Edward Ravenscroft's *The Anatomist* and the "Tyburn Riots Against the Surgeons"', *Restoration*, 32, 1: 19–35.

Cressy, David 2004, 'Lamentable, Strange, and Wonderful: Headless Monsters in the English Revolution', in *Monstrous Bodies/Political Monstrosities in Early Modern Europe*, edited by Laura Lunger Knoppers and Joan B. Landes, Ithaca: Cornell University Press.

Cvetkovich, Ann 1992, *Mixed Feelings: Feminism, Mass Culture and Victorian Sensationalism*, New Brunswick: Rutgers University Press.

Dabyden, David 1985, *Hogarth's Blacks: Images of Blacks in Eighteenth Century English Art*, Mundelstrup: Dangaroo Press.

Daniel, Trenton 2004, 'Nollywood Confidential, Part 2', *Transition*, 95: 110–28.

Dante, Alighieri 1984, *The Divine Comedy, Volume I: Inferno*, trans. Mark Musa, Harmondsworth: Penguin Books.

Davies, Ioan 1966, *African Trade Unions*, Harmondsworth: Penguin Books.

Davis, Angela Y. 1981, *Women, Race and Class*, New York: Vintage Books.

Davis, David Brion 2006, *Of Human Bondage: The Rise and Fall of Slavery in the New World*, Oxford: Oxford University Press.

Davis, Mike 2004, 'Planet of Slums', *New Left Review*, II, 26: 5–34.

De Boeck, Filip 1998, 'Beyond the Grave: History, Memory and Death in Postcolonial Congo/Zaire', in *Memory and the Postcolony: African Anthropology and the Critique of Power*, edited by Richard Werbner, London: Zed Books.

—— 1999, 'Domesticating Diamonds and Dollars: Identity, Expenditure and Sharing in Southwestern Zaire (1984–1997)', in Meyer and Geschière (eds.) 1999.

De Brosses, Charles 1756, *Histoire des navigations aux terres australes*, Volume 1, Paris: Durand.

De Bruyn, Frans 1996, *The Literary Genres of Edmund Burke: The Political Uses of Literary Form*, Oxford: Clarendon Press.

De Sainte Croix, Geoffrey E.M. 1981, *The Class Struggle in the Ancient Greek World*, London: Duckworth.

Deleuze, Gilles and Félix Guattari 1983, *Anti-Oedipus: Capitalism and Schizophrenia*, Minneapolis: University of Minnesota Press.

Delius, Peter 2001, 'Witches and Missionaries in Nineteenth Century Transvaal', *Journal of Southern African Studies*, 27, 3: 429–43.

Dendle, Peter 2001, 'Night of the Living Dead', in *The Zombie Movie Encyclopedia*, Jefferson: McFarland and Co.

—— 2007, 'The Zombie as Barometer of Cultural Anxiety', in Scott (ed.) 1997.

Derrida, Jacques 1994, *Specters of Marx*, trans. Peggy Kamuf, London: Routledge.

Descartes, René 1968, 'Discourse on Method', in *Discourse on Method and the Meditations*, trans. F.E. Sutcliffe, Harmondsworth: Penguin Books.

Diawara, Manthia 1998, 'Toward a Regional Imaginary in Africa', in *The Cultures of Gobalization*, edited by Fredric Jameson and Masao Miyoshi, Durham, NC.: Duke University Press.

Dickens, Charles 1989, *Our Mutual Friend*, edited by Michael Cotsell, Oxford: Oxford University Press.
—— 2003, *Barnaby Rudge*, edited by John Bowen, Harmondsworth: Penguin Books.
Dickinson, H.T. (ed.) 1982, *The Political Works of Thomas Spence*, Newcastle upon Tyne: Avero Publication.
Dobson, Michael and Stanley Wells (eds.) 2001, *The Oxford Companion to Shakespeare in Literature*, Oxford: Oxford University Press.
Drohan, Madelaine 2000, 'Gruesome Tales Show Nigeria's Desperate State', *Globe and Mail*, 25 September.
—— 2003, *Making a Killing: How Corporations Use Armed Force to Do Business*, Toronto: Random House.
Du Bois, W.E.B. 1994 [1903], *The Souls of Black Folk*, New York: Dover.
Dubois, Laurent 2004, *Avengers of the New World: The Story of the Haitian Revolution*, Cambridge, MA.: Harvard University Press.
Dubois, Page 1994, 'Subjected Bodies, Science and the State: Francis Bacon, Torturer', in *Body Politics: Disease, Desire and the Family*, edited by Michael Ryan and Avery Gordon, Boulder: Westview.
Eagleton, Terry 1990, *The Ideology of the Aesthetic*, Oxford: Blackwell.
Edgcliffe-Johnson, Andrew 2008, 'Vampires Set to Provide Ray of Hope Amid Gloom', *Financial Times*, 20 November.
Eichengreen, Barry 1996, *Globalizing Capital: A History of the International Monetary System*, Princeton: Princeton University Press.
El Jack, Amani 2007, 'Gendered Implications: Development Induced Displacement in Sudan', in *Development's Displacements: Ecologies, Economies, and Cultures at Risk*, edited by Peter Vandergeest, Pablo Idahosa, and Pablo S. Bose, Vancouver: UBC Press.
Elliott, Marianne 1982, *Partners in Revolution: The United Irishmen and France*, New Haven: Yale University Press.
Emmison, F.G. 1970, *Elizabethan Life: Disorder (Mainly from Essex and Assize Records)*, Chelmsford: Essex County Council.
Erdman, D.V. 1991, *Blake: Prophet Against Empire*, London: Dover.
Fage, J.D. 2002, *A History of Africa*, 4th edition, London: Routledge.
Fanon, Frantz 1967, *Black Skin, White Masks*, New York: Grove Press.
—— 1968, *The Wretched of the Earth*, New York: Grove Press.
Federici, Silvia 2004, *Caliban and the Witch: Women, the Body and Primitive Accumulation*, New York: Autonomedia.
Ferrari, Giovanna 1987, 'Public Anatomy Lessons and the Carnival: The Anatomy Theatre of Bologna', *Past and Present*, 117: 50–106.
Fine, Ben 2009, 'Development as Zombieconomics in the Age of Neoliberalism', *Third World Quarterly*, 30, 5: 885–904
Finn, Margot C. 2003, *The Character of Credit: Personal Debt in English Culture, 1740-1914*, Cambridge: Cambridge University Press.
Fisiy, Cyprian F. and Peter Geschière 1991, 'Sorcery, Witchcraft and Accumulation: Regional Variations in South and West Cameroon', *Critique of Anthropology*, 11, 3: 251–78.
—— 2001, 'Witchcraft, development and paranoia in Cameroon', in Henrietta L. Moore and Todd Sanders (eds.) 2001.
Fletcher, Anthony and Diarmid MacCulloch 1997, *Tudor Rebellions*, 4th edition, New York: Longman.
Foot, Paul 1984, *Red Shelley*, London: Bookmarks.
Forstater, Matthew 2005, 'Taxation and Primitive Accumulation: The Case of Colonial Africa', *Research in Political Economy*, 22: 51–64.
Foucault, Michel 1979, *Discipline and Punish: The Birth of the Prison*, trans. Alan Sheridan, New York: Vintage Books.
—— 1981, 'The Order of Discourse', in *Untying the Text*, edited by Robert Young, Boston: Routledge.
Fox, Loren 2003, *Enron: The Rise and Fall*, Hoboken: Wiley and Sons.

Fraser, Robert 2002, *Ben Okri: Towards the Invisible City*, Horndon: Northcote House.

Freud, Sigmund 1997, 'Fetishism', in *On Sexuality*, Volume 7 of the Penguin Freud Library, trans. James Strachey, Harmondsworth Penguin Books.

Friedman, John Black 1981, *The Monstrous Races in Medieval Art and Thought*, Cambridge, MA.: Harvard University Press.

Frykman, J. and O. Lofgren 1987, *Culture Builders: A Historical Anthropology of Middle Class Life*, New Brunswick: Rutgers University Press.

Gallop, G.I. (ed.) 1982, *Pig's Meat: Selected Writings of Thomas Spence* Nottingham: Spokesman.

Gandy, Matthew 2005, 'Learning from Lagos', *New Left Review*, II, 33: 36–52.

Genovese, Eugene D. 1976, *Roll, Jordan, Roll: The World the Slaves Made*, New York: Vintage Books.

Geschière, Peter 1997, *The Modernity of Witchcraft: Politics and the Occult in Postcolonial Africa*, trans. Peter Geschière and Janet Roitman, Charlottesville: University of Virginia Press.

—— 1999, 'Globalization and the Power of Indeterminate Meaning: Witchcraft and Spirit Cults in Africa and East Asia', in Meyer and Geschière (eds.) 1999.

Geyer-Ryan, Helga 1994, *Fables of Desire*, Cambridge: Polity Press.

Gibson, Andrew 1996, *Towards a Postmodern Theory of Narrative*, Edinburgh: Edinburgh University Press.

Gilroy, Paul 1993, *The Black Atlantic: Modernity and Double Consciousness*, Cambridge, MA.: Harvard University Press.

Giola, Ted 1977, *The History of Jazz*, Oxford: Oxford University Press.

Giroux, Henry A. 2009, 'Zombie Politics and Other Late Modern Monstrosities in the Age of Disposability', *Truthout*, 17 November, available at: <http://www.truth-out.org/111709Giroux>.

Gitler, Ira 1985, *Swing to Bop: An Oral History of the Transition in Jazz in the 1940s*, Oxford: Oxford University Press.

Global Observatory 2003, *Slums of the World: The Urban Face of Poverty in the New Millennium?*, New York: United Nations.

Godwin, William 1985, *Enquiry Concerning Political Justice*, Harmondsworth: Penguin Books.

Goethe, Johann Wolfgang von 1949, *Faust*, Part One, trans. Philip Wayne, Harmondsworth: Penguin Books.

—— 1959, *Faust*, Part Two, trans. Philip Wayne, Harmondsworth: Penguin Books.

—— 1961, *Goethe's Faust*, trans. Walter Kaufmann, New York: Doubleday.

Gohhen, Miriam 1998, 'Land Accumulation and Local Control: the Manipulation of Symbols and Power in Nso, Cameroon', in *Land and Society in Contemporary Africa*, edited by R.E. Downs and S.P. Reyna, Hanover, NH.: University Press of New England.

Gonzalez, G.M. James 1997, 'On Property: Of "Captive" "Bodies", Hidden "Flesh" and Colonization', in Gordon (ed.) 1997.

Gordon, Avery F. 1997, *Ghostly Matters: Haunting and the Sociological Imagination*, Minneapolis: University of Minnesota Press.

Gordon, Jane Anna and Lewis R. Gordon 2009, *Of Divine Warning: Reading Disaster in the Modern Age*, Boulder: Paradigm Publishers.

Gordon, Lewis R. 1997a, 'Existential Dynamics of Theorizing Black Invisibility', in *Existence in Black: An Anthology of Black Existential Philosophy*, edited by Lewis R. Gordon, London: Routledge.

—— (ed.) 1997, *Existence in Black: An Anthology of Black Existential Philosophy*, New York: Routledge.

Gramsci, Antonio 1971, *Selections from the Prison Notebooks*, trans. Quintin Hoare, New York: International Publishers.

—— 1985, 'Observations on Folklore: Giovanni Crocioni', in *Selections from Cultural Writings*, Cambridge, MA.: Harvard University Press.

Greenblatt, Stephen 1983, 'Murdering Peasants: Status, Genre, and the Representation of Rebellion', *Representations*, 1, 1: 1–29.

Grossman, Lev 2009, 'Zombies are the New Vampires', *Time*, 9 April.

Gruzinski, Serge 1988, *La colonisation de l'imaginaire*, Paris: Gallimard.

—— 2001, *Images at War: Mexico from Columbus to Blade Runner (1492–2019)*, trans. Heather MacLean, Durham, NC.: Duke University Press.

—— 2002, *The Mestizo Mind: The Intellectual Dynamics of Colonization and Globalization*, trans. Deke Dusinberre, London: Routledge.

Guerrini, Anita 2005, 'The Creativity of God and the Order of Nature: Anatomizing Monsters in the Early Eighteenth Century', in *Monsters and Philosophy*, edited by Charles T. Wolfe, London: College Publications.

Gutierrez, David 2009, 'Singapore to Legalize Financial Compensation for Organ Donors', *NaturalNews.com*, 14 July.

Guyer, Jane I. 1998, 'Wealth in People and Self-Realisation in Equatorial Africa', *Man*, new series, 28, 2: 243–66.

Gwynne, S.C. 1986, *Selling Money*, London: Weidenfeld and Nicolson.

Habermas, Jürgen 1984, *The Theory of Communicative Action*, Volume 1, trans. Thomas McCarthy, Boston: Beacon Press.

Habib, Irfan 2002, 'Marx's Perception of India', in *Essays in Indian History: Towards a Marxist Perception*, London: Anthem Press.

Hammar, Amanda 2001, '"The Day of Burning": Eviction and Reinvention in the Margins of Southwest Zimbabwe', *Journal of Agrarian Change*, 1, 4: 550–74.

Hammond, J. L. and Barbara Hammond 1978, *The Village Labourer*, London: Longman.

Hampsher-Monk, Iain 1991, 'John Thelwall and the Eighteenth-Century Radical Response to Political Economy', *Historical Journal*, 34: 1–20.

Handwerk, Gary and A.A. Markley (eds.) 2000, *Caleb Williams*, Toronto: Broadview Press.

Harley, David 1994, 'Political Post-Mortems and Morbid Anatomy in Seventeenth-Century England', *Social History of Medicine*, 7, 1: 1–28.

Harman, Chris 2009, *Zombie Capitalism: Global Crisis and the Relevance of Marx*, London: Bookmarks Publications.

Harms, Robert 2002, *The Diligent: A Voyage Through the World of the Slave Trade*, New York: Basic Books.

Harris, H.S. 1972, *Hegel's Development: Toward the Sunlight, 1770–1801*, Oxford: Clarendon Press.

Harvey, David 2003, *The New Imperialism*, Oxford: Oxford University Press.

Hattaway, Michael 1988, 'Rebellion, Class Consciousness, and Shakespeare's 2 *Henry VI*', *Cahiers Elisabethains*, 33: 13–22.

Hawkes, David 2001, *Idols of the Marketplace: Idolatry and Commodity Fetishism in English Literature, 1580–1680*, London: Palgrave Macmillan.

Haynes, Jonathan 2005, 'Nollywood, What's in a Name?', *Guardian*, 3 July.

Heckscher, William S. 1958, *Rembrandt's Anatomy of Dr. Nicolaas Tulp*, New York: New York University Press.

Hegel, Georg W.F. 1977, *Phenomenology of Spirit*, trans. A.V. Miller, Oxford: Oxford University Press.

—— 1991, *The Philosophy of History*, trans. J. Sibree, Buffalo: Prometheus Books.

Higginson, John 1988, 'Steam without a Piston Box: Strikes and Popular Unrest in Katanga, 1943–45', *International Journal of African Historical Studies*, 21, 1: 97–117.

Hill, Christopher (ed.) 1973, *The Law of Freedom and Other Writings*, Harmondsworth: Penguin Books.

—— 1966, 'The Many-Headed Monster in Late Tudor and Early Stuart Political Thinking', in *From the Renaissance to the Counter-Reformation*, edited by Charles H. Carter, London: Jonathon Cape.

—— 1972, *The World Turned Upside Down: Radical Ideas During the English Revolution*, Harmondsworth: Penguin Books.

Hilton, Rodney 1975, 'A Study in the Pre-history of English Enclosure in the Fifteenth Century', in *The English Peasantry in the Later Middle Ages*, Oxford: Clarendon Press.

Hitchcock, Susan Tyler 2007, *Frankenstein: A Cultural History*, New York: W.W. Norton.

Hobsbawm, Eric 1962, *The Age of Revolution, 1789–1848*, New York: New American Library.
—— 1965, 'The Crisis of the Seventeenth Century' in *Crisis in Europe, 1560–1660*, edited by T. Aston, London: Routledge & Kegan Paul.
—— 1989, *The Jazz Scene*, London: Weidenfeld and Nicolson.
Hochschild, Adam 1999, *King Leopold's Ghost: A Story of Greed, Terror and Heroism in Colonial Africa*, New York: Houghton Miflin.
Hoeveler, Diane Long 2003, '*Frankenstein*, Feminism and Literary Theory', in *The Cambridge Companion to Mary Shelley*, edited by Esther Schor, Cambridge: Cambridge University Press.
Holmes, Richard 1974, *Shelley: The Pursuit*, London: Weidenfeld and Nicholson.
Holzapfel, Amy Strahler 2008, 'The Body in Pieces: Contemporary Anatomy Theatres', *PAJ*, 89, 30, 2: 1–16.
Hoogvelt, Ankie 2002, 'Globalisation, Imperialism and Exclusion: The Case of Sub-Saharan Africa', in *Africa in Crisis: New Challenges and Possibilities*, London: Pluto Press.
Horkheimer, Max and Theodor Adorno 1972, *Dialectic of Enlightenment*, trans. John Cumming New York: Herder and Herder.
Humphries, Jane 1990, 'Enclosure, Common Rights, and Women: The Proletarianization of Families in the Late Eighteenth and Early Nineteenth Century', *Journal of Economic History*, 50, 1: 17–42.
Hutton, Luke 1930, 'The Black Dog of Newgate', in *The Elizabethan Underworld*, edited by A.V. Judges, London: Routledge and Sons.
Hyman, Stanley Edgar 1962, *The Tangled Bank: Darwin, Marx, Frazier and Freud as Imaginative Writers*, New York: Atheneum.
Idahosa, Pablo and Bob Shenton 2004, 'The Africanist's "New" Clothes', *Historical Materialism*, 12, 4: 67–114.
Iyayi, Festus 1986, 'The Primitive Accumulation of Capital in a Neo-Colony: The Nigerian Case', *Review of African Political Economy*, 35: 27–39.
James, C.L.R. 1963, *The Black Jacobins*, 2nd edition, New York: Random House.
James, C.L.R., George Breitman, Edgar Keemer et al. 1980, *Fighting Racism in World War Two*, New York: Monad Press.
Jameson, Fredric 1981, *The Political Unconscious: Narrative as a Socially Symbolic Act*, Ithaca: Cornell University Press.
—— 1991, *Postmodernism, or the Cultural Logic of Late Capitalism*, London: Verso Books.
Johnson, Barbara 1982, 'My Monster, My Self', *Diacritics*, 12, 2: 2–10.
Johnson, Matthew 1996, *An Archaeology of Capitalism*, Oxford: Blackwell.
Johnson, Nancy E. 2004, *The English Jacobin Novel on Rights, Property and the Law*, London: Palgrave Macmillan.
Jones, Frederick L. (ed.) 1944, *The Letters of Mary W. Shelley*, Volume 1, Norman: University of Oklahoma Press.
—— (ed.) 1947, *Mary Shelley's Journal*, Norman: Oklahoma University Press.
Jones, Leroi 1963, *Blues People*, New York: Morrow Quill.
Jones, Timothy S. and David A. Sprunger (eds.) 2002, *Marvels, Monsters, and Miracles: Studies in the Medieval and Early-Modern Imaginations*, Kalamazoo: Western Michigan University.
Joyner, Charles 1984, *Down by the Riverside: A South Carolina Slave Community*, Urbana: University of Illinois Press.
Kafka, Franz 1961, 'In the Penal Colony', in *The Penal Colony: Stories and Short Pieces*, New York: Schocken Books.
Kant, Immanuel 1952, *Critique of Judgment*, trans. James Creed Meredith, Oxford: Clarendon Press.
—— 1998, 'Religion with the Boundaries of Mere Reason', in *Religion with the Boundaries of Mere Reason and Other Writings*, edited by Allen W. Wood and George Di Giovanni, Cambridge: Cambridge University Press.
Kearney, Richard 2002, *On Stories*, London: Routledge.

—— 2003, *Strangers, Gods and Monsters: Interpreting otherness*, London: Routledge.

Kelley, Robin D.G. 1996, *Race Rebels: Culture, Politics and the Black Working Class*, New York: Free Press.

—— 2002, *Freedom Dreams: The Black Radical Imagination*, Boston: Beacon Press.

—— 2009, *Thelonius Monk: The Life and Times of an American Original*, New York: Free Press.

Kelly, Gary 1976, *The English Jacobin Novel, 1780–1805*, Oxford: Oxford University Press.

Kemple, Thomas M. 1995, *Reading Marx Writing: Melodrama, the Market and the 'Grundrisse'*, Stanford: Stanford University Press.

Kerridge, Eric 1953, 'The Movement of Rent, 1540–1640', *Economic History Review*, 6: 16–34.

Kesteven, G.R. 1967, *Peterloo, 1819*, London: Chatto and Windus.

Kindelberger, Charles P. 1978, *Manias, Panics, and Crashes: A History of Financial Crises*, New York: Basic Books.

Knoppers, Laura Lunger 2004a, '"The Antichrist, the Babilon, the Great Dragon": Oliver Cromwell, Andrew Marvell, and the Apocalyptic Monstrous', in Knoppers and Landes (eds.) 2004.

Knoppers, Laura Lunger and Joan B. Landes (eds.) 2004, *Monstrous Bodies/Political Monstrosities in Early Modern Europe*, edited by Laura Lunger, Ithaca: Cornell University Press.

Kojève, Alexandre 1969, *Introduction to the Reading of Hegel*, trans. James H. Nichols, Jr., New York: Basic Books.

Lachmann, Richard 1987, *From Manor to Market: Structural Change in England, 1536–1640*, Madison: University of Wisconsin Press.

Landes, Joan B. 2004, 'Revolutionary Anatomies', in Knoppers and Landes (eds.) 2004.

Laqueur, Thomas 1983, 'Bodies, Death, and Pauper Funerals', *Representations*, 1, 1: 109–31.

Laroche, Maximilien 1976, 'The Myth of the Zombi', in *Exile and Tradition: Studies in African and Caribbean Literature*, edited by Rowland Smith, New York: Africana Publishing.

Lattas, Andrew 1993, 'Sorcery and Colonialism: Illness, Dreams and Death as Political Languages in New West Britain', *Man*, new series, 28, 1: 51–77.

Lazarus, Neil 1999, *Nationalism and Cultural Practice in the Postcolonial World*, Cambridge: Cambridge University Press.

—— 2002, 'The Fetish of the "West" in Postcolonial Theory', in *Marxism, Modernity and Cultural Studies*, edited by Crystal Bartolovich and Neil Lazarus, Cambridge: Cambridge University Press.

Lebowitz, Michael A. 1992, *Beyond Capital: Marx's Political Economy of the Working Class*, New York: St. Martins Press.

Lefebvre, Henri 1991, *The Production of Space*, trans. Donald Nicholson-Smith, Oxford: Blackwell.

Leslie, Esther 1997, 'Breaking-Up and Making-Up: Woman and Ware, Craving and Corpse in Walter Benjamin's *Arcades Project*', *Historical Materialism*, 1: 66–89.

Levine, David 1984, 'Production, Reproduction and the Proletarian Family in England, 1500–1851', in *Proletarianization and Family History*, edited by David Levine, Orlando: Academic Press.

Lewis, David Levering 1993, *W.E.B. Du Bois: Biography of a Race, 1868–1919*, New York: Henry Holt.

Lewis, Peter and Howard Stein 1997, 'Shifting Fortunes: The Political Economy of Financial Liberalization in Nigeria', *World Development*, 25, 1: 5–22.

Lindgren, J. Ralph (ed.) 1967, *The Early Writings of Adam Smith*, London: Kelley.

Linebaugh, Peter 1975, 'The Tyburn Riot Against the Surgeons', in *Albion's Fatal Tree: Crime and Society in Eighteenth-Century England*, edited by Douglas Hay et al., New York: Pantheon Books.

—— 1982, 'Labour History without the Labour Process: A Note on John Gast and His Times', *Social History*, 7, 3: 319–28.

—— 2003, *The London Hanged*, 2nd edition, London: Verso Books.

Linebaugh, Peter and Marcus Rediker 2000, *The Many-Headed Hydra: Sailors, Slaves, Commoners, and the Hidden History of the Revolutionary Atlantic*, Boston: Beacon Press.

Lis, Catharina and Hugo Soly 1979, *Poverty and Capitalism in Pre-Industrial Europe*, Brighton: Harvester Press.

Lovejoy, Paul 1986, *Africans in Bondage: Studies in Slavery and the Slave Trade*, Madison: University of Wisconsin Press.

Lowry, Edward and Richard deCordova 2004, 'Enunciation and the Production of Horror in *White Zombie*', in *Planks of Reason: Essays on the Horror Film*, revised edition, edited by Barry Keith Grant and Christopher Sharrett, Lanham: Scarecrow Press.

Lucchetti, Aaron 2007, "Innovation, Imagination' Drive Derivatives-Investment Contracts', *Wall Street Journal*, 20 March.

Lugalla, Joe L.P. 1997, 'Development, Change and Poverty in the Informal Sector during the Era of Structural Adjustment in Tanzania', *Canadian Journal of African Studies*, 31, 3: 424–51.

Lukács, Georg 1971a, *Theory of the Novel*, trans. Anna Bostock, London: Merlin Books.

—— 1971b, *History and Class Consciousness*, trans. Rodney Livingstone, London: Merlin Books.

Lynch, Deirdre Shauna 1998, *The Economy of Character: Novels, Market Culture, and the Business of Inner Meaning*, Chicago: University of Chicago Press.

Maddison, Ben 2006, 'Commodification and the Construction of Mainstream Australian Economic Historiography', *Journal of Australian Political Economy*, 58: 114–37.

Maier, Karl 2002, *This House Has Fallen: Nigeria in Crisis*, Boulder: Westview Press.

Mandeville, Bernard 1964, *An Enquiry in the Causes of the Frequent Executions at Tyburn*, Los Angeles: University of California Press.

—— 1970, 'An Essay on Charity Schools', in *The Fable of the Bees*, Harmondsworth: Penguin Books.

Manning, Roger B. 1988, *Village Revolts: Social Protest and Popular Disturbances in England, 1509–1640*, Oxford: Clarendon Press.

Manuel, Frank E. 1967, *The Eighteenth Century Confronts the Gods*, New York: Atheneum.

Marcuse, Herbert 1955, *Eros and Civilization: A Philosophical Inquiry into Freud*, Boston: Beacon Press.

Marshall, Tim 1995, *Murdering to Dissect: Grave-Robbing, Frankenstein and the Anatomy Literature*, Manchester: Manchester University Press.

Martin, John E. 1983, 'The Midland Revolt of 1607', in *An Atlas of Rural Protest in Britain 1548–1900*, edited by Andrew Charlesworth, Philadelphia: University of Pennsylvania Press.

—— 1986, *From Feudalism to Capitalism: Peasant and Landlord in English Agrarian Development*, London: Macmillan.

Marx, Eleanor 1973, 'Recollections of Mohr', in *Marx and Engels on Literature: A Selection of Writings*, edited by Lee Baxandall and Stefan Morawski, St. Louis: Telos Press.

Marx, Karl 1952, *Wage Labour and Capital*, Moscow: Progress Publishers.

—— 1963, *The Poverty of Philosophy*, New York: International Publisher.

—— 1967, *Capital*, Volume 1, trans. Moore and Aveling, New York: International Publishers.

—— 1969, *Le Capital*, Paris: Garnier-Flammarion.

—— 1970, *A Contribution to the Critique of Political Economy*, New York: International Publishers.

—— 1971, *Theories of Surplus Value*, Moscow: Progress Publishers.

—— 1973, *Grundrisse*, trans. Martin Nicolaus, Harmondsworth: Penguin Books.

—— 1973a, 'The Future Results of the British Rule in India', in *Surveys from Exile*, edited by David Fernbach, Harmondsworth: Penguin Books.

—— 1975, *Early Writings*, trans. Rodney Livingstone and Gregor Benton, Harmondsworth: Penguin Books.

—— 1976, *Capital*, Volume 1, trans. Ben Fowkes, Harmondsworth: Penguin Books.
—— 1981, *Capital*, Volume 3, trans. David Fernbach, Harmondsworth: Penguin Books.
Marx, Karl and Frederick Engels 1975a, *Collected Works of Marx and Engels*, Volume 1, New York: International Publishers.
—— 1975b, *Collected Works of Marx and Engels*, Volume 4, New York: International Publishers.
—— 1979, *Collected Works of Marx and Engels*, Volume 12, New York: International Publishers.
—— 1987, *Collected Works of Marx and Engels*, Volume 42: Letters 1864–68, New York: International Publishers.
—— 1988, *Collected Works of Marx and Engels*, Volume 30, New York: International Publishers.
Masquelier, Adeline 1992, 'Encounter with a Road Siren: Machines, Bodies and Commodities in the Imagination of a Mawri Healer', *Visual Anthropology Review*, 8, 1: 56–69.
—— 2000, 'Of Headhunters and Cannibals: Migrancy, Labour, and Consumption in the Mawri Imagination', *Cultural Anthropology*, 15, 1: 84–126.
Matthews G.M. 1968, 'A Volcano's Voice in Shelley', in *Shelley: Modern Judgements*, edited by R. B. Woodings, London: Macmillan.
Mbembe, Achille 2001, *On the Postcolony*, Berkeley: University of California Press.
McCall, John C. 2004, 'Nollywood Confidential', *Transition*, 95: 98–109.
McCalman, Iain 1988, *Radical Underworld: Prophets, Revolutionaries and Pornographers in London, 1795–1840*, Cambridge: Cambridge University Press.
McCarthy, Wyatt 1994, 'African Objects and the Idea of the Fetish', *Res*, 25: 123–31.
McClintock, Anne 1995, *Imperial Leather: Race, Gender and Sexuality in the Colonial Conquest*, London: Routledge.
McGowen, Randall 1987, 'The Body and Punishment in Eighteenth-Century England', *Journal of Modern History*, 59, 4: 651–79.
McManners, John 1981, *Death and the Enlightenment: Changing Attitudes to Death among Christians and Unbelievers in Eighteenth-Century France*, Oxford: Clarendon Press.
McNally, David 1988, *Political Economy and the Rise of Capitalism: A Reinterpretation*, Berkeley: University of California Press.
—— 1989, 'Locke, Levellers and Liberty: Property and Democracy in the Thought of the First Whigs', *History of Political Thought*, 10, 1: 17–40.
—— 1993, *Against the Market*, London: Verso Books.
—— 1998, 'Marxism in the Age of Information', *New Politics*, 6, 4: 99–106.
—— 2000, 'Political Economy to the Fore: Burke, Malthus and the Whig Response to Popular Radicalism in the Age of the French Revolution', *History of Political Thought*, 21: 427–48.
—— 2001, *Bodies of Meaning: Studies on Language, Labor and Liberation*, Albany: State University of New York Press.
—— 2002, *Another World Is Possible: Globalization and Anti-Capitalism*, Winnipeg: Arbeiter Ring Publishing.
—— 2004, 'Language, Praxis and Dialectics', *Historical Materialism*, 12, 2: 149–68.
—— 2006, *Another World Is Possible: Globalization and Anti-Capitalism*, 2nd edition, Winnipeg and London: Arbeiter Ring Publishing and Merlin Press.
—— 2009, 'From Financial Crisis to World-Slump: Accumulation, Financialisation and the Global Slowdown', *Historical Materialism*, 17, 2: 35–83.
—— 2010, *Global Slump: The Economics and Politics of Crisis and Resistance*, Oakland: PM Press.
McNiece, Gerald 1969, *Shelley and the Revolutionary Idea*. Cambridge, MA.: Harvard University Press.
Mellor, Anne K. 1988, *Mary Shelley: Her Life, Her Fiction, Her Monsters*, London: Routledge.
—— 2003, 'Making a "Monster": An Introduction to *Frankenstein*', in Schor (ed.) 2003.

Merriam Webster Collegiate Dictionary 1996, 10th edition, Springfield, MA.

Métraux, Alfred 1957, *Le vaudou haitien*, Paris: Gallimard.

Meyer, Birgit 1995, '"Delivered from the Powers of Darkness": Confessions of Satanic Riches in Christian Ghana', *Africa*, 65, 2: 236–55.

—— 1999, 'Commodities and the Power of Prayer: Pentecostalist Attitudes Towards Consumption in Contemporary Ghana', in Meyer and Geschière (eds.) 1999.

Meyer, Birgit and Peter Geschière (eds.) 1999, *Globalization and Identity: Dialectics of Flow and Closure*, Oxford: Blackwell Publishers.

Miéville, China 2002, 'Symposium: Marxism and Fantasy. Editorial Introduction', *Historical Materialism*, 10, 4: 39–49.

Michie, Jonathan and John Grieve Smith (eds.) 1995, *Managing the Global Economy*, Oxford: Oxford University Press.

Milner, Andrew 1996, *Literature, Culture and Society*, London: UCL Press.

Moore, Henrietta L. and Todd Sanders (eds.) 2001, *Magical Interpretations, Material Realities: Modernity, Witchcraft and the Occult in Postcolonial Africa*, London: Routledge.

Moore, Lucy 1997, *The Thieves' Opera*, New York: Harcourt Brace.

Moretti, Franco 1983, *Signs Taken for Wonders*, London: Verso.

Morgan, Jack 1998, 'Toward an Organic Theory of the Gothic: Conceptualizing Horror', *Journal of Popular Culture*, 32, 1: 59–80.

Morris, Martin 2001, *Rethinking the Communicative Turn: Adorno, Habermas, and the Problem of Communicative Freedom*, Albany: State University of New York Press.

Morrison, Toni 1989, 'Unspeakable things Unspoken: The Afro-American Presence in American Literature', *Michigan Quarterly Review*, 28, 1: 1–34.

Mudimbe, V.Y. 1988, *The Invention of Africa: Gnosis, Philosophy and the Order of Knowledge*, Bloomington: Indiana University Press.

Mulvey-Roberts, Mary 2000, 'The Corpse in the Corpus: *Frankenstein*, Rewriting Wollstonecraft, and the Abject', in *Mary Shelley's Fictions: From Frankenstein to Falkner*, edited by Michael Eberle-Sinatra, London: Macmillan.

Myers, Gregory W. 1994, 'Competitive Rights, Competitive Land Claims: Land Access in Post-War Mozambique', *Journal of Southern African Studies*, 20, 4: 603–32.

Nanga, Jean 2003, 'The Marginalization of Sub-Saharan Africa', *International Viewpoint*, 355, available at: <http://www.internationalviewpoint.org/spip.php?article115>.

Neeson, J.M. 1993, *Commoners: Common Right, Enclosure and Social Change in England, 1700–1820*, Cambridge: Cambridge University Press.

Negri, Antonio 2008, 'The Political Monster: Power and Naked Life', in *In Praise of the Common: A Conversation on Philosophy and Politics*, edited by Cesare Casarino and Antonio Negri, Minneapolis: University of Minnesota Press.

Neocleous, Mark 2003, 'The Political Economy of the Dead: Marx's Vampires', *History of Political Thought*, 24, 4: 668–84.

New York Times 2003, 'Malawi: Vampire Hunt Continues', 10 January.

Nicolaievsky, Boris and Otto Maenchen-Helfen 1973, *Karl Marx: Man and Fighter*, Harmondsworth: Penguin Books.

Niehaus, Isak 1995, 'Witches of the Transvaal Lowveld and their Familiars. Conceptions of Duality, Power and Desire', *Cahiers d'Etudes Africaines*, 138–9: 513–40.

Norris, Christopher 1992, *Uncritical Theory: Postmodernism, Intellectuals and the Gulf War*, London: Lawrence and Wishart.

Nyambara, Pius S. 2001 'The Closing Frontier: Agrarian Change, Immigrants and the 'Squatter Menace' in Gwoke, 1980s–1990s', *Journal of Agrarian Change*, 1, 4: 534–49.

Nyamnjoh, Francis P. 2001, 'Delusions of Development', in Moore and Sanders (eds.) 2001.

O'Flinn, Paul 1983, 'Production and Reproduction: The Case of Frankenstein', *Literature and History*, 9, 2: 194–213.

O'Brien, Paul 2004, *Shelley and Revolutionary Ireland*, London: Bookmarks.

O'Connor, Mary 1991, 'Subject, Voice and Women in Some Contemporary Black American Women's Writing', in *Feminism, Bakhtin, and the Dialogic*, edited by Dale M. Bauer and S. Jaret McKinstry, Albany: State University of New York Press.

Ochsner, Beate 2005, 'More than a Word: From a Portent to Anomaly, the Extraordinary Career of Monsters', in *Monsters and Philosophy*, edited by Charles T. Wolfe, London: College Publications.

Offiong, Daniel A. 1991, *Witchcraft, Sorcery, Magic and the Social Order Among the Ibibio of Nigeria*, Enugu: Fourth Dimension Publishing.

Okri, Ben 1980, *Flowers and Shadows*, London: Longman Drumbeat.

—— 1988, *Stars of the New Curfew*, London: Secker and Warburg.

—— 1992a, *The Famished Road*, London: Vintage.

—— 1992b, *An African Elegy*, London: Jonathon Cape.

—— 1993, *Songs of Enchantment*, London: Vintage.

—— 1997, 'Redreaming the World', in *A Way of Being Free*, London: Phoenix House.

—— 1998, *Infinite Riches*, London: Phoenix House.

—— 1999, *Mental Fight*, London: Phoenix.

Onimode, Bade 1988, *The Political Economy of the African Crisis*, London: Zed Books.

Osborne, Peter 1995, *The Politics of Time: Modernity and Avant-Garde*, London: Verso.

Otchet, Amy 1999, 'Lagos: The Survival of the Determined', *UNESCO Courier*, June.

Outram, Quentin 1997 '"It's Terminal Either Way": An Analysis of Armed Conflict in Liberia, 1989–1996', *Review of African Political Economy*, 73: 355–71.

Oxford English Dictionary Online 1989, 2nd edition.

Paine, Thomas 1984, *The Rights of Man*, Harmondsworth: Penguin Books.

Palmer, Bryan 2000, *Cultures of Darkness: Night Travels in the History of Transgression [From Medieval to Modern]*, New York: Monthly Review Press.

Panic, Mica 1995, 'The Bretton Woods System: Concept and Practice', in Michie and Smith (eds.) 1995.

Parish, Jane 2001, 'Black Market, Free Market: Anti-Witchcraft Shrines and Fetishes among the Akan', in Moore and Sanders (eds.) 2001.

Park, Katharine and Lorraine J. Daston 1981, 'Unnatural Conceptions: The Study of Monsters in Sixteenth- and Seventeenth-Century France and England', *Past and Present*, 92: 20–54.

Partnoy, Frank 2003, *Infectious Greed*, New York: Times Books.

Paster, Gail Kern 1987, 'Leaky Vessels: The Incontinent Women of City Comedy', *Renaissance Drama*, 18: 43–65.

Patterson, Annabel 1991, *Fables of Power: Aesopian Writing and Political History*, Durham, NC.: Duke University Press.

Patterson, Orlando 1998, *Rituals of Blood: Consequences of Slavery in Two American Centuries*, Washington: Civitas/Counterpoint.

Pels, Peter 1998, 'The Magic of Africa: Reflections on a Western Commonplace', *African Studies Review*, 41, 3: 193–209.

Peters, Pauline E. 1984, 'Struggles Over Water, Struggles Over Meaning: Cattle, Water and the State in Botswana', *Africa*, 54, 3: 29–49

—— 2002, 'Bewitching Land: The Role of Land Disputes in Converting Kin to Strangers and in Class Formation in Malawi', *Journal of Southern African Studies*, 28, 1: 155–78.

—— 2004, 'Inequality and Social Conflict Over Land in Africa', *Journal of Agrarian Change*, 4, 3: 269–314.

Petras, James and Henry Veltmeyer 2001, *Globalization Unmasked*, Halifax: Fernwood Books.

—— 2003, *System in Crisis: the Dynamics of Free Market Capitalism*, Halifax: Fernwood Books.

Petty, William 1963, 'Political Anatomy of Ireland', in *The Economic Writings of Sir William Petty*, Volume 1, edited by Charles Henry Hull, New York: Augustus M. Kelley.

Philips, Matthew 2008, 'The Monster that Ate Wall Street', *Newsweek*, 6 October.

Pietz, William 1985, 'The Problem of the Fetish, I', *Res*, 9: 5–17.

—— 1988, 'The Problem of the Fetish, IIIa', *Res*, 16: 105–23.

Pinchbeck, Ivy 1985, *Women Workers and the Industrial Revolution, 1750–1850*, London: Virago.

Plato 1941, *The Republic*, trans. Francis MacDonald Cornford, London: Oxford University Press.

Platt, Peter J. (ed.) 1999, *Wonders, Marvels and Monsters in Early Modern Culture*, Newark: University of Delaware Press.

Polanyi, Karl 1957, *The Great Transformation: The Political and Economic Origins of Our Time*, Boston: Beacon Press.

—— 1968, *Primitive, Archaic and Modern Economies*, Boston: Beacon Press.

Polidori, John 1997, 'The Vampyre', in *The Vampyre and Other Tales of the Macabre*, edited by Robert Morrison and Chris Baldick, Oxford: Oxford University Press.

Poovey, Mary 1984, *The Proper Lady and the Woman Writer*, Chicago: University of Chicago Press.

—— 1987, '"My Hideous Progeny": The Lady and the Monster', in *Mary Shelley's Frankenstein*, edited by Harold Bloom, New York: Chelsea House.

Prashad, Vijay 2003, *Fat Cats and Running Dogs: The Enron Stage of Capitalism*, Monroe: Common Courage Press.

Prawer, S.S. 1976, *Karl Marx and World Literature*, Oxford: Oxford University Press.

Pred, Allan and Michael John Watts 1992, *Reworking Modernity: Capitalisms and Symbolic Discontent*, New Brunswick: Rutgers University Press.

Pryke, Michael and John Alleyn 2000, 'Monetized Time-Space: Derivatives – Money's 'New Imaginary'?', *Economy and Society*, 29, 2: 264–84.

Puma, Edward Li and Benjamin Lee 2004, *Financial Derivatives and the Globalization of Risk*, Durham, NC.: Duke University Press.

Punter, David 1980, *The Literature of Terror: A History of Gothic Fictions from 1795 to the Present Day*, London: Longman.

Quayson, Ato 1997, *Strategic Transformations in Nigerian Writing: Rev. Samuel Johnson, Amos Tutuola, Wole Soyinka, Ben Okri*, Bloomington: University of Indiana Press.

Quigley, Christine 1996, *The Corpse: A History*, Jefferson: McFarland.

Rader, Melvin 1979, *Marx's Interpretation of History*, Oxford: Oxford University Press.

Radoki, Carole (ed.) 1997, *The Urban Challenge in Africa: Growth and Management of Its Large Cities*, Tokyo: United Nations University Press.

—— 1997a, 'Global Forces, Urban Change and Urban Management in Africa', in Radoki (ed.) 1997.

Radzinowicz, Leon 1947–56, *A History of the Criminal Law*, Volume 3, London: Stevens.

Read, Jason 2003, *The Micro-Politics of Capital*, Albany: State University of New York Press.

Rediker, Marcus 1987, *Between the Devil and the Deep Blue Sea*, Cambridge: Cambridge University Press.

—— 2007, *The Slave Ship: A Human History*, New York: Viking.

Reid, Robert 1986, *Land of Lost Content: The Luddite Revolt of 1812*, London: Cardinal/Sphere Books.

Reno, William 1998, *Warlord Politics and African States*, Boulder: Lynne Rienner.

Reuters 2008a, 'Ecuador Defaults, Says to Fight "Monster" Creditors', 12 December.

—— 2008b, 'Banks Turned Markets into "Monster": German President', 14 December.

Reynault, Claude 1998, 'Aspects of the Problem of Land Concentration in Niger', in *Land and Society in Contemporary Africa*, edited by R.E. Downs and S.P. Reyna, Hanover, NH: University Press of New England.

Rhodes, Gary D. 2001, *White Zombie: Anatomy of a Horror Film*, Jefferson: McFarland and Co.

Richardson, Ruth 1987, *Death, Dissection and the Destitute*, London: Routledge.

Rinehart, James W. 1996, *The Tyranny of Work: Alienation and the Labour Process*, 3rd edition, Toronto: Harcourt Brace.

Robinson, Lukin 1973, 'The Decline of the Dollar', *Socialist Register 1973*, edited by Ralph Miliband and John Saville, London: Merlin Press.

Rogers, Nicholas 1990, 'Crowd and People in the Gordon Riots', in *The Transformation of Political Culture: England and Germany in the Late Eighteenth Century*, edited by Eckhart Helmut, Oxford: Oxford University Press.

—— 1994, 'Vagrancy, Impressment and the Regulation of Labour in Eighteenth-Century Britain', *Slavery and Abolition*, 15, 2: 102–13.

Rogerson, Christian M. 1997, 'Globalization or Informalization? African Urban Economies in the 1990s', in Radoki (ed.) 1995.

Rowe, Katherine 1999, *Dead Hands: Fictions of Agency, Renaissance to Modern*, Stanford: Stanford University Press.

Rowe, William and Vivian Schelling 1991, *Memory and Modernity: Popular Culture in Latin America*, London: Verso.

Rowlands, Michael and Jean-Pierre Warnier 1988, 'Sorcery, Power and the Modern State in Cameroon', *Man*, new series, 23, 1: 118–32.

Royle, Edward and James Walvin 1982, *English Radicals and Reformers 1760-1848*, Sussex: Harvester.

Rudé, George 1974, 'The Gordon Riots', in *Paris and London in the Eighteenth Century*, London: Fontana/Collins.

Rule, John 1982, *Outside the Law: Studies in Crime and Order 1650–1850*, Exeter: University of Exeter Press.

Russell, Ross 1973, *Bird Lives! The High Life and Hard Times of Charle 'Yardbird' Parker*, London: Quartet Books.

Russo, Mary 1994, *The Female Grotesque: Risk, Excess, Modernity*, London: Routledge.

Sahlins, Marshall 1972, *Stone Age Economics*, Chicago: Aldine Publishing.

Sale, Kirkpatrick 1995, *Rebels Against the Future: The Luddites and Their War on the Industrial Revolution*, Reading, MA.: Addison-Wesley.

Sanders, Todd 1999, 'Modernity, Wealth and Witchcraft in Tanzania', *Research in Economic Anthropology*, 20: 117–31.

—— 2001, 'Save Our Skins: Structural Adjustment, Morality and the Occult in Tanzania', in Moore and Sanders (eds.) 2001.

—— 2003, 'Invisible Hands and Visible Goods: Revealed and Concealed Economies in Millennial Tanzania', in *Transparency and Conspiracy*, edited by Harry G. West and Todd Sanders, Durham, NC.: Duke University Press.

Saro-Wiwa, Zina 2009, 'No Going Back', in *Nollywood*, photographs by Hugo Pieter with texts by Chris Abani, Stacy Hardy and Zina Saro-Wiwa, Munich: Prestel.

Saul, Scott 2003, *Freedom Is, Freedom Ain't: Jazz and the Making of the Sixties*, Cambridge, MA.: Harvard University Press.

Sawday, Jonathon 1995, *The Body Emblazoned: Dissection and the Human Body in Renaissance Culture*, London: Routledge.

Scarry, Elaine 1985, *The Body in Pain: The Making and Unmaking of the World*, Oxford: Oxford University Press.

Schama, Simon 1987, *The Embarrassment of Riches: An Interpretation of Dutch Culture in the Golden Age*, London: Fontana Press.

Scheper-Hughes, Nancy 1996, 'Theft of Life: The Globalization of Organ Stealing Rumours', *Anthropology Today*, 12, 3: 3–11.

Scheper-Hughes, Nancy and Loic Wacquant (eds.) 2002, *Commodifying Bodies*, London: Sage.

Schmoll, Pamela G. 1993, 'Black Stomachs, Beautiful Stones: Soul-Eating among Hausa in Niger', in Comaroff and Comaroff (eds) 1993.

Schneller, Johanna 2009, 'Who Knew Bloodsucking Could Be so Marketable', *Globe and Mail*, 1 August.

Schor, Esther (ed.) 2003, *The Cambridge Companion to Mary Shelley*, Cambridge: Cambridge University Press.

Schumpeter, Joseph A. 1950, *Capitalism, Socialism and Democracy*, 3rd edition, New York: Harper and Row.

Scott, Niall (ed.) 2007, *Monsters and the Monstrous: Myths and Metaphors of Enduring Evil*, Amsterdam, NY: Rodopi.

Seabrook, William 1929, *The Magic Island*, New York: Blue Ribbon Books.

Sekine, Thomas T. 1997, *An Outline of the Dialectic of Capital*, London: Macmillan.

Sekyi-Otu, Ato 1996, *Fanon's Dialectic of Experience*, Cambridge, MA.: Harvard University Press.

Semonin, Paul 1996, 'Monsters in the Marketplace: The Exhibition of Human Oddities in Early Modern England', in *Freakery: Cultural Spectacles of the Extraordinary Body*, edited by Rosemarie Garland Thomson, New York: New York University Press.

Sharp, Buchanan 1980, *In Contempt of All Authority: Rural Artisans and Riot in the West of England, 1586–1660*, Berkeley: University of California Press.

Sharp, Leslie A. 2000, 'The Commodification of the Body and its Parts', *American Review of Anthropology*, 29: 287–328.

Shaviro, Steve 2002, 'Capitalist Monsters', *Historical Materialism*, 10, 4: 281–90.

Shaw, Rosalind 1997, 'The Production of Witchcraft/Witchcraft as Production: Memory, Modernity, and the Slave Trade in Sierra Leone', *American Ethnologist*, 24, 4: 856–76.

—— 2001, 'Cannibal Transformations: Colonialism and Commodification in the Sierra Leone Hinterland', in Moore and Sanders (eds.) 2001.

—— 2002, *Memories of the Slave Trade: Ritual and the Historical Imagination in Sierra Leone*, Chicago: University of Chicago Press.

Shelley, Mary 1996a, 'Rambles in Germany and Italy', in *The Novels and Selected Works of Mary Shelley*, Volume 8, edited by Nora Crook with Pamela Clemit, London: Pickering & Chatto.

—— 1996b, 'Falkner', in *The Novels and Selected Works of Mary Shelley*, Volume 7, edited by Nora Crook with Pamela Clemit, London: Pickering & Chatto.

—— 1999, *Frankenstein*, edited by D.L. Macdonald and Kathleen Sherf, Toronto: Broadview Press.

Shelley, Percy B. 1960, 'Prometheus Unbound', in *The Complete Poetical Works of Percy Bysshe Shelley*, edited by Thomas Hutchinson, London: Oxford University Press.

—— 1990, 'A Philosophical View of Reform', in *Shelley's Revolutionary Year: The Peterloo Writings of the Poet Shelley*, edited by Paul Foot, London: Redwords.

Shildrick, Margrit 2002, *Embodying the Monster: Encounters with the Vulnerable Self*, London: Sage Publications.

Sidney, Philip 1922, 'Arcadia', in *The Complete Works of Philip Sidney*, Volume 1, edited by A. Feuillerat, Cambridge: Cambridge University Press.

Silko, Leslie Marmon 1992, *Almanac of the Dead*, New York: Penguin Books.

Simmel, Georg 1997, 'The Metropolis and Modern Mental Life', in *Reflections on Commercial Life: Classic Texts from Plato to the Present*, edited by Patrick Murray, London: Routledge.

Simon, David 1997, 'Urbanization, Globalization and Economic Crisis in Africa', in Radoki (ed.) 1997.

Singh, Kavaljit 2000, *Taming Global Financial Flows*, London: Zed Books.

Sipple, Susan 1991, '"Witness to the Suffering of Women": Poverty and Sexual Transgression in Meridel Le Sueur's *Women on the Breadlines*', in *Feminism, Bakhtin, and the Dialogic*, edited by Dale M. Bauer and S. Jaret McKinstry, Albany: State University of New York Press.

Smith, Adam 1969, *The Theory of Moral Sentiments*, Indianapolis: Liberty Press.

—— 1976, *The Wealth of Nations*, edited by E.R. Campbell and A.S. Skinner, Oxford: Oxford University Press.

Smith, Andrew 2005, 'Ben Okri and the Freedom Whose Walls Are Closing in', *Race and Class*, 47, 1: 1–13.

Smith, Daniel Jordan 2001a, '"The Arrow of God": Pentecostalism, Inequality, and the Supernatural in South-Eastern Nigeria', *Africa*, 71, 4: 587–613.

—— 2001b, 'Ritual Killing, 419, and Fast Wealth: Inequality and the Popular Imagination in Southeastern Nigeria', *American Ethnologist*, 28, 4: 803–26.

Smith, David Norman 2002, 'Accumulation and the Clash of Cultures', *Rethinking Marxism*, 14, 4: 73–84.

Smith, Mark M. 1997, *Mastered by the Clock: Time, Slavery, and Freedom in the American South*, Chapel Hill: University of North Carolina Press.

Sohn-Rethel, Alfred 1978, *Intellectual and Manual Labour: A Critique of Epistemology*, London: Macmillan.

Solomon, Robert C. 1983, *In the Spirit of Hegel*, Oxford: Oxford University Press.

Spivak, Gayatri Chakravorty 1985, 'Three Women's Texts and a Critique of Imperialism', *Critical Inquiry*, 12: 254–9.

St. Clair, William 1989, *The Godwins and the Shelleys: The Biography of a Family*, London: Faber and Faber.

Stallybrass, Peter 1986, 'Patriarchal Territories: The Body Enclosed', in *Rewriting the Renaissance*, edited by Margaret W. Ferguson et al., Chicago: University of Chicago Press.

—— 1998, 'Marx's Coat', in *Border Fetishisms: Material Objects in Unstable Spaces*, edited by Patricia Spyer, London: Routledge.

Stearns, Marshall W. 1958, *The Story of Jazz*, London: Oxford University Press.

Sterrenburg, Lee 1979, 'Mary Shelley's Monster: Politics and Psyche in *Frankenstein*', in *The Endurance of Frankenstein*, edited by George Levine and U.C. Knoepflmacher, Berkeley: University of California Press.

Stubbes, Philip 1877–9, *Anatomy of the Abuses in England*, edited by F.J Furnival, London: New Shakespeare Society.

Suvin, Darko 1982, 'Transubstantiation of Production and Creation: Metamorphic Imagery in the *Grundrisse*', *Minnesota Review*, 18: 102–15.

Taibbi, Matt 2009, 'Inside the Great American Bubble Machine', *Rolling Stone*, 2 July.

Taussig, Michael T. 1980, *The Devil and Commodity Fetishism in South America*, Chapel Hill: University of North Carolina Press.

Tawney, R.H. 1967 [1912], *The Agrarian Problem in the Sixteenth Century*, New York: Harper and Row.

The Concise Oxford Dictionary of English Etymology 1996, edited by T.F. Hoad, Oxford: Oxford University Press.

Thirsk, Joan 1976, 'The Common Fields', in *Peasants, Knights and Heretics: Studies in Medieval English Social History*, edited by Rodney Hilton, Cambridge: Cambridge University Press.

Thirsk, John and J.P. Cooper (eds.) 1972, *Seventeenth Century Economic Documents*, Oxford: Clarendon Press.

Thomas, Keith 1971, *Religion and the Decline of Magic: Studies in Popular Beliefs in Sixteenth and Seventeenth Century England*, London: Weidenfeld and Nicolson.

Thomis, Malcolm 1970, *The Luddites*, Newton Abbott: Archon Books.

Thompson, Edward P. 1963, *The Making of the English Working Class*, New York: Vintage Books.

—— 1975, *Whigs and Hunters: The Origin of the Black Act*, New York: Pantheon.

—— 1978, 'Eighteenth-Century English Society: Class Struggle Without Class?', *Social History*, 3, 2: 133–65.

—— 1991, 'Time, Work-Discipline and Industrial Capitalism', in *Customs in Common*, New York: New Press.

—— 1993, *Witness Against the Beast*, Cambridge: Cambridge University Press.

Thornton, John 1992, *Africa and Africans in the Making of the Atlantic World, 1400-1680*, Cambridge: Cambridge University Press.

Tillyard, E.M.W. 1991, *Shakespeare's History Plays*, Harmondsworth: Penguin Books.

Tutuola, Amos 1984, *The Palm-Wine Drinkard and My Life in the Bush of Ghosts*, New York: Grove Press.

Underdown, David 1985, 'The Taming of the Scold: the Enforcement of Patriarchal Authority in Early Modern England', in *Order and Disorder in Early Modern England*, edited by A. Fletcher and J. Stevenson, Cambridge: Cambridge University Press.

Uno, Kozo 1977, *Principles of Political Economy: Theory of a Purely Capitalist Society*, trans. Thomas T. Sekine, Sussex: Harvester Press.

Valenze, Deborah 2006, *The Social Life of Money in the English Past*, Cambridge: Cambridge University Press.

Van Dijk, Rijk 2001, 'Witchcraft and Scepticism by Proxy: Pentecostalism and Laughter in Urban Malawi', in Moore and Sanders (eds.) 2001.

Vickers, Nancy 1997, 'Members Only: Marot's Anatomical Blazons', in *The Body In Parts: Fantasies of Corporeality in Early Modern Europe*, London: Routledge.

Viinikka, Jussi 2009, '"There Shall be No Property": Trade Unions, Class and Politics in Nigeria', in *Class Struggle and Resistance in Africa*, edited by Leo Zeilig, Chicago: Haymarket.

Vlasopolos, Anca 1983, '*Frankenstein's* Hidden Skeleton: The Psycho-Politics of Oppression', *Science Fiction Studies*, 10: 125–36.

Volney, C.F. 1990, *The Ruins, or, Meditation on the Revolutions of Empires: and the Law of Nature*, Baltimore: Blacks Classic Press, published from the Peter Eckler edition of 1890.

Voloshinov, Valentin N. 1986, *Marxism and the Philosophy of Language*, trans. Ladislav Matejka and I.R. Titunik, Cambridge, MA.: Harvard University Press.

Wachtel, Nathan 1994, *Gods and Vampires: Return to Chipaya*, trans. Carol Volk, Chicago: University of Chicago Press.

Wade, Robert and Frank Veneroso 1998, 'The Asian Crisis: The High Debt Model Versus the Wall Street-Treasury-IMF Complex', *New Left Review*, I, 228: 3–23.

Wallerstein, Immanuel 1985, 'Three Stages of African Involvement in the World-Economy', in *The Political Economy of Contemporary Africa*, edited by Peter C.W. Gutkind and Immanuel Wallerstein, Beverley Hills: Sage.

Weiss, Brad 1999, 'Electric Vampires: Haya Rumours of the Commodified Body', in *Bodies and Persons: Comparative Perspectives from Africa and Melanesia*, edited by Michael Lambek and Andrew Strathern, Cambridge: Cambridge University Press.

Wells, Roger 1986, *Insurrection: The British Experience, 1795–1803*, Gloucester: Alan Sutton.

Wheen, Francis 1999, *Karl Marx*, London: Fourth Estate.

White, Luise 2000, *Speaking with Vampires: Rumor and History in Colonial Africa*, Berkeley: University of California Press.

Wilkinson, Jane 1990, *Talking with African Writers*, London: James Currey.

Williams, Gwyn A. 1968, *Artisans and Sans-Culottes: Popular Movements in France and Britain during the French Revolution*, London: Edward Arnold.

Williams, Mary Lou 1954, 'In her own words...Mary Lou Williams Interview', *Melody Maker*, April–June.

Williams, Tony 1983, '*White Zombie*: Haitian Horror', *Jump Cut: A Review of Contemporary Media*, 28: 18–20.

Wilson, Charles 1968, *The Dutch Republic*, New York: McGraw-Hill.

Wilson, Edmund 1973, *To the Finland Station: A Study in the Writing and Acting of History*, New York: Farrar, Strauss and Giroux.

Wise, Sarah 2004, *The Italian Boy: A Tale of Murder and Body Snatching in 1830s London*, New York: Metropolitan Books.

Witt, Judith 1979, '*Frankenstein* as Mystery Play', in *The Endurance of Frankenstein*, edited by George Levine and U.C. Knoepflmacher, Berkeley: University of California Press.

Wolff, Robert Paul 1988, *Moneybags Must Be So Lucky: On the Literary Structure of Capital*, Amherst: University of Massachusetts Press.

Wollstonecraft, Mary 1993, 'An Historical and Moral View of the French Revolution', in *Political Writings*, edited by Janet Todd, Toronto: University of Toronto Press.

Wood, Andy 1997, 'The Place of Custom in Plebeian Political Culture: England, 1550–1800', *Social History*, 22, 1: 46–60.

Wood, Ellen Meiksins 1989, *Peasant-Citizen and Slave*, London: Verso.

—— 1999, *The Origin of Capitalism*, New York: Monthly Review Press.

—— 2002, 'The Question of Market Dependence', *Journal of Agrarian Change*, 2, 1: 50–87.

—— 2003, *Empire of Capital*, London: Verso.

—— 2006, 'Logics of Power: A Conversation with David Harvey', *Historical Materialism*, 14, 4: 9–34.

Wood, Michael 2005, *In Search of Shakespeare*, London: BBC Books.

Wood, Robin 2004, 'An Introduction to the American Horror Film', in *Planks of Reason: Essays on the Horror Film*, revised edition, edited by Barry Keith Grant and Christopher Sharrett, Lanham: Scarecrow Press.

Woodhouse, Philip et al. 2001, *African Enclosures? The Social Dynamics of Wetlands in Drylands*, Trenton: Africa World Press.

Wordie, J.R. 1983, 'The Chronology of English Enclosure, 1500–1914', *Economic History Review*, 36, 4: 483–505.

World Bank 2001a, *Global Development Finance*. Washington, DC.: World Bank.

—— 2001b, *World Development Report 2000/2001*, Oxford: Oxford University Press.

—— 2003, *Nigeria: Country Brief*, September, available online.

Yamba, C. Bawa 1997, 'Cosmologies in Turmoil: Witchfinding and AIDS in Chiawa, Zambia', *Africa*, 67, 2: 200–23.

Yelling, J.A. 1977, *Common Field and Enclosure in England 1450–1850*, London: Macmillan.

Zack-Williams, Alfred B. 1999, 'Sierra Leone: The Political Economy of Civil War', *Third World Quarterly*, 20, 1: 143–62.

Zeilig, Leo and David Seddon 2009, 'Introduction: Resisting the Scramble for Africa', in *Class Struggle and Resistance in Africa*, edited by Leo Zeilig, Chicago: Haymarket.

Index